They Dared

Copyright © 2012 by Yvette Quarles Chatman

Illustrations Copyright© 2012 by Yvette Quarles Chatman

All rights reserved

No part of this publication may be reproduced, stored in a retrieval system, or transmitted in any form or by any means, electronic, mechanical, recording or otherwise without written permission of the author.

Publisher- CreateSpace Independent Publishing Platform

ISBN-10:14023088X

ISBN-13:978-140230880

History is not dead.

It is consistently growing with each generation and experience we add. It is teaching, repeating lessons not learned. It is revealing, each forgotten or hidden experience we unearth.

<u>They Dared</u>, is a history lesson for students of all ages and ethnicities.

Yvette Chatman references the iconic contributions to the Afrikan experience in both revealing and reaffirming prose. Her voice and this book are a welcome addition to the record of contemporary black voices in America and throughout the Afrikan Diaspora.

Kwabena Dinizulu- National Teaching Artist, Poet and Griot

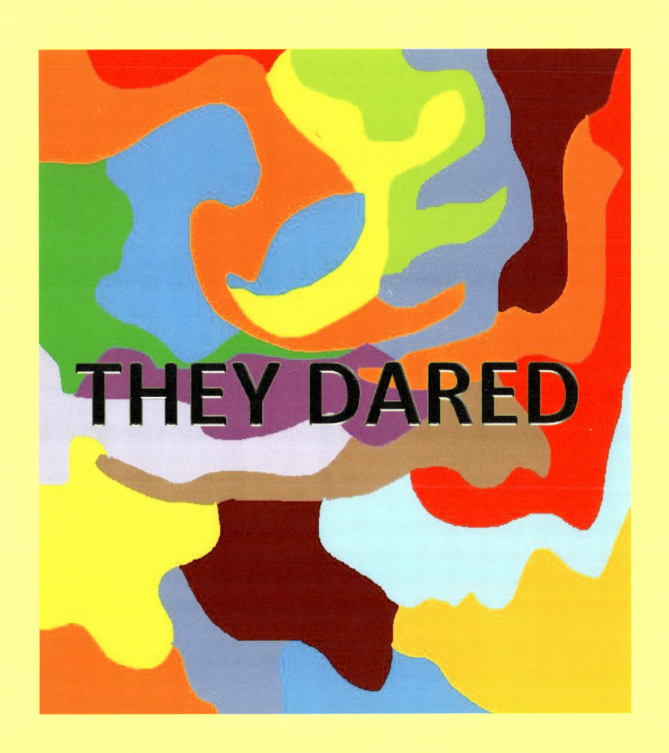

For all the little people in my life

Phillip, Cameron, Maya, Carter, Samuel, Ladybug, Seven, EJ, Kwest and Nia, Masani, Aminah

Thanks so much to my loving and-oh-so-understanding husband, Joseph and my favorite daughter Tamiika, my favorite oldest son Adam , and my favorite youngest son Joseph. "Truly, the wind beneath my wings."

To my brothers; John, Leon, Calvin, Douglas, Ronnie and sisters; Aleatha and Yvonne- I am because You are. THANKS!

A loving thanks to Mamma Edgeworth, who has prayed for me for as long as I can remember.

A special thanks to my Birmingham Civil Rights Institute family! Your love, encouragement, and insight is beyond measure.

Like India and Maya, I'm full of poetry.
They sang their songs for me.
For me, for me; they sang their songs for me!

Like Gabby and Jesse, I'm full of energy.
They ran their best for me.
For me, for me; they ran their best for me!

Like President Obama and Michelle, I'm full of democracy.
They dared to hope for me.
For me, for me; they dared to hope for me!

Like Synthia and Jacob, I'm full of creativity.
They painted life for me.
For me, for me; they painted life for me!

Like Lola and Audrey, I'm full of history.
They spoke their truths for me.
For me, for me; they spoke their truths for me!

Like Ali and Thurgood, I'm full of tenacity.
They fought the fight for me.
For me, for me; they fought the fight for me!

Like Porter and Martin, I'm full of empathy.
They dreamed their dreams for me.
For me, for me; they dreamed their dreams for me!

Like Daniel and Mae, I'm full of discovery.
They answered questions for me.
For me, for me; they answered questions for me!

**Like Shuttlesworth and Mandela, I'm full of ministry.
They shared their love for me.
For me, for me; they shared love for me!**

Biographical information taken from individuals' official websites, unless otherwise noted.

Page 1

Poetry- *The art of rhythmical composition, written or spoken, for exciting pleasure by beautiful, imaginative, or elevated thoughts.*

India Arie

(October 3, 1975---)

India Arie is known and cherished by fans and fellow musicians as a poet, a songwriter, a producer, a musician, a singer, an advocate, a friend and a philanthropist -- but she is possibly best known for the love in her music that has inspired and motivated people worldwide. With over eight million albums sold, her last studio album Testimony Vol. 2; Love & Politics, hit # 1 on Billboard R&B Chart and #3 on the Billboard Top 200 Chart. Praised by both the New York Times, "one of the most determinedly virtuous songwriters in R&B or pop, strives to make faith, goodness and positive thinking seductive." (soulbird.com)

Maya Angelou

(April 4, 1928---)

Dr. Maya Angelou is one of the most renowned and influential voices of our time. Hailed as a global renaissance woman, Dr. Angelou is a celebrated poet, memoirist, novelist, educator, dramatist, producer, actress, historian, filmmaker, and civil rights activist. Published in 1970, I Know Why the Caged Bird Sings was published to international acclaim and enormous popular success. The list of her published verse, non-fiction, and fiction now includes more than 30 bestselling titles. She served on two presidential committees, was awarded the Presidential Medal of Arts in 2000, the Lincoln Medal in 2008, and has received 3 Grammy Awards.   (mayaangelou.com)

Page 2

Energy *-the capacity for vigorous activity; available power.*

Cleveland "Jesse" Owens

(September 12, 1913 – March 31, 1980)
Jesse Owens was an American track and field athlete who specialized in the sprints and the long jump. He participated in the 1936 Summer Olympics in Berlin, Germany, where he achieved international fame by winning four gold medals: one each in the 100 meters, the 200 meters, the long jump, and as part of the 4x100 meter relay team. He was the most successful athlete at the 1936 Summer Olympics. (jeseowens.com)

Gabrielle Christina Victoria "Gabby" Douglas

(December 31, 1995 ---)
"Gabby Douglas" is an American gymnast. As a member of the U.S. Women's Gymnastics team at the 2012 Summer Olympics, she won gold medals in both the individual and team all-around competitions. Douglas is the first woman of color and the first African-American gymnast in Olympic history to become the individual all-around champion, and the first American gymnast to win gold in both the individual all-around and team competitions at the same Olympics. She was also a member of the gold-winning U.S. team at the 2011 World Championships. (gabrielledouglas.com)

Democracy- *government by the people; a form of government in which the supreme power is vested in the people and exercised directly by them or by their elected agents under a free electoral system.*

President Barack Hussein Obama II

(August 4, 1961---)

President Obama is the first African American to hold the office of the United States Presidency. He is the 44th president and was re-elected for a second term in Nov 2012. His story is the American story — values from the heartland, a middle-class upbringing in a strong family, hard work and education as the means of getting ahead, and the conviction that a life so blessed should be lived in service to others. (www.whitehouse.gov)

Michelle LaVaughn Robinson Obama

(January 17, 1964---)

Michelle Obama is the wife of the 44th and incumbent President of the United States, Barack Obama, and the first African-American First Lady of the United States. She is an attorney, while in law school, Michelle Robinson worked to help local residents unable to afford legal advice and representation, on issues ranging from divorce, custody and tenant rights. She also served as Assistant to the Mayor, City of Chicago, 1991-1992. (www.whitehouse.gov)

Page 4

Creativity- 1. the state or quality of being creative. 2. the ability to transcend traditional ideas, rules, patterns, relationships, or the like, and to create meaningful new ideas.

Synthia Saint James

(February 11, 1949---)
Synthia St. James is an international award winning artist and designer of the first United States Postal Stamp for the Kwanzaa holiday. She has to date written and or illustrated 13 children's picture books, 3 poetry and prose books, 4 children's activity books, a cookbook, and a postcard book. She is the recipient of The 2008 Woman of the Year Award for the 26th Senate District, and has garnered numerous other awards including the Parent's Choice Silver Honor, a Coretta Scott King Honor, and an Oppenheim Gold Award all for her books. (synthiasaintjames.com)

Jacob Lawrence

(September 7, 1917 – June 9, 2000)
Jacob Lawrence was an American painter. He is among the best-known 20th-century African-American painters, a distinction shared with Romare Bearden. Lawrence was only in his twenties when his "Migration Series" made him nationally famous. A part of this series was featured in a 1941 issue of Fortune magazine. The series depicted the epic Great Migration of African Americans from the rural South to the urban North.
(jacoblawrence.org)

Page 5

History- the branch of knowledge dealing with past events. 2. the record of past events and times, especially in connection with the human race.

Lola Mae Hendricks
(December 1932---)

In 1956, Alabama state officials outlawed the National Association for the Advancement of Colored People (NAACP) for its role in the Montgomery bus boycott. In response, Lola Mae Hendricks joined civil rights leader Fred Shuttlesworth and other African Americans to form the Alabama Christian Movement for Human Rights (ACMHR). The ACMHR organized demonstrations and boycotts to protest segregation in Birmingham's schools and businesses. In 1961, the ACMHR won a lawsuit to integrate Birmingham's 67 city parks. Public Safety Commissioner Eugene "Bull" Connor retaliated by closing the parks. Hendricks later worked for the Southern Christian Leadership Conference (SCLC), headed by Martin Luther King Jr., where she served as secretary to the SCLC's executive director, Wyatt T. Walker. (teachersdommain.org)

Audrey Hendricks

(May 22, 1953- March 1, 2009)
Audrey Hendricks was born in Birmingham, Alabama in 1953. Her childhood spanned the busiest years of the Civil Rights movement. In 1954, the Supreme Court ruled in Brown v. Board of Education that segregated schools were unconstitutional. In the spring of 1963, just before her tenth birthday, Hendricks and other students left school and joined civil rights leaders in a march to Birmingham's Sixteenth Street Baptist Church, the staging area for the demonstrations. Together with students from schools in other parts of the city, they were organized into protest groups and spent the next four days demonstrating against discrimination in Birmingham. (teachersdomain.org)

Tenacity *1. the quality or property of being tenacious (holding or grasping firmly; forceful: a tenacious grip.*

Muhammad Ali

(January 17, 1942)

Muhammad Ali is an American former professional boxer, heavyweight champion, philanthropist and social activist. His success as a boxer is widely respected, but Ali's greatest triumph lies in his legacy as a leader, humanitarian, and artist. As a boxer, Muhammad brought unprecedented speed and grace to his sport, while his charm and wit changed forever what the public expected a champion to be. (ali.com)

Thurgood Marshall

(July 2, 1908- Jan. 24, 1993)

Thurgood Marshall was the first African American to serve on the Supreme Court. As counsel to the NAACP, he utilized the judiciary to champion equality for Black Americans. In 1954, he won the Brown v. Board of Education case, in which the Supreme Court ended racial segregation in public schools. He promoted affirmative action -- preferences, set-asides and other race conscious policies -- as the remedy for the damage remaining from the nation's history of slavery and racial bias. Marshall was appointed to the Supreme Court in 1967 and served for 24 years. As counsel to the NAACP, he utilized the judiciary to champion equality for black Americans. He worked on behalf of black Americans, but built a structure of individual rights that became the cornerstone of protections for all Americans. He succeeded in creating new protections under law for women, children, prisoners, and the homeless. (thurgoodmarshall.com)

Empathy - *the action of understanding, being aware of, being sensitive to, and vicariously experiencing the feelings, thoughts, and experience of another of either the past or present.*

John Thomas Porter

(April 4, 1931 - February 15, 2006)
A native of Birmingham, Porter was educated at Alabama State University in Montgomery, where he assisted Rev. Martin L. King, Jr. at Dexter Avenue Baptist in King's first year as pastor of that congregation. Porter went on to study religion at Morehouse in Atlanta, where he worked with King's father, Martin L. King, Sr. at Ebenezer Baptist Church. On Easter Sunday 1963, Porter was arrested leading a march in downtown Birmingham along with Reverend N.H. Smith and King's brother, Reverend A.D. King

Dr. Martin Luther King, Jr.

(January 15, 1929 – April 4, 1968)
Dr. King was an American clergyman, activist, and prominent leader in the African-American Civil Rights Movement. He is best known for his role in the advancement of civil rights using nonviolent civil disobedience. In 1957 he was elected president of the Southern Christian Leadership Conference, an organization formed to provide new leadership for the now burgeoning civil rights movement. He led a massive protest in Birmingham, Alabama, that caught the attention of the entire world, providing what he called a coalition of conscience. and inspiring his "Letter from a Birmingham Jail", a manifesto of the Negro revolution; he planned the drives in Alabama for the registration of Negroes as voters; he directed the peaceful march on Washington, D.C., of 250,000 people to whom he delivered his address, "I Have a Dream". At the age of thirty-five, Martin Luther King, Jr., was the youngest man to have received the Nobel Peace Prize. (NobelPrize.org)

Page 8

Discovery *- the act or process of discovering.*

Williams, Daniel Hale

(1858–1931,)
American surgeon, b. Hollidaysburg, Pa., M.D. Northwestern Univ., 1883. As surgeon of the South Side Dispensary in Chicago (1884–91), he became keenly aware of the lack of facilities for training African Americans like himself as doctors and nurses. As a result he organized the Provident Hospital, the first black hospital in the United States. In 1893, Williams performed the first successful closure of a wound of the heart and pericardium. (infoplease.com)

Dr. Mae Jemison

(October 17, 1956---)
Dr. Mae Jemison was the science mission specialist on a cooperative mission between the United States and Japan. She was the first African American female astronaut. The eight-day mission was accomplished in 127 orbits of the Earth, and included 44 Japanese and U.S. life science and materials processing experiments. Dr. Mae Jemison was a co-investigator on the bone cell research experiment flown on the mission. The Endeavour and her crew launched from and returned to the Kennedy Space Center in Florida. In completing her first space flight, Dr. Mae Jemison logged 190 hours, 30 minutes, 23 seconds in space. (maejemison.com)

Ministry- *a person or thing through which something is accomplished*.

Reverend Fred Shuttlesworth

(March 18, 1922 – October 5, 2011)
African American Baptist pastor and the central leader of the civil rights movement in Birmingham, Fred Lee Shuttlesworth was one of the pioneering figures in the civil rights era. The organization he founded in 1956, the Alabama Christian Movement for Human Rights (ACMHR), joined with Martin Luther King Jr.'s Southern Christian Leadership Conference (SCLC) to protest segregation in Birmingham in 1963. Partly as a result of those direct-action demonstrations, the U.S. Congress passed the Civil Rights Act of 1964. He was a co-founder of the Southern Christian Leadership Conference, and was instrumental in the 1963 Birmingham Children's Movement. (encyclopediaofalabama.com)

Nelson Mandela

(July 18, 1918—)
Nelson Mandela is a South African politician who served as President of South Africa from 1994 to 1999, the first ever to be elected in a fully representative democratic election. In 1962 he was arrested and convicted of treason, sabotage and other charges, and sentenced to life imprisonment. Mandela went on to serve 27 years in prison, spending many of these years on Robben Island. Following his release from prison on 11 February 1990, Mandela led his party in the negotiations that led to the establishment of democracy in 1994. He was awarded the Nobel Peace Prize in 1993. (NobelPeaceprize.org)

Biography

Yvette Quarles Chatman is the author of the new children's book "They Dared". She is currently employed at the Birmingham Civil Rights Institute and is responsible for community and family literacy initiatives, parent education and assisting with youth programming. She and her family own Homecoming Coffee & Gifts in Birmingham, Al.

She holds Associate Degrees in Child Development and Biblical Studies and a B.A. in Children and Family Studies.

She is a mother, grandmother, wife, auntie, neighbor but most of all she is my twin and sister-friend. She is a combination of Mary Poppins and Angela Davis. "They Dared", is a historical book of prose that is as simple and complex as its writer. Her use of trouble-free limerick and rhyme exemplifies and mimics her attitude toward life and living.

Like Yvette Quarles Chatman;

>   I seek boldness and humility

>   She defines the world for me,

>   For me, for me, she defines the world for me!

~~Yvonne Quarles-Thomas

.

Made in the USA
Lexington, KY
05 February 2013

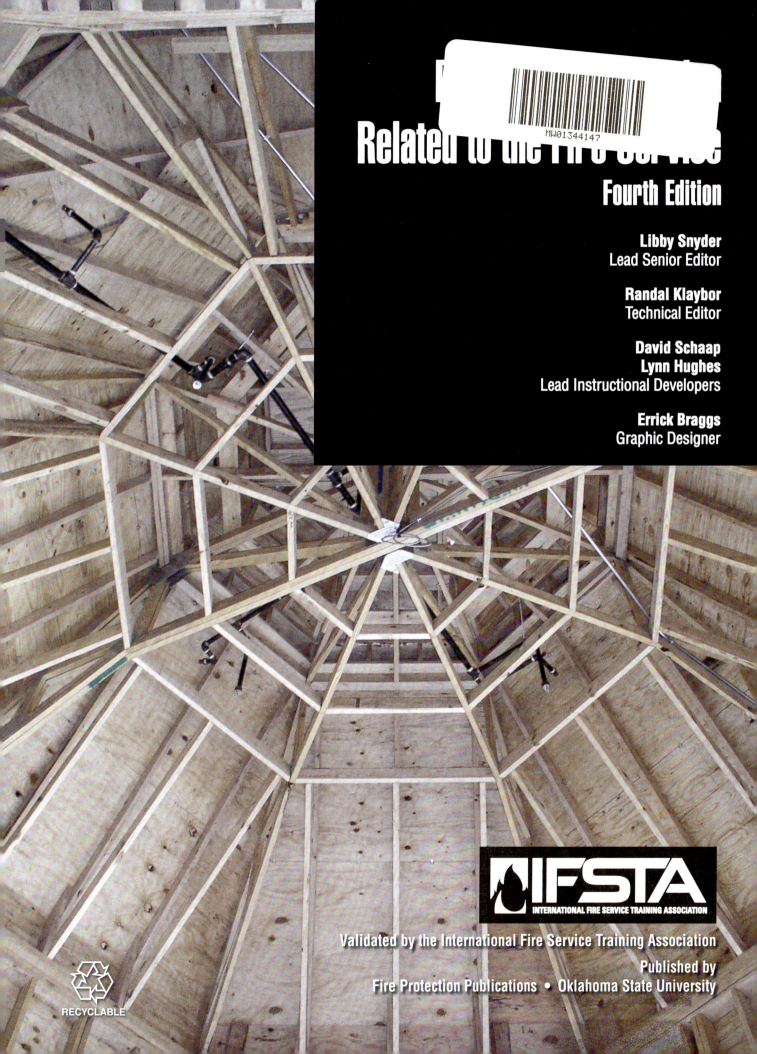

Related to the Fire Service

Fourth Edition

Libby Snyder
Lead Senior Editor

Randal Klaybor
Technical Editor

David Schaap
Lynn Hughes
Lead Instructional Developers

Errick Braggs
Graphic Designer

IFSTA
INTERNATIONAL FIRE SERVICE TRAINING ASSOCIATION

Validated by the International Fire Service Training Association

Published by
Fire Protection Publications • Oklahoma State University

The International Fire Service Training Association (IFSTA) was established in 1934 as a *nonprofit educational association of fire fighting personnel who are dedicated to upgrading fire fighting techniques and safety through training*. To carry out the mission of IFSTA, Fire Protection Publications was established as an entity of Oklahoma State University. Fire Protection Publications' primary function is to publish and distribute training materials as proposed, developed, and validated by IFSTA. As a secondary function, Fire Protection Publications researches, acquires, produces, and markets high-quality learning and teaching aids consistent with IFSTA's mission.

IFSTA holds two meetings each year: the Winter Meeting in January and the Annual Validation Conference in July. During these meetings, committees of technical experts review draft materials and ensure that the professional qualifications of the National Fire Protection Association® standards are met. These conferences bring together individuals from several related and allied fields, such as:

- Key fire department executives, training officers, and personnel
- Educators from colleges and universities
- Representatives from governmental agencies
- Delegates of firefighter associations and industrial organizations

Committee members are not paid nor are they reimbursed for their expenses by IFSTA or Fire Protection Publications. They participate because of a commitment to the fire service and its future through training. Being on a committee is prestigious in the fire service community, and committee members are acknowledged leaders in their fields. This unique feature provides a close relationship between IFSTA and the fire service community.

IFSTA manuals have been adopted as the official teaching texts of many states and provinces of North America as well as numerous U.S. and Canadian government agencies. Besides the NFPA® requirements, IFSTA manuals are also written to meet the Fire and Emergency Services Higher Education (FESHE) course requirements. A number of the manuals have been translated into other languages to provide training for fire and emergency service personnel in Canada, Mexico, and outside of North America.

Copyright © 2016 by the Board of Regents, Oklahoma State University

All rights reserved. No part of this publication may be reproduced in any form without prior written permission from the publisher.

ISBN 978-0-87939-594-0   Library of Congress Control Number: 2016937290

Fourth Edition, First Printing, May 2016   *Printed in the United States of America*

10   9   8   7   6   5   4   3

If you need additional information concerning the International Fire Service Training Association (IFSTA) or Fire Protection Publications, contact:

Customer Service, Fire Protection Publications, Oklahoma State University
930 North Willis, Stillwater, OK 74078-8045
800-654-4055   Fax: 405-744-8204

For assistance with training materials, to recommend material for inclusion in an IFSTA manual, or to ask questions or comment on manual content, contact:

Editorial Department, Fire Protection Publications, Oklahoma State University
930 North Willis, Stillwater, OK 74078-8045
405-744-4111   Fax: 405-744-4112   E-mail: editors@osufpp.org

Oklahoma State University in compliance with Title VI of the Civil Rights Act of 1964 and Title IX of the Educational Amendments of 1972 (Higher Education Act) does not discriminate on the basis of race, color, national origin or sex in any of its policies, practices or procedures. This provision includes but is not limited to admissions, employment, financial aid and educational services.

Chapter Summary

Chapter

1. Building Construction and the Fire Service ... 6
2. Building Classifications and Structure Fire Resistance ... 40
3. Structural Design Features of Buildings ... 62
4. Building Systems ... 90
5. Interior Finishes and Passive Fire Protection ... 135
6. Foundations ... 166
7. Wood Construction ... 178
8. Masonry and Ordinary Construction ... 214
9. Steel Construction ... 236
10. Concrete Construction ... 254
11. Roofs ... 274
12. Special Structures and Design Features ... 306
13. Buildings under Construction, Remodeling, Expansion, and Demolition ... 342
14. Non-Fire Building Collapse ... 356

Appendices

A. Chapter and Page Correlation to FESHE Outcomes ... 379
B. Metric Conversions ... 380

Glossary ... 383
Index ... 399

Table of Contents

Introduction 1
Purpose and Scope 2
Terminology 2
Resources 2
Key Information 3
Metric Conversions 3
Key Term 4
Signal Words 4

1   Building Construction and the Fire Service 6
Case History 9
History of Building Construction 11
The Design and Construction Process 12
    Concept 12
        Design Principles 13
        Professional Design 13
        Materials 13
        Engineering Specialties 13
    Financing 14
    Documentation and Bids 14
    Building Permits 15
    Construction 15
    Inspection and Testing 16
    Renovation and Remodeling 17
Law-Based Construction Variables 18
    Building Code Requirements 18
        Life Safety Codes 19
        Construction Type 20
        Occupancy and Use 21
    Accessibility Requirements 21
Engineering-Based Construction Variables 22
    Climate 22
    Building Site Properties 22
    Configuration of Internal Spaces 23
    Automatic Fire Suppression Systems 23
    Age of Construction 25
        Advantages of Older Construction 25
        Gentrification 26
    Energy Conservation (Green Design) 26
Economics-Based Construction Variables 27
    Building Use 27
    Existing Infrastructure 27
    Fire Loss Management 28
Other Variables 28
    Owner's Needs and Desires 28
    Investment of Wealth 28
    Aesthetics and Culture 29
Community Fire Defense 30
    Heat Transfer 30
    Exposures and Fire Spread Factors 31
Design-Caused Structural Failure 33
    Loss of Structural Integrity 34
    Building System Failure 34
    Design Deficiencies 35
Preincident Planning in Building Construction .. 36
    Geographic Information Systems 36
    Fire Fighting Strategy 37
Chapter Summary 37
Review Questions 37
Chapter Notes 38

2   Building Classifications and Structural Fire Resistance 40
Case History 43
Basic Building Classifications 43
    Type I Construction – Fire Resistive 46
        Noncombustible Materials 46
        Combustible Materials 47
    Type II Construction – Protected Noncombustible or Noncombustible 47
    Type III Construction – Exterior Protected/Ordinary 48
    Type IV Construction – Heavy Timber 49
        Features of Type IV Construction 49
        Usage of Type IV Construction 50
    Type V Construction – Wood Frame 50
        Limitations of Type V Construction 50
        Type V Construction Methods 51
    Mixed Construction 51
Occupancy Classifications 51
    International Building Code® (IBC) Occupancy Classifications 51
    NFPA® Occupancy Classifications 52
    Mixed Occupancies 52
    Change of Occupancy 53
Fire and Fuel Load 54
    Combustibility of Materials 54
    Fire Load versus Structural Load 54
Fire Resistance 55
    Laboratory-Tested Data 56
        Limitations of Test Findings 58
        E-119 Test 58
        Testing Laboratories 59
        Publishing Fire Test Results 59
    Mathematical Models Based on Collected Data 60
Chapter Summary 60

Review Questions **61**
Chapter Notes **61**

3 Structural Design Features of Buildings 62
Case History **65**
Forces, Stresses, and Loads **66**
    Forces 67
    Stresses 68
    Load Types 70
        Dead and Live Loads *70*
        Static and Dynamic Loads *70*
        Concentrated and Distributed Loads *72*
    Rain and Snow Loads 72
    Water Loads 73
    Wind Loads 73
    Seismic Loads 74
        Location of Seismic Activity *74*
        Seismic Load Types *76*
        Structural Accommodations Unique to Seismic Activity *76*
        Structural Stiffening Accommodations *77*
    Soil Pressure Load 78
Structural Accommodations for Loads **79**
    Beams 79
    Columns 80
    Arches 80
    Cables 82
    Trusses 82
        Truss Construction *83*
        Truss Loads and Failure *84*
    Space Frames 84
Composite Structural Systems **84**
    Structural Bearing Walls 84
    Frame Structural Systems 85
        Steel Stud Walls *85*
        Post and Beam Construction *86*
        Rigid Frames *86*
        Slab and Column Frames *87*
    Membrane and Shell Systems 87
        Membrane Structures *87*
        Shell Structures *88*
Chapter Summary **88**
Review Questions **88**
Chapter Notes **88**

4 Building Systems 90
Case History **93**
Stairs **94**
    Basic Components 94
    Prefabricated Stairs 95
    Types of Stairs 95
        Straight-Run Stairs *95*
        Return Stairs *95*
        Scissor Stairs *96*
        Circular Stairs *96*
        Spiral Stairs *97*
        Folding Stairs *97*
    Stairs as Part of the Means of Egress 98
        Protected Stairs *98*
        Exterior Stairs *98*
        Fire Escapes *98*
    Smokeproof Stair Enclosures 99
        Active Smokeproof Enclosures *100*
        Passive Smokeproof Enclosures *100*
    Open Stairs 101
Mechanical Conveyor Systems **101**
    Moving Stairs 101
    Moving Walkways 102
Elevators **102**
    Emergency Use of Elevators 103
    Types of Elevators 104
        Hydraulic Elevators *104*
        Electric Elevators *104*
    Safety Features 108
    Elevator Hoistways 109
    Elevator Doors 111
    Elevator Access Panels 112
        Emergency Exits in Elevators *112*
        Blind Hoistway *112*
    Elevator Shafts 114
Vertical Shafts and Utility Chases **114**
    Vertical Shaft Enclosures 114
        Refuse and Laundry Chutes *114*
        Grease Ducts *115*
    Pipe Chases 116
Air Handling Systems **116**
    HVAC System Components 118
        Outside Air Intakes *118*
        Fans *118*
        Air Filtration *118*
        Air Heating and Cooling Equipment *119*
        Air Ducts *119*
    Simple Ventilation and Exhaust Systems 120
    Forced-Air System 120
    Smoke Control Systems 121
        Automatic Smoke Control *123*
        Manual Smoke Control *123*
    Smoke and Heat Vents 124
        Vent Types *124*
        Vent Limitations *125*
        Vent Hazards *125*
    Smoke Towers 125
    Pressurized Stairwells 126

Types of Pressurization Systems................... 126
Calibration of Pressurization Systems......... 126
Electrical Equipment... 128
Transformers.. 128
Air-Cooled Transformers............................ 129
Oil-Cooled Transformers............................ 129
Emergency and Standby Power Supplies 130
Generators 130
Emergency Power Batteries........................ 131
Chapter Summary 131
Review Questions.. 132
Chapter Notes.. 132

5 Interior Finishes and Passive Fire Protection 134
Case History... 137
Interior Finishes 138
Surface Burning Characteristics 139
Thin Surface Treatments 140
Floor Coverings.. 140
Fire-Retardant Coatings 140
Testing Interior Finishes 141
ASTM E-84.. 141
Flame Spread Ratings 142
Smoke Developed Ratings........................... 143
NFPA® Interior Finish Tests 143
Limitations of Test Findings............................ 144
Ceilings 145
Walls and Partitions.. 145
Compartmentation... 145
Fire Walls 146
Freestanding Walls 146
Tied Walls 147
Parapet Walls 147
Fire Resistance Ratings of Fire Walls 147
Negative Perception of Fire Walls 148
Fire Partitions.. 149
Enclosure and Shaft Walls............................... 149
Curtain Walls... 150
Fire Doors.. 152
Fire Door Classifications 152
Fire Door Requirements 153
Rolling (Overhead) Doors............................ 154
Horizontal Sliding Fire Doors 155
Swinging Fire Doors 156
Special Fire Doors....................................... 157
Fire Door Hardware and Features 158
Fire Door Closing Devices 159
Glazing... 161
Louvers 162
Fire Door Maintenance 162
Fire Door Testing 162

Criterion Referenced Testing 163
Marking Rated Fire Doors..........................164\
Chapter Summary 165
Review Questions.. 165
Chapter Notes.. 165

6 Foundations 166
Case History... 169
Soil Properties... 169
Types of Foundations 170
Shallow Foundations....................................... 171
Deep Foundations 172
Piles 173
Piers... 173
Foundation Walls.. 174
Concrete and Mortared Masonry 174
Stone 174
Wood... 174
EPS 174
Building Settlement 175
Shoring and Underpinning 176
Chapter Summary 177
Review Questions.. 177

7 Wood Construction 178
Case History... 181
Material Properties of Wood and Manufactured Components.. 181
Solid Lumber... 182
Engineered Wood 183
Laminated Wood... 184
Glulam Beams 185
Structural Composite Lumber 186
Thermoplastic Composite Lumber 187
Panels.. 187
Plywood 187
Nonveneered Panels 188
Composite Panels 189
Firestopping 189
Exterior Wall Materials 190
Sheathing... 190
Building Wrap 190
Foam Insulation 191
Siding Materials... 192
Brick or Stone Veneer 193
Interior Finish Materials 194
Manufactured Components 194
Quality Control of Lumber.............................. 195
Combustion Properties of Wood 196
Ignition Temperature 196
Heat of Combustion 197
Surface Area and Mass................................ 198

      Fire-Retardant Treatment of Wood 198
      Void Spaces 200
   Ignition-Resistant Construction 200
   Calculating Structural Endurance under Fire Conditions 201
Wood Structural Systems **202**
   Light Wood Framing 203
      Balloon Framing 203
      Platform Framing 204
   Heavy Timber Framing 205
   Post and Beam Framing 208
   Box Beams and I-Beams 208
   Trusses 209
Structural Collapse of Wood Construction **210**
Chapter Summary **211**
Review Questions **211**
Chapter Notes **211**

8 Masonry and Ordinary Construction 214
Case History **217**
Material Properties of Masonry Construction ... **217**
   Stone 219
   Bricks 219
   Concrete Blocks 220
   Other Masonry Units 220
   Mortar 221
   Fire Resistance of Masonry Walls 221
Features and Functions of Masonry Structures . **221**
   Code Classification of Masonry Buildings 222
   Construction of Masonry Walls 223
      Nonload-Bearing Masonry Walls 223
      Load-Bearing Masonry Walls 223
      Reinforced Masonry Walls 226
   Interior Framing 227
   Openings in Masonry Walls 228
   Parapets 229
   False Fronts and Voids 230
Structural Failure of Masonry Construction **230**
   Collapse of Masonry Construction 230
   Tie Rods and Bearing Plates 232
   Nonfire-Related Deterioration 233
Chapter Summary **235**
Review Questions **235**

9 Steel Construction 236
Case History **239**
Material Properties of Steel and Iron **240**
   Steel Ductility 241
   Steel Expansion and Deterioration 242
   Fire Protection of Steel 243
      Spray-Applied Materials 243
      Cementitious 244

      Gypsum 244
      Intumescent and Mastic Coatings 245
      Membrane Ceilings 245
Steel-Framed Structures **246**
   Beam and Girder Frames 247
      Rigid Frame 247
      Simple Frame 247
      Semi-Rigid Frame 247
   Steel Trusses 248
   Gabled Rigid Frames 249
   Steel Arches 249
   Steel Suspension Systems 250
   Steel Columns 250
   Floor Systems in Steel-Framed Buildings 251
      Open-Web Joists 251
      Steel Beams and Light-Gauge Steel Joists ... 251
   Code Modifications 251
Collapse of Steel Structures **252**
Chapter Summary **253**
Review Questions **253**

10 Concrete Construction 254
Case History **257**
Material Properties of Concrete **257**
   Reinforced Concrete 259
      Ordinary Reinforcing 259
      Prestressing Reinforcing 261
      Collapse of Prestressed Concrete 263
   Applications of Concrete 263
   Quality Control of Concrete 264
      Water-to-Cement Ratio 264
      Hydration 264
      Temperature 264
      Concrete Quality Tests 265
   Fire Resistance of Concrete Construction 266
      Spalling 267
      Heat Sink Effect 267
Concrete Framing Systems **267**
   Flat-Slab Concrete Frames 267
   Slab and Beam Framing 268
   Waffle Construction 268
   Concrete Plus Structural Steel 268
   Precast Concrete 268
      Advantages and Disadvantages 269
      Tilt-Up Construction 270
      Precast Connections 270
Chapter Summary **272**
Review Questions **272**
Chapter Notes **272**

11 Roofs 274
Case History **277**

Roofs and Fire Fighting 278
Architectural Styles of Roofs 279
    Flat Roofs 279
    Pitched Roofs 279
    Curved Roofs 281
        Lamella Arch *282*
        Geodesic Domes *282*
    Dormers 283
Roof Support Systems 283
    Flat Roof Support 283
        Box Beams and I-Beams *284*
        Inverted Roofs *285*
    Conventional Roof Framing 285
    Pre-Engineered Roof Framing 287
        Bowstring Trusses *288*
        Wood and Steel Trusses *289*
    Arches 289
Roof Decks 289
    Function of the Roof Deck 289
    Roof Deck Materials 290
Roof Coverings 291
    Flat Roof Coverings 292
        Vapor Barrier *292*
        Thermal Insulation *292*
        Roofing Membrane *292*
        Drainage Layer *294*
        Wear Course *294*
    Pitched Roof Coverings 294
        Asphalt Shingles and Tiles *294*
        Wood Shingles and Shakes *295*
        Clay, Slate, and Cement Tiles *296*
        Metal Roof Coverings *297*
    Fire Ratings of Roof Coverings 298
    Rain Roofs 299
Green Design Roofs 300
    Photovoltaic Roofs 301
    Vegetative Roof Systems 302
Roof Openings 303
    Penthouses 303
    Skylights 303
Chapter Summary 304
Review Questions 304
Chapter Notes 304

12 Special Structures and Design Features 306
Case History 309
High-Rise Buildings 310
    Early versus Modern High-Rise Buildings 311
        High-Rise Construction Height *311*
        Occupancy and Use *311*
        Ventilation and Vertical Enclosures *311*

        High-Rise Construction Type *313*
    Fire Protection Systems in High-Rise
        Buildings 314
        Standpipes *314*
        Automatic Sprinklers *315*
        Fire Alarm Systems *316*
        Smoke Control Systems *317*
        Fire Command Center/Central Control
            Station *317*
    Fire Extension in High-Rise Buildings 318
    Emergency Use of Elevators in High-Rise
        Buildings 319
        Safety during Emergency Elevator Use *319*
        Phase I Elevator Operation *320*
        Phase II Elevator Operation *321*
Limited or Controlled Access Buildings 322
    Underground Buildings 322
        Smoke and Fire Considerations *323*
        Special Provisions *324*
        Below Grade Spaces *324*
    Membrane Structures 325
        Air-Supported and Air-Inflated
            Structures *325*
        Limitations of Air Inflated and Supported
            Structures *326*
        Fire Fighting Considerations *327*
    Cable- and Frame-Membrane Structures 327
    Covered Mall Buildings 328
        Hazards and Access *329*
        Configuration *329*
        Construction and Systems *330*
    Detention and Correctional Facilities 330
Special Features within Buildings 332
    Atriums 332
    Explosion Venting of Buildings 334
        Types of Explosions *334*
        Containment and Venting *334*
    Areas of Refuge 337
    Rack Storage 337
        Sprinklers *339*
        Structure of Surrounding Building *339*
Chapter Summary 340
Review Questions 340
Chapter Notes 340

13 Buildings under Construction, Remodeling, Expansion, and Demolition 342
Case History 345
Tactical Problems of Construction Sites 345
    Construction Site Access 346
        Access Roads and Water Supply *347*
        Construction Elevators *347*

   Material Hoists *348*
   Stairways *348*
  Fire Hazards at Construction Sites 348
   Electrical Wiring... *349*
   Uses of Fuels *349*
   Storage of Fuels... *349*
   Construction Processes................................. *350*
   Combustible Debris *350*
  Structural Integrity 350
  Fire Protection.. 351
   Temporary Fire Protection Systems............. *351*
   Fire Extinguishers *352*
Structural Changes and Expansion **352**
  Building Renovating and Remodeling 352
  Building Expansion 353
  Life Safety Features 354
Demolition of Buildings **354**
  Scavenging Scrap Materials 354
  Unique Hazards of Demolition......................... 355
Chapter Summary **355**
Review Questions.. **355**

14 Non-Fire Building Collapse 356
Case History **359**
Human Related Causes of Building Collapse..... **360**
  Inadequate Structural Design........................... 360
  Change in Building Use..................................... 360
  Poor or Careless Construction Methods.......... 361
   Temporary Loads *361*
   Sequencing.. *361*
   Weakness of Building Frame....................... *361*
   Instability of Building Frame...................... *362*
  Poor or Careless Demolition Methods............. 362
  Explosions 363
  Other Human-Related Causes.......................... 364
Nature-Related Causes of Building Collapse **365**
  Earthquakes 365
  Landslides, Subsidence, and Sinkholes 367
   Landslides... *367*
   Subsidence *368*
   Sinkholes... *368*
  Wind-Related Hazards 369
   Tornadoes *370*
   Hurricanes *370*
  Snow and Water Loads...................................... 371
  Floods 372
Wide Area Incidents **373**
Chapter Summary **375**
Review Questions.. **375**
Chapter Notes.. **375**

Appendix A Chapter and Page Correlation to FESHE Outcomes **379**
Appendix B Metric Conversions **380**

Glossary **383**

Index **399**

List of Tables

Table 2.1	2015 International Building Code® Fire-Resistance Rating Requirements for Building Elements (Hours)	45
Table 3.1	Minimum Uniformly Distributed Live Loads, International Building Code®	71
Table 5.1	Flame Spread Ratings of Common Materials	142
Table 7.1	Dimensions of Softwood Lumber Products	182
Table 7.2	Fire-Resistance Requirements for Mill Construction	207
Table 8.1	Ultimate Compressive Strengths of Masonry	218
Table 8.2	Density of Masonry Materials	218
Table 11.1	A Comparison of Various Rigid-Roof Insulating Materials	293

Acknowledgements

The fourth edition of **Building Construction Related to the Fire Service** is designed to meet the objectives listed for FESHE courses.

Acknowledgement and special thanks are extended to the members of the IFSTA validating committee who contributed their time, wisdom, and knowledge to the development of this manual.

Technical Editor

The fourth edition of **Building Construction Related to the Fire Service** could not have been completed without the skill and hard work of contracted technical editor Randal Klaybor. Mr. Klaybor revised the early drafts of all manual chapters to the validation committee for their review, revision, and approval. He also assisted the committee and project manager with changes to chapter content from validation discussions.

IFSTA Building Construction Related to the Fire Service Fourth Edition Validation Committee

Chair

Don Turno
Area Operations Manager (Operations Chief)
Savannah River Nuclear Solutions
Aiken, SC

Vice Chair

David Hanneman
Fire Chief
Idaho Falls Fire Department
Idaho Falls, ID

Secretary

Kris Cooper
Deputy Fire Marshal
Colorado Springs Fire Department
Colorado Springs, CO

Committee Members

Mark Butterfield
Principal Senior Instructor
Butterfield & Associates
Hutchinson, KS

Randal E. Novak
Bureau Chief
Iowa Fire Service Training Bureau
Ames, Iowa

Michael Dalton
Battalion Chief/Shift Commander
Colorado Springs Fire Department
Colorado Springs, CO

Steven Parker
Deputy Fire Marshal
Arvada Fire Protection District
Arvada, CO

Tim Frankenberg
Deputy Chief/Fire Marshal
Washington Fire Dept
Washington, MO

Edward Prendergast, PE
Fire Protection Engineer
Chicago Fire Department (Retired)
Chicago, IL

Steven Martin
Deputy Director
Delaware State Fire School
Dover, DE

Thomas Rullo
Deputy Fire Chief
Mashpee Fire & Rescue Department
Mashpee, MA

IFSTA Building Construction Related to the Fire Service Fourth Edition Validation Committee
Committee Members (cont.)

David Sullivan
Battalion Chief
Orange County Fire Rescue Department
Winter Park, FL

Brad Tadlock
Fire Chief
Hilton Head Island Fire Rescue
Hilton Head Island, SC

Special thanks go to **Crown Fire Doors** for allowing us to watch, document, and ask questions during a UL test burn of their fire door hardware. Much appreciation is given to the following individuals and organizations for contributing information, an invitation for a photography session, photographs, and technical assistance instrumental in the development of this manual:

- American Plywood Association
- City of Norman (OK) Fire Department
- Colorado Springs (CO) Fire Department
- Crown Fire Doors
- Dave Coombs
- District Chief Chris E. Mickal, NOFD Photo Unit
- Donald Ouilette
- Donny Howard
- Doug Allen
- Edward Prendergast, PE
- Ed Steiner
- FEMA News Photography
- Gala and Associates
- Gregory Havel, Burlington, WI
- Hoover Wood Products
- Jerry Howell
- Jim Shirreffs III
- Loretta Hall
- McKinney (TX) Fire Department
- Michael Boub
- Natural Resources Canada 2015
- Rich Mahaney
- San Diego County Sheriff's Department
- Scott Strassburg
- Sturzenbecker Construction Company, Inc.
- Tanya Hoover
- Todd Mesick
- Underwriters Laboratories
- U.S. Geological Survey (USGS) Department of the Interior
- Vermont Timber Works
- West Allis (WI) Fire Department
- Wil Dane

Last, but certainly not least, gratitude is extended to the following members of the Fire Protection Publications staff whose contributions made the final publication of this manual possible.

Building Construction Related to the Fire Service, Fourth Edition, Project Team

Lead Senior Editor
Libby Snyder, Senior Editor

Technical Editor
Captain Randal Klaybor (ret.)
Fire Instructor
Milwaukee Area Technical College
Oak Creek, Wisconsin

Director of Fire Protection Publications
Craig Hannan

Curriculum Managers
Leslie Miller
Lori Raborg
Elkie Burnside

Editorial Manager
Clint Clausing

Production Coordinator
Ann Moffat

Editors
Veronica A. Smith, Senior Editor
Anthony E. Peters, Senior Editor

Illustrators and Layout Designer
Errick Braggs, Senior Graphic Designer
Clint Parker, Senior Graphic Designer
Ben Brock, Senior Graphic Designer
Missy Hannan, Senior Graphic Designer

Curriculum Development
Lynn Hughes, Lead Instructional Developer
Angel Musik, Instructional Developer
Crystal Griggs, Instructional Developer
David Schaap, Instructional Developer
Brittany Cook, Curriculum Writer
Beth Ann Fulgenzi, Instructional Developer
Lindsey Dugan, Curriculum Writer
Rachel Ware, Curriculum Writer
Brad McLelland, Instructional Developer
Jayne Ann Williamson, Instructional Developer
Angela Greenroy, Curriculum Writer
Frank Carter, Technical Editor
Alyssa Bullock, Intern

Photographers
Veronica A. Smith, Senior Editor
Leslie A. Miller, Senior Editor

Technical Reviewer
Kris Cooper
Deputy Fire Marshal
Colorado Springs Fire Department
Colorado Springs, CO

Editorial Staff
Tara Gladden, Editorial Assistant

Indexer
Nancy Kopper

The IFSTA Executive Board at the time of validation of Building Construction Related to the Fire Service was as follows:

IFSTA Executive Board

Executive Board Chair
Stephen Ashbrock
Fire Chief
Madeira & Indian Hill Fire Department
Cincinnati, OH

Vice Chair
Bradd Clark
Fire Chief
Ocala Fire Department
Ocala, FL

Executive Director
Mike Wieder
Fire Protection Publications
Stillwater, Oklahoma

Board Members

Steve Austin
Past President
Cumberland Valley Volunteer FF Association
Newark, DE

Mary Cameli
Assistant Chief
City of Mesa Fire Department
Mesa, AZ

Dr. Larry Collins
Associate Dean
Eastern Kentucky University
Richmond, KY

Chief Dennis Compton
Chairman
National Fallen Firefighters Foundation
Mesa, AZ

John W. Hoglund
Director Emeritus
Maryland Fire & Rescue Institute
New Carrollton, MD

Scott Kerwood
Fire Chief
Hutto Fire Rescue
Hutto, TX

Wes Kitchel
Assistant Chief
Sonoma County Fire & Emergency Services
Cloverdale, CA

Brett Lacey
Fire Marshal
Colorado Springs Fire Department
Colorado Springs, CO

Robert Moore
Division Director
TEEX
College Station, TX

Dr. Lori Moore-Merrell
Assistant to the General President
International Association of Fire Fighters
Washington, DC

Jeffrey Morrissette
State Fire Administrator
State of Connecticut Commission on
Fire Prevention and Control
Windsor Locks, CT

Josh Stefancic
Division Chief
Largo Fire Rescue
Largo, FL

IFSTA Executive Board
Board Members (cont.)

Don Turno
Operations Chief
Savannah River Nuclear Solutions
Aiken, SC

Paul Valentine
Senior Engineer
Nexus Engineering
Oakbrook, IL

Steve Westermann
Fire Chief
Central Jackson County Fire Protection District
Blue Springs, MO

Dedication

This manual is dedicated to the men and women who hold devotion to duty above personal risk, who count on sincerity of service above personal comfort and convenience, who strive unceasingly to find better and safer ways of protecting lives, homes, and property of their fellow citizens from the ravages of fire, medical emergencies, and other disasters

...The Firefighters of All Nations.

Introduction

Introduction Contents

Introduction	1
Purpose and Scope	2
Terminology	2
Resources	2
Key Information	3
Safety Alert	3
Information	3
Case Study	3
Case History	3
Metric Conversions	3
Key Term	4
Signal Words	4
Warning	4
Caution	4
Note	4

Introduction

The basic mission of the firefighter is, when called upon, to enter a burning structure to rescue occupants and to extinguish the fire; therefore, the true workplace of a firefighter is inside a building on fire. The firefighter enters a hostile and unknown environment and if the fire is not controlled, it will only become worse. To extinguish a fire in a building efficiently and safely without injury, the firefighter must be a master of that dangerous environment.

The firefighter must understand building construction to understand the behavior of buildings under fire conditions. However, firefighters cannot perform a detailed engineering analysis of buildings while performing their firefighting duties on the fire ground. Therefore, a fundamental knowledge of building components and systems is an essential prerequisite component of the decision-making process in successful fire ground operations.

While the idea of firefighters having a basic knowledge of buildings may seem simple or even self-evident, two fundamental aspects of building construction make it difficult. First, the field of building construction is constantly changing. Second, the life span of a building may be more than 100 years.

Firefighters face an enormous number of challenges and risk factors during an emergency related to building construction. Common factors that may affect a building's stability during a fire include:

- Use of lightweight construction materials that leave structures vulnerable to quick collapse during a fire.
- Obsolete materials and methods that may be obsolete.
- Materials manufactured to look like something else. For example, polyurethane siding designed to look like stone.
- Change in owner, occupancy type, and/or function; any of which may not have been legal or structurally sound.
- Reinforced structural elements that impair access.
- Renovations that exceed the capacity of the original building's structural components.
- Reliance on sprinklers for structural protection instead of mass of building elements.

These factors and more require that firefighters have a working knowledge of building construction materials and their behavior during a fire as well as pre incident planning procedures that will identify and lessen the hazards to firefighters during an emergency.

Purpose and Scope

This manual is intended to furnish the reader with basic information about how buildings are designed and constructed. This information will aid in decision making related to fire prevention and fire control. Whether enforcing fire codes, inspecting buildings, developing preincident plans, fighting fires, directing fire ground operations, overseeing firefighter safety, or investigating fires, a thorough understanding of building construction principles and practices as these relate to fire behavior and fire load will enable firefighters to make better, safer, and more timely decisions to protect people and property from potential and actual fires. Although this manual is not based on an NFPA® standard, many principles discussed in this text mirror NFPA® job performance requirements from standards such as NFPA® 1001, 1006, 1021, and 1031.

This manual is designed to meet the objectives delineated in the model course outline for Building Construction for Fire Protection as established by the Fires and Emergency Services Higher Education (FESHE) initiative of the United States Fire Administration (USFA).

This initiative brings together leaders in fire service higher education for the purpose of establishing model core curriculums for Associate's, Bachelor's, and Master's level fire service degree programs. This initiative is intended to encourage growth in the fire service higher education field and support commonality of the information that is taught to all students who will become responsible for the work of entering burning buildings.

Terminology

This manual is written with a global, international audience in mind. For this reason, it often uses general descriptive language in place of regional- or agency-specific terminology (often referred to as *jargon*). Additionally, in order to keep sentences uncluttered and easy to read, the word *state* is used to represent both state and provincial-level governments (or their equivalent). This usage is applied to this manual for the purposes of brevity and is not intended to address or show preference for only one nation's method of identifying regional governments within its borders.

The glossary at the end of the manual will assist the reader in understanding words that may not have their roots in the fire and emergency services. The IFSTA *Fire Service Orientation and Terminology* manual is the source for the definitions of fire and emergency services-related terms in this manual.

Resources

To help you increase your knowledge of occupational safety and health issues, this manual contains references to additional materials. Books, articles, journals, and websites are included in the Suggested Readings section at the end of the manual. These materials were used in the development of this manual and are recommended by the members of the validation committee for your use.

Additional educational resources to supplement this manual are available from IFSTA and Fire Protection Publications (FPP).

Key Information

Various types of information in this book are given in shaded boxes marked by symbols or icons. See the following definitions:

Safety Alert

Safety Alert boxes are used to highlight information that is important for safety reasons. Safety-related information that requires an in-depth explanation or is too lengthy for use in a CAUTION or WARNING box may be emphasized in these boxes.

Information

Information boxes give facts that are complete in themselves but belong with the text discussion. It is information that needs more emphasis or separation. (In the text, the title of information boxes will change to reflect the content.)

Case Study

Case Study boxes, like Case History boxes, present information analyzing an actual event. A Case Study describes an incident and its development, action taken, investigation results, and lessons learned.

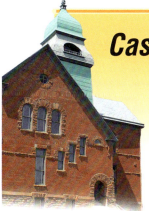

Case History

Each chapter in the manual will begin with a Case History. Case History boxes present information analyzing an actual event relevant to the topic of the chapter. Case Histories can include figures and illustrations.

Metric Conversions

Throughout this manual, U.S. units of measure are converted to metric units for the convenience of our international readers. Be advised that we use the Canadian metric system. It is very similar to the Standard International system, but may have some variation. The Tables and Guidelines used for Metric Conversions in this manual are explained in **Appendix B**.

Fire Hazard — Any material, condition, or act that contributes to the start of a fire or that increases the extent or severity of fire.

Key Term

A **key term** is designed to emphasize key concepts, technical terms, or ideas that the student in an associate's degree program in a fire-related field need to know. They are listed at the beginning of each chapter and the definition is placed in the margin for easy reference. An example of a key term is:

Fire Hazard — Any material, condition, or act that contributes to the start of a fire or that increases the extent or severity of fire.

Signal Words

Three key signal words are found in the book: **WARNING, CAUTION,** and **NOTE.** Definitions and examples of each are as follows:

- **WARNING** indicates information that could result in death or serious injury to the student in an associate's degree program in a fire-related field needs to be aware of. See the following example:

> **WARNING!**
> Truss constructed buildings have been known to fail in as little as 5 to 10 minutes of fire exposure. Firefighters should exercise extreme caution when operating in or on any building of lightweight construction in which the structural elements have been exposed to heat or fire.

- **CAUTION** indicates important information or data that the student in an associate's degree program in a fire-related field needs to be aware of in order to perform their duties safely. See the following example:

> **CAUTION**
> Cable and telephone lines are utility wires that generally are not thought of as posing a major hazard. However, these lines carry current and may pose a threat in certain hazardous environments. In addition, these wires are often run in close proximity to electrical lines, and under certain conditions they may become charged.

- **NOTE** indicates important operational information that helps explain why a particular recommendation is given or describes optional methods for certain procedures. See the following example:

NOTE: More information concerning fire and life safety education follows in a subsequent section.

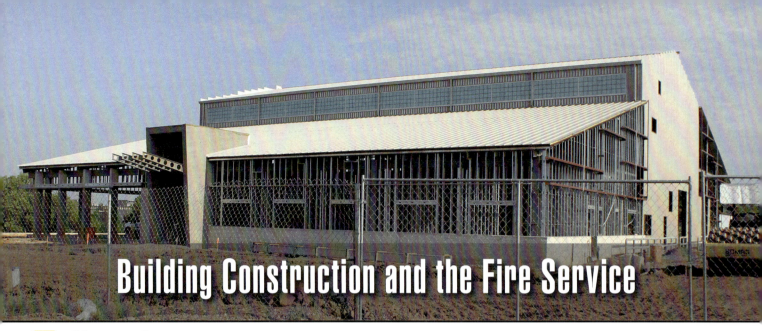

Building Construction and the Fire Service

Chapter Contents

Case History 9	Building Use 27
History of Building Construction 11	Existing Infrastructure 27
The Design and Construction Process 12	Fire Loss Management 28
Concept 12	**Other Variables** **28**
Financing 14	Owner's Needs and Desires 28
Documentation and Bids 14	Investment of Wealth 28
Building Permits 15	Aesthetics and Culture 29
Construction 15	**Community Fire Defense** **30**
Inspection and Testing 16	Heat Transfer 30
Renovation and Remodeling......................17	Exposures and Fire Spread Factors 31
Law-Based Construction Variables **18**	**Design-Caused Structural Failure** **33**
Building Code Requirements 18	Loss of Structural Integrity 34
Accessibility Requirements 21	Building System Failure 34
Engineering-Based Construction	Design Deficiencies 35
Variables................................... **22**	**Preincident Planning in Building**
Climate 22	**Construction**............................... **36**
Building Site Properties 22	Geographic Information Systems 36
Configuration of Internal Spaces 23	Fire Fighting Strategy 37
Automatic Fire Suppression Systems 23	**Chapter Summary** **37**
Age of Construction 25	**Review Questions** **37**
Energy Conservation (Green Design) 26	**Chapter Notes** **38**
Economics-Based Construction	
Variables................................... **27**	

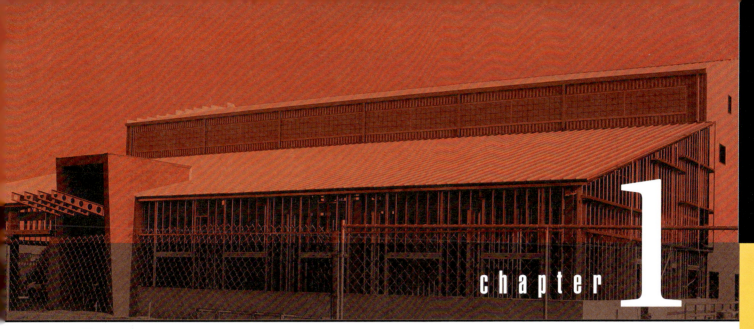

chapter 1

Key Terms

Aesthetics 29	Fuel Load..20
Americans with Disabilities Act (ADA) of 1990 - Public Law 101-336 20	Gentrification 26
Area of Refuge 20	Geographic Information Systems (GIS) 36
Authority Having Jurisdiction 12	Green Design 27
Board of Appeals 15	Heat Release Rate (HRR) 20
Building Code 13	Heat Transfer...31
Building Permit 15	*International Building Code® (IBC®)* 18
Combustion...35	International Code Council (ICC) 18
Conflagration 30	Noncombustible 20
Convection 31	Preincident Planning 16
Design Principles 13	Preincident Survey 16
Design-Build 12	Setback...23
Exposure 31	Spec Building..28
Fast-Track Construction 16	Thermal Radiation 31
Fire Spread..30	Wildland/Urban Interface........................33

Building Construction and the Fire Service

FESHE Outcomes Addressed In This Chapter

Fire and Emergency Services Higher Education (FESHE) Outcomes: *Building Construction for Fire Protection*

1. Describe building construction as it relates to firefighter safety, building codes, fire prevention, code inspection, firefighting strategy, and tactics.
2. Classify major types of building construction in accordance with a local/model building code.
8. Identify the indicators of potential structural failure as they relate to firefighter safety.
9. Identify the role of GIS as it relates to building construction.

Learning Objectives

After reading this chapter, students will be able to:

1. Recognize how changes in building construction can influence fire fighting operations.
2. Describe the building design and construction process from concept to renovation and remodeling.
3. Identify laws and other regulation variables that affect building design.
4. Identify engineering variables that affect building design.
5. Identify economic variables that affect building design.
6. Identify other variables that affect building design.
7. Explain fire behavior principles as they apply to community fire defense.
8. Identify factors of structural failure caused by design.
9. Explain the role of preincident planning in building construction.

Chapter 1
Building Construction and the Fire Service

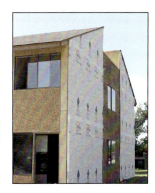

Case History

Part 1: Bowstring Truss Collapse, 1988

Event Description:

Five firefighters were killed in a bowstring truss roof collapse while fighting a fire in an automotive dealership in 1988. The fire was reported to be in the roof area when firefighters arrived and crews vented the roof and extended hand lines into the shop area in an attempt to control the fire.

After approximately twenty minutes, little progress had been made in controlling the fire, prompting the crews to withdraw. Before the crews could exit, a portion of the truss roof collapsed trapping the firefighters in an area engulfed in fire. This occurred thirty-three minutes after the first fire unit arrived on scene.

Lessons Learned:

- Fire in the attic area involved the five wood trusses that spanned the service area.
- The attic area was used for storage and the additional fuel load affected the spread and growth of the fire.
- Operating under a truss roof is just as dangerous operating on top of the roof when the structural members are involved.

Source: NFPA

Part 2: Basement Fire, 1991

Event Description:

In 1991, four volunteer firefighters were killed during a fire in Western Pennsylvania. The fire began in the basement of a two-story building storing flammable and combustible materials including lacquer, paints, varnish, a spray booth, dip tanks, and furniture.

Responding firefighters found evidence of fire in the basement but could not initially determine the fire's extent. As fire fighting operations began, one fire team entered from the front of the building to the first floor. Approximately forty-two minutes after the initial alarm, a large section of the concrete first floor collapsed at the front of the building. The floor surface was concrete, but it was supported by unprotected steel beams and steel columns with severe rust in the front of the building.

The collapsed floor, and fire erupting from the basement, cut off the firefighters' avenue of escape. Subsequent medical examination determined that the firefighters died from burns.

Lessons Learned:
- The nature and condition of the first floor construction was not apparent from the outside. Therefore, its behavior when exposed to the fire below could not be anticipated.
- A furniture refinishing operation with its associated fuel and fire hazards was located in a basement where it might not have been expected.
- The below grade location of the fire made access difficult.
- Preincident surveys are essential, especially after a change of occupancy.

Part 3: Structural Collapse, 2006

Event Description:

Two volunteer firefighters were killed when an exterior wall and awning collapsed during defensive overhaul operations in 2006. The fire occurred in a structure that had undergone several renovations and additions. The one-story building was built of ordinary construction with concrete block walls and a heavy timber truss roof with sheet metal decking. The front block wall had been covered with brick veneer, wood, and sheet metal siding. The metal awning was covered with sheet metal.

When the initial offensive attack was unsuccessful, efforts to control the fire changed to a defensive strategy. After several hours, the roof collapsed and the fire slowly burned out. Many crews were released from the scene and operations were suspended so the remaining firefighters could rehabilitate.

Firefighters began exterior overhaul operations after the break, and small fires were noticed in the building. A hand line was re-positioned at the front door. Firefighters had already pulled down areas of the side walls due to noticeable instability. While the two person crew was operating at the front, the awning pivoted down, striking the two firefighters. The front wall then immediately collapsed, burying the firefighters.

Lessons Learned:
- Firefighters should be trained on the different building construction types, the associated hazards, and the potential methods of collapse when exposed to fire.
- Collapse zones should be established and monitored during and after the fire because the structure has been weakened and may collapse.
- Conduct preincident planning on buildings to identify construction types and gather information on various features that will aid in the development of safe and effective fireground operations.

Source: NIOSH

In a scientific sense, the laws of physics and chemistry that govern fire behavior never change. At the same time, no two fires are exactly identical because no two buildings are exactly identical. Knowledge of building structures and construction allows investigators and first responders to determine reasonable and safe options while evaluating conditions. This chapter will introduce the following topics:

- History of building construction
- The design and construction process
- Law-based construction variables
- Engineering-based construction variables
- Economics-based construction variables

- Other variables
- Community fire defense
- Design-caused structural failure
- Preincident planning in building construction

History of Building Construction

Because each building type reacts to fire conditions in a different way, the firefighter's ability to recognize configuration features and component pieces of a structure is critically important. The history of building construction provides the basis for understanding the differences between buildings in a jurisdiction. Factors such as technology and economics affect the configuration and materials used at structures in any specific time and place. A building's life span can range from months to full centuries; therefore, most communities include buildings that vary widely in age. Buildings may appear drastically different or be camouflaged to look similar despite differences in age, configuration, and construction materials **(Figure 1.1)**.

Figure 1.1 The building in the foreground, constructed in 2005, was designed to coordinate with the aesthetic of the building in the background, constructed in 1911.

Construction technology is continually evolving. Buildings in a community may represent a wide range of construction types, each presenting challenges to firefighters. Older buildings may include features now considered obsolete or dangerous. Newer buildings use technology that may not be fully tested, or include unexpected hazards. For example, a modern building with electricity-powered air conditioning and natural gas heating units on the roof may be built next to a building constructed in the 1920s with no central air conditioning and a coal powered heating plant.

This chapter will review construction types and materials common to most jurisdictions in the US and Canada. Every individual jurisdiction is strongly encouraged to survey its response area to determine the construction types that will be encountered in local incidents.

Authority Having Jurisdiction (AHJ) — An organization, office, or individual responsible for enforcing the requirements of a code or standard, or approving equipment, materials, an installation, or a procedure.

Scope of This Manual

The information provided in this manual is intended to serve as general information to address many aspects of building systems and is not intended to indicate specific code requirements in any jurisdiction. Applicable codes and the **Authority Having Jurisdiction** will dictate the building system specifications within any specific jurisdiction. The student should understand common local construction methods and codes.

The Design and Construction Process

Before studying building construction, it is useful to examine the overall design process. The building's design and construction is a process that begins as an idea and ends with a substantial structure. The process may take weeks or years and requires many resources including:

- Legal expertise
- Technical knowledge
- Financial resources
- Management skills
- Creative talent

Buildings are diverse. In some cases, the reasons behind building design features may shift with time, availability, and utility. For example, log cabins are modernly erected mainly for appearance rather than structural or economic advantage, but they were originally built because logs were readily available and useful. This manual includes many insights into diverse philosophies of building design, appearance, use, and the construction process.

Common variables in building construction are described later in this chapter, categorized by their primary focus, although several have implications across multiple categories. The following sections describe the factors that influence a building's design and construction in the usual order in which the steps are taken.

Concept

The building process begins when a developer or project owner perceives a need. The owner may contact an architect with a concept of the finished project, or solicit proposals from several architectural firms. The architects and their associates will have meetings with the owner to determine the owner's needs and desires. If the building is not large, such as an ordinary house, the process may begin with a contractor. The contractor may retain an architect, who will produce a preliminary presentation to the owner. Once the building's concept appears on paper, it begins to be quantifiable, and the owner has the opportunity to evaluate and change the design.

The owner may contract with a single firm to undertake both the building's design and construction. Such an arrangement is known as a **design-build** project. A design-build firm is usually a general contractor with architects and engineers on staff. In other cases, separate contracting and design firms may affiliate through a joint venture for a particular project.

Design-Build — The use of a single organization to design and build a facility to minimize risks for the project owner. May also refer to a design-build firm.

Design Principles

During the concept phase, the variables may be discussed in terms of **design principles** [1]. The design principles of a building include many subcategories that influence the building's final appearance in addition to construction techniques and safeguards against structural failure.

Design Principles — Guidelines applied to basic units of a project that cause the items to work together as a unified, completely finished item that serves a purpose within established parameters. Units can include the materials, concepts, and setting.

Architectural Perspectives

Buildings and their design is the topic of much writing and discussion. One of America's most prominent architects, Frank Lloyd Wright, called buildings "machines for living." A few years prior, Chicago architect Louis A. Sullivan, known for his stately commercial buildings, summarized his design philosophy with the statement, "Form follows function."

Buildings are a composite of many diverse elements and systems that are designed with a purpose. First responders must understand the essential purposes behind building design and construction in order to predict how the fire will affect the structure, occupants, and contents, and how best to mitigate those effects.

Professional Design

The design and construction process is a serious and expensive undertaking. Many people are involved and many decisions must be made. An architect will use **building codes** relevant to the jurisdiction as a primary resource when choosing major building aspects and eliminating alternatives.

NOTE: More information on building codes is included later in this chapter.

Building Code — A set of rules developed by a standards organization and adopted as law by a governmental body to regulate the minimum requirements for construction, renovation, and maintenance of buildings.

Materials

Some buildings may be designed using predesigned, prefabricated components and techniques. A design may also involve old materials used in innovative ways **(Figure 1.2)**. Using established resources reduces the time and cost of the design work. Other buildings involve unique architecture and newly developed methods and materials.

Engineering Specialties

In addition to architecture, the major engineering specialties required during building construction activities include:

- Civil engineering
  - Water supply
  - Sanitary sewers
  - Surveying
  - Site preparation and excavation
  - Roadways
  - Storm water drainage

Figure 1.2 This 2009 renovation of a building constructed in 1919 includes original features in innovative ways.

- Structural engineering
  - Determination of loads
  - Foundation design
  - Structural behavior
  - Structural members
  - Structural erection
- Mechanical engineering
  - Heating, ventilation, and air conditioning
  - Pumping systems
  - Elevators
  - Plumbing systems
- Electrical engineering
  - Lighting
  - Power
  - Communications
- Fire protection engineering
  - Automatic sprinklers
  - Standpipes
  - Fire alarm
  - Smoke control
  - Building code compliance

The final consideration in the building design process is landscaping. A local building code may specify a type or amount of landscaping required in the interest of community beautification; this work will be assigned to a landscape architect.

Financing

When the initial design has been selected, the owner must secure financing for construction. A financial institution providing the construction loan will have certain requirements, which may include a market analysis to evaluate the project's economic feasibility. For example, in projects like an office building or a shopping center, the lending institution will want to know that tenants have expressed a willingness to rent space when the building is completed. The lending institutions' technical requirements will necessitate a review of the architect's design drawings and may include engineering documents such as:

- Land surveys
- Preliminary budgets
- Soil test reports

Documentation and Bids

When financing has been secured, the building's engineering design can proceed. Final modifications and design decisions are settled. At this time, the building's details become more specific and involve everything within the scope of the final building, including common items such as door handles, and lighting fixtures. Bids are received from subcontractors who will perform specialized work, such as installing electrical wiring, and contracts are signed.

Building Permits

Before a building is constructed, a government unit, such as a city, county, province, or state, typically requires a **building permit** to be issued. Before the permit is issued, the proposed design must meet the applicable building code's provisions. Fire officials may be actively involved in the permitting process in some jurisdictions.

NOTE: For more information about the permitting process, see the IFSTA **Plans Examiner for Fire and Emergency Services and Fire Inspection and Code Enforcement** manuals.

A building permit is obtained from the local building department. Normally, building plans are submitted to the building department for review as part of the permit process. If the building official notes conditions in the plan that do not comply with the code, further changes may be necessary. Unusual designs or circumstances may require the use of compensatory measures or equivalencies rather than strict compliance with a prescriptive code.

If a building official rejects a proposed building design, an architect may appeal the decision to the **Board of Appeals**. Building codes provide an appeals process to resolve differences in interpretation of the specific code provisions or to review an alternative means of compliance.

Building Permit — Authorization issued from the appropriate authority having jurisdiction (AHJ) before any new construction, addition, renovation, alteration, or demolition of buildings or structures occurs.

Board of Appeals — Group of people, usually five to seven, with experience in fire prevention, building construction, and/or code enforcement, who are legally constituted to arbitrate differences of opinion between fire and building officials, property owners, occupants or builders.

In the case of large projects such as a high-rise building that will take many months to construct, the building department may issue a permit for the initial phase of work so construction can begin while the final design details are being completed. A permit may be issued for the foundation so that the excavation and construction can begin, thus saving both time and money.

In some jurisdictions, the fire authorities have legal authority to review building plans. In jurisdictions where the fire department does not have formal authority, fire department officials or representatives may establish a cooperative relationship with building officials. In this type of relationship, the building department gains aid in determining fire safety compliance, and the fire department gains information on the construction types within the jurisdiction **(Figure 1.3)**. When the fire department is involved in the planning process, fire safety issues can be addressed before construction begins. Identifying and correcting problems before construction starts improves efficiency and cost effectiveness.

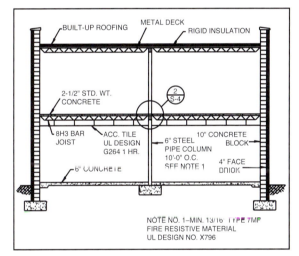

Figure 1.3 Fire and code enforcement officials must have the opportunity to evaluate building plans before construction begins. The details of structural fireproofing are just one aspect that needs to be reviewed.

Construction

The construction process requires coordination and scheduling. Some tasks must be performed before others; for example, the structural components must be in place before the roof can be constructed. The need for coordination also extends to suppliers, who need to know when materials will be needed at the job site. For example, if a hotel is being constructed, a plumbing supplier may have a contract to supply 1,000 bathtubs. If the bathtubs are not ready when they are needed, construction will be delayed; at the same time, storage may not be available for the bathtubs before installation.

A technique known as **fast-track construction** may be used to shorten the construction time by overlapping the design and construction phases. Construction work starts on completed early design phases while later phases are still in process. This method can greatly reduce total construction time, making it attractive to owners.

The timing of some construction phases may affect the fire department. For example, the street must be paved and water supply established before combustible building materials arrive on site. Water supply and road work may be delayed during cold weather conditions, but the builders may continue construction.

> **Fast-Track Construction** — Strategy to reduce the overall time for completion of a project by merging the design and construction phases. Often used in conjunction with design-build.

Inspection and Testing

Knowledgeable inspectors must work closely with architects and contractors during construction. Inspections take place during construction and upon a project's completion to ensure that proper materials and construction techniques are used. Seemingly minor changes to an architect's or engineer's plans may directly cause or contribute to structural failure.

During inspections, the following building features may be tested for function and compliance with standards and codes:

- Materials (such as concrete)
- Systems (such as fire pumps)
- Components (such as emergency generators)

Several entities perform inspections to evaluate unique factors. Examples include:

- Building department inspects the building during construction and after completion for compliance with the building code
- Owner's representative inspects the building and communicates any findings to the general contractor
- Architect or the architect's representative inspects the building as construction nears completion
- Fire inspector inspects fire protection system installation and operation in new construction

NOTE: The fire inspector witnesses system tests. The actual system tests are performed by the installing contractor's representatives. This practice helps minimize fire service liability should a system component fail.

> **Preincident Survey** — Assessment of a facility or location made before an emergency occurs, in order to prepare for an appropriate emergency response. *Also known as* Preplan.

> **Preincident Planning** — Act of preparing to manage an incident at a particular location or a particular type of incident before an incident occurs. *Also known as* Prefire Inspection, Prefire Planning, Preincident Inspection, Preincident Survey, or Preplanning.

Fire department involvement in new construction testing and inspection provides the fire department with first-hand information from a **preincident survey** that is useful in **preincident planning**. The fire prevention bureau should document fire protection system test results. This practice serves several purposes including:

- Establishing that the systems were installed in accordance with the fire code and that the system operated properly.

- Facilitating re-inspection and subsequent testing over the life of the systems by establishing performace benchmarks.
- Documenting system features and functions so the information is maintained as personnel changes occur in the fire department and the building's management.

NOTE: More information on preincident surveys is included later in this chapter.

Renovation and Remodeling

Permits for building renovation and remodeling are also included in the building permit process **(Figure 1.4)**. Building departments require that structural modifications be designed by structural engineers and performed by licensed contractors. Minor renovations, such as adding an electrical receptacle, must also be performed by licensed contractors. A jurisdiction may not require that plans be submitted for minor renovations; however, an inspector will determine whether the work was completed in an acceptable manner.

In some cases, a building may be exempt from current code requirements. The *International Existing Building Code (IEBC)* determines the extent of work in relation to the building as a whole, which may range from repairs, to renovations, to change of occupancy, and building additions. The conditions established in the code will determine how much of the existing structure can be considered *existing/non-conforming*. Occupancy changes may not be required to comply with current codes if the new occupancy classification is considered to be a lesser hazard than the original use.

Depending on the extent of the renovation, the owners may have to bring the building to current code. In some cases, planned renovations may violate the provisions of a building code; for example, the construction of corridor partitions that do not have the required fire resistance because compliance with the specific requirements of a building code would be more costly.

Figure 1.4 Renovation and remodeling work may be regulated per the codes adopted in a city.

If renovation or remodel work is not carried out properly, unsafe conditions could result. A building department should watch for any of the following potentially dangerous changes:

- Removal or penetration of bearing walls
- Modification of beams or trusses
- Structural overloading of roofs
- Creation of mezzanine floors in attic spaces
- Rooftop additions
- Remodeling that creates additional voids
- Illegal remodeling or overloading that causes extreme hazards
- Subdivision of existing spaces that creates maze-like floor plans

Law-Based Construction Variables

Laws and other regulations may govern the features required in structures. These types of variables are discussed in the following sections.

Building Code Requirements

A building code is a body of law that determines the minimum standards that buildings must meet in the interest of community safety and health. Although jurisdictions can write and adopt their own codes, they typically adopt all or a portion of a model code package as their building and fire code. By adopting model codes, government entities do not need to write their own complex documents to provide a fundamental degree of uniformity among jurisdictions. Model codes are not intended to address all features unique to a jurisdiction, so the AHJ may amend a model code through appropriate legislation to suit local conditions.

International Building Code Origin

The International Building Code is the successor to three earlier model codes:

- The Uniform Building Code (UBC) published by International Conference of Building Officials (ICBO).
- The Standard Building Code published by Southern Building Code Congress International.
- The Building Officials and Code Administrators (BOCA) National Building Code published by the Building Officials and Code Administrators International.

> **International Building Code® (IBC®)** — Code that is dedicated to providing safety regulations for life safety, structural, and fire protection issues that occur throughout the life of a building.

> **International Code Council (ICC)** — Organization that develops the *International Building Code® (IBC®)* and the *International Fire Code® (IFC®)*, for city and state adoption. Was formed by the merger of the Building Officials and Code Administrators (BOCA) International, Inc., the International Conference of Building Officials (ICBO), and the Southern Building Code Congress International (SBCCI).

The most widely used model building code in the United States is the ***International Building Code® (IBC®)*** published by **International Code Council® (ICC)**. The International Building Code has a companion fire code, the *International Fire Code*. The building and fire codes complement each other and are intended to be used together during facility design. This interdependence underscores the desirability for building and fire officials to work together in applying and enforcing building and fire codes.

Some jurisdictions may adopt and use codes developed by the National Fire Protection Association® (such as NFPA® 1, *Uniform Fire Code*, and NFPA® 5000, *Building Construction and Safety Code*. A commonly adopted NFPA® code is the *Life Safety Code* (NFPA® 101). This code is often adopted by a governmental agency with a specific area of responsibility, such as a state health department.

In Canada, a widely used building code is the *National Building Code of Canada* published by National Research Council of Canada. This document is a model code and is adopted or adapted by most of the provinces and territories in Canada.

Building codes impose restrictions on designers that may conflict with their creative intentions. On the other hand, all designers have an ethical and legal responsibility to provide a safe end product.

Many building codes quantify common sense requirements. For example, a building must have sufficient structural strength to prevent collapse. In addition to supporting its own weight, the structural system must be able to withstand environmental forces common to the area such as wind, snow, and earthquakes.

Significant portions of building codes are also devoted to fire safety because buildings include many features that affect fire behavior. Provisions address the following elements:

- Structural fire resistance
- Flammability of interior finishes
- Adequacy of means of egress
- Enclosure of vertical openings
- Fire protection systems
- Exposure protection
- Occupancy separation
- Electrical systems
- Natural gas

Life Safety Codes

Many safety codes are developed in reaction to catastrophic incidents. Life safety during an incident in a structure must include considerations for the safety of firefighters and civilians. Numerous occupational safety standards and regulations address the inherent danger of fire fighting. The most prominent of these come from the NFPA® and the U.S. Occupational Safety and Health Administration (OSHA). Additional safety programs are also available through the National Fallen Firefighters Foundation's Everyone Goes Home® program and the International Association of Fire Chiefs' annual safety stand-down. The United States Fire Administration maintains a national map that indicates location and frequency of fire fatalities [2].

Life safety codes require that specific types of structures include fire- and smoke-resistant features, which often equates to a longer time span between ignition and the development of an environment immediately dangerous to life or health. Occupant safety must also be considered in the following areas:

- Design of stairs and walking surfaces
- Balcony railings
- Overhead obstacles
- Electrical systems (electrical shock prevention)
- Elevator operation

The following are life safety considerations for first responders and the public during a structural incident:

- Annunciator panels should be easily viewed near entrances to help company officers know the type and location of the alarm
- Standpipe connections must have standard threads to ensure compatibility with fire department equipment

Noncombustible — Incapable of supporting combustion under normal circumstances.

Fuel Load — The total quantity of combustible contents of a building, space, or fire area, including interior finish and trim, expressed in heat units of the equivalent weight in wood.

Heat Release Rate (HRR) — (1) Total amount of heat produced or released to the atmosphere from the convective-lift phase of a fire, per unit mass of fuel consumed per unit time. (2) Heat released when a material burns, expressed in kilowatts or British Thermal Units (Btu).

Americans with Disabilities Act (ADA) of 1990 - Public Law 101-336 — Federal statute intended to remove barriers, physical and otherwise, that limit access by individuals with disabilities.

Area of Refuge — (1) Space protected from fire in the normal means of egress either by an approved sprinkler system, separation from other spaces within the same building by smokeproof walls, or location in an adjacent building. (2) Area where persons who are unable to use stairs can temporarily wait for instructions or assistance during an emergency building evacuation.

- Generator systems must have a switch that takes circuits off line to prevent feedback to unintended areas
- Air handling units that recirculate interior air must address air quality during incidents.

NOTE: Building ventilation systems and smoke control systems are described in depth in Chapter 4.

Construction Type

First the insurance industry, and then model building code publishers, recognized that fire behavior differed based on a building's features, and began to classify buildings by their construction type. More currently, the *International Building Code® (IBC®)* establishes numerical designations for the following construction types:

- Type I — Fire-Resistive
- Type II — Protected **Noncombustible** or Noncombustible
- Type III — Exterior Protected (Masonry or Ordinary)
- Type IV — Heavy Timber
- Type V — Wood Frame

Each classification is further divided into sub classifications. For example, wood-frame construction is divided into two sub-classifications that indicate whether the wood framing is provided with a protection such as gypsum board.

NOTE: Construction classifications are explained in detail in Chapter 2.

In many cases, the actual construction type is not obvious, or multiple construction types may be used in combination. The combination of classifications is especially likely when an older structure is renovated **(Figure 1.5)**. When a building encompasses multiple construction classifications, the building should be considered to meet the lesser construction classification.

Figure 1.5 During renovations, an additional building construction classification may be added to an existing structure.

Occupancy and Use

Occupancy and use are often addressed in model codes because they affect the **fuel load**, which in turn influences fire behavior within the structure. As a general rule, greater quantities of fuel or highly volatile fuels will generate a higher **heat release rate**. For example, an automobile body shop will contain high fuel load resources such as gasoline, solvents, and torches. A fire in this environment will develop rapidly and subject the structure to high temperatures. Other types of occupancies, such as a bank, typically have relatively low quantities of combustibles (low fuel load) with only a few potential sources of ignition.

Over time, many buildings undergo one or more changes in occupancy type. More than a simple change in decoration and contents, this is a change to a building's overall use. For example, a cold-storage warehouse may be converted to a residential apartment building **(Figure 1.6)**.

Figure 1.6 Extreme renovations may change the occupancy type of a building. For example, this photo shows a building that was converted from a cold storage building to apartments. *Courtesy of Ed Prendergast.*

The fire ratings and life safety features of one occupancy type may not address the needs of another. Changes in occupancy are monitored through the process of reviewing the plan during renovation. While not optimal, a change of occupancy may also be discovered when a fire or building inspector visits the property for a routine inspection. Communication between code officials and fire departments is essential in this process.

Accessibility Requirements

In 1990, the ***Americans with Disabilities Act (ADA)*** was signed into law in the US. The Act requires the removal of architectural barriers and the addition of other features to provide accessibility for persons with recognized impairments **(Figure 1.7)**. Some building elements that may be altered to improve access include:

- Building entrances
- Parking and passenger loading zones
- Elevators
- Alarms (visible and/or audible)
- Means of egress

In cases where building codes allow ADA-inaccessible structural features, such as stairs, alternate protection must be made available, such as an **area of refuge** where a person may wait safely until further assistance or instructions are available. Areas of refuge may not be required in buildings equipped with an automatic sprinkler system.

Figure 1.7 Fire alarm pull stations may be located at a lower level in a wall for easier access by a person in a wheelchair.

Where required, the area of refuge must be equipped with two-way communication so occupants can call for assistance. Firefighters must be prepared to respond to anyone calling for assistance. Areas of refuge may include arrangements such as:

- Stairway landing in a smoke proof enclosure
- Balcony located adjacent to an exterior stair
- Protected vestibule adjacent to an exit enclosure

Engineering-Based Construction Variables

Regardless of the building's purpose, it must be designed so it can actually be built. The strength of the building materials and the mathematics of structural mechanics must match the proposed building design and the expected loads and forces.

NOTE: Loads and forces are discussed in Chapter 3.

Common building designs must meet a wide range of engineering variables, as described in the following sections. In addition to those variables, buildings that include exotic or innovative design elements may challenge the engineer and architect. Buildings that defy conventional planning and may require special resources in case of an emergency include:

- The Golden Gate Bridge
- Willis Tower, formerly known as the Sears Tower
- St. Louis Gateway Arch

Climate

Building heating and cooling requirements are determined by the region's historical temperature variations. In all climates, insulating materials increase the structure's energy conservation.

Climatic concerns affect other aspects of building design. For example, in areas with heavy annual rainfall, buildings may be designed with overhangs or enclosed walkways between them to protect pedestrians.

Building Site Properties

Engineering-based variables must take into consideration the features of the building site itself. Soil conditions and properties vary by region and must be evaluated before the foundation of a building is designed. The type of foundation used will be determined partially by the soil's strength, resistance to strain, and stability.

NOTE: Soil properties and foundation types are described in Chapter 6.

Natural terrain and developed terrain features will also affect the features of a completed building **(Figure 1.8)**. These factors may also affect fire fighting tactics, and they must be identified before an incident so the response team can plan an appropriate response. Natural and developed terrain features that may complicate access by emergency responders include:

- Steep slopes
- Rivers

- Landscaping
- Narrow roadways
- **Setbacks**
- Security barriers

Other building site factors that influence the overall building height and the practicality of below-grade spaces include:

- Level of the water table
- Frost line
- Presence or absence of a solid bedrock layer

Configuration of Internal Spaces

The configuration of a building refers to its general shape or layout. While building code requirements address fire behavior and containment, building designers rarely consider fire fighting strategies as a principle design element. Designers tend to focus on the structure's non-fire functionality and visual appeal.

Design choices can significantly affect fire behavior and the response of building elements to a fire. For example, designers or the building's owners may favor vertical openings for aesthetic reasons although vertical openings create a chute for unimpeded fire and smoke travel **(Figure 1.9)**.

NOTE: Atriums are discussed in Chapter 12.

Automatic Fire Suppression Systems

Inclusion of fire protection systems, especially an automatic sprinkler system, will affect the planned building design. For example, codes may reduce other aspects of building design, such as required fire resistance or allowable area, when a sprinkler system is provided.

An automatic fire protection system, especially an automatic sprinkler system, is the first line of defense in many buildings. When the sprinkler system is properly designed and maintained, incipient stage fires will be promptly detected and controlled. Even where an automatic suppression system cannot be effective in controlling a fire, such systems can constrain fire growth and notify emergency responders.

NOTE: For additional information on fire suppression systems, refer to Chapter 4 in this manual and IFSTA's **Fire Protection and Detection and Suppression Systems** manual.

Figure 1.8 The river adjoining this condominium renders one entire side of the structure inaccessible to land-based emergency vehicles. *Courtesy of Ed Prendergast.*

Figure 1.9 High-ceiling atriums have few features to contain smoke from a fire.

Setback — Distance from the street line to the front of a building.

Dupont Plaza Hotel

An example of how building configuration affects fire behavior and life safety can be seen in the 1986 fire in the Dupont Plaza hotel in Puerto Rico that killed 97 people[3]. The Dupont Plaza Hotel fire was the second deadliest hotel fire in U.S. history.

The hotel was a 20-story, nonsprinklered, fire-resistive structure. The first floor was a ballroom. The second floor was compartmentalized with a gambling casino, lobby, and shops **(Figure 1.10)**. The following points correspond to the four points of fire spread:

1. At 3:22 p.m. fire was discovered in the ballroom on the first floor. The fire had been deliberately set in a stack of recently delivered furniture.

2. A glass partition wall separated the ballroom from an adjacent open stairwell that extended to the lobby level above. The glass partition wall failed from the fire's heat, and products of combustion spread up the open stairwell.

3. The gambling casino had two exits but they both led into the lobby where the open stairwell spread fire from the ballroom level. The open stairwell not only provided a path for fire travel through the structure, it also blocked the two exits from the casino.

4. Eighty-five of the victims were located in the casino because there was no safe means of egress for them to escape the fire.

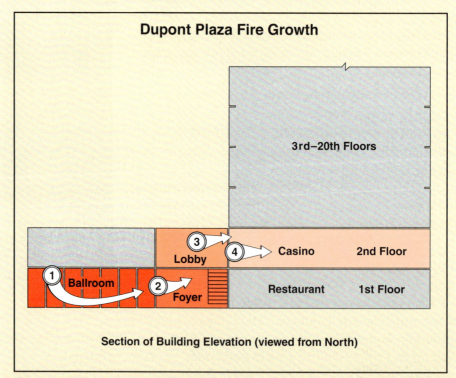

Figure 1.10 The growth area of the Dupont Plaza hotel fire is diagrammed in this illustration. *Source: NIST Engineering Analysis of the Early Stages of Fire Development – The Fire at the Dupont Plaza Hotel and Casino – December 31, 1986.*

Age of Construction

All new construction is a product of its place and time. Factors that influence a building's condition at any given time include:

- Older codes
- Materials
- Construction methods
- Maintenance over time

The effects of age are not uniform. Examples of factors that may require maintenance and upgrading over time include:

- Physical systems such as the electrical wiring and heating plant
- Exterior protection from the weather, such as roofs
- Settling foundations

Of course, real estate can outlive its useful economic life. When buildings become obsolete and unmarketable, they frequently become a target for arson or may be left to degrade with weather and time.

Advantages of Older Construction

In some cases, older buildings offer advantages to the firefighter. Structures built before computer aided design (CAD) were often designed with greater structural mass than was absolutely necessary. This greater mass often results in greater structural stability under fire conditions.

Modern design methods allow more efficient techniques, resulting in less material being used for similar structural members. These more slender and lighter structural members are structurally sound under normal climate and seismic conditions; however, under fire conditions, they may fail more quickly than older, heavier supports.

World War II Influences on Construction Codes and Styles

After WWII, significant changes in building construction started, based in part on advances in engineering, math, and science during the war effort. In reaction to the urban conflagrations in the early 1900s, ways to limit the fire risk in growing cities were sought. The Building Officials and Code Administrators International (BOCA) published the BOCA Basic Building Code in 1950 and ushered in an era of building safety conformity. Building construction increased its pace after these efforts, to provide factories for new industries such as aviation and electronics. Several factors contributed to the sudden need for a large quantity of housing, including:

- The Baby Boom increased the overall American population
- Veterans returning from the war needed houses and jobs
- A higher percentage of Americans reached the middle class and could afford new construction

Figure 1.11 This 100-year-old home has been renovated and modernized. *Courtesy of Ed Prendergast.*

Figure 1.12 Green design uses renewable resources to conserve energy. *Courtesy of Colorado Springs (CO) Fire Department.*

Gentrification

Older neighborhoods sometimes undergo **gentrification** in which older properties are extensively rehabilitated to satisfy the desires of a modern real estate market **(Figure 1.11)**. During renovation for gentrification, the effects of aging can be negated, although other problems may be discovered. For example, an old paint warehouse converted to a church may require minimal structural work, but may require extensive renovations to remove hazardous materials and add essential life-safety provisions to meet the occupancy rating.

Misleading Exteriors

Older buildings may be completely renovated with only the exterior left the same. It is impossible to determine the construction materials and building type simply by looking at the exterior.

Energy Conservation (Green Design)

Effort to increase the energy efficiency of structures and their component materials is known as **green design** **(Figure 1.12)**. For example, as the need for heating fuels is decreased, greenhouse gas emissions are lowered. Other efforts include decreasing use of electrical power and water.

Green design can have an indirect effect on fire fighting[4]. Energy efficient features, for example, include dual-pane windows and tighter fitting doors and seals. These affect the firefighters' ability to quickly ventilate a building. When doors and windows are tightly fitted, the flow of air to a fire is reduced, which results in a fire burning in an oxygen-poor environment. Under these circumstances, when ventilation does occur, a rapid development of the fire can result. As a benefit, it is also possible in some cases that a fire can be so starved for oxygen that it burns itself out.

A primary hazard of green design is the tendency of components to increase the combustibility of the overall building. For example, green insulators such as recycled cotton denim contribute to fire spread much more than fiberglass. Green construction elements are often engineered to be more energy- and material-efficient, so they may have smaller dimensions and be more likely to fail under fire and fire suppression conditions. For example, engineered structural components may not tolerate the same conditions as large dimensional timber. These structures are also designed to minimize heat loss, and as a consequence, they tend to hold the heat from a fire inside the building and may make ventilation more difficult.

Economics-Based Construction Variables

Funds often determine a building's overall appearance and size. For example, a community may ask for a school that is attractive architecturally and is equipped with modern classrooms, laboratories, and athletic facilities. Available tax dollars, however, may force the architect to design a less costly facility by reducing or eliminating other spaces such as the library or music instruction rooms.

Cutting costs may also lead to difficulties during an emergency. For example, an owner may decide to reduce the size of an emergency generator to afford marble flooring in an office building lobby. The rationale for the decision may be that the lobby decor is visible and marketable while the generator is hidden from view and, presumably, will be used infrequently.

> **Gentrification** — Process of restoring rundown or deteriorated properties by more affluent people, often displacing poorer residents.

> **Green Design** — Incorporation of environmental principles including energy efficiency and environmentally friendly building materials into design and construction.

Building Use

A building may be designed to meet the minimum requirements of the intended function and not include significant adornment **(Figure 1.13)**. Common examples of buildings that are designed for a specific use include:

- Grain silos
- Aircraft hangars
- Fire stations
- Movie theaters

Figure 1.13 This fire station has been designed according to its intended use. *Courtesy of Ed Prendergast.*

A building's end use also dictates more subtle requirements. For example, in mercantile buildings, the floor plan is usually arranged to maximize the customers' exposure to products while minimizing the opportunities for shoplifting. In hospitals, the nurses' station is centrally located so the staff can observe the corridors and have a minimum travel distance to the patients' rooms.

Existing Infrastructure

Public utility availability must be considered early in the design process. For example, virtually all buildings require sewer service. Where a building is to be constructed where public sewers do not exist, a septic tank may be needed. For a large project, such as a residential subdivision, it may be appropriate to construct or enhance a sewer treatment facility.

Water availability is an essential consideration in the design of fire protection systems. The primary concern is the water quantity needed for the fire protection system's flow rate. A test may be necessary to determine if existing water mains can supply the required flow and pressure. If the existing water mains cannot supply the required flow, it may be necessary to increase the size of the mains or provide for on-site storage and fire pumps. If public water mains are not readily accessible, a well and storage tank may be necessary. Any requirements that are not provided or supplemented by the existing infrastructure will add to the cost of the project; the developer may bear those costs or share them with the local community.

Fire Loss Management

Fire loss management is systematic and includes many factors including life safety, engineering, and administrative controls to protect community resources. Properly applied loss management activities generate benefits before and after a fire.

Before a fire, loss management activities will:

- Minimize risk present in specific occupancy classifications
- Identify violations or vulnerabilities in business practices/behaviors

During and after a fire, loss management activities:

- Minimize damage to the structure, exposures, and contents
- Eliminate the chance that a fire will reignite in the structure
- Reduce the amount of time needed to repair and reopen the business
- Create goodwill for the fire department within the community
- Minimize financial loss for the owner, occupant, insurance company, and the community

Other Variables

Buildings are designed to provide people and their property with security from outside forces. Buildings also provide stability and privacy for the activities carried out within a society, such as in office buildings and factories. As a society evolves, variables described in the following sections may also change.

Owner's Needs and Desires

The building and its design belong to the owner. The architect works for the owner so it is appropriate for the owner, who will pay for and occupy the building, to have the final word in many design matters. For example, the specific atmosphere desired or the owner's practical knowledge of restaurant operations may influence restaurant design.

Often, the architect cannot address all design considerations presented by the owner. For example, a conflict can exist between the maximum surface flammability allowed by a code and a particular intended interior finish material. The design process involves compromises and prioritization. The final building design always involves a balance of what is wanted, what is needed, and what is practical.

Investment of Wealth

Buildings are repositories of wealth and are frequently constructed as investment tools because they provide security, and because energy and resources are expended in the construction of buildings.

When buildings are constructed without a known occupant, they are referred to as **spec buildings**. This type of construction is often developed primarily as an investment rather than to meet specific needs. Examples of this type of construction include:

- Office plazas
- Shopping malls

Spec Building — Building built before securing a tenant or occupant. Spec is short for speculation.

- Light industrial buildings
- Condominiums

Aesthetics and Culture

Although normally of little interest to the fire service, **aesthetics**, or the art in building design, is a major force in architecture. As with other art forms, architectural styles are subject to change over time and are influenced by the communal environment.

Buildings take on cultural as well as functional characteristics. The design of a building frequently serves as an expression of taste or to convey a certain image. Projections of an owner's wealth or a corporation's sense of permanence are frequently incorporated into the design **(Figure 1.16)**. Designers strive for building designs that are appealing, comfortable, and enhance human endeavors.

Figure 1.16 Buildings are often designed to convey a particular message, including the social status of the occupant.

Aesthetics — Branch of philosophy dealing with the nature of beauty, art, and taste.

Aesthetics over Time

Prominent architect Mies van der Rohe introduced the International Style, a distinctive aesthetic, in the early 1930s. The style was characterized by rectangular lines and was used in many buildings in that era **(Figure 1.14)**. The geometric simplicity used by van der Rohe is different from other designs from other eras **(Figure 1.15)**.

Figure 1.14 (left) Simple and clean architectural lines are features of the International Style aesthetic. *Courtesy of Ed Prendergast.*

Figure 1.15 (above) Some buildings are designed to make a strong impression through their distinctive design. *Courtesy of Ed Prendergast.*

Figure 1.17 Exposed piping and ductwork are a relatively common design choice.

Aesthetics frequently clash with fire safety concerns. For example, an architect may conceal or disguise the fire department connection (FDC) or a pump test header because of its "clunky" appearance. Conversely, the architect may leave piping and other mechanical equipment exposed for visual interest **(Figure 1.17)**.

Community Fire Defense

In the past, entire communities have been destroyed by fire. For example, in 1871, the Great Chicago Fire destroyed much of the city's central business district and killed up to 300 people.

In some cases, this and similar **conflagrations** have been encouraged by construction practices that assist fire travel.

Building construction methods and practices that resist fire and smoke spread are much more effective at preventing **fire spread** between structures. The earliest building codes were developed to prevent future conflagrations from destroying whole neighborhoods or large sections of a city. For example, some of the earliest fire regulations adopted in colonial Boston prohibited thatched roofs to prevent the spread of fire. The following sections describe heat transfer mechanisms between exposures and ways to protect communities from fire spread.

NOTE: The 3rd edition of this manual used the phrase "communication of fire" to indicate the movement of fire between a source and an exposure. This edition will use "fire spread" to match NFPA® 921.

Heat Transfer

Fire spread is often expressed in terms of **heat transfer** through two methods: **convection**, and **thermal radiation** **(Figure 1.18)**. The third method of heat transfer, conduction, is not usually considered a factor in spreading fire between buildings. Descriptions of the two primary methods of heat transfer are:

> **Conflagration** — Large, uncontrollable fire covering a considerable area and crossing fire barriers such as streets and waterways; usually involves buildings in more than one block and causes a substantial fire loss. Forest fires can also be considered conflagrations.

> **Fire Spread** – The movement of fire from one material (source) to another (exposure). May occur within a compartment or across a break.

Figure 1.18 Convection spreads fire vertically. Radiation spreads fire in all directions.

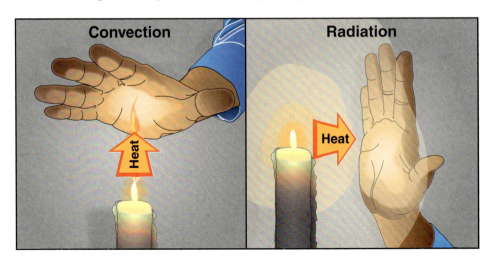

30 Chapter 1 • Building Construction and the Fire Service

- **Convection** — Convection usually involves the transfer of heat energy through the movement of hot smoke and fire gases. Depending on the wind direction, convective plumes are also significant when the exposed building is higher than the exposing building.

- **Thermal Radiation** — Thermal radiation is the transfer of heat energy through space by electromagnetic waves. All bodies emit thermal radiation at a rate dependent on their absolute temperature. When two bodies, such as two buildings, have different temperatures, a net transfer of energy will move from the body of higher temperature to the body of lower temperature, allowing the fire to travel horizontally. A relatively small increase in temperature produces a large increase in thermal radiation (see Information Box).

Heat Transfer — Flow of heat from a hot substance to a cold substance; may be accomplished by convection, conduction, or radiation.

Convection — Transfer of heat by the movement of heated fluids or gases, usually in an upward direction.

Thermal Radiation — Transmission or transfer of heat energy, from one body to another body at a lower temperature, through intervening space by electromagnetic waves similar to radio waves or X-rays.

Exposure — (1) Structures or separate parts of the fireground to which a fire could spread. (2) The heat effect from an external fire that might cause ignition of or damage to an exposed building.

Calculating Thermal Radiation Intensity

Thermal radiation can ignite a building across a wide street. The Stefan-Boltzmann law (physics) states that the intensity of thermal radiation (T) is a function of the fourth power of the absolute temperature of the thermal radiation source (T^4) **(Formula 1.1)**.

Formula 1.1

When a building's exterior wood frame wall is involved in fire, its temperature increases from the ambient temperature to the fire temperature. This example will assume an ambient temperature of 70°F (21°C) (530R) and a fire temperature of 1,000°F (538°C) (1460R).

NOTE: Fahreinheit can be converted to Rankine (R) using the formula: R = (°F - 32) + 491.67

The relative increase in the intensity of thermal radiation emitted in this example can be calculated:

(Fire temperature in R)^4 / (Ambient temperature in R)^4

$(1{,}460R)^4 / (530R)^4 = 57.6$

Exposures and Fire Spread Factors

During fires, heat transfer becomes a problem in communities because of exposures and certain fire progression factors. This section will explore how exposures contribute to fire progression and how code provisions work to prevent the problem.

An **exposure** can refer to any number of surfaces that may be ignited or damaged by the heat of an external fire **(Figure 1.19)**. Exposures include structures and other objects, such as fuel storage tanks.

Some known ways that fires spread to an exposed building include:

- Ventilation pulls in flames, hot brands, or superheated convective currents
- Openings, such as doors, allow convection currents to enter the structure

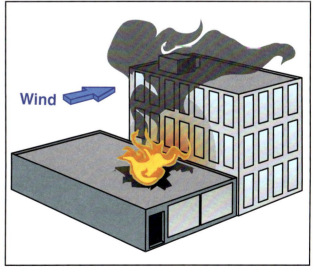

Figure 1.19 Exposures in this illustration include the facing surfaces of the taller building.

- Roof materials ignite readily from convection
- Siding materials ignite readily from convection or radiant heat
- Windows and window dressings allow radiant heat to start fire directly inside
- Structures or other fire loads placed in close proximity to each other
- Lack of organized fire protection and/or systems to limit fire size

Fire temperature is one factor in determining whether a fire will progress to an exposure. The flame's height and width are also relevant. For example, flames emitting from a window in a masonry wall can expose an adjacent building. A wider window opening will increase the amount of thermal radiation against the exposure.

NFPA 80®A, *Recommended Practice for Protection from Exterior Fire Exposure*, describes three levels of exposure based on the potential severity of the exposing fire: light, moderate, or severe. The levels are based on the fire load and the flame spread rating of the wall and ceiling finishes of the burning building. For example, a lumber yard will represent a much greater exposure fire risk than an office building.

Despite the longstanding awareness of the risk and principles of fire transfer, exposure fires remain a significant problem, especially in older urban environments with closely spaced combustible construction **(Figure 1.20)**. In modern suburban communities, building-to-building fire spread has been reduced as a result of code requirements including greater separation between buildings resulting from features including:

- Building setbacks
- Building sizes in relation to lot sizes
- Off-street parking and loading

Figure 1.20 Closely spaced garages may present exposure risks to each other. *Courtesy of Ed Prendergast*.

As cities evolve and grow, building codes develop with the goal of preventing the spread of fire between buildings. Fire protection methods used to protect buildings from exposing fires include:

- Clearing space between buildings, including roadways
- Imposing limits on the height and area of combustible construction
- Eliminating or reducing openings in exterior walls

In addition to these methods, fire protection features specified in building codes provide minimum requirements for several systems including:

- Fire detection and suppression systems:
  — Water-based sprinkler systems
  — Fire-retardant distribution systems
  — Automatic outside deluge systems
- Passive barriers:
  — Self-supporting barrier walls between the fire building and the exposure
  — Blank walls of noncombustible construction

- Parapets on exterior masonry walls
- Glass block panels in openings
- Wired glass in steel sash windows

• Active Barriers:
- Automatic fire shutters or dampers on wall openings
- Automatic fire doors on door openings

In the **wildland/urban interface**, fire can travel in either direction between the built and unbuilt environments. Wildland/urban interface codes now address these exposures by regulating types of roofing and siding materials, and require the creation of defensible space through fire-resistant vegetation.

Wildland/Urban Interface — Line, area, or zone where an undeveloped wildland area meets a human development area.

Design-Caused Structural Failure

Depending on the structure's intended purpose, structural failure can be caused by any number of factors including unplanned loads and design flaws. Unwillingness to spend additional money may entice a building owner to continue work without the necessary permits at any phase of work, but primarily during renovation.

To the firefighter, building failure usually equates to structural collapse. In the broader sense, however, it can mean that the building or part of it is no longer performing its required function in a satisfactory (designed) manner. Thus, fire spread through a fire-rated barrier is considered a failure. The unsatisfactory performance of a fire protection system is also a failure. The following sections describe common causes of building failure.

Hyatt Regency Collapse

A tragic example of structural failure occurred in Kansas City, Missouri on July 17, 1981 at the Hyatt Regency Hotel. Construction was completed in July, 1980 after many delays and extensions in the construction plan. On the evening of July 17, the second and fourth level walkways collapsed while a dance competition was being held in the atrium. The collapse resulted in the deaths of 144 persons and injuries to an additional 200 people.

The hotel complex included an atrium 50 feet (15 m) high that was used for various functions. The atrium was spanned by three walkways at the second, third, and fourth floor levels. The walkway for the fourth floor was located above the walkway for the second floor.

In the original design for the hotel, the walkways for the second and fourth floors were to be supported by a series of continuous steel rods from a truss system at the roof of the atrium **(Figure 1.21, p. 34)**. The rods were to pass through box beams used to support the walkway at the fourth level and continue to the box beams used to support the second floor level walkway. In both the original and redesigned plan, the box beams were supported by a steel nut and washer at the bottom of the box beam.

The change to the support system of the walkways used two rods to support both walkways. One rod started at the truss system, and terminated at the underside of the box beam supporting the fourth-level walkway.

A second rod extended down from the top of the fourth level box beam to the underside of the box beam to support the second level walkway.

The structural engineers reviewed this change, but did not recognize the full implications of the altered stresses. Because of the change, the nut and washer assembly pulled out of the box beams at the fourth level walkway.

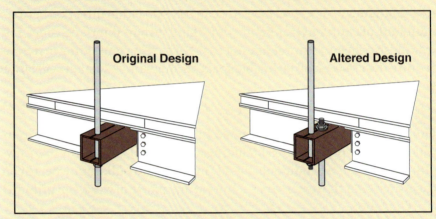

Figure 1.21 An alteration from original plans weakened supports in a hotel walkway, and ultimately resulted in the failure of the system.

Loss of Structural Integrity

A building that maintains its structural integrity allows firefighters to more effectively attack an interior fire. Under fire conditions, a building's structural integrity is related to the fire resistance and combustibility of its construction materials **(Figure 1.22)**. Any building that collapses, under any conditions, has lost structural integrity. Construction materials have limitations unique to their properties, including:

Figure 1.22 Buildings constructed of combustible materials will collapse under severe fire conditions. *Courtesy of District Chief Chris E. Mickal, NOFD Photo Unit.*

- Combustible materials may possess some initial fire resistance, as with heavy plank flooring, and be able to act as a barrier to fire, but ultimately they will be consumed.

- Depending on their physical dimensions, noncombustible materials such as steel or glass may also retain structural integrity at first but will fail from the effects of heat.

- Fire-resistive materials possess the ability to maintain structural integrity under fire conditions (though not necessarily under other types of conditions).

NOTE: Chapter 2 includes analysis of fire resistive materials.

Building System Failure

Modern buildings function as total systems to provide a healthy, productive, and comfortable environment using complicated systems including:

- Heating, ventilation, and air conditioning (HVAC)
- Electrical power
- Communications
- Plumbing
- Transportation such as elevators and conveyors

Well-designed building systems utilize provisions to prevent the spread of **combustion** products, including such measures as smoke detectors to initiate the shutdown of units or to operate dampers in ducts. Improper or inadequate design of these systems can contribute to building failures under fire conditions. For example, a ventilation system's ductwork and circulating fans can spread combustion products throughout a building.

NOTE: Building systems are discussed in greater detail in Chapter 4.

Electrical systems are essential to all modern buildings. Their design and installation should include fire stopping at the openings where conduits penetrate floor slabs and firewalls. Electrical systems should also include a provision for emergency power that is protected from fire and highly unlikely to fail as a backup system. If both electrical systems fail, firefighting operations become much more difficult. For example, a fire penetrating a single utility closet at the 1991 Meridian Plaza fire in Philadelphia resulted in the failure of the primary and the emergency power to the entire high-rise building, resulting in loss of power to fire pumps and elevators.

NOTE: The Meridian Plaza fire is described in Chapter 12.

Design Deficiencies

In the design process, codes and standards are followed closely, and often narrowly, because competing priorities, including economics, may discourage measures that exceed the safety provisions outlined in codes. Unfortunately, building codes are limited in their scope because:

- Codes cannot address every situation that may arise.
- Codes are subject to political processes, competing interests, and economic priorities.
- Codes can only provide a baseline level of protection for the most commonly encountered situations.

In addition to these limitations, a code may not provide an adequate level of safety, or compliance with the provisions of a code may not be possible. In these cases, technical analysis research with a goal toward meeting the safety requirements of the building may be conducted and submitted to the AHJ. Design deficiencies refer to any failure to provide a level of fire safety appropriate to the ultimate use of the building, regardless of the reason but including:

- Oversight
- Incorrect assumption
- Oversimplification
- Underestimation

Buildings must have a minimum number of exits based on the expected occupancy capacity and classification. This aspect can be difficult to plan,

Combustion — A chemical process of oxidation that occurs at a rate fast enough to produce heat and usually light in the form of either a glow or flame. (Reproduced with permission from NFPA® 921-2011, Guide for Fire and Explosion Investigations, Copyright© 2011, National Fire Protection Association®).

based on fluctuations in the uses of the structure. For example, an exhibition hall may be used for an industrial trade show with a restricted attendance; the same hall may also be used for a rock concert with a highly dense and volatile crowd. The difference in these two occasions is enormous in terms of emergency evacuation.

Preincident Planning in Building Construction

The building permit process is a resource that can be used by firefighters to develop knowledge of building construction in their jurisdiction. As buildings are permitted for construction, a fire service representative may be involved in the process, or information can be passed from the building department to the fire department. The information can then be shared between fire companies and with the fire prevention bureau.

Tracking permits is particularly useful in the construction of large structures. In the case of smaller buildings such as single-family dwellings and small commercial buildings, however, it is impractical to track a large number of projects through the permit process. The following sections include other information sources that can be used while developing a preincident plan.

The availability of useful information and the effectiveness of emergency response are closely related. Preincident plans should include:

- Occupancy type
- Industrial processes conducted on site
- Hazardous materials in the vicinity
- Location and function of fire protection system controls and outlets
- Building access routes
- Utilities present

Geographic Information Systems

Geographic information systems (GIS) technology is another means of obtaining, analyzing, and using data based on a specific location. GIS has multiple uses across many disciplines and is also becoming more widely used in building construction applications. For large-scale construction projects, GIS allows a large project to be divided into smaller areas or sectors. This subdivision makes the project more manageable and allows for logistical, planning, and tracking functions to take place with greater efficiency. By pairing global positioning systems (GPS) with survey information, GIS applications also provide a means for determining the exact locations necessary for placement of critical building elements such as foundations and structural steel. GIS may be used as a design aid in several types of construction. Modern beams are stamped with a rated weight and intended structural application/location; for example, higher ratings are used for loadbearing applications.

Graphic representation of resource response within a jurisdiction is a powerful application of GIS. Data from inspections and preplans, including building construction type, can be entered into GIS for a specific occupancy and then retrieved on districting or dispatching maps. Through Computer Aided Dispatch (CAD), these maps can be interactive for the dispatcher calling for a response and on a laptop for the company officer heading to the incident site.

> **Geographic Information Systems (GIS)** — Computer software application that relates physical features on the earth to a database to be used for mapping and analysis. The system captures, stores, analyzes, manages, and presents data that refers to or is linked to a location.

These building construction types must be labeled appropriately to convey the necessary information. A jurisdiction's GIS can potentially provide tools for functions including:

- Evaluating department performance
- Dispatching emergency responses
- Code enforcement
- Zoning and taxing

Fire Fighting Strategy

Building construction types influence the strategies that will be effective at a structural fire. In addition, the building's exterior appearance may not match the interior. For example, an older building that was completely gutted during renovation may leave only the existing shell as original construction. Each chapter that discusses materials will include some strategic considerations. Actual fire suppression tactics at any level are beyond the purpose and scope of this manual.

There are only three primary strategies in a fire incident: offensive, defensive, and transitional. Offensive strategies address:

- Life hazards
- Structural stability
- Risk (benefit outweighs risk)

Defensive strategies address:

- Volume of fire
- Structural deterioration
- Risk (risk outweighs benefit)
- Structural conditions

Transitional strategies include all strategies that include a change in either direction between an offensive or defensive focus. For more information on these three strategies and how they are used, refer to IFSTA's **Structural Fire Fighting: Initial Response Strategy and Tactics** manual.

Chapter Summary

The physical and chemical laws that govern fire behavior never change, but the buildings in which fires occur vary greatly. The tactical firefighter must understand the design, construction, and functioning of a building so that emergency operations can be carried out effectively.

Review Questions

1. How does the history of building construction help in understanding different types of buildings?
2. What are the phases of the design and construction process?
3. What are two major types of legal requirements that affect building design?
4. What types of engineering variables affect building design?

5. How can economic variables influence building design?
6. What are some other variables that affect building design?
7. How do heat transfer, exposures, and fire spread threaten community fire defense?
8. How can design factors lead to structural failure of a building?
9. What is the role of preincident planning in building construction?

Chapter Notes

1. Lidwell, William, Kritina Holden, Jill Butler. *Universal Principles of Design: 125 Ways to Enhance Usability, Influence Perception, Increase Appeal, Make Better Design Decisions, and Teach through Design.* Rockport Publishers, Inc; 2010.

2. United States Fire Administration. Residential Fire Fatalities in the News. http://apps.usfa.fema.gov/civilian-fatalities/incident/reportMap

3. Klem, Thomas J. "Ninety seven die in arson fire at Dupont Plaza Hotel." *NFPA® Fire Journal*, Vol. 81, No.3, 1987, pp. 74-82.

4. Duval, Robert. "Perfect Storm." *NFPA® Journal*. January 6, 2014. http://www.nfpa.org/newsandpublications/nfpa-journal/2014/january-february-2014/features/perfect-storm

Building Classifications and Structural Fire Resistance

Chapter Contents

Case History **43**	NFPA® Occupancy Classifications 52
Basic Building Classifications **43**	Mixed Occupancies 52
Type I Construction – Fire Resistive 46	Change of Occupancy 53
Type II Construction – Protected Noncombustible	**Fire and Fuel Load** **54**
or Noncombustible 47	Combustibility of Materials................................... 54
Type III Construction – Exterior Protected/Ordinary 48	Fire Load versus Structural Load 54
Type IV Construction – Heavy Timber 49	**Fire Resistance** **55**
Type V Construction – Wood Frame 50	Laboratory-Tested Data 56
Mixed Construction 51	Mathematical Models Based on Collected Data 60
Occupancy Classifications **51**	**Chapter Summary** **60**
International Building Code® (IBC)	**Review Questions** **61**
Occupancy Classifications 51	

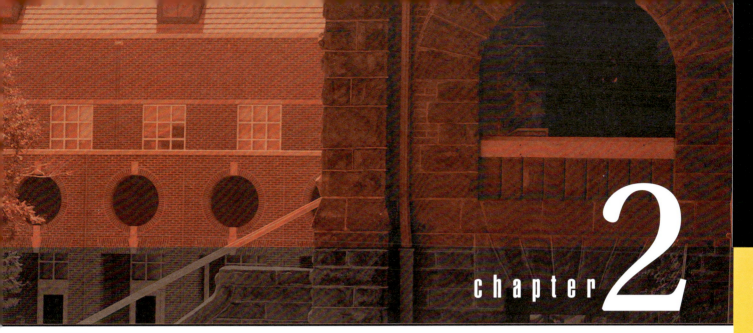

chapter 2

Key Terms

Fire Load 54	Fire Stop 49
Fire Resistance 55	Heat of Combustion 54
Fire Resistance Rating 55	Occupancy 51
Fire Retardant 47	

FESHE Outcomes Addressed In This Chapter

Fire and Emergency Services Higher Education (FESHE) Outcomes: *Building Construction for Fire Protection*

1. Describe building construction as it relates to firefighter safety, building codes, fire prevention, code inspection, firefighting strategy, and tactics.
2. Classify major types of building construction in accordance with a local/model building code.
3. Analyze the hazards and tactical considerations associated with the various types of building construction
4. Explain the different loads and stresses that are placed on a building and their interrelationships.
6. Differentiate between fire resistance, flame spread, and describe the testing procedures used to establish ratings for each.
7. Classify occupancy designations of the building code.

Building Classifications and Structural Fire Resistance

Learning Objectives

After reading this chapter, students will be able to:

1. Describe building classifications used in the fire service.
2. Explain the function of occupancy classifications.
3. Describe ways that fire and fuel load are determined.
4. Explain methods for determining fire resistance.

Chapter 2
Building Classifications and Structural Fire Resistance

Case History

The Windsor Tower in Madrid, Spain was a 32-story concrete building with a reinforced concrete central core. A typical floor included a concrete slab supported by internal columns with additional steel I-beams, and steel perimeter columns. The building featured two heavily reinforced concrete transfer structures between the 2nd and 3rd floors, and between the 16th and 17th floors respectively. The perimeter columns were supported by the transfer structures at the 17th and 3rd floor levels.

When the fire occurred on February 12th, 2005, the building was partially through a three year refurbishment with the goal of adding a sprinkler system, and fire protection to perimeter steel columns and internal steel beams. Fire protection elements were added systematically, floor by floor, starting from the bottom floor. At the time of the fire, the fire protection had been completed through the 17th floor. No sprinklers were operable at the time of the fire. Originally, the perimeter columns and internal steel beams were left unprotected in accordance with the Spanish building code at the time of construction.

The fire started at 11:00 p.m. at the 21st floor. Within one hour, all floors above the 21st floor were on fire. A large number of the floor slabs above the 17th floor progressively collapsed during the fire when the unprotected steel perimeter columns on the upper levels buckled and collapsed. The reinforced concrete of the 17th floor was able to sustain the impact and, as a result, the collapse did not continue below this floor. Fire continued below to the 4th floor without collapse until extinguishment. Among other lessons learned, this fire demonstrated the differences in buildings with protected and nonprotected concrete supports.

For a firefighter, the effects of fire conditions on a building are extremely significant. Factors that influence fire behavior include:

- Basic building classifications
- Occupancy classifications
- Fire or fuel load
- Fire resistance

Basic Building Classifications

As explained in Chapter 1, building codes (including IBC) initially classify structures by the materials used in their construction. In the fields of fire protection and building code enforcement, buildings are grouped into five major classifications commonly designated as follows:

- Type I – Fire-resistive
- Type II – Noncombustible or protected noncombustible
- Type III – Exterior protected (masonry)
- Type IV – Heavy timber
- Type V – Wood frame

Building classifications are fundamental from both fire fighting and fire safety standpoints. These classifications can help firefighters determine the likelihood of structural collapse under fire conditions. They also indicate the degree of occupant safety provided by the building's construction.

Building Type Terminology

Building codes use only the numerical designations to indicate a building's classification. This manual includes descriptive terms used in building construction and related fields because these terms are helpful in describing and understanding building characteristics.

The building classifications used in the building codes are based on the materials used in construction and the fire resistance ratings required for the structural components. With the exception of Type IV, heavy timber, the major classifications are further divided into two or three subclassifications. The highest requirements for fire resistance are for Type I construction, with lower requirements for other types of construction.

Generic Language

This manual discusses a large number of structural elements from several perspectives including application, fire resistance, and load-bearing capability. To prevent an unwieldy level of detail in the nonspecific chapters, two terms will be used to indicate a wider focus.

The phrase *structural components* will refer to a wide pool of diverse elements. For example, structural components that work together to maintain the structural integrity of a building include structural supports, fasteners, and other reinforcing materials.

The term *member* will refer generically to a specific type of component that may have a wide range of variation of material and design but serves a defined purpose. For example, roof structural members can include wooden or metal beams, among other options.

NFPA® 220, *Standard on Types of Building Construction*, details the requirements for each of the classifications and subclassifications. In NFPA® 220, each classification is designated by a three-digit number code. For example, Type I construction can be either 4-4-3 or 3-3-2. The digits are explained as follows:

- First digit – Fire resistance rating (in hours) of exterior bearing walls.
- Second digit – Fire resistance rating of structural frames or columns and girders that support loads of more than one floor.

- Third digit – Fire resistance rating of the floor construction.

The *International Building Code® (IBC)* uses construction classifications similar to NFPA® 220, although the requirements for individual structural components differ **(Table 2.1)**.

Table 2.1
2015 International Building Code® Fire-Resistance Rating Requirements for Building Elements (Hours)

Building Element	Type I A	Type I B	Type II A[d]	Type II B	Type III A[d]	Type III B	Type IV HT	Type V A[d]	Type V B
Primary Structural Frame[g] (see Section 202)	3[a]	2[a]	1	0	1	0	HT	1	0
Bearing Walls Exterior[f, g] Interior	3 3[a]	2 2[a]	1 1	0 0	2 1	2 0	2 1/HT	1 1	0 0
Nonbearing Walls and Partitions Exterior	See Table 602								
Nonbearing Walls and Partitions Interior[e]	0	0	0	0	0	0	See Section 602.4.6	0	0
Floor Construction and Secondary Members (see Section 202)	2	2	1	0	1	0	HT	1	0
Floor Construction and Secondary Members (see Section 202)	1½[b]	1[b, c]	1[b, c]	0[c]	1[b, c]	0	HT	1[b, c]	0

For SI: 1 foot = 304.8 mm.

a. Roof supports: Fire-resistance ratings of primary structural frame and bearing walls are permitted to be reduced by 1 hour where supporting a roof only.

b. Except in Group F-1, H, M and S-1 occupancies, fire protection of structural members shall not be required, including protection of roof framing and decking where every part of the roof construction is 20 feet or more above any floor immediately below. Fire-retardant-treated wood members shall be allowed to be used for such unprotected members.

c. In all occupancies, heavy timber shall be allowed where a 1-hour or less fire-resistance rating is required.

d. An approved automatic sprinkler system in accordance with Section 903.3.1.1 shall be allowed to be substituted for 1-hour fire-resistance-rated construction, provided such system is not otherwise required by other provisions of the code or used for an allowable area increase in accordance with Section 506.3 or an allowable height increase in accordance with Section 504.2. The 1-hour substitution for the fire resistance of exterior walls shall not be permitted.

e. Not less than the fire-resistance rating required by other sections of this code.

f. Not less than the fire-resistance rating based on fire separation distance (see Table 602).

g. Not less than the fire-resistance rating as referenced in Section 704.10

Source: International Code Council, *2015 International Building Code®,* Table 601.

NOTE: Table 2.1, shows basic requirements that are permitted to be reduced. This table will be referenced frequently in this chapter. For more information, see the IFSTA **Fire Inspection and Code Enforcement** manual.

Type I Construction – Fire Resistive

Type I (fire-resistive) construction is classified by the presence of noncombustible structural components that have fire resistance ratings within a specified range. Construction materials may be supplemented to attain the necessary ratings. For example, steel is noncombustible, but not fire-resistive, and must be protected to attain fire resistance.

The addition of fire resistance increases structural integrity during a fire. The fire-resistive compartmentation provided by partitions and floors tends to limit or slow the spread of fire through a building. These features allow time for occupant evacuation and interior fire fighting. In a Type I structure, the building is less likely to collapse on the firefighters.

Examples of the variation in fire resistance by application include:

- Bearing walls, columns, and beams – Two to four hours, as specified by the local code and the construction classification
- Floor construction – Two or three hours
- Roof deck and construction supporting the roof – One to two hours
- Interior partitions enclosing stairwells and corridors – As specified by the local code; usually one or two hours
- Partitions separating occupancies or tenants – As specified by the local code

Noncombustible Materials

Type I buildings are most commonly constructed using a protected steel frame or reinforced concrete **(Figure 2.1)**. Although the structural components do not contribute to the combustible materials in a Type I building, the contents will contribute most of the fuel for a fire. The fire-resistive components of this type of construction do not contribute to fire extinguishment, but do collect heat from a fire and give off radiant heat.

Unprotected steel has no fire resistance. When steel is used in fire-resistive designs, it must be protected by an insulating material. The combination of the structural strength of steel and the insulation produce a fire-resistive structural assembly. Several insulating materials are commonly used to protect the steel. The thickness of the insulating material can be adjusted to meet a number of fire ratings.

NOTE: See Chapter 9 for more information on steel structures.

Concrete is an inherently noncombustible material with good thermal insulating properties. These two attributes result in a material that is fundamentally fire-resistive, although the degree of fire resistance will vary with the specific

Figure 2.1 Steel is often used to increase the structural strength of concrete.

type of concrete assembly. Reinforced concrete can fail under an explosion or intense fire of long duration.

NOTE: Several techniques can be used in designing a reinforced concrete building. See Chapter 10 for more information on concrete structures.

Combustible Materials

As a practical matter, building codes usually permit a limited use of combustible materials in Type I construction. A code may also allow the use of **fire retardant**-treated wood in roofs or interior partitions. Combustible materials typically are permitted for such uses as the following:

- Roof coverings
- Interior floor finishes
- Interior wall finishes and trims
- Doors and door frames
- Window sashes and frames
- Platforms
- Nailing and furring strips
- Light-transmitting plastics
- Foam plastics subject to restrictions

NOTE: Chapter 7 includes more information on wood treatments.

> **Fire Retardant** — Any substance, except plain water, that when applied to another material or substance will reduce the flammability of fuels or slow their rate of combustion by chemical or physical action.

Type II Construction – Protected Noncombustible or Noncombustible

Type II construction allows a wider range of materials than Type I construction. In addition to steel and concrete block, glass and aluminum can be used with a limited structural role. Building codes also allow the use of combustible material in Type II construction for applications similar to those in Type I construction.

Some building codes contain a provision to omit the fire-resistive rating for a roof construction for some occupancy types when the roof is located more than 20 feet (6 m) above the floor **(Figure 2.2)**. This omission can cause a Type II (noncombustible) construction building to be classified and inspected as a Type I (fire-resistive) building, which can be significant in the event of a fire. For example, if a fire were to break out in an exhibition hall when it contained a higher fuel load, the roof construction can be subject to failure.

Type II-A (protected) requires that structural components have one-hour fire resistance. Protected noncombustible construction is similar to Type I but with a lower requirement for fire resistance. Protected, noncombustible construction provides a degree of structural fire protection similar to Type I, which will depend on the degree of fire resistance provided.

Figure 2.2 The walls of this church are Type I construction (fire-resistive), but part of the roof covering includes combustible materials. *Courtesy of McKinney (TX) Fire Department.*

Figure 2.3 Unprotected steel is most commonly used in unprotected, noncombustible construction. *Courtesy of McKinney (TX) Fire Department.*

Figure 2.4 Type III construction may survive many decades. *Courtesy of Dave Coombs.*

Figure 2.5 Gypsum is an extremely common interior covering.

Type II-B (unprotected) allows structural components to remain unprotected. In unprotected noncombustible construction, the major structural components have no fire resistance. The use of unprotected steel is the most common characteristic of unprotected, noncombustible construction **(Figure 2.3)**. An unprotected, noncombustible building cannot be expected to provide structural stability under fire conditions. The failure of unprotected steel from the heat of burning contents must be anticipated. The speed at which unprotected members will fail, however, depends on the following factors:

- Ceiling height of the building
- Size of the unprotected steel members
- Intensity and duration of the exposing fire

Type III Construction – Exterior Protected/Ordinary

Type III construction has been commonly referred to as "ordinary construction." Type III construction is frequently constructed with exterior walls of masonry, but from a technical standpoint, any noncombustible material with the required fire resistance can be used for the exterior walls **(Figure 2.4)**. Interior structural components that are permitted to be partially or wholly combustible include:

- Walls
- Columns
- Beams
- Floors
- Roofs

Type III construction has two subclassifications, allowing the interior structural components to be protected or unprotected. When the structural components of Type III construction are required to have a fire rating (such as for IBC Type III A and NFPA® Type III 2-1-1 construction), they can be protected by several means, including plaster in older buildings and gypsum board in newer buildings **(Figure 2.5)**. In NFPA® Type III 2-0-0 and IBC Type III B, unprotected steel is sometimes used to support combustible members. For example, unprotected steel trusses can be used to support a combustible roof deck. Type III construction commonly uses nominal 2 inch x 10 inch (50 mm x 250 mm) joists for floor construction.

NOTE: Nominal dimensions are not exact measurements. See Chapter 7, Wood Construction, for more information.

A fundamental fire concern with Type III construction is the combustible concealed spaces that are created between floor and ceiling joists and between studs in partition walls when they are covered with interior finish materials. These spaces provide combustible paths for the communication of fire through a building. Fire can enter these spaces when openings exist in the interior finish materials or when a fire is of sufficient magnitude to destroy the material. Concealed spaces in Type III construction must contain appropriate **fire stops**.

Fire Stop — Solid materials, such as wood blocks, used to prevent or limit the vertical and horizontal spread of fire and the products of combustion; installed in hollow walls or floors, above false ceilings, in penetrations for plumbing or electrical installations, in penetrations of a fire-rated assembly, or in cocklofts and crawl spaces.

Hazards of Dropped Ceilings

In older Type III construction, dropped ceilings may have been installed during renovations. These ceilings are typically installed several inches or several feet beneath the original ceiling. Dropped ceilings can mask the location of fires and allow products of combustion to travel easily.

Firefighters cannot assume any level of structural stability where the structural components are combustible. When combustible materials become involved in a fire, they will be consumed and collapse. Without interior supports, the exterior masonry walls will lose stability and may collapse **(Figure 2.6)**.

Type IV Construction – Heavy Timber

Type IV construction is commonly known as heavy-timber or "mill" construction. Like Type III construction, the exterior walls are normally of masonry construction and the interior structural components are combustible. Two important distinctions between Type III and Type IV construction are:

- In Type IV construction the beams, columns, floors, and roofs are made of solid or laminated wood with dimensions greater than in Type III construction.
- Concealed spaces are not permitted between structural components in Type IV construction **(Figure 2.7)**.

Features of Type IV Construction

Type IV construction is the only construction type that does not include A and B subdivisions. Instead, the designation 2HH is used. The structural components so indicated are of heavy timber with minimum dimensions greater than those used in Type III or Type V construction.

Type IV construction uses wood components with greater mass than are used in Type III construction. These components' features provide greater structural endurance under fire conditions because the larger timbers are slower to ignite and burn. If the members have not been exposed to a prolonged fire, they may be cleaned of charring and remain in place after a fire.

Figure 2.6 Regardless of materials, loss of interior supports can lead to collapse of walls.

Figure 2.7 In Type IV construction, concealed spaces are not permitted between structural members. *Courtesy of McKinney (TX) Fire Department.*

Even heavy timber components are combustible and ultimately will be consumed in a fire. The exterior masonry walls can then become unstable and collapse because of the loss of the interior bracing provided by the floors and columns. Type IV (heavy timber) construction requires minimum nominal dimensions of 6 inch x 10 inch (150 mm x 250 mm) for floor construction, which is thicker than needed in Types III and V construction.

NOTE: See Chapter 7 for more discussion on the hazards of Type IV (heavy timber) construction.

Usage of Type IV Construction

Modern heavy timber wood frame construction is primarily used for aesthetic purposes. Type IV construction is not commonly used in new construction for multistory buildings, although many buildings of this type remain in use.

Many Type IV (heavy-timber) buildings built in the 19th and early 20th centuries have been converted to residential use from original applications including:

- Factories
- Mills
- Warehouses

NOTE: For more information about heavy-timber construction, including hazards that can remain in older, gentrified buildings, see Chapter 7, Wood Construction.

Fire Hazards of Type IV (Heavy-Timber) Construction

The primary fire hazard associated with Type IV construction is the relatively large amount of fuel present in structural supports. In addition, the interior of the building may have traces of oils and residues from previous industrial use.

Type V Construction – Wood Frame

In Type V construction, all major structural components are permitted to be of combustible construction. The basic method of construction in a Type V building consists of using a wood frame to provide the primary structural support **(Figure 2.8)**. Many Type V structures are required to have a 1-hour fire resistance for structural components. The addition of plaster or fire-rated gypsum board typically provides enough protection for combustible frame members.

Limitations of Type V Construction

The fundamental problem with Type V construction is the presence of extensive concealed voids. These concealed spaces provide avenues for extension of fire within a building. Because of its inherent combustibility, a Type V building can become totally involved and completely destroyed in a fire.

Figure 2.8 The definitive characteristic of Type V construction is the wood framing components.

A heavily involved wood-frame building also presents an exposure threat to adjacent structures; therefore, building codes impose restrictions on the maximum allowable heights and areas of Type V (wood frame) buildings. The building codes may also require a separation distance between a Type V (wood frame) building and an adjacent property line.

Type V Construction Methods

Several different methods can be used to construct a Type V (wood frame) building. In modern practice, wood-frame buildings are most often constructed using a method known as light-frame construction. This technique was introduced to the United States in the 1830s. Light-frame construction eliminated heavy posts and beams and made use of smaller studs, joists, and rafters. This change permitted a building to be erected faster and more cheaply. Light-frame construction is considered "the common currency of small residential and commercial buildings in North America today."[1]

Mixed Construction

Mixed construction occurs where a new structure is built onto an existing structure of a different construction type. Mixed structures may present special challenges for emergency responders. For example, the addition of one type of construction to another can result in a building that exceeds the height restrictions for one of the types of construction.

Occupancy Classifications

Building construction and **occupancy** classifications are used together in building codes to establish limitations on the permissible heights and open areas of buildings. These classifications reflect the life safety issues inherent to specific types of occupancies. For example, a building code may restrict wood-frame (Type V-A) schools to one story. A two-story school will have to include an automatic sprinkler system or a type of construction with greater fire resistance. A 15-story apartment building will be required to be of Type I-A construction in the IBC (NFPA® 4-4-2). However, an 11-story or lower apartment building can be of Type I-B construction (NFPA® 3-3-2).

Classifying buildings according to occupancy facilitates the administration of a code. Grouping building uses into a relatively small number of classifications allows for the use of less cumbersome code language. The occupancy classifications assign building occupancies into groups with broadly similar fire risks. For example, one important occupancy factor is the capacity of the building because crowd density can affect the rate of egress during an emergency. The IBC and NFPA® maintain code requirements for occupancies, as described in the following sections.

> **Occupancy** — Building code classification based on the use to which owners or tenants put buildings or portions of buildings. Regulated by the various building and fire codes. *Also known as* Occupancy Classification.

International Building Code® (IBC) Occupancy Classifications

The building codes group building occupancies into occupancy classifications. The *International Building Code® (IBC)* contains ten major occupancy classifications:

- Assembly Group A
- Business Group B

- Educational Group E
- Factories Group F
- High Hazard Group H
- Institutional Group I
- Mercantile Group M
- Residential Group R
- Storage Group S
- Utility and Miscellaneous Group U

Ten classifications is a relatively small number in which to group all the potential uses for a building, and considerable variation of hazards can exist within the classifications **(Figure 2.9)**. The IBC contains a total of 26 subgroups within the 10 major occupancy classifications.

NOTE: The IBC also separately addresses one-and two-family dwellings not more than three stories high. Although these buildings are classified as R in the IBC, they are governed by a separate code, the *International Residential Code (IRC)*.

Figure 2.9 A parking garage with noncombustible construction may shelter combustible materials, which would alter the hazards within the space. *Courtesy of McKinney (TX) Fire Department.*

NFPA® Occupancy Classifications

In contrast to the IBC, NFPA® 5000, *Building Construction and Safety Code*, and NFPA® 101, Life Safety Code®, identify 12 major occupancy classifications:

- Assembly
- Educational
- Day care
- Health care
- Ambulatory health care
- Detention and correctional
- Residential
- Residential board and care
- Mercantile
- Business
- Industrial
- Storage

Mixed Occupancies

Buildings frequently contain occupants that represent more than one occupancy classification. For example, a building may contain mercantile and residential occupancies. The different occupancies will present different types and levels of hazards to each other. For example, a mercantile occupancy sharing building space with a nightclub can endanger the occupants of a nightclub if a fire occurred in the mercantile occupancy.

To alleviate this problem, building codes may require fire-resistive separations between various occupancies. For example, an infant care center and a restaurant located in the same building can be required to be separated by a 2-hour fire-resistive separation.

The specific requirements for occupancy separation will depend on the local building code. Required separations can range from one to four hours and not all occupancies will require a separation. Furthermore, a building code may permit a reduction in the required occupancy separation if a building is sprinklered.

Change of Occupancy

Buildings frequently undergo an occupancy change. As was noted in Chapter 1, a change of occupancy can create serious problems when the safety features required by the new occupancy are not to be fully implemented.

E2 Nightclub Disaster

In the early morning hours of February 16, 2003, a crowd later estimated at 1,150 persons was occupying the E2 nightclub on the south side of Chicago. At approximately 1:00 a.m., a disturbance occurred as a result of a fight between two patrons. A security guard discharged mace in an attempt to quell the disturbance. The crowd began to surge toward the front entrance in an effort to flee the effects of the mace. Twenty-one persons were crushed to death in the stairway that led from the second floor where the club was located to the street-level main entrance.

The E2 nightclub was located on the second floor of a two-story building that had been constructed as an automobile dealership. The building had first and second floors of reinforced concrete and exterior walls of masonry. The roof was wood deck supported by wood bowstring trusses. A mezzanine used for VIP suites had been constructed in the space between the upper and lower chords of the trusses. At the time of the incident the first floor was occupied by a restaurant that was a separate operation from the nightclub.

The net area of the second floor was 4,260 square feet (400 m^2). The mezzanine had a net area of 1,491 square feet (140 m^2). Under the provisions of the Chicago building code, the calculated occupant load was 1,040 persons for the second floor and mezzanine. The building code required that exits be provided for this number of people.

There were three exits from the second floor. These consisted of two rear stairways and a front stairway that served as the main entrance. The exits had not been modified from the time the building was originally occupied as an automobile dealership (more than 70 years earlier). The combined capacity of the three existing stairs under the provisions of was only 240 persons total; therefore, the existing exits were insufficient for 800 people.

To provide enough exits to handle the occupant load, it would have been necessary to construct additional stairways from the second floor to grade level: a costly undertaking. The operators of the club had not completed the necessary work. At the time of the incident, city building inspectors had cited the nightclub for code violations and the case was in court.

> **Fire Load** — Maximum amount of heat that can be released if all fuel in a given area is consumed; expressed in pounds per square foot and obtained by dividing the amount of fuel present by the floor area. Used as a measure of the potential heat release of a fire within a compartment. *Similar to* Fuel Load *and* Heat of Combustion.

> **Heat of Combustion** — Total amount of thermal energy (heat) that could be generated by the combustion (oxidation) reaction if a fuel were completely burned. The heat of combustion is measured in British Thermal Units (Btu) per pound, kilojoules per gram, or Megajoules per kilogram.

Fire and Fuel Load

Fuel load, the total quantity of combustible material in a compartment, is a critical factor when determining the fire safety requirements of a space. The fuel load contributes to the calculation of the **fire load**, the maximum amount of heat that can be released if all fuel is consumed. The fire load will vary depending on the **heat of combustion** of the fuel load.

The fire load is the product of the weight of the combustibles multiplied by their heat of combustion, expressed in pounds per square foot (kg/m^2). The fire load can be used as an estimate of the total potential heat release or thermal energy to which a building may be subjected if all combustibles become fully involved in fire. Buildings with combustible structural components (Types III, IV, and V) have an inherently greater fire load than noncombustible construction (Types I or II) because the structural framing materials contribute a significant amount of fuel to a fire.

Combustibility of Materials

Because of the variety of materials used in building construction, the difference between noncombustible products and materials capable of supporting combustion must be clearly established. This is especially important where materials are used in combination or have been treated in some manner to alter their properties.

Building codes contain explicit criteria for determining what constitutes a combustible material. The *International Building Code®* defines a noncombustible material as being "in the form in which used and under the conditions anticipated, will not ignite, burn, support combustion, or release flammable vapors, when subjected to fire or heat." The most commonly used test for determining combustibility is ASTM E 136, *Standard Test Method for Behavior of Materials in a Vertical Tube Furnace at 750°C.*

Fire Load versus Structural Load

A fire load may not directly translate into an equivalent structural load. For example, a Type IV (heavy-timber) warehouse containing iron radiators would have a high structural load but a light fire load. Conversely, a toy store would have a moderate structural load but a high fire load because most toys are combustible with combustible packaging.

The severity of a fire is a factor of the fire load plus the rate at which the fuel burns. The faster the available fuel burns, the greater will be the heat release rate (HRR). A greater heat release rate results in a faster developing fire. Another factor is the rate at which fuel and the available oxygen combine. Materials that have a high exposure surface to the surrounding oxygen will burn more rapidly with a correspondingly higher heat release rate.

Figure 2.10 This illustration shows the specifications for a floor and ceiling assembly with a 1-hour rating from the UL Fire Resistance Directory.

Design No. G507
Restrained Assembly Rating - 1 Hr.
Unrestrained Assembly Rating - 1 Hr.

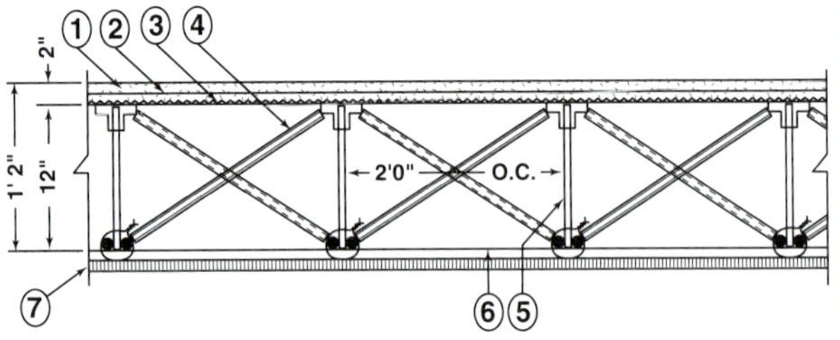

1. **Normal Weight Concrete** - Siliceous or carbonate aggregate, 150 (+or-) 3 pcf unit weight, 4000 psi compressive strength.
2. **Welded Wire Fabric** - 6 x 6, 8/8 SWG.
3. **Metal Lath** - 3/8 in. rib, 3.4 lb/sq yd expanded steel; tied to each joist at every other rib, and midway between joists at side lap with 18 SWG galv steel wire.
4. **Bridging** - 3/4 in., 16 USS gauge box channels or min 1/2 in. diam steel bars.
5. **Steel Joists** - Type 12J4 min size; spaced 24 in. OC and welded to end supports.
6. **Furring Channel** - 3/4 in. 0.30 lb furring channel or 7/8 in. 24 MSG nailing channels, 16 in. OC, fastened to each joist with double tie of galv 18 SWG wire, double furring at each butt joint of wallboard.
7. **Wallboard, Gypsum*** - 5/8 in. thick, secured to furring channels with No.6 flathead sheet-metal screws spaced 8 in. OC or to nailing channels with fetter ring barbed nails 1-1/4 in. long with 11 SWG shanks and 3/8 in. heads, spaced 6 in. OC. Joint treatment not required for this rating, except for tapered, rounded-edge wallboard where edge joints are covered with paper tape and joint compound.

    Celotex Corp. - Type B, C or FRP.
    Continental Gypsum Company - Type CG5-5.
    G-P Gypsum Corp. - Type 5 or C.
    James Hardie gypsum Inc. - Types Fire X, Max"C".
    Republic Gypsum Co. - Type RG-1 or Rg-3.

*Bearing the UL Classification Marking.

Fire Resistance

Fire resistance describes several properties of a material, including:

- Combustibility
- Thermal conductivity
- Chemical composition
- Density
- Dimensions

Fire resistance indicates the ability of a structural assembly to maintain its load-bearing capacity and structural integrity under fire conditions. Fire-resistive construction is not prone to structural failure under fire conditions. In the case of walls, partitions, and ceilings, fire resistivity also means the ability to act as a barrier to fire.

The **fire resistance rating** can be evaluated quantitatively and expressed in time units including hours and fractions of hours **(Figure 2.10)**. The fire resistance ratings incorporated into the building codes include minimum requirements for structural components such as:

- Beams
- Columns
- Walls and partitions
- Floor and ceiling assemblies
- Roof and ceiling assemblies

For example, a building code will typically require that columns supporting the floors in a fire-resistive building have a fairly high fire resistance rating **(Figure 2.11)**. The walls enclosing an exit stairwell, which may or may not be load bearing, typically have a lower fire resistance rating. Fire doors and windows will have a fire resistance rating specific to their function and location.

Laboratory testing is the most common method used to determine fire resistance. Results from laboratory tests are also incorporated into building codes. The standard test is ASTM E-119, also known as NFPA® 251, *Standard Method of Tests of Fire Endurance of Building Construction and Materials.* Other methods of determining fire resistance include the development of mathematical models based on data collected during nonstandard testing, and the use of statistical data to determine probability of fire resistance based on standard test results.

The earliest known fire tests on building materials were conducted in Germany in 1884-86. In the United States, the first known fire tests were conducted in Denver, Colorado in 1890, with subsequent tests in New York City in 1896.

NOTE: See Chapter 5 for more information on testing interior finishes.

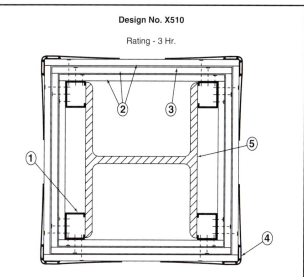

Figure 2.11 Testing material inside furnace. *Courtesy of Underwriters Laboratories.*

Fire Resistance — The ability of a structural assembly or material to maintain its load-bearing ability under fire conditions.

Fire Resistance Rating — Rating assigned to a material or assembly after standardized testing by an independent testing organization; identifies the amount of time a material or assembly will resist a typical fire, as measured on a standard time-temperature curve.

Laboratory-Tested Data

The standard fire-resistance test is widely used in fire protection to establish the required performance standards in building codes. The primary means used to determine a fire resistance rating is to subject the component to be evaluated to the heat of a fire regulated to maintain a standard temperature in a laboratory test furnace. In the standard test, the furnace temperature is regulated to conform to a uniform time-temperature curve. In other words, the temperature in the test furnace is raised along a time scale (**Figure 2.12**).

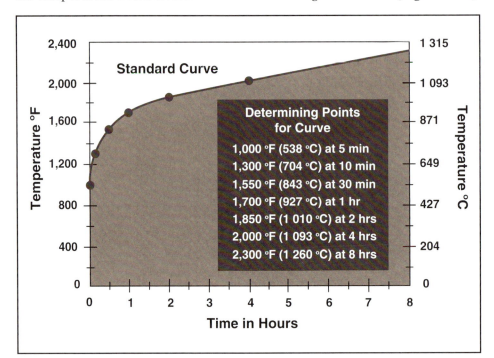

Figure 2.12 The testing protocol includes a standardized time-temperature curve.

The fire resistance of structural systems is affected by the manner in which they are used in the field. In the test the structural components are loaded in a manner that will approximate the working stresses expected in the design (**Figure 2.13**). The test results will be classified as either *load-bearing* or *nonload-bearing*. In addition, the fire resistance ratings are developed for *restrained* and *unrestrained* floor and ceiling assemblies because end restraints affect the extent to which an assembly may expand or rotate at its ends when exposed to high temperatures, affecting its ability to support a load.

Figure 2.13 Before the test, the company testing its materials ensures that the item is properly aligned and placed for best results.

The test continues until the specimen fails or the required time reached **(Figure 2.14)**. For example, a test will be stopped at two hours if the tested material does not fail before the two hours are over. Normally, assemblies are not tested beyond four hours because this is the maximum time that the building code requires.

The failure criteria are specific to the specimen being tested. The primary points of failure for the test are:

- Failure to support an applied load
- Temperature increase on the unexposed side of wall, floor, and roof assemblies of 250°F (121°C) above ambient temperatures
- Passage of heat or flame through the assembly sufficient to ignite cotton waste
- Excess temperature on steel members

NOTE: The failure point temperature of steel will depend on the application of the component. Other factors include maximum temperatures indicated for identified points in the assembly, and the average overall temperature.

In addition, certain wall, partition, and door assemblies are subjected to the application of a hose stream to duplicate the impact and thermal shock of water that may occur during firefighting operations **(Figure 2.15)**. This test is intended to simulate firefighting operations after a prolonged fire.

Figure 2.14 During the test, sensors indicate the temperature on the nonexposed side of the door.

Figure 2.15 The fire hose test simulates suppression operations after a building has been involved in fire for a significant amount of time.

An assembly may fail at any time during the test, for any number of reasons. To provide more accurate and useful data, fire resistance ratings for test specimens are expressed in standard intervals such as 15 minutes, 30 minutes, 45 minutes, 1 hour, 1½ hours, 2 hours, 3 hours, and 4 hours. The number is rounded down to the nearest interval, so an assembly that fails after one hour and ten minutes into a test is rated as one hour.

Limitations of Test Findings

Fire resistance ratings are established using a standardized laboratory test fire. In uncontrolled conditions, rated assemblies may perform satisfactorily for longer or shorter periods of time than in laboratory conditions. This variation is due partly to workmanship and materials that may vary substantially from those used in test specimens. Other variables include the specific conditions used during testing, as described below.

The standard time-temperature curve maintained in a laboratory may not duplicate uncontrolled fires. For example, the standard test fire uses an endless fuel supply and adequate ventilation to produce increasing temperatures; these conditions are not matched in a light-hazard occupancy with limited ventilation. In contrast, a fire involving flammable liquids can produce higher temperatures more quickly than in the controlled fire. For this purpose, a more severe test fire may be used for applications including evaluating the structural members used in petroleum refineries. That test is described in *ASTM Standard 1529, Standard Test Methods for Determining Effects of Large Hydrocarbon Pool Fires on Structural Members and Assemblies.*

Laboratory size restrictions do not permit testing entire buildings. For example, the test furnace used by Underwriters Laboratories, Inc. (UL) for the testing of beams, floor, and roof assemblies replicates the behavior of materials in relatively small compartments. The behavior of identical materials or assemblies in larger configurations may be different in uncontrolled conditions because of the effects of thermal expansion in larger members.

E-119 Test

Despite the limitations of laboratory-controlled testing, the E-119 test is the only standardized test method currently universally accepted by building codes. The use of the fire ratings developed over the years has contributed significantly to the safety of individual buildings and collectively to the fire safety of communities.

The standard test evaluates the ability of structural assemblies to carry a structural load and to act as a fire barrier. The test does not provide the following information:

- Information about performance of assemblies constructed with components or lengths other than those tested
- Evaluation of the extent to which the assembly may generate smoke, toxic gases, or other products of combustion
- Measurement of the degree of control or limitation of the passage of smoke or products of combustion
- Measurement of flame spread over the surface of the tested material
- The effect on fire endurance of openings in an assembly such as electrical outlets and plumbing openings unless specifically provided for in the construction tested

Fire behavior of joints between building elements such as floor-to-wall or wall-to-wall connections are also not evaluated via the E-119 test. Joint systems for floor-to-wall and wall-to-wall connections are tested in accordance with UL Standard 2079, *Standard for Fire Tests of Joint Systems.*

Although all of the above limitations are important, the last point is of particular interest to building and fire prevention inspectors. When the continuity of an assembly is destroyed, it cannot function as a fire barrier. Over time, and particularly during renovation, fire-resistive assemblies may be penetrated. Penetrations of fire-resistive assemblies may be made for ductwork, plumbing, electrical, and communication purposes and not be adequately fire-stopped.

Testing Laboratories

The furnaces used to determine fire resistance ratings are very large and materials are tested at high temperatures. Consequently, the test is beyond the capability of local fire and building departments. Laboratories equipped for such work must conduct the testing **(Figure 2.16)**. Some of these organizations use their furnaces primarily for research and product development.

Figure 2.16 Certified laboratories have equipment that is unavailable to most fire departments.

Some of the organizations that perform fire-resistance testing include:

- Underwriters Laboratories
- Underwriters Laboratories of Canada
- Building Research Division of the National Research Council of Canada
- Southwest Research Institute
- Intertek Testing
- University of California at Berkeley, Forest Products Laboratory
- Armstrong Cork Company
- National Gypsum Company

Publishing Fire Test Results

To make the results of fire-resistance testing available and useful to engineers, architects, and building officials, the testing laboratories publish the results of their tests. Probably the best known of the laboratories is Underwriters Laboratories. Underwriters Laboratories annually publishes a Fire Resistance Directory, which lists assemblies that have been tested and their fire resistance ratings. Notice that the listings specify all the details of the assemblies. Deviation from the materials or dimensions specified will alter the test results. In the same way, field inspections must enforce correct conditions to ensure the best performance of the assemblies. For example, the method of attachment of gypsum wall board to a steel column is especially important to ensure the best performance of all elements.

Mathematical Models Based on Collected Data

Because testing materials in a furnace is costly, and because some structural members may not match those that have been previously tested, mathematical equations have been developed to predict the behavior of materials under test conditions without the need for direct testing. These equations have evolved into mathematical models that utilize the mechanical and thermal properties of materials at high temperatures.

The NFPA® 251 standard time-temperature test is the most commonly used method of satisfying building code requirements for structural fire resistance. As was noted earlier, however, the standard time-temperature curve may not reflect conditions in an uncontrolled structural fire.

For example, the NFPA® 251 test can be too severe or not severe enough for a given situation. Updates to the testing methodology include the calculation of fire resistance based on a time-temperature curve that reflects a more realistic fire occurrence for a given set of circumstances. In some cases, this will be a less severe fire exposure than provided in the NFPA® 251 time-temperature curve. Consequently, fire resistance ratings determined analytically using a different time-temperature curve must be interpreted cautiously.

In 1997, the American Society of Civil Engineers (ASCE) and the Society of Fire Protection Engineers (SFPE) jointly developed a standard for the calculation of fire resistance of structural elements. That standard, known as ASCE/SFPE 29, *Standard Calculation Methods for Structural Fire Protection*, provides the methods for calculating fire resistance ratings that are equivalent to the results obtained from the standard fire test. These calculation methods are limited to use with the following materials:

- Structural steel
- Plain and reinforced concrete
- Timber and wood
- Concrete masonry
- Clay masonry

The calculation methods are based in part on data obtained over time during laboratory testing of materials. These methods may not provide accurate results when applied to materials that have not been used in the actual tests. For example, structural steel designated A7 or A36 is the most prevalent steel used in compiling the test data. If high-strength steel such as A242 were to be used, the calculated results may be inaccurate. Some calculation methods may be relatively simple **(Formula 2.1)**. Others may be more detailed.

Chapter Summary

Building codes classify construction into major types depending on the construction material used and the structural fire resistance. The codes also classify buildings according to their occupancy, which roughly relates to how many people are inside and how the building is being used. Occupancies within the individual occupancy groups present roughly similar fire risk factors. The fire behavior in a building is determined in large measure by the building's materials and fire resistance. The structural fire resistance of building components is determined most often through laboratory testing.

Formula 2.1

Fire Endurance of Steel Beams and Columns with Light Insulation

In standard units, the equation is:

$R = \{[(C_1 \times M) + C_2] \times I\} \div D$

Where:

R = Fire endurance in minutes

M = Mass of the member in lb/ft

D = Heated perimeter in inches

I = Thickness of protection in inches

In metric units the equation is:

$R = \{[(0.672 \times C_1 \times M) + (0.039 \times C_2)] \times I\} \div D$

Where:

R = Fire endurance in minutes

M = Mass of the member in kg/m

D = Heated perimeter in mm

I = Thickness of protection in mm

C1 and C2 are constants that are empirically derived for the insulating units. C1 and C2 are the same for U.S. and metric units.

The constant C1 is calculated thus:

$C_1 = 1200 \div r$

In this formula, r is the insulating material density in pounds per cubic foot.

C2 has a value of 30 for low-density insulating materials such as mineral fibers, U, and perlite. For common insulating materials such as cement pastes or gypsum with similarly high densities, C2 = 72.

Review Questions

1. What are the five basic building classifications used to classify structures by the materials used in their construction?
2. What is the purpose of occupancy classifications?
3. What are some fire and fuel load considerations when determining fire safety?
4. What methods are used to determine and calculate fire resistance of building materials?

Chapter Notes

1. Allen, Edward and Joseph Iano. *Fundamentals of Building Construction: Materials and Methods.* John Wiley and Sons; Hoboken, New Jersey, 2009.

Structural Design Features of Buildings

Chapter Contents

Case History **65**
Forces, Stresses, and Loads **66**
Forces 67
Stresses 68
Load Types 70
Rain and Snow Loads 72
Water Loads 73
Wind Loads 73
Seismic Loads 74
Soil Pressure Load 78
Structural Accommodations for Loads **79**
Beams 79

Columns 80
Arches 80
Cables 82
Trusses 82
Space Frames 84
Composite Structural Systems **84**
Structural Bearing Walls 84
Frame Structural Systems 85
Membrane and Shell Systems 87
Chapter Summary **88**
Review Questions **88**
Chapter Notes **88**

chapter 3

Key Terms

Arch 81	Dynamic Load 71	Post and Beam Construction 86
Axial Load 69	Eccentric Load 69	Resonance 77
Bar Joist 83	Elastomer 77	Rigid Frame 86
Base Isolation 77	Equilibrium 66	Seismic Effect 74
Beam 78	Expansion Joints 77	Seismic Forces 74
Bearing Wall Structures ... 85	Factor of Safety 69	Seismic Load 76
Bending Moment 67	Failure Point 69	Shear Stress 68
Bending Stress 79	Fault 74	Shell Structure 88
Bowstring Truss 83	Flange 81	Slab and Beam Frame 87
Cables 83	Force 66	Space Frames 84
Cantilever 78	Frame 85	Static Load 70
Capital 87	Gravity (G) 67	Stress 66
Chord 83	Gusset Plates 83	Structural Stiffness 77
Column 81	Horizontal Motion 77	Stud 85
Compression 68	Joists 78	Surface Systems 87
Concentrated Load 72	Kinetic Energy 73	Tensile Stress 68
Concrete Block 85	Lateral Load 77	Tension 68
Cross-Section 68	Live Load 70	Torsional Load 69
Damping Mechanism 77	Load 66	Transverse Load 86
Dead Load 70	Load-Bearing Wall 85	Truss 83
Dewatering 73	Membrane Structure 87	Web 81
Drop Panel 87	Negative Pressure 73	Wind 67

Chapter 3 • Structural Design Features of Buildings

Structural Design Features of Buildings

FESHE Outcomes Addressed In This Chapter

Fire and Emergency Services Higher Education (FESHE) Outcomes: *Building Construction for Fire Protection*

4. Explain the different loads and stresses that are placed on a building and their relationships.
5. Identify the function of each principle structural component in typical building design.

Learning Objectives

After reading this chapter, students will be able to:

1. Explain various forces, stresses, and loads exerted on the structural design features of a building.
2. Describe common load-bearing structural components.
3. Identify commonly encountered composite structural systems.

Chapter 3
Structural Design Features of Buildings

Case History

Just after midnight, units responded to a reported chimney fire. Light smoke was visible from the eaves. A truck company captain conferred with a sheriff's deputy who had arrived on scene ahead of the fire fighters. The captain verified the reported conditions, and called for a team, supplies, and a 35-foot ladder to the back of the house to find the attic fire.

Thick black smoke began to bank down during operations, obscuring the team's ability to see hazards that had been identified during the walk-around. Fortunately, no injuries occurred as the team established scene lighting and continued operations.

Fire spread advanced quickly into the attic and in the void spaces between the first and second floors. Teams began pulling down the ceiling to access the void spaces. Visibility within the structure was high – minimal smoke had entered the first floor.

Shortly into the operation, the Operations Chief recognized signs of rapid deterioration from outside of the structure, including fire venting out of the roof, and called for a change to a defensive attack mode. As the last of the fire fighters exited the building, the ceiling collapsed behind them from the weight of the heavy Spanish tile roofing no longer supported by the compromised roof trusses. During post-incident analysis, the roof construction was confirmed to be parallel core truss and joist construction with multiple large open sections and no fire stopping.

Source: NEAR-MISS EVENT, NO INJURY OR DAMAGE #09-0000042

Accommodating the type and magnitude of the forces to which the structure will be subjected is the most critical aspect of engineering design. The ability to understand and evaluate these forces distinguishes a casual knowledge of buildings from a professional knowledge. This chapter discusses the following topics relevant to structural design:

- Forces, stresses, and loads
- Structural accommodations for loads
- Composite structural systems

Force — In physics: Any interaction that may change the motion of an object. Simple measure of weight, usually expressed in pounds (kilograms).

Load — Any effect that a structure must be designed to resist, including the forces of gravity, wind, earthquakes, or soil pressure.

Stress — Factors that work against the strength of any piece of apparatus, equipment, or structural support. Measurement of force intensity is calculated as force divided by area.

Equilibrium — Condition of balance that exists when a structural system is capable of supporting the applied load.

Forces, Stresses, and Loads

To calculate the structural supports needed to allow a building to withstand common **forces**, **loads** are categorized and calculated. The direction of forces from loads acting on the interior of structural members is expressed as **stress**.

The forces within a structural support system that resist applied loads are referred to as *reactions R* (**Figure 3.1**). When a structural support system can support a load equal to or greater than the applied loads L, **equilibrium** exists (**Figure 3.2**). Loss of equilibrium can lead to partial or total collapse. In a sense, when the building disintegrates into a pile of debris on the ground, equilibrium is reestablished.

Figure 3.1 (right) A uniformly applied load on a beam will stress each of the supports equally.

Figure 3.2 (below) Reactions R must equal or surpass the applied loads L to achieve structural equilibrium.

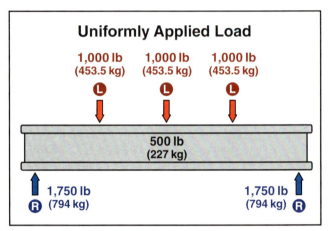

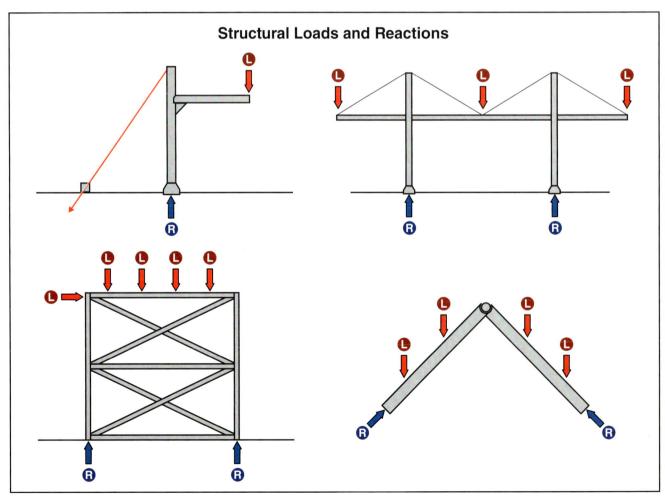

One common type of reaction is a **bending moment** within a horizontal structural component that is loaded vertically. When the vertical load exceeds the strength of the component, the component will bend and possibly fail.

Forces

The force of **gravity** is the most common load imposed on a structure via the weight of the structure's components, contents, and any occupancy activity. Gravity-related factors significantly influence structural plans **(Figure 3.3)**.

> **Bending Moment** – A reaction within a structural component that opposes a vertical load. When the bending moment is exceeded, the component will fail. Bending stress can be calculated from the bending moment.

> **Gravity (G)** — Force acting to draw an object toward the earth's center; force is equal to the object's weight.

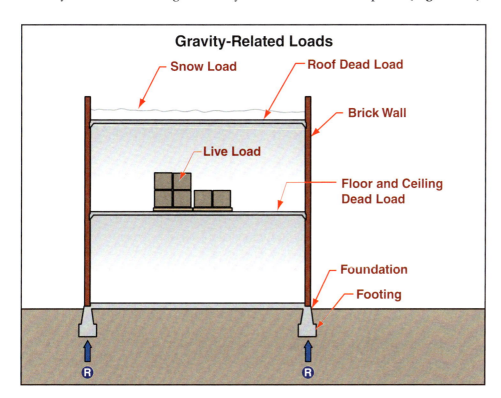

Figure 3.3 The force of gravity manifests as different types of loads on a structure.

Additional forces added to the structure will also increase the load that must be supported by a building's supports, and in turn, the soil beneath the structure. For example:

- Vibration – Shaking motion. Sources of vibration can include:
    - Natural: **Wind**, seismic
    - Building-related: Ventilation system motors
    - External: Vehicular traffic, trains
- Temperature – Temperature changes external to the building may cause peripheral structural members to expand and contract at a rate different from internal members that are held at a more constant temperature. These differences can change the direction of forces between structural elements.
- Shrinkage – As lumber dries over time, the dimensions of wooden structural components shrink. This change of dimension can affect the direction of forces within structural components.

NOTE: The properties of wood components and their loads are explained further in Chapter 7.

> **Wind** – Horizontal movement of air relative to the surface of the earth.

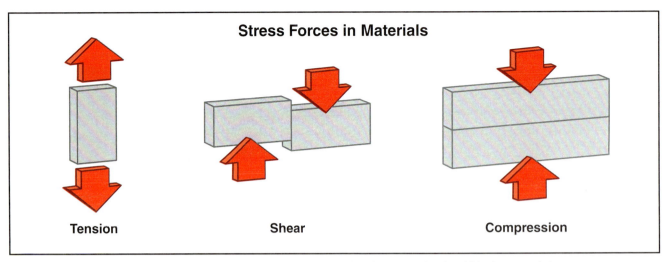

Figure 3.4 Stresses are classified according to the direction in which they exert loads within the material.

Tension — Vertical or horizontal force that pulls material apart; for example, the force exerted on the bottom chord of a truss.

Tensile Stress — Stress in a structural member that tends to stretch the member or pull it apart; often used to denote the greatest amount of force a component can withstand without failure.

Compression — Vertical and/or horizontal forces that push the mass of a material together; for example, the force exerted on the top chord of a truss.

Shear Stress — Stress resulting when two forces act on a body in opposite directions in parallel adjacent planes.

Cross-Section – Theoretical slice of a 3-dimensional structural component to enable area and stress calculations.

Stresses

Stresses within a material are classified according to the direction of the force (**Figure 3.4**):

- **Tension** – Pulls the material apart; referred to as **tensile stress**.
- **Compression** – Squeezes the material; referred to as compressive stress.
- **Shear** – Slides one plane of a material past an adjacent plane.

The direction of the interior stresses is important because material properties have unique tolerances. For example, concrete has high compressive strength but low tensile strength.

Structural members may be constructed in specific shapes and sizes to control multiple stresses within the allowable values for the particular material being used. For example, loads create tension stresses in the bottom of a beam and compressive stresses in the top of a beam. Shear stress is also created across the vertical **cross-section** of the beam (**Figure 3.5**).

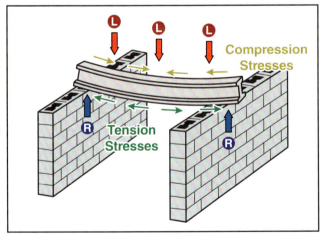

Figure 3.5 Structural members may be shaped, arranged, and supported in specific ways to manage the expected stresses.

Loads applied to the exterior of a structural member create internal stresses within the member based on the placement of the load. External forces often can be visually identified and evaluated; interior forces must be calculated.

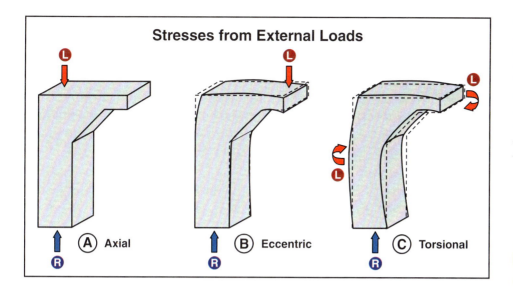

Figure 3.6 (A) Axial loads are applied along the center of the cross-section, and may evenly load the component. (B) Eccentric loads are applied to one side of the cross-section, and may bend the component. (C) Torsional loads are applied at an angle to the cross-section, and may twist the component.

Unique stresses are caused by external load alignments including **(Figure 3.6)**:

- **Axial load**
- **Eccentric load**
- **Torsional load**

The total stresses within structural members must be lower than the **failure point** of the material for the structure to remain intact. A ratio of the failure point of the material to the maximum supportable design stress is added to the minimum-required strength as a **factor of safety**. This added allowance adds tolerance for variations in the properties of the construction materials, workmanship, and live and dead loads. Failure due to stress may include visible indicators, such as cracking, crumbling, bending, and breaking **(Figure 3.7)**.

Axial Load — Load applied to the center of the cross-section of a member and perpendicular to that cross-section. It can be either tensile or compressive, and creates uniform stresses across the cross-section of the material.

Eccentric Load — Load perpendicular to the cross-section of the structural member, but which does not pass through the center of the cross-section. An eccentric load creates stresses that vary across the cross-section and may be both tensile and compressive.

Torsional Load — Load applied off-center from the cross-section of the structural component and at an angle to or in the same plane as the cross-section; produces a twisting effect that creates shear stresses in a material.

Failure Point — Point at which material ceases to perform satisfactorily; depending on the application, this can involve breaking, permanent deformation, excessive deflection, or vibration.

Factor of Safety — Ratio of the failure point of a material to the maximum design stress; indicates the strength of a structure beyond the expected or actual loads.

Figure 3.7 Structural failure of one component may compromise others, as in this failed heavy timber beam that collapsed onto a main gas line while the electrical panels in the building were still energized. *Courtesy of West Allis (WI) Fire Department.*

> **Dead Load** — Weight of the structure, structural members, building components, and any other features permanently attached to the building that are constant and immobile.

> **Live Load** — (1) Items within a building that are movable but are not included as a permanent part of the structure. (2) Force placed upon a structure by the addition of people, objects, or weather.

Load Types

Loads may shift slowly over time, or more quickly when affected by large-magnitude forces. Any change can increase the probability of structural failure. Loads must be anticipated and supported for a structure to remain upright during its working life. Load types can meet multiple categories that are based on factors such as change over time, load application velocity, and weight distribution, as described in the following sections.

Dead and Live Loads

A **dead load** is fixed in location and quantifiable. For example, a building's permanent structural elements are considered part of the dead load **(Figure 3.8)**.

Figure 3.8 Dead loads include any structural elements that do not change significantly over the lifetime of the structure.

In some cases, dead loads can increase or decrease over time. For example, an air conditioning unit installed on the roof of a building is considered a dead load. A new, larger unit replacing an old unit is still considered a dead load, but any change in size, weight, and placement will place new stresses on the existing supports.

> **Static Load** — Load that is steady, motionless, constant, or applied gradually.

A **live load** is not fixed or permanent. The actual weight and distribution of live loads are often not precisely quantifiable **(Figure 3.9)**. In addition, live loads vary by occupancy. Therefore, building codes specify minimum live loads to be used in the design process for different occupancies **(Table 3.1)**. When the actual live load for a given occupancy is known and exceeds the values contained in the code, the actual load must be used in the design calculations.

Static and Dynamic Loads

Loads applied to buildings may be classified according to the rate of speed at which they are applied to a structure. **Static loads** are steady or are applied gradually. When evaluating static loads, an engineer can reasonably pre-

Figure 3.9 Live loads change significantly at relatively short intervals. For example, parking garages hold live loads.

70 Chapter 3 • Structural Design Features of Buildings

Table 3.1
Minimum Uniformly Distributed Live Loads
International Building Code®

Occupancy	Pounds per Square Foot (psf)	Kilograms per Square Meter (kgsm)
Assembly Areas and Theaters		
Fixed Seats	60	293
Lobbies	100	488
Movable Seats	100	488
Stages	125	610
Catwalks	40	195
Balconies (exterior)	100	488
On One-and Two-Family Residences Not Exceeding 100 ft² (m²)	60	293
Bowling Alleys	75	366
Dining Rooms and Restaurants	100	488
Fire Escapes	100	488
Gymnasiums	100	488
Manufacturing		
Light	125	610
Heavy	250	1221
Residential		
Uninhabitable Attics without Storage	10	49
Uninhabitable Attics with Storage	20	98
Habitable Attics and Sleeping Areas	30	146
All Other Areas except Balconies	40	195
Stores		
Retail, First Floor	100	488
Retail, Upper Floors	75	366
Wholesale, all Floors	125	610

Source: 2006 International Building Code®, modified from Table 1607.1.

dict that the constant force needed to be supported will equal the weight of the object. With the exception of mechanical equipment that produces vibrations, dead loads are generally static loads. Many types of live loads are also static.

Dynamic loads involve motion and are capable of delivering energy greatly in excess of the weight of the object involved **(Formula 3.1)**. Dynamic loads may include impact from any of the following:

Formula 3.1
Kinetic Energy of a Falling Object

$E = \frac{1}{2}mv^2$

Where E = Kinetic energy (foot-pounds or Newton-meters)

m = The mass of an object (pounds or kilograms)

v = Velocity (feet or meters per second)

> **Dynamic Load** — Loads that involve motion, including impact from wind, falling objects, and vibration. *Also known as* Shock Loading.

- Wind
- Moving vehicles
- Earthquakes
- Vibration
- Falling objects
- Emergency or maintenance work

For a dynamic load to stop moving, the surface it impacts must absorb the kinetic energy. Whether the surface can withstand the dynamic load depends on the design strength and energy-absorbing properties of the materials used to support the surface.

Dynamic loads may cause structural failure. Even when a single impact does not result in failure, repeated impacts may cause the structure to lose resiliency. For example, garage floor deterioration commonly occurs because of repeated impact loads from the movement of heavy vehicles.

Concentrated and Distributed Loads

Concentrated Load — Load that is applied at one point or over a small area.

Loads may be widely distributed, or they may be contained in a small area. The differences in the structural loads from a uniformly distributed load and a **concentrated load** of the same magnitude can be significant.

Concentrated loads produce highly localized forces and non-uniform loads in the supporting structural members (**Figure 3.10**). Structural supports must be designed to accommodate the anticipated loads. When a concentrated load is known and exceeds the uniform load values contained in the code, the minimum support needed for the concentrated load must be used in the design calculations.

Figure 3.10 Concentrated loads include heavy machinery such as an industrial paper cutter.

Rain and Snow Loads

Rain and snow are live loads. Roofs normally include features that facilitate drainage so rain water runs off, although some *ponding* (water accumulation) can occur on large flat roofs that are not uniformly level.

Snow, however, does not drain off quickly and can accumulate to a considerable depth. The expected *snow load* exerted on a roof can range from virtually none in states in the southern U.S. to a significant load in northern and mountainous regions. The amount of snow that accumulates on a roof also depends on the slope or shape of the roof and the effect of adjacent structures. The snow load expected on the ground is used as a starting point in calculating the snow load on a roof.

Building codes contain requirements for snow loads depending on the particular region. Even in high snowfall regions, the snow load calculated for a roof may be considerably lower than the live loads used for floors.

Water Loads

Water from firefighting operations can add an additional live load to a building. This load may be dynamic as fire flow, or static as accumulated water. For example, the dynamic load of a stream discharging 250 gallons per minute (1 000 L/min) may impact its target with 2,080 pounds of water per minute (945 kg/min).

In a high-rise building, most accumulated water will drain from upper floors through elevator shafts and stairwells. Some older multistory industrial buildings have scuppers through the outside walls to drain water from the upper floors. In some cases, **dewatering** operations will be necessary because water at a depth of 3 inches (75 mm) adds a static load of 21 pounds per square foot (1 kPa).

Dewatering — Process of removing water from a building.

Kinetic Energy — Energy possessed by a moving object because of its motion.

Negative Pressure — Air pressure less than that of the surrounding atmosphere; a partial vacuum.

Wind Loads

The air that makes up the atmosphere is a gas that, like all substances, has mass. The **kinetic energy** of air manifests as wind that presents a force that can be calculated (**Formula 3.2**).

Formula 3.2
Kinetic Energy of Wind

$E = \frac{1}{2}mv^2$

Where E = energy

m = Mass of a body

v = Velocity

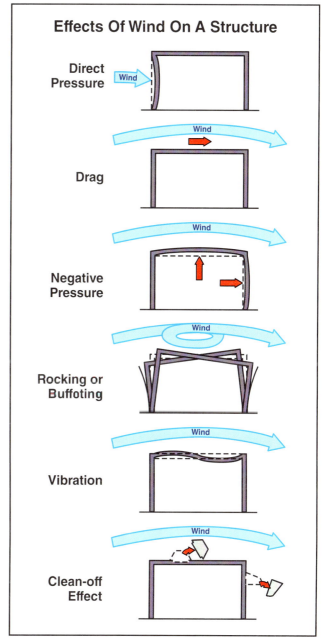

The effects of wind can be simple or complex, and can occur simultaneously with each other. Factors such as wind speed and direction may influence the overall effect of wind. Other effects of wind include (**Figure 3.11**):

- Direct pressure – Straight-line winds apply force to a surface.
- Drag – Wind flowing around the object may catch (drag) along a building's surface.
- **Negative pressure** – Wind may produce a suction effect on the downwind side of the building resulting in outward pressure.
- Rocking – Wind may cause the building to sway in a back-and-forth motion.
- Vibration – Wind passing over a surface, such as a roof, may shake the surface.
- Clean-off – Wind may dislodge or move objects from a building's surface.

In designing buildings to withstand wind forces, direct pressure is used as the primary consideration. Other factors considered include wind velocity and static

Figure 3.11 Structures must be hardened against individual and combination effects of wind.

air pressure, and they assume a wind direction perpendicular to the building wall. Wind pressure increases with increases in wind velocity. Buildings located in a region susceptible to hurricanes must include sufficient supports and braces for the anticipated conditions.

Building design can influence the effects of wind. For example, larger buildings are affected more strongly because winds contact more surface area. Smooth-contoured buildings may shed the force; other contour features, such as canopies and parapets, can catch the wind **(Figure 3.12)**. In addition to horizontal wind effects and building design, engineers must account for complex factors including:

Figure 3.12 Smooth contours in a building will shed wind forces more easily than contour features that catch the wind.

> **Seismic Forces** — Forces produced by earthquakes travel in waves. These are the most complex forces that can be exerted on a building.
>
> **Fault** — Area of discontinuity in the earth's crust associated with movement by tectonic plates.
>
> **Seismic Effect** — Movement of a shock wave through the ground or structure after a large detonation; may cause additional damage to surrounding structures.

- Building height
- Surrounding terrain
- Adjacent urban development

Wind forces are particularly dangerous against walls with insufficient supports. Common locations where walls may be insufficiently braced include:

- Construction sites
- Demolition sites
- Fire-damaged buildings

Seismic Loads

Seismic forces apply the most complicated load that must be accommodated by structural design. These forces result from movement between tectonic plates along a **fault** line or zone. As the plates move and slip, they produce vibrations (waves) at the earth's surface, known as *earthquakes*. An earthquake's vibrational motion can be very destructive to buildings, as history has shown. Explosive detonations may cause a **seismic effect** similar to earthquakes.

Location of Seismic Activity

Earthquakes can occur anywhere on Earth, but some places have a higher probability of seismic events during a 50 year period – the typical expected "life span" of a building. Earthquake-prone areas are mapped by organizations such as the United States Geological Survey (USGS) and National Geographic **(Figure 3.13)**.

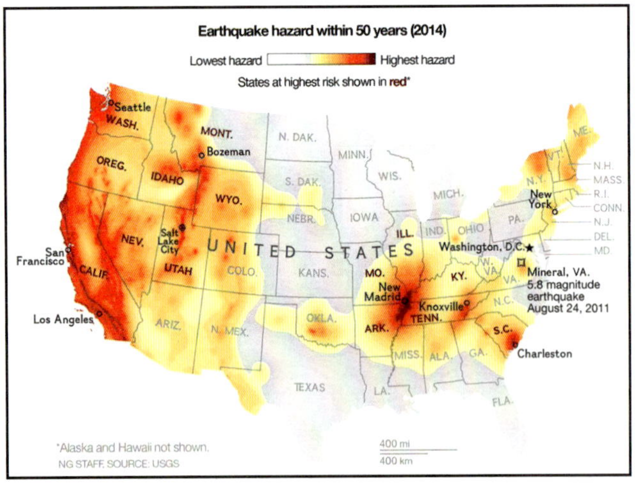

Figure 3.13 Seismic maps of the United States show areas that are susceptible to earthquake activity. *Illustration courtesy of U.S. Geological Survey (USGS) Department of the Interior.*

Earthquake High Risk Locations

- Alaska
- Hawaii
- Canadian coasts **(Figure 3.14)**
- South Carolina
- Pacific coast: California, Washington
- U.S. intermountain west: Montana, Nevada, Oregon, Utah, Wyoming
- U.S. states bordering the Mississippi River: Arkansas, Illinois, Kentucky, Missouri, and Tennessee

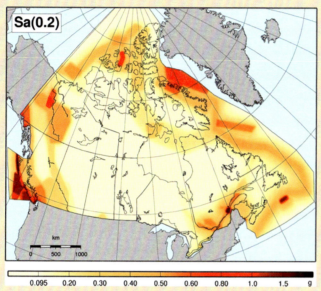

Figure 3.14 The National Building Code of Canada includes a map of seismic hazards. *Reproduced with the permission of Natural Resources Canada 2015.*

All model building codes provide seismic maps. Building codes also contain provisions for design based on the duration and magnitude of seismic forces. In cases where the expected seismic loads are different than the structural provisions for wind or gravitational loads, the structural design plan must accommodate the more stringent requirements. Per code, some buildings require stronger bracing than the seismic activity map indicates. Examples include:

- Office buildings
- Public assembly buildings
- Schools

Other buildings must be designed for greater seismic loads because they are essential for community recovery after an earthquake. Examples include:

- Fire and police stations
- Hospitals
- Communication centers
- Emergency preparedness centers
- Generating stations

Seismic Load — Application of forces caused by earthquakes.

Seismic Load Types

The overall effect of the **seismic load** against a structure depends on the acceleration of the ground beneath the building more than the total movement. Seismic loads may be far more complex than wind loads because the movement of the ground beneath a building can be three-dimensional. Directional movement includes:

- Lateral – **Lateral loads** that create **horizontal motion** are the most significant force generated by an earthquake **(Figure 3.15)**. Inertia holds the upper portion of the building in its initial position as the lower portion moves with the ground, and shear stress develops between the upper and lower portions of the building. Low buildings are less susceptible to this type of motion than tall buildings.

- Torsional – Torsional loads are applied to a structural member that is twisted by seismic motion.

- Resonant – Seismic waves affect some buildings differently than others due to the **resonance** of the earthquake and each building's features.

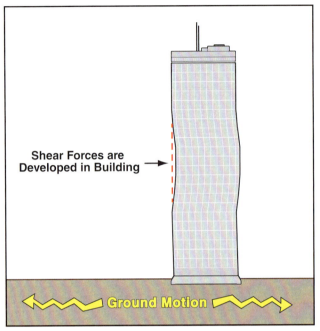

Figure 3.15 Seismic waves may transmit wave-like forces along the height of a building.

Structural Accommodations Unique to Seismic Activity

The significance of the forces developed within a building during an earthquake depends on many factors, and the expected forces from seismic forces may exceed other types of expected forces. Accommodations for seismic forces may be included in new construction or retrofitted to existing buildings. Three types of accommodations are described below:

- Expansion joints
- Damping mechanisms
- Base isolation

A building's basic architecture influences the degree to which it is affected by seismic activity. For example, buildings with geometric irregularities are inherently more susceptible to damage from earthquakes than buildings with symmetrical design. Tall and shorter sections in a single building will respond differently to seismic vibrations, which can produce damaging forces at the sections' junction **(Figure 3.16)**. In buildings with height variations or large floor plans, seismic **expansion joints** can be added to increase the flexibility of the connection.

Damping mechanisms absorb resonant energy as the structure begins to move. These mechanisms are typically installed at the connections between columns and beams, and operate on a principle similar to mechanical door equipment that controls the movement of an automatic door.

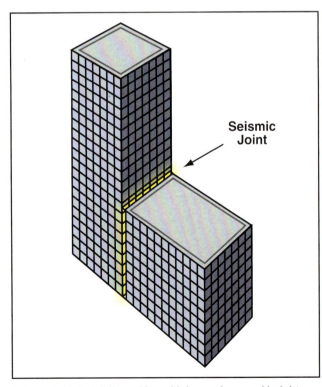

Figure 3.16 A building with multiple sections and heights may be constructed with seismic joints to accommodate differences in how seismic activity will affect the sections.

> **Expansion Joints**
>
> Partitions fitted with seismic expansion joints must include joints that also meet any relevant fire rating. In 1980, openings in seismic joints significantly contributed to the spread of fire gases at the MGM Grand in Las Vegas. In that incident, 87 people died and 650 were injured, including 14 firefighters[1].

Base isolation isolates the building from the horizontal movement of the earth's surface. This strategy is increasingly popular and includes two common methods:

- **Shear systems** – **Elastomeric** bearings placed in a layer between the building and the foundation **(Figure 3.17)**. The bearings change the fundamental resonance of the building. Several buildings in the U.S. have been built or retrofitted with these bearings, including the City Hall of Oakland, California.

- **Sliding systems** – Special plates that slide on each other to isolate the building from horizontal shear force. This system is a less common method of building isolation.

Figure 3.17 Elastomeric bearings used in base isolation prevent some seismic force from travelling into a building. *Courtesy of San Diego County Sheriff's Department.*

Figure 3.18 Cross bracing reinforcements increase a building's ability to resist earthquake forces. *Courtesy of Tanya Hoover.*

Structural Stiffening Accommodations

Structural stiffening is a strategy used to *harden* a structure against expected loads. Some types of **structural stiffness** are particularly effective against seismic loads. Two types are explained below:

- Shear walls and cross bracing
- Structural support redundancy

Shear walls and cross bracing are effective against ground motions with a relatively long (slow) vibrational period **(Figure 3.18)**. Because cross bracing components must be symmetrically located in a building to prevent torsional forces from developing, this type of bracing may not be suitable for all locations.

Lateral Load — Load that exerts a horizontal force against a structure. Calculated as a live load; includes seismic activity and soil pressure against vertical restraints such as retaining walls and foundations.

Horizontal Motion — Side-to-side, swaying motion.

Resonance — Movements of relatively large amplitude resulting from a small force applied at the natural frequency of a structure.

Expansion Joints — Structural accommodation that allows building sections to move independently of each other; often installed in concrete. Modern expansion joints may be fire-rated.

Damping Mechanism — Structural element designed to control vibration from resonance.

Base Isolation — A system of structural elements that create a joint between a building and its base to minimize seismic force effects on the main structure. The type of system may be customized to the type of seismic forces expected in an area.

Elastomer — Generic term for rubber-like materials including natural rubber, butyl rubber, neoprene, and silicone rubber used in facepiece seals, low-pressure hoses, and similar SCBA components.

Structural Stiffness — The use or addition of structural supports to improve the ability of a structure to withstand forces imposed by loads. Often indicates supplemental reinforcement to accommodate specific types of loads, such as earthquake forces. *Also known as* Stiffening.

Redundant structural members support the entire system, making collapse less likely to occur **(Figure 3.19)**. This type of building stiffening also uses continuous joints that have a greater ability to absorb energy, in contrast to joints with less support. For example, a poured-in-place concrete structure is easier to design for earthquake resistance than a structure using precast concrete.

NOTE: Concrete construction methods are discussed further in Chapter 10.

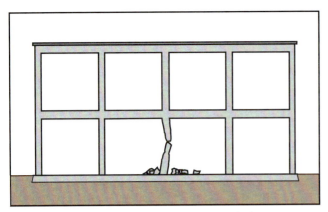

Figure 3.19 Redundant structural supports help prevent a building from falling after being damaged.

Soil Pressure Load

Soil exerts a lateral load (pressure) against a foundation **(Figure 3.20)**. This load must be evaluated in the design process. As with wind and earthquakes, the loads associated with soils may be difficult to predict accurately, but estimates based on historical data are provided via codes.

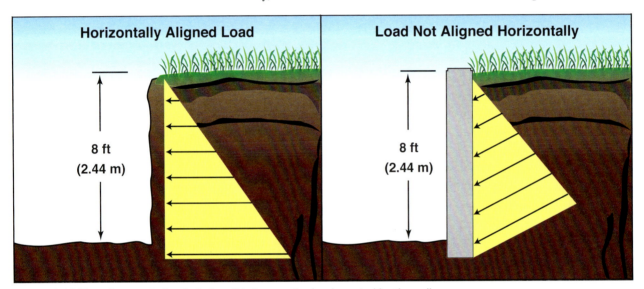

Figure 3.20 The alignment of soil strata will influence the load exerted by the soil.

Beam — Structural component loaded perpendicular to its length. Primarily resists bending stress characterized by compression in the top portion and tension in the bottom portion.

Joists — Horizontal structural members used to support a ceiling or floor. Drywall materials are nailed or screwed to the ceiling joists, and the subfloor is nailed or screwed to the floor joists.

Cantilever — Projecting beam or slab supported at one end.

The magnitude of the pressure depends on the soil's properties, as explained in Chapter 6. The pressure exerted by the soil against the foundation is known as the *active soil pressure*. The force of the foundation against the soil is known as the *passive soil pressure*. In determining the force created by the active soil pressure, the soil is assumed to behave similarly to a fluid. Thus, the pressure would range from zero at the top of a foundation wall to the maximum pressure at the base, which depends on the depth and density of the soil **(Formula 3.3)**. Firefighters should recognize the importance of foundation shifts over time, especially as the shifts change the alignment of forces being supported within a structure.

Sand content in soil is particularly relevant when surveying sites with high seismic activity. Sandy soil usually has some cohesive properties during seismic activity. In contrast, *soil liquefaction* occurs when sandy soil near water sources is looser and saturated with water, and entrapped water prevents the sand particles from moving closer together, reducing the ability of the soil to support a structure.

Formula 3.3
Simple Soil Pressure Formula

The basic equation used to determine soil pressure is:

P = CWH

Where P = Pressure

H = Depth of soil

W = Density of soil

C = Numerical constant that depends on the physical properties of the soil.

Structural Accommodations for Loads

Structural support components work in tandem within a support system to enable the capability of larger structures to withstand their own weight plus the expected loads. The following sections describe common load-bearing structural components.

Beams

A **beam** is a structural member that carries loads perpendicular to its longitudinal dimension. The primary design consideration of beams is their ability to resist being deformed from the applied loads. Materials used in beams can include:

- Steel
- Wood
- Reinforced concrete

Common support systems for beams include **(Figure 3.21)**:

- **Simply supported beams** — Supported beneath both ends and free to rotate. A wood **joist** resting on a masonry wall is an example of a simply supported beam.
- **Restrained beams** — Rigidly supported at each end. Under fire conditions, a rigidly supported beam may retain its load-bearing ability longer than a simply supported beam because the end restraints provide more resistance to the applied stresses.
- **Cantilever beams** — Supported at one end; must be able to support a vertical load in addition to resisting **bending stresses**. **Cantilever beams** often support balconies.
- **Overhanging beams** — Similar to cantilever beams but with additional support.
- **Continuous beams** — May span several vertical supports.

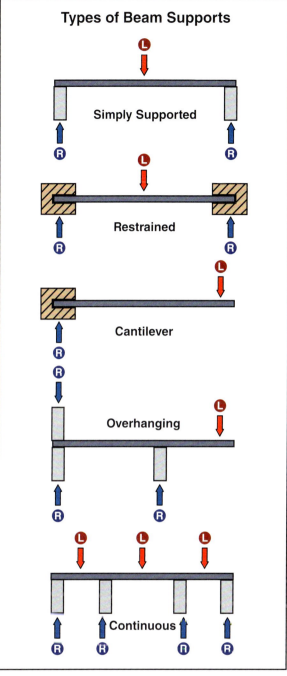

Figure 3.21 Beams may be supported in several standard ways to serve specific purposes.

Bending Stress — Compressive and tensile stresses in a beam. When the stresses are not held in equilibrium, the beam will bend and ultimately fail. Bending stresses are calculated from the *Bending Moment* (the amount of stress at which a structural member bends from its original alignment).

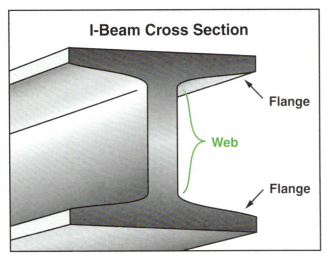

Figure 3.22 The cross-section of an I-beam shows the manufactured sections that include more material in sections that support greater stresses and less material in areas with lower stresses.

Figure 3.23 A constructed I-beam made of wood maximizes the beam's ability to carry a load while minimizing the materials required for each component. *Courtesy of Dave Coombs.*

Figure 3.24 Cast-iron is less commonly used as a structural support, but may still be found in older structures.

The top **flange** of the beam carries compressive stresses, and the bottom flange of the beam carries tensile stresses. The center horizontal line of the **web** is known as the *neutral axis* because the tension and compression stresses are zero, but the neutral axis is the maximum point of shear stress **(Figure 3.22)**.

As shown earlier in this chapter, beams may be shaped to maximize the ability of the beam to carry the expected load while minimizing the material needed for the purpose.

Shaping the beam increases the efficient use of material and reduces the weight of the beam.

Some thickness can be removed from the web without greatly affecting the strength of the beam. This engineering principle results in many beams being constructed in the shape of the capital letter "I". This construction is effective because the top and bottom flanges of the beam carry most of the load of resisting the bending stress. I-beams are generally constructed using a web and two flanges that are affixed to each other, rather than carved from one piece **(Figure 3.23)**.

The stresses on the elements of an I-beam can be calculated mathematically. The stresses are a function of the cross-sectional area of the flanges and the vertical dimension of the beam. Tall beams are capable of supporting greater loads than short beams, even if they have the same cross-sectional area.

Columns

Columns are structural members designed to support an axial load **(Figure 3.24)**. The stresses created within a column are primarily compressive. Materials used in columns can include:

- Wood
- Steel
- Cast iron
- Concrete
- Masonry

Columns are not primarily designed to withstand bending stresses. Columns are likely to fail if the support beneath the column or beams attached to a column shift out of alignment. Tall, thin columns fail by buckling; short, squat columns fail by crushing.

Arches

An **arch** is a curved structural member with primarily compressive interior stresses. Arches produce *inclined*

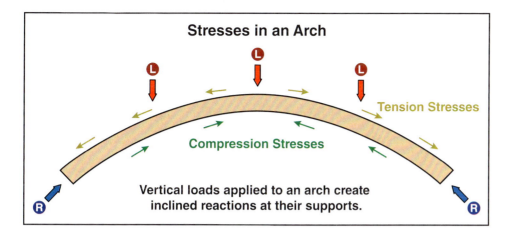

Figure 3.25 The supports on the ends of the arch hold the arch in place.

forces at their end supports, which the supports must resist **(Figure 3.25)**. Arches are used to carry loads across a distance. They are often used as support for roofs and entrances in masonry buildings. Materials used in arches can include:

- Masonry
- Steel
- Concrete
- Laminated wood

If the supports at the ends of the arches shift because of settling soil or thermal expansion, bending stresses may develop in the arch. To provide for minor adjustments, arches are sometimes designed with hinges **(Figure 3.26)**. If the end supports of an arch are removed, the arch becomes unstable. Supports added after the fact, for example, by adding a wood column under the arch and a steel rod anchored in the masonry wall, are not ideal solutions. If the end supports cannot maintain the arch, horizontal tie rods can be used to prevent the arch from spreading.

Flange — Single or paired external ridges or rims on a beam that do most of the work of supporting a load.

Web — (1) Wide vertical part of a beam between thick ridges (flanges) at the top and bottom of the beam. (2) Secondary member of a truss contained between the chords. *Also known as* Diagonals.

Column — Vertical member designed to support an axial load and compressive stresses.

Arch — Curved structural member using compressive internal stresses. Arches develop inclined reactions at their supports.

Figure 3.26 Hinges may replace a keystone to allow an arch to move under specific conditions.

Chapter 3 • Structural Design Features of Buildings

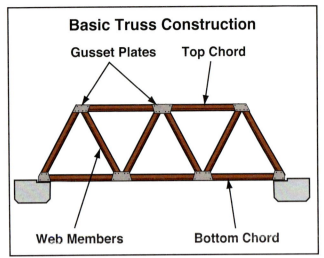

Figure 3.27 Trusses are constructed as a series of triangles arranged in a plane.

Cables

Although **cables** are essentially straight, a cable used to support loads over a distance will assume a curved shape. The stresses in a cable are tension stresses. Cables are usually made of steel strands, although aluminum may be used where weight is a critical factor.

Trusses

Trusses are framed structural units made up of a group of triangles in one plane **(Figure 3.27)**. A true truss is made only of straight members. The top and bottom members of a truss are called **chords**. The middle section of a truss is also called the *web* or *diagonals*.

Geometrically speaking, triangles provide an inherently rigid frame. If a diagonal brace is added to a framework, the resulting triangulation creates a stronger assembly.

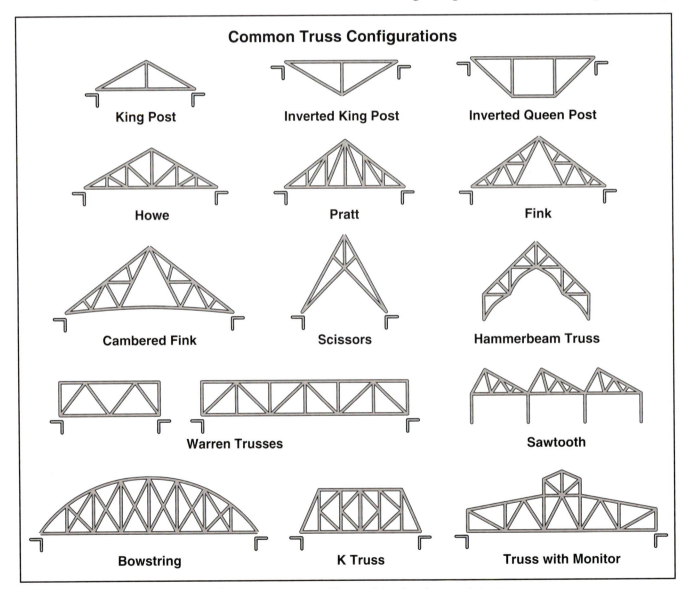

Figure 3.28 Common configurations of trusses may be used in a variety of roof support structures.

Trusses may be arranged in a wide variety of styles **(Figure 3.28)**. Typical truss shapes span distances of 22 to 70 feet (7 m to 21 m), but truss spans in modern construction may exceed 100 feet (30 m).

Some types of roof trusses, such as the **bowstring truss**, have a curved top chord. These curved members are unavoidably subjected to bending stresses.

Truss Construction

Most trusses are prefabricated. They are able to span a set distance using less material and weight than a comparable beam.

Materials used in trusses include wood, steel, or a combination of wood and steel. Lightweight wood or metal trusses, known as truss joists, have become common in floor construction, taking the place of solid joists. Lightweight wood trusses are also commonly used in roof construction. Lightweight steel trusses, known as **bar joists**, are also used for floor and roof construction in fire-resistive and noncombustible construction **(Figure 3.29)**.

NOTE: Roof trusses that are even lighter in weight than steel bar joists are available. In effect, these trusses are made of galvanized steel studs or channels similar to them, and assembled with self-drilling screws.

The material used in the truss members will affect the materials used in the connections. Connectors used with steel trusses include:

- Steel gusset plates
- Rivets
- Welds

Connectors used with wood trusses include:

- Pins or bolts
- **Gusset plates**
- Structural adhesives
- Brackets
- Metal straps

Figure 3.29 Lightweight trusses can be used to support a roof. *Courtesy of McKinney (TX) Fire Department.*

Cables — Flexible structural members designed to withstand tension stresses. Commonly used to support roofs, brace tents, and restrain pneumatic structures.

Truss — Structural member used to support a roof or floor with triangles or combinations of triangles to provide maximum load-bearing capacity with a minimum amount of material. Connections are likely to fail in intense heat.

Chord — Top or bottom longitudinal member of a truss; main members of trusses, as distinguished from diagonals.

Bowstring Truss — Lightweight truss design noted by the bow shape, or curve, of the top chord

Bar Joist — Open web truss constructed entirely of steel, with steel bars used as the web members.

Gusset Plates — Metal or wooden plates used to connect and strengthen the joints of two or more separate components (such as metal or wooden truss components or roof or floor components) into a load-bearing unit.

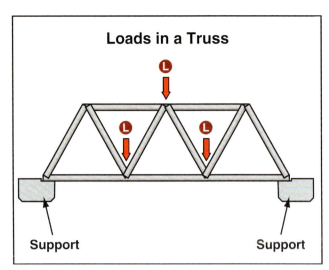

Figure 3.30 Loading a truss at the strongest points, at the intersections of web members, will apply compressive or tensile stresses to the top and bottom beams of the truss.

Figure 3.31 A space frame is a series of trusses connected with diagonal members between each truss. In this roof assembly, the black piping is part of the sprinkler system. *Courtesy of Ed Prendergast.*

> **Space Frames** — Aluminum skeleton upon which an aluminum, plastic, or composite skin is attached. The internal structure provides structural support, while the skin provides styling and protection from the elements.

Truss Loads and Failure

When loads are applied only at the point of intersection of the truss members, only compressive or tensile stresses will affect the members of the truss (**Figure 3.30**). In addition, loads applied to the truss between the intersection points of the members will also create bending stresses. Trusses may fail under adverse conditions because the stresses in the top and bottom chords balance each other; failure of either results in failure of the truss.

The connectors in truss assemblies are a critical factor in the strength of the truss. Failure of a connector will result in failure of the truss. Quality control in the manufacture of trusses can affect the behavior of trusses under fire conditions. A gusset connector that is not properly seated may work loose under fire conditions. In some wood truss assemblies, a small gap may exist between the ends of the horizontal members at the joint.

NOTE: Connectors are discussed in more detail in later chapters.

Space Frames

Space frames are three-dimensional truss structures (**Figure 3.31**). They offer many of the advantages of two-dimensional trusses in terms of economic use of material. Space frames are well-suited to support uniformly distributed loads. The design of space frames is more complicated than with two-dimensional trusses because the forces must be analyzed in three dimensions.

Composite Structural Systems

Individual structural components are of little value unless they can be assembled into a composite system that will support a building. Just as architectural styles can vary widely, an almost infinite number of structural designs can be created. As with building types, practical necessity and economics result in a number of commonly encountered structural systems. General types of structural systems share fundamental characteristics. Each system has advantages or disadvantages related to materials, cost, and applications.

Structural Bearing Walls

Load-bearing walls are commonly placed at the exterior of a structure, but they may also include internal walls. Load-bearing walls carry compressive loads and provide lateral support to the structure along the length of the wall. Common materials used in bearing walls include:

- **Concrete blocks** (concrete masonry units)
- Brick
- Stone

- Solid wood
- Concrete panels

Bearing walls may be constructed as a continuous barrier or interrupted for door and window openings. **Bearing wall structures** use walls to support spanning elements, including:

- Beams
- Trusses
- Precast concrete slabs

Frame Structural Systems

A **frame** structure uses structural supports in a manner similar to the way the skeleton supports the human body. The walls act as the 'skin' to enclose the frame. The walls may also provide lateral stiffness but provide no structural support.

In the fire service, the term *frame construction* often refers to a wood-frame building, but frame structural systems are also built using other materials. Components of a frame may be constructed using a series of trusses **(Figure 3.32)**. The following sections describe types of structural frame construction.

> **Load-Bearing Wall** — Wall that supports itself, the weight of the roof, and/or other internal structural framing components, such as the floor beams and trusses above it; used for structural support. *Also known as* Bearing Wall.

> **Concrete Block** — Large rectangular brick used in construction; the most common type is the hollow concrete block. *Also known as* Concrete Masonry Units (CMU).

> **Bearing Wall Structures** — Common type of structure that uses the walls of a building to support spanning elements such as beams, trusses, and pre-cast concrete slabs.

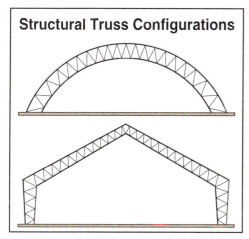

Figure 3.32 In addition to roof supports, truss systems can be arranged in a wide variety of structural frame configurations.

Figure 3.33 Cross bracing may be added to resist lateral movement. *Courtesy of Colorado Springs (CO) Fire Department.*

Steel Stud Walls

Steel **stud** wall construction includes frames built from relatively closely spaced vertical steel studs connected by top and bottom horizontal members. Studs are placed 12 to 16 inches (300 to 400 mm) apart.

A steel stud wall is frequently provided with diagonal bracing for stability **(Figure 3.33)**. Both sides of a stud wall may be covered with paneling and sheathing. The use of steel studs has become more common in recent years. Historically, stud-wall frame construction has been associated with the use of 2 inch x 4 inch (50 mm x 100 mm) wood studs.

> **Frame** — Internal system of structural supports within a building.

> **Stud** — Vertical structural member within a wall in frame buildings; most are made of wood, but some are made of light-gauge metal.

Post and Beam Construction

Post and beam construction framing uses a series of vertical elements (posts) to support horizontal elements (beams) that carry **transverse loads** (**Figure 3.34**). Post and beam construction requires the addition of other members, such as diagonal braces, to withstand lateral loads.

Materials that can be used in post and beam construction include masonry for the posts and steel and precast concrete for the posts and beams. Historically, this system evolved from the use of tree trunks for framing and is still commonly associated with wood beams and columns.

The distinctive characteristic of post and beam framing is the spacing of the vertical posts and the cross-sectional dimension of the members, because the dimensions are often greater than used in stud wall construction. For example, posts may be 6 x 8 inches (150 x 200 mm) when supporting roofs only.

NOTE: Post and beam construction is discussed further in Chapter 7.

> **Post and Beam Construction** — Construction style using vertical elements to support horizontal elements. Associated with heavy beams and columns; historically constructed of wood.

> **Transverse Load** — Structural load that exerts a force perpendicular to structural members.

> **Rigid Frame** — Load bearing system constructed with a skeletal frame and reinforcement between a column and beam.

Figure 3.34 Post and beam framing is identifiable by the spacing of the vertical posts and the dimensions of the members.

Rigid Frames

A **rigid frame** structural system is characterized by columns and beams reinforced to transmit the bending stress through the joints. Rigid frame buildings are often single story in height with a gabled roof (**Figure 3.35**). Rigid frames are also used in other types of structures including multistory and multispan designs. Materials used in rigid frames include:

- Steel
- Laminated wood
- Reinforced concrete

The peak of the roof is usually provided with a hinged connection to allow for slight movement between the two halves of the frame. The joints will be the last portion of the assembly to fail under fire conditions.

Figure 3.35 Rigid-frame buildings may be constructed with steel frames. *Courtesy of McKinney (TX) Fire Department.*

Slab and Column Frames

One common concrete framing system uses concrete floor slabs supported by concrete columns. The floors of a multistory, reinforced-concrete building can be designed by several methods, depending on the loads to be supported. In addition to concrete slabs, horizontal systems that can be used to support floor loads include wood decks and metal decks supported by beams and columns. Because of the high stress load at the connection, the intersection between the slab and column is usually reinforced by additional material in the form of a **capital** or a **drop panel** (**Figure 3.36**).

NOTE: Slab and column framing is different than **slab and beam framing**. More information on the latter is covered in Chapter 10.

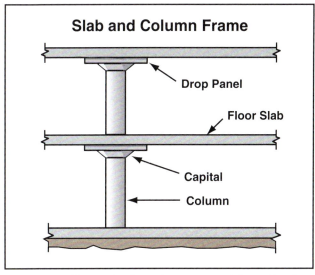

Figure 3.36 Slab and column frames are reinforced by the addition of a capital and drop panel.

Membrane and Shell Systems

Surface systems consist primarily of an enclosing, waterproof surface; the stresses resulting from the applied loads occur within the bearing wall structures.

Membrane Structures

Membrane structures are similar to fabric tents, but differ in that they are intended to be permanent structures. Building codes typically address membrane structures with a life of 180 days or more, while fire codes address those used for less than 180 days. Recent designs use polytetraflouroethylene (PTFE) coated glass fiber for the fabric. In early permanent membrane structures, polyvinyl-coated polyester fabric was used. Fabrics cannot resist compressive forces; therefore, frameworks must support the fabrics (**Figure 3.37**). Types of frames include:

- Cables and masts
- Tubular
- Solid

Membrane structures possess several design advantages over traditional construction, including:

- Fabrics weigh less than other roof systems: about 2 pounds per square foot (0.1 kPa).
- Membrane structures can usually be erected in less time than a rigid structural system.
- Fabrics can flex and absorb some of the stresses caused by seismic and wind forces.

NOTE: Structures supported only by air are discussed in Chapter 12.

Figure 3.37 Fabrics cannot resist compressive forces, therefore, membrane structures must be supported by materials other than the membrane itself. *Courtesy of Ed Prendergast.*

Capital — Broad top surface of a column or pilaster, designed to spread the load held by a column.

Drop Panel — Type of concrete floor construction in which the portion of the floor above each column is dropped below the bottom level of the rest of the slab, increasing the floor thickness at the column.

Slab and Beam Frame — Construction technique using concrete slabs supported by concrete beams.

Surface Systems — System of construction in which the building consists primarily of an enclosing surface, and in which the stresses resulting from the applied loads occur within the bearing wall structures.

Membrane Structure — (1) Structure with an enclosing surface of a thin stretched flexible material. (2) Weather-resistant, flexible or semiflexible covering consisting of layers of materials over a supporting framework.

In the U.S. and Canada, frames are usually steel and sometimes aluminum. Other materials used in the frame of membrane structures include:

- Wood
- Concrete
- Steel

Shell Structures

Shell structures are rigid, three-dimensional structures having thin components, as compared to other structural material dimensions. Shell structures are most commonly constructed of concrete, although it is possible to construct them using plywood or fiberglass. Shell structures lend themselves to regular geometric shapes such as cones, domes, barrel vaults, and folded plates **(Figure 3.38)**.

Figure 3.38 Shell structures are often constructed with concrete in regular geometric shapes. *Courtesy of Ed Prendergast.*

Shell Structure — Rigid, three-dimensional structure with an outer "skin" thickness that is small compared to other dimensions.

Chapter Summary

Buildings must withstand a wide variety of forces, loads, and stresses. Firefighters must have a basic understanding of the forces acting on structures so they can be aware of structural hazards and collapse dangers. Under fire conditions, the loads and stresses exerted on a structural system are subject to change in magnitude and direction resulting in structural failure.

A structural engineer will apply calculations and requirements by model building codes to design supports. While determining the supports required, a variety of structural components may be used, because these components support loads in different ways.

Review Questions

1. What common forces, stresses, and loads may impact the structural design of a building?
2. What components may enable structures to withstand their own weight plus the expected loads?
3. What are types of commonly encountered composite structural systems?

Chapter Notes

1. *Casey, Heather. "Vegas MGM Grand Fire 20 Years Ago Among the Worst." Firehouse.com news*

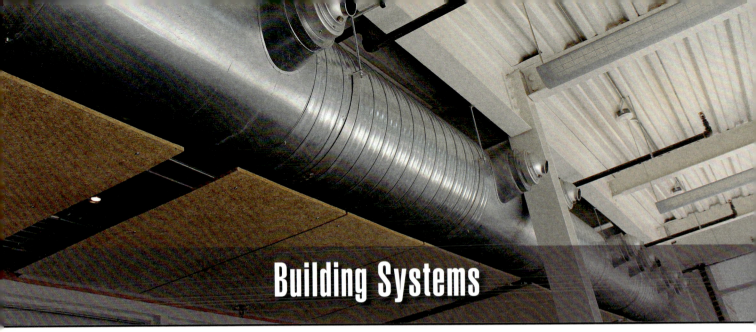

Building Systems

Chapter Contents

Case History 93	Elevator Shafts 114
Stairs **94**	**Vertical Shafts and Utility Chases** **114**
Basic Components 94	Vertical Shaft Enclosures 114
Prefabricated Stairs 95	Pipe Chases 116
Types of Stairs 95	**Air Handling Systems** **116**
Stairs as Part of the Means of Egress 98	HVAC System Components 118
Smokeproof Stair Enclosures 99	Simple Ventilation and Exhaust Systems ..120
Open Stairs 101	Forced-Air System 120
Mechanical Conveyor Systems **101**	Smoke Control Systems 121
Moving Stairs 101	Smoke and Heat Vents 124
Moving Walkways 102	Smoke Towers 125
Elevators **102**	Pressurized Stairwells 126
Emergency Use of Elevators 103	**Electrical Equipment** **128**
Types of Elevators 104	Transformers 128
Safety Features 108	Emergency and Standby Power Supplies ..130
Elevator Hoistways 109	**Chapter Summary** **131**
Elevator Doors 111	**Review Questions** **132**
Elevator Access Panels 112	**Chapter Notes** **132**

90 Chapter 4 • Building Systems

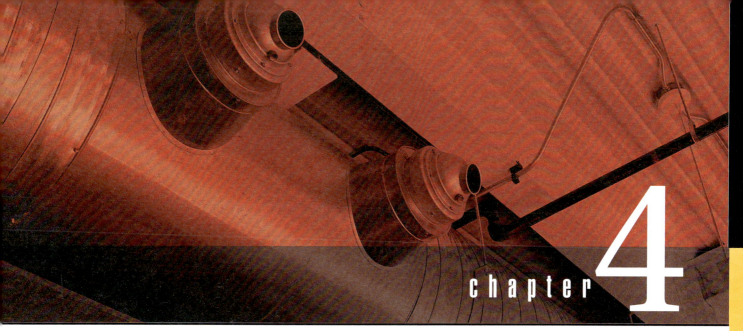

chapter 4

Key Terms

Alternating Current (AC) Circuit 106	Landing 95
Arc 129	Machine Room-Less 108
Blind Hoistway 112	Means of Egress 94
Compensated System 128	Multiple-Injection System 126
Convenience Stair 94	Mushrooming 110
Cooling Tower 120	Overpressure 128
Cupola 117	Passive Smoke Control 99
Dielectric 129	Pipe Chase 116
Direct Current (DC) Circuit 106	Polychlorinated Biphenyl (PCB) 129
Draft Curtains 124	Products of Combustion 98
Dumbwaiter 108	Recirculation 120
Elevator 103	Refuse Chute 114
Elevator Pit 109	Return-Air Plenum 119
Escalator 101	Rise 94
Exhaust System 120	Riser.. 94
Exterior Stairs 98	Run 94
Fire Damper 119	Shear Wall 110
Fire Escape 98	Single-Injection System 126
Firefighter's Smoke Control Station (FSCS).. 123	Smoke Control 121
Forced–Air System 120	Smoke Control Mode 121
Generator 130	Smoke Damper 119
Heating, Ventilating, and Air Conditioning (HVAC) System.......................... 116	Smoke Tower 125
Hoistway 105	Smokeproof Stair Enclosures 99
Hurricane Glazing 121	Stationary Storage Battery System 131
Hydronic System 120	Transformer 128
	Tread 94
	Utility Chase 114

Building Systems

FESHE Outcomes Addressed In This Chapter

Fire and Emergency Services Higher Education (FESHE) Outcomes: *Building Construction for Fire Protection*

1. Describe building construction as it relates to firefighter safety, building codes, fire prevention, code inspection, firefighting strategy, and tactics.

Learning Objectives

After reading this chapter, students will be able to:

1. Describe the building system functions of stairs.
2. Describe mechanical conveyor systems used in buildings.
3. Describe the building system functions of elevators.
4. Identify types of vertical shafts and utility chases.
5. Explain various functions of building air handling systems.
6. Identify types of electrical equipment used for building systems.

Chapter 4
Building Systems

Case History

In the early morning hours on January 27, 2013, a fire broke out in the Boate Kiss nightclub in Santa Maria, Brazil. As a result of this blaze, 235 people were killed and an additional 200 people were injured. Numerous issues arose as a result of the fire; however, interior finishes covering the nightclub's walls and ceiling was a main contributor to the toxic smoke production and flame spread within the nightclub. Reports indicate eerily similar causes and outcomes as the Station nightclub fire that occurred in West Warwick, Rhode Island.

That night, the Boate Kiss nightclub was hosting a party for students from six colleges from the University of Santa Maria. Over 2,000 people packed this small nightclub to see the two bands that had been booked to play. A member of one of the bands shot off a flare or firework that ignited flammable acoustic foam that lined the walls and ceiling of the club. The acoustic foam allowed for quick flame spread and the production of copious amounts of thick black smoke. Polyurethane foam, in addition to the conditions listed above, creates a super-heated environment, which produces untenable conditions that result in death within minutes of ignition. The incorrect installation of the acoustical materials was the main contributing factor to the deaths and injuries at the nightclub.

Buildings, like complex machines, contain many basic systems to address the convenience, access, comfort, efficiency, and, most important, life safety for occupants. All building systems may significantly influence any fire event. Any defects in a system can impair the building's functionality. The building design team is responsible to ensure that the necessary building systems initially provide the intended level of fire and life safety. Subsequently, the building owner and/or management must maintain these systems over time. Building systems discussed in this chapter include:

- Stairs
- Mechanical Conveyor Systems
- Elevators
- Vertical Shafts and Utility Chases
- Air Handling Systems
- Electrical Equipment

Means of Egress — Continuous and unobstructed path of exit travel from any point in a building or structure to a public way; consists of three separate and distinct parts: exit access, exit, and exit discharge. (Source: NFPA® 101, Life Safety Code®).

Convenience Stair — Stair that usually connects two floors in a multistory building.

Tread — Horizontal face of a step.

Riser — Vertical part of a stair step.

Run — The horizontal measurement of a stair tread or the distance of the entire stair length.

Rise — Vertical distance between the treads of a stairway, or the height of the entire stairway.

NOTE: For more information on building systems, consult the IFSTA **Plans Examiner, Fire Protection, Detection, and Suppression Systems**, and **Fire Inspection and Code Enforcement** manuals.

Stairs

Most stairs provide a dual role as a building system. First, they enable access to multiple levels of the structure. Second, they serve as a basic component of building egress during an emergency. Stairs that are NOT part of the **means of egress** are often referred to as **convenience stairs**. Typically, these stairs are open and connect only two levels per code limitations. Buildings that are four or more stories in height may be required to include one stairway that extends to the roof for access to mechanical equipment, and is identified by signage in the stairway.

Basic Components

All stair types have basic components in common. The step itself consists of the **tread** and the **riser**, commonly referred to as the **run** and **rise**. For safety purposes, the measurements of stair treads and risers must be consistent throughout the same set of stairs. Stairs with open sides must also include handrails and guards to prevent people or objects from falling onto adjacent spaces **(Figure 4.1)**. Other components may be added as required by the application.

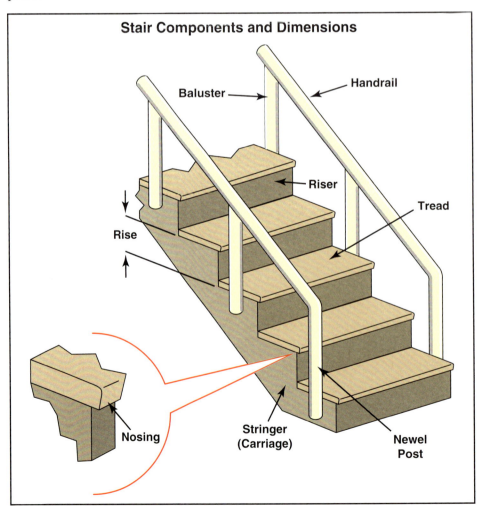

Figure 4.1 Stair components include features that are regulated for the safety of the people who will use them.

Prefabricated Stairs

Stairs can be prefabricated using lightweight materials and techniques. The components are held together using metal gussets, which are known to fail under specific conditions, having been tested for applications including roof and floor joists. First responders recognize the hazard presented by other engineered products when safeguards, such as drywall sheeting, are shortcut, eliminated, or destroyed. However, at the time of this printing, no credible source indicates that this type of construction is likely to fail at a rate higher than heavier types of construction when safeguards are in place.

NOTE: Chapter 7 includes information on lightweight materials used in construction.

Types of Stairs

The design or layout of a set of stairs may take any of several different forms, depending on their length, location, and purpose **(Figure 4.2)**. The following sections describe six common types of stairs.

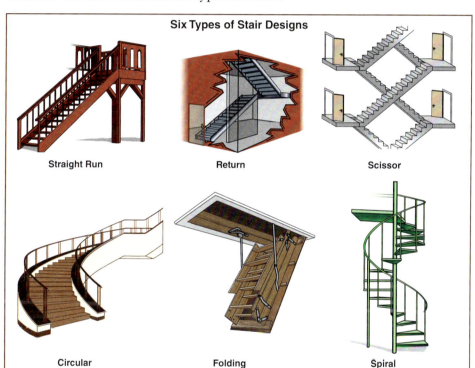

Figure 4.2 The six most common types of stairs may be found in a wide variety of occupancy types.

Straight-Run Stairs

Straight-run stairs extend in one direction for their entire length. **Landings** may be used between sections of vertical travel.

Landing — Horizontal platform where a flight of stairs begins or ends.

Return Stairs

Return stairs have an intermediate landing between floors and reverse direction at that point. Return stairs may have more than one landing where the height between floors is greater than normal. This type of stair design is common in modern construction.

Scissor Stairs

Scissor stairs are two separate sets of stairs constructed in a common shaft **(Figure 4.3)**. Scissor stairways are cheaper and more space efficient than two separate stair enclosures.

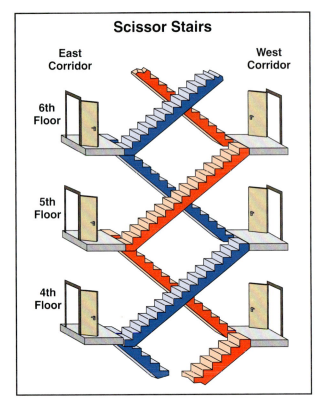

Figure 4.3 Older designs of scissor stairs may exit the stairwell on every other floor; newer designs have exits on each floor.

Scissor stairs often use a pair of return stairs for assembly occupancies that have large floor-to-ceiling heights. In these instances, the ingress/egress access is from the same corridor, but several feet apart. This arrangement positions the standpipe on the same stair side at each floor. Buildings that often include scissor stairs include:

- Airport terminals
- Convention centers
- Malls
- Cinema complexes

The modern design arrangement for scissor stairs allows for ingress and egress at each floor landing; this feature is used to provide additional exit capacity. Older scissor stairs may return to every second floor. This older design restricts egress from the stairway into one corridor on even-numbered floors and into the opposite corridor on odd-numbered floors. This arrangement can be confusing, particularly during a fire. Firefighters may need additional hose to connect to a standpipe on the floor below the fire.

Circular Stairs

Circular stairs are often found as grand stairs or convenience stairs serving only two levels. The minimum width of the run is usually 10 inches (250 mm). A special requirement for circular stairs is that the small radius of the full circle is greater than or equal to twice the widest part of the stair tread.

Spiral Stairs

Spiral stairs consist of a series of steps spiraling around a single column to fit in a very small space. Each tread is tapered and connects to the column (baluster) at the tread's narrow end. Typically, custom-made spiral stairs are not enclosed.

Spiral stairs are primarily used in residential occupancies, but may also be found in commercial occupancies for limited use. Because they can be difficult to traverse, spiral stairs are generally allowed as part of the means of egress only within residences. Steel spiral stairs are sometimes used for access to permit-required confined spaces, as a dry-well in a sewage pumping station, and in industrial applications.

Folding Stairs

Folding stairs are actually ladders used to provide access to an attic space that does not have a permanent access stair. These stairs are most commonly found in residential occupancies, and added after construction to provide attic access. This type of stair is most often located away from the building's usual functional spaces.

Folding stairs usually have three wooden sections: the main section that hinges from the frame, and two articulating sections **(Figure 4.4)**. After the lower stair sections are folded together, the stair swings up into the attic space and is held in place by coil or gas springs, or counterbalances. A light wooden panel, usually plywood, is attached to the main section and conceals the stair when it is folded into the ceiling.

Firefighters should be aware that springs in folding stairs lose tension rapidly when exposed to heat, and the stair assembly may swing down into the structure during a fire. The stair opening can also provide a vertical path for fire and smoke spread.

Some buildings may use fixed ladders (ship's ladders) in similar applications to provide access to areas including:

- Mechanical spaces
- Roof hatches at the top of stairways
- Between roof levels with portions at different elevations

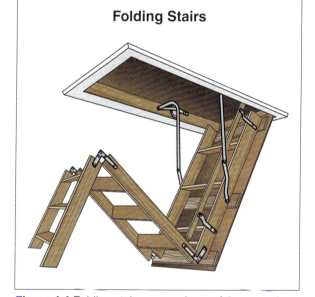

Figure 4.4 Folding stairs are made up of three sections that unfold as the stairs are lowered.

Both folding stairs and fixed ladders may have weight limitations lower than the weight of a firefighter wearing full PPE. Many departments recommend against using these stairs for fire fighting purposes.

Gas Springs

Gas springs, also known as *struts*, are increasingly used with the hinge in folding stairs. These struts replace traditional coil springs in new construction because they function more cheaply, quietly, efficiently, and easily. Unfortunately, under sudden exposure to fire temperatures or compression, gas springs can fail with explosive force.[1]

Stairs as Part of the Means of Egress

Exit stairs, as a component of the required means of egress, must meet strict requirements to ensure safe passage during building evacuation. Features include:

- Fire-resistance rating of the enclosure
- Separation when exterior stairs are utilized
- Features to ensure safety during both nonemergency and emergency use.

Some types of exit stairs provide egress but not access, that is, they do not allow building re-entry onto any floor except the ground floor, for security reasons. These types of stairs are commonly found in hotels or other multistory buildings. Types of stairs specifically indicated for egress are discussed in the following sections.

Protected Stairs

Products of Combustion — Materials produced and released during burning.

Protected stairs must resist the effects of the **products of combustion**. This protection is extremely important in the overall life safety of a building because studies show that even minor impairment in visibility significantly impairs occupants' ability to safely egress.

Measures indicated in building codes to protect stair enclosures include:

- Limited penetrations in the enclosure for light, fire protection, and environmental control
- Required self- or automatic-closing fire-rated doors
- Separation from the rest of the building
- Stairway vestibules

Other measures indicated in building codes may be regulated or prohibited. For example, penetrations for services not required for the stair enclosure itself are generally prohibited. Also, stair enclosures may include horizontal exit passageways with the same life safety requirements.

Exterior Stairs

Exterior Stairs — Stairs separated from the interior of a building by walls.

Exterior stairs are naturally ventilated on one or more sides (**Figure 4.5**). Fully enclosed exterior stairs are subject to the same regulations as enclosed interior stairs.

When provided as a part of the means of egress, open exterior stairs may feature limited or protected openings in the building's outside wall near the stairs. Thus, these stairs have some degree of protection from products of combustion from inside the building.

Fire Escapes

Fire Escape — Means of escaping from a building in case of fire; usually an interior or exterior stairway or slide, independently supported and made of fire-resistive material.

Fire escapes include open metal stairs and landings attached to the outside of a building (**Figure 4.6**). The lowest flight may consist of a swinging stair section to limit unauthorized access. Stairs exposed to weather must be routinely inspected and maintained.

NOTE: Fire escapes have not been permitted in new construction for many decades, though many still exist.

Figure 4.5 (left) The arrows in this photo point to exterior stairs that provide a means of egress that is open to the elements.

Figure 4.6 (right) Fire escapes are not permitted in new construction, and existing fire escapes cannot be considered safe for use today.

Fire escapes are usually anchored to the building, and the anchor points may fail without warning due to factors including:

- Damage from the freeze-thaw cycle
- Corrosion from pollution and weather
- Inadequate mortar holding the anchors

Smokeproof Stair Enclosures

Building codes have traditionally required a minimum of one **smokeproof stair enclosure** for stairs serving buildings five stories or higher. More recently, codes also require protection for stairs serving floor levels more than 30 feet (10 m) below the level of exit discharge. Smokeproof stair enclosures may use either active or **passive smoke control**. Smokeproof stair enclosures are typically located on the exterior perimeter of the building and are entered through ventilated vestibules or open exterior balconies.

Smokeproof Stair Enclosures — Stairways that are designed to limit the penetration of products of combustion into a stairway enclosure that serves as part of a means of egress.

Passive Smoke Control — Smoke control strategies that incorporate fixed components that provide protection against the spread of smoke and fire. Passive smoke control components include fire doors, fire walls, fire stopping of barrier penetrations, and stair and elevator vestibules.

Active versus Passive Fire Protection

Active fire protection uses moving mechanical or electric parts that work as a system and require a power source for operation. Systems that may be linked directly into a building's systems may include automatic sprinkler systems (plumbing) or fire alarm systems (electrical). Other power sources may be manual, for example, portable fire extinguishers.

Passive fire protection does not require any system activation or movement. Passive fire protection relies on building construction and materials to contain fire or products of combustion. Examples of passive fire protection include fire walls or stair enclosures.

NOTE: Active and passive systems are also discussed in the IFSTA manual **Fire Protection, Detection, and Suppression Systems**.

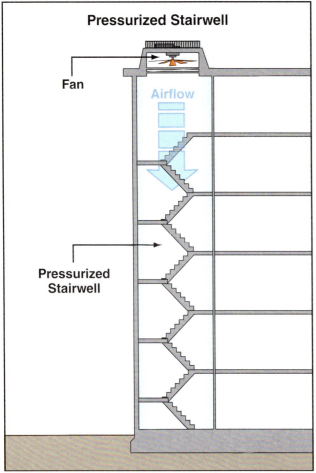

Figure 4.7 A pressurized stairwell uses a ventilation system to maintain a higher air pressure in the stairwell than on the individual floors to prevent smoke from entering the stairwell.

Active Smokeproof Enclosures

Stairwells may be designed to pressurize when the fire alarm system is activated **(Figure 4.7)**. In this arrangement, a dedicated mechanical air-handling system will generate enough pressure to keep smoke out of the stair enclosure, even when a door is open to the fire floor. A correctly operating system should allow firefighters to begin suppression operations concurrently with occupant egress. In high rise structures, codes require dedicated, pressurized stairways designed solely to provide firefighters a safe route to access and attack a fire.

Building codes specify maximum and minimum allowable pressure differentials between the stair enclosure and the building to allow the doors in the enclosure to be opened with a reasonable amount of force. Earlier versions of codes allowed the stair door to open directly from a corridor; newer versions typically require a vestibule between the corridor and stairway. These vestibules are also pressurized to assist in keeping smoke out of the stairway.

NOTE: Additional information about protection of stairwells and towers is provided later in this chapter.

Passive Smokeproof Enclosures

Passive smokeproof enclosures protect the stairway enclosure and provide a means of smoke ventilation before the smoke enters the stair enclosure. These enclosures are accessed through a vestibule or an exterior balcony **(Figure 4.8)**.

NOTE: More information on passive containment measures is included in Chapter 5.

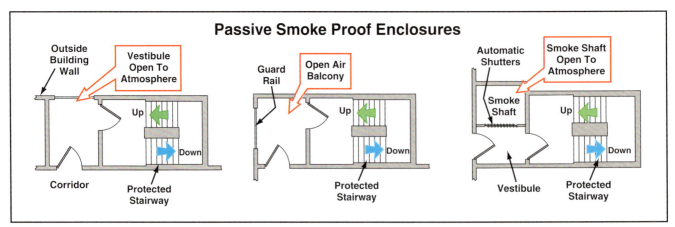

Figure 4.8 Passive smoke containment prevents the spread of products of combustion between a building and stairwell.

Open Stairs

Open stairways are not enclosed with fire-rated construction. Therefore, they may provide a path for products of combustion to spread, and will not protect anyone from those hazards. Building codes typically allow the use of open stairs in buildings only when they connect no more than two adjacent floors above the basement level **(Figure 4.9)**.

Mechanical Conveyor Systems

A conveyor system is used to transport items and materials. Some conveyors, such as screw or pneumatic systems, work in enclosed compartments. Material conveyors are typically found in manufacturing or storage occupancies, and airport baggage handling facilities.

Figure 4.9 Open stairs connect different levels of a building without compartmentation from the building.

Conveyor systems often penetrate fire barriers, and are protected by features such as:

- Fire doors
- Shutters
- Water spray fixed fire suppression systems

Escalator – Belt-driven moving stairs that move in one direction at a fixed rate of speed.

Incomplete door or shutter closure is a primary safety hazard at conveyor penetrations during a fire. Safeguards against incomplete closure include:

- Automatic stop controls
- Breaks in the conveyor
- Multiple layers of doors or shutters

Conveyor systems that are intended to carry people are similar but have more stringent regulations. Regardless of the specific operation method and use, conveyor functions should be routinely inspected and tested.

Moving Stairs

Escalators are a conveyor transport device aligned as a stairway with electrically powered steps that move continuously in one direction. Escalators are commonly found in facilities that contain large numbers of people **(Figure 4.10)**. The driving machinery is located under an access plate at the upper landing.

Escalator speeds are standardized at 100 feet per minute (fpm) [30 meters per minute (m/min)]. Older escalators usually operate at speeds of either 90 or 120 feet per minute (27 or 36 m/min). The elements of moving stairways work as follows:

- Each individual step rides a track.
- The steps are linked by a *step chain* and move around the escalator frame.
- Continuous handrails also move at the same speed as the steps.

Figure 4.10 Escalators and moving walkways move along a track in one direction; continuous handrails move at the same rate of speed.

Chapter 4 • Building Systems **101**

An emergency stop switch will stop the escalator and set the brake **(Figure 4.11)**. The location of the emergency stop switch may vary by manufacturer or other factors. Stopped escalators may be used as fixed stairs. Escalators may be stopped for reasons, including:

- Routine, periodic maintenance
- Emergency operations
- Periods of low-capacity in the building

Vertical penetrations for escalators serving more than two floors must be protected. The most common protection for the vertical opening is to use closely spaced sprinklers and draft stops around the opening **(Figure 4.12)**. Combined, these two features may be arranged as an 18-inch (450 mm) deep draft stop with a row of automatic sprinklers on all sides outside the draft stop. A rolling shutter at the top of the escalator can also provide vertical opening protection. Partial enclosures use separate fire-rated enclosures for the up escalator and the down escalator.

Moving Walkways

Moving walkways are similar to escalators but are only used to move people horizontally or up slight inclines. Moving walkways are often found in airports to move passengers long distances between the main terminal and remote concourses. Typically, they use metal plates attached in a continuous pathway, equipped with moving handrails. Some installations use moving rubber-like belts over metal rollers.

Elevators

Elevators are complex mechanical building systems with the following features:

- Serves two or more levels or landings
- Includes hoisting and lowering mechanisms **(Figure 4.13)**
- Provides access to above- or below-grade stories
- Uses a car or platform that moves along guide rails

Depending on the application, firefighters may view elevators negatively or positively during a fire response. Elevators are uniquely useful when upper floors of a high-rise building must be accessed, especially in non-fire situations such as medical emergencies. Conversely, elevators are uniquely dangerous when the system malfunctions or the electrical power system is disrupted[2,3].

Figure 4.11 Firefighters should be aware of the location of emergency shutoffs for escalators. Properly stopped escalators may be used as fixed stairs during emergency conditions.

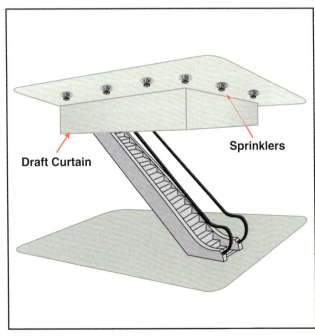

Figure 4.12 Sprinklers may be included in protection systems provided over escalators.

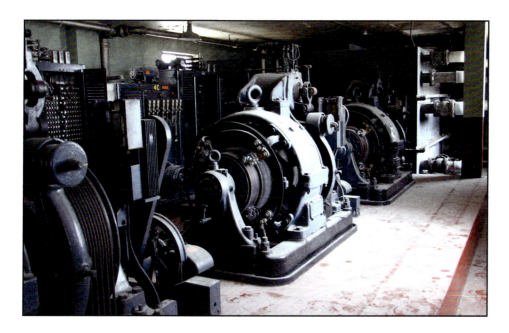

Figure 4.13 Complex mechanical elements used in an elevator include motors used for hoisting and lowering the car.

Over time and because of their importance, the safe and reliable use of elevators has grown as a topic of regulation at multiple levels of government, especially in regard to elevator design, construction, and operation. Most elevator regulations are based on ASME/ANSI A17.1, *Safety Code for Elevators*, published by the American Society of Mechanical Engineers (ASME). Elevators have also increased in importance in multistory buildings because of the accessibility requirements in the *Americans with Disabilities Act* (ADA). For example, the ADA requires either ramp or elevator access within multistory buildings; elevators require significantly less floor space than ramps.

Historically, stairs have been the only recognized means of emergency egress for floors above or below the exit discharge. In recent years, elevators have gained new importance. For example, some elevators are now used for applications including:

- Dedicated elevator cars for firefighter use
- Designated means of emergency egress in high rise structures
- Emergency evacuation of individuals with disabilities, when properly designed

Elevator — Vertical traveling mechanical system used to transport people and items in a multistory building.

Emergency Use of Elevators

The purpose of this manual is not to advocate any standard operating procedures for the use of elevators during fire operations; rather, it describes some basic safety precautions and common practices. Each jurisdiction must establish its own set of policies and procedures regarding the use of elevators during fires and practice these procedures during drills.

When an elevator meets the necessary qualifications, it may be used during emergency response. Before such use, firefighters should recall the elevator to the lobby and open the door from a floor level above the recalled elevator to check the shaft for smoke infiltration.

NOTE: Emergency use of elevators is covered in Chapter 12. This manual does not address emergency elevator rescue techniques.

Types of Elevators

Elevators can be classified according to their use:

- Passenger elevators carry people **(Figure 4.14)**.
- Freight elevators carry resources that may be bulky or heavy **(Figure 4.15)**.
- Service elevators are passenger elevators designed to also carry freight.

All types of elevators use some form of power to perform the hoisting and lowering operations. The two most common types of power used in elevators are hydraulic and electric.

Figure 4.14 Common passenger elevators deliver passengers to designated floors. *Courtesy of McKinney (TX) Fire Department.*

Figure 4.15 Freight elevators are scaled larger than passenger elevators to carry heavier and bulkier loads, and may deliver to a small range of floors.

Hydraulic Elevators

Hydraulic elevators operate via fluid forced, under pressure, into a cylinder containing a piston or ram. Pumping in fluid raises the ram and moves the car upward. Draining the fluid allows the car to lower through gravity. Hydraulic elevators do not have brakes; cars are controlled through the flow of the hydraulic fluid.

Because the elevator car is attached to the top of the ram, the ram must be long enough to reach the highest service floor. In newer construction, hydraulic elevators can use a multi-stage hydraulic cylinder rather than a single-stage ram, reducing the overall length of the cylinder. Historically, the practical upper limit for hydraulic elevators was about six stories, and the elevator shaft required a deep well for the ram to extend into the ground to reach the lowest service floor.

Electric Elevators

Electric elevators use a hoisting cable and a drum, but the exact configuration of those components is different among the styles **(Figure 4.16)**. Modern elevator cables are flat polyethylene-coated steel belts that increase energy efficiency. Historically, elevator cables have been made of conventional wire cables. Four common styles of elevators are:

Figure 4.16 Electric elevators use a hoisting cable or belt and a drum to raise and lower elevator cars or platforms. *Copyrighted material courtesy of Jim Shirreffs III.*

Figure 4.17 Traction elevators are commonly used in modern construction. *Copyrighted material courtesy of Jim Shirreffs III.*

Figure 4.18 Hoistways, described later in this chapter, often house elevator components such as cables and rails.

- Drum elevators, intended for passenger use
- Traction elevators, intended for passenger use **(Figure 4.17)**
- Machine Room-Less (MRL) Elevators, intended for passenger use
- Dumbwaiters, intended for cargo use

Drum elevators use a hoisting cable wound on a drum located in a motor room directly over the **hoistway** **(Figure 4.18)**. The car is connected to a set of moving counterweights to reduce the effort the motor must produce to raise

Hoistway — The vertical shaft in which the elevator car travels; includes the elevator pit.

Chapter 4 • Building Systems   **105**

the car. Like hydraulic elevators, drum-type elevators have practical height limitations because the size of the drum increases with the lifting distance. Drum elevators are obsolete and found only in very old structures or in use as freight elevators.

Traction elevators are the most common type of elevator in buildings over six stories. Traction elevators are fast and do not have the height limitations of either hydraulic or drum-type elevators. The drive equipment for traction elevators is contained in a machine room that is usually located directly over the hoistway **(Figure 4.19)**. Similar to drum elevators, traction elevators use counterweights to reduce the amount of energy needed to raise the elevator.

Figure 4.19 Traction elevators are especially common in buildings over 6 stories. *Copyrighted material courtesy of Jim Shirreffs III.*

Hoist cables attached to the elevator car run up and over the drive sheave at the top of the hoistway and then down the back wall of the hoistway to connect to the movable counterweights **(Figure 4.20)**. The hoist cables do not wind around the drive sheave; they merely pass over it. Friction between the cable and the sheave hold the cable in place.

Even though counterweights reduce the amount of energy needed to raise the elevators, the operating heights may require them to have as much as a 500-volt power supply. The drive motors may be either **direct current (DC)** or **alternating current (AC)** types. Firefighters must be extremely careful when conditions require them to work in the vicinity of high-voltage equipment.

Alternating Current (AC) Circuit — Electrical circuit in which the current can move through the circuit in both directions and the flow can be constantly reversing.

Direct Current (DC) Circuit — Electrical circuit in which the current moves through the circuit in only one direction.

Electrical Utility Safety
Lock-out/tag-out procedures should be identified and followed when working with electrical and mechanical equipment. Utility company personnel should be called to the scene if electrical hazards are a substantial concern during incident response.

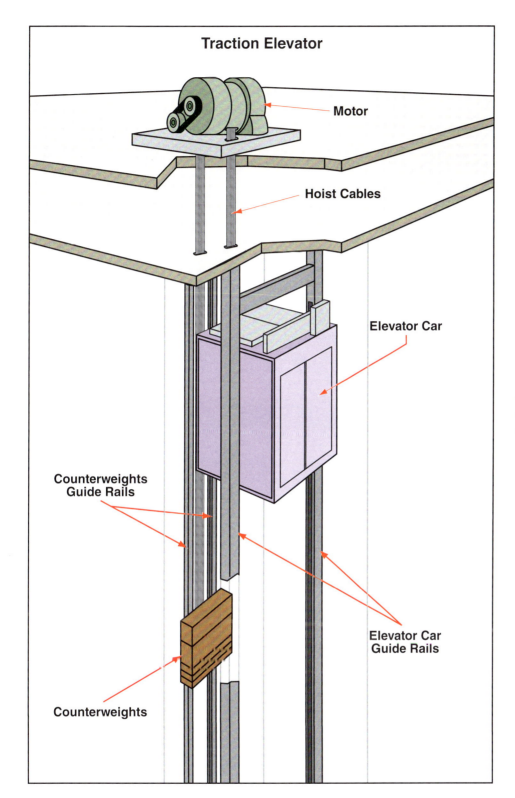

Figure 4.20 Traction elevators use a series of components to safely raise and lower an elevator car in normal and emergency modes.

Traction motors have a braking system that operates during both normal operation and malfunctions. The system employs a brake drum located on the shaft of the drive motor.

Under normal conditions, the spring-operated brake shoes hold electromagnets away from the drum. During normal operation, the brakes on traction elevators with AC motors aid directly in stopping the car at the correct

Chapter 4 • Building Systems **107**

Figure 4.21 Elevator control panels can indicate at a glance the location and status of individual elevator cars. *Courtesy of Colorado Springs (CO) Fire Department.*

Machine Room-Less (MRL) – Elevator hoistway that includes all components, including motors, mounted within the hoistway itself to eliminate the need for a machine room at the top of the hoistway. The elevator controls may be located remotely from the elevator system.

Dumbwaiter – Small freight elevators that carry items, not people, and generally have a small weight and size capacity.

floor. On elevators with DC motors, the brakes do not play any part in actually stopping the elevator car. The motor stops the car and then the brakes are applied to hold the car in place.

In the event of power failure, the electromagnets release and the brake shoes are forced against the drum. This results in the car being stopped wherever it was when the power failed.

Machine Room-Less (MRL) elevators feature controls that may be remote from the elevator system. The other components may all fit within the hoistway.

Dumbwaiters are small freight elevators that move along a hoistway and transport items of small weight and size between floors. Dumbwaiters found within modern structures, including commercial, public, and private buildings, may be powered with an electric motor and accessible at multiple levels. Historically, they were drawn with ropes and used to move food from a kitchen to upper floors in occupancies including:

- Restaurants
- Schools
- Hospitals
- Retirement homes

Safety Features

Equipment that can safely stop a car in the event of a failure will help maintain the maximum protection of passengers. The excellent safety record of elevators can be attributed to several factors including **(Figure 4.21)**:

- Strict regulation of equipment
- Rigorous engineering to reduce the likelihood of failure
- Numerous safety devices designed to limit the effects of failures that do occur

Passenger safety devices found on elevators may include:

- Terminal device – An electric switch that terminates power before the elevator reaches the upper or lower limits of the hoistway.
- Buffers – Large springs or hydraulic cylinders and pistons located at the bottom of the pit that act as shock absorbers should the terminal switch fail. Buffers cannot safely stop a free-falling car; they only stop a car traveling at its normal rate of speed.
- Speed-reducing switch – Also known as the speed governor. This switch slows the drive motor when an elevator starts to exceed a safe speed. If the car continues to accelerate, the switch trips the overspeed switch and applies the car safeties.
- Overspeed switch – Also connected to the speed governor. This switch is activated if the speed-reducing switch fails to slow the car sufficiently.

- Car safeties – Tapered pairs of steel jaws that wedge against the guide rails and bring the elevator to a stop. Elevator safeties are designed to stop a free-falling car.

Elevator Hoistways

An elevator hoistway is the vertical shaft in which the elevator car travels, and includes the **elevator pit**. The pit extends down from the lowest floor landing to the bottom of the hoistway **(Figure 4.22)**. Hoistways are required to be constructed of fire-resistive materials and are equipped with fire-rated door assemblies. However, some hoistways, such as those located in an atrium, are not required to be enclosed.

Elevator Pit – Depression at the base of an elevator hoistway that contains equipment and maintenance access.

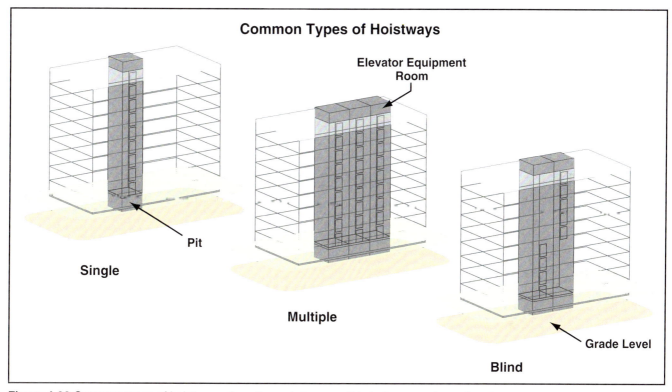

Figure 4.22 Common types of hoistways show the variation possible in the same type of enclosure.

In low-rise buildings, the entire hoistway enclosure may consist of gypsum, cement block, or other easily penetrated material. In tall buildings of reinforced concrete construction, the elevator hoistway may be enclosed on three sides with poured concrete, with only the wall that faces the elevator car doors built of block. This construction serves to harden the entire building against the wind load. Firefighters must plan for hardened elevator hoistways when considering making openings in elevator shafts during emergency operations because these hoistways will be difficult to breach.

Elevator hoistway enclosures usually are required to be a fire-rated assembly with a 1- or 2-hour rating, depending on the height of the building. Therefore, the integrity of the rated hoistway assembly must be maintained. Any necessary penetrations through the hoistway walls must be protected with an appropriately rated assembly. No wiring, ductwork, or piping should be run within the hoistway unless it is required for the elevator itself.

Shear Wall – Wall panels that are braced against lateral loads. May be load bearing or nonload bearing.

Elevator and stair shafts are built early in the construction process, and often use **shear walls** (Figure 4.23). An elevator's lobby may be used as an area of refuge if it is appropriately hardened. When used as a means of egress, an elevator's shaft must be equipped with safety lights and fire ratings suitable to the height of the structure.

Figure 4.23 Shear walls constructed early in the process of erecting a building support structures against lateral loads. *Courtesy of Rich Mahaney.*

Hoistways may act as a vertical chimney to spread fire and smoke throughout a building. As the elevator car moves along the shaft, it acts like a pump, drawing smoke into the shaft and pushing it out on other floors. If the hoistway is not vented at the top, the accumulated hot gases and smoke tend to **mushroom** or spread horizontally into the upper floors. To prevent mushrooming, building codes require venting at the top of most hoistways. The codes also require fire-rated vestibules, or equivalent, at each floor to prevent smoke and hot gases from moving throughout the building.

A building with three or fewer elevators may contain all three in a single hoistway. Four or more elevators must have a minimum of two separate hoistways. This requirement minimizes the possibility that a fire will compromise all elevator services.

Where more than one hoistway is provided, up to four elevators may be located in one hoistway. Elevators that share a hoistway are not usually separated.

In very tall buildings, express elevators are divided into zones, with each set serving a separate zone. A zone often includes 15 to 20 consecutive floors. Upper zone cars operate in express mode (without stops) from the first floor to the lowest floor of the upper zone. Express elevators serving upper levels have no entrances to the hoistway shaft between the main entrance and the lowest floor served. Single-elevator hoistways that only serve upper levels have regularly spaced access doors for rescue purposes in the portion without normal hoistway doors.

Mushrooming — Tendency of heat, smoke, and other products of combustion to rise until they encounter a horizontal obstruction; at this point they will spread laterally until they encounter vertical obstructions and begin to bank downward.

Blind Hoistway — Used for express elevators that serve only upper floors of tall buildings. There are no entrances to the shaft on floors between the main entrance and the lowest floor served.

Blind hoistways are used for express elevators that serve the upper elevator zones in tall buildings. There will be no entrances to the hoistway on floors between the main floor and the lowest floor served. If a single-car hoistway is used, access doors will be provided for rescue purposes. Generally, these are placed every three floors.

Hoistway Innovations

Elevators and space in high rise buildings are both expensive. In some cases, innovations that minimize the expense may be implemented. Two examples that may be found in some jurisdictions are mentioned here. Further discussion of this type of innovation is beyond the scope of this manual.

Sky lobbies are building floors some distance up a high-rise that are used as a common discharge floor for two separate elevator systems. Often, the two systems will use two separate elevator cars that may use the same hoistway, but in different zones. In many cases, the sky lobby will separate types of occupancies. For example, in the John Hancock Center in Chicago, Illinois, the lower zone occupancy is office space, and the upper zone occupancy is residential.

Double-deck elevators are two cars that are permanently connected to each other vertically, and travel in the same hoistway. Normally, the bottom car will serve only odd-numbered floors and the top car will serve only even-numbered floors. Because the cars move in tandem and may not aim for similarly stacked destinations, the passengers in one car may be held while the passengers in the other are discharged.

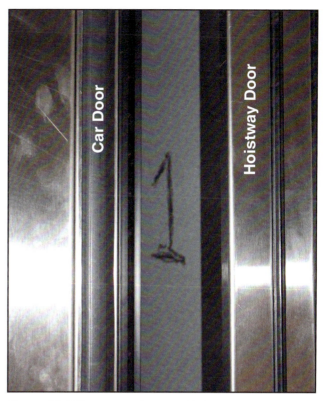

Figure 4.24 Elevator car doors and hoistway doors open and close simultaneously during normal operation.

Elevator Doors

Doors in elevator installations include both car doors and hoistway doors **(Figure 4.24)**. The two are usually designed to open and close together, in the same direction. Elevator doors are designed to open and close automatically when the car stops at the floor where it has been summoned. The operations are sequenced in the following order:

- When the elevator stops at the correct level, the driving vane attached to the car door holds the door open **(Figure 4.25)**.
- As the car door opens, the vane strikes a roller that releases the hoistway door lock **(Figure 4.26, p. 112)**.
- The car doors then push the hoistway doors completely open.

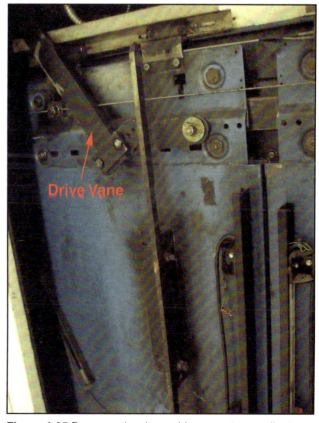

Figure 4.25 Doors work using a drive vane to coordinate opening and closing. *Copyrighted material courtesy of Jim Shirreffs III.*

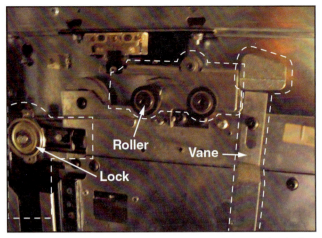

Figure 4.26 The drive vane trips a roller that trips the lock. *Copyrighted material courtesy of Jim Shirreffs III.*

- When the controller signals the doors to close, a weight forces the hoistway doors closed, the driving vane moves away from the roller, and the hoistway doors are relocked **(Figure 4.27)**.

Passenger elevator car doors use the power of an electric motor mounted on top of the elevator car. The car door does not have locks and can be pushed open at any time. However, electric interlocks will not allow a car to move when the car doors are open and a moving car will immediately stop if the doors are pushed open **(Figure 4.28)**. When the doors are closed again, most elevator cars will start to move again. Some types will not start moving again until they have been reset.

Elevator Access Panels

Only trained personnel should attempt an evacuation of passengers from a stalled elevator car. ASME Standard A17.4, *Guide for Emergency Personnel*, contains procedures to follow in performing evacuations.

Emergency Exits in Elevators

A top exit is provided on all electric traction elevators. On hydraulic elevators, a top exit may be provided depending on whether the system is equipped with a manual lowering valve. This valve permits the lowering of the car in the event of malfunction. A top exit is optional otherwise.

Some top panels are designed to be opened from inside the car, but all can be opened from outside and all open outward. Some cars are also provided with electrical interlocks that prevent movement of the car while the panel is open. This feature is not required and is not found on all models, especially freight elevators.

In multiple-elevator hoistways, most elevator cars are equipped with side exits to allow passengers to be transferred laterally from a stalled car to a functioning car next to it. Side exits can be opened from outside the hoistway where a permanent handle is provided. Some panels are locked from the inside and cannot be opened without a special key or handle **(Figure 4.29)**. Side exits are required to have electrical interlocks to prevent car movement when the panels are open. Side exits may not be provided on cars in hydraulic elevator systems where a manual lowering valve is provided.

Figure 4.27 Elevator components may be difficult to access during normal operation. *Copyrighted material courtesy of Jim Shirreffs III.*

Blind Hoistway

If the car is stopped in a blind hoistway, the emergency exits from the car must be used. These exits consist of either a hinged access hatch through the top of the car or hinged or removable panels on the sides of the car. Using either of these exits is time-consuming and involves some added risk to passengers, so should be done only if no other options are possible.

Figure 4.28 The door clutch provides a safety measure to prevent the elevator car from operating if all systems are not working correctly. *Copyrighted material courtesy of Jim Shirreffs III.*

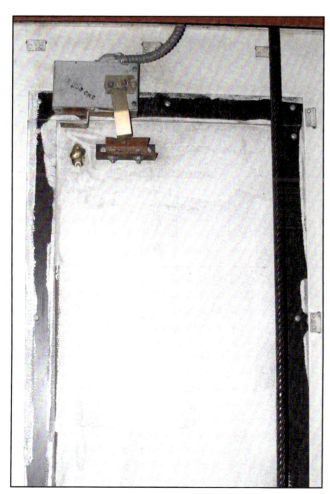

Figure 4.29 Maintenance and emergency access side doors may be equipped with electronic locks and minimal inside handle.

Chapter 4 • Building Systems   **113**

Elevator Shafts

First responders should be able to access elevators and elevator shafts in their jurisdiction. The local AHJ should have procedures in place for obtaining elevator keys for preincident planning, training, and emergency operations. Elevator keys may be secured in a lock box. Relevant codes or the AHJ may determine the location of the lock box.

Vertical Shafts and Utility Chases

Vertical shafts and **utility chases** can provide a path for smoke and fire travel as well as serve as the area of origin for fires. Common types of vertical and utility openings are described in the following sections.

Vertical Shaft Enclosures

Vertical shaft enclosures are built using fire-rated construction methods, but may contain combustible materials, depending on their function. Vertical openings often do not include any horizontal fire barriers along the length of the shaft. In addition to the types of shafts used in stairways and elevators, types of vertical openings include chutes described below.

NOTE: Air ducts are discussed in the HVAC section of this chapter.

> **Utility Chase** — Vertical pathway (shaft) in a building that contains utility services such as laundry or refuse chutes, and grease ducts.

> **Refuse Chute** — Vertical shaft with a self-closing access door on every floor; usually extending from the basement or ground floor to the top floor of multistory buildings.

Refuse and Laundry Chutes

A **refuse chute** provides a space for the gravity-aided removal of trash or laundry from upper floors of buildings such as residential properties. These chutes extend through the building and have openings on each floor for depositing trash or linen **(Figure 4.30)**. The chute often terminates in a room at grade level or in the basement where the refuse or laundry is collected.

Because the trash or laundry deposited in the chute is mostly combustible, refuse chutes are required to be constructed of noncombustible material with rated doors and a fire-rated shaft enclosure **(Figure 4.31)**. Sprinklers are required at the top of the chute and in its termination room. There may also be intermittent sprinklers within the chute. These sprinklers must be protected from damage from the refuse or laundry falling down the shaft.

Current codes require access openings for chutes to be in a separate room from the corridor, but older buildings often have the openings directly on the corridor. A fire in a properly designed, installed, and maintained refuse or laundry chute should be contained within the chute. It is not uncommon, however, that some smoke will leak out of the chute through the access doors in older installations because of poor maintenance or loss of operational integrity. Smoke can then be transferred throughout multiple floors and there may be heavy smoke in upper floors.

Figure 4.30 Refuse and laundry chutes remove deposited items from a designated place to another destination for further processing.

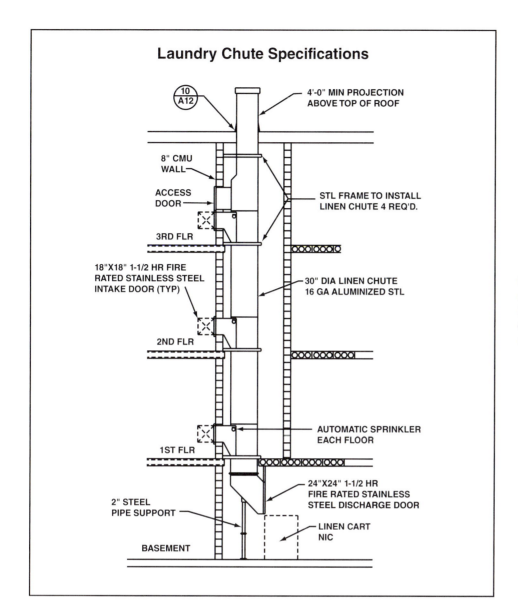

Figure 4.31 Construction of refuse and laundry chutes includes requirements for the enclosure, intake points, and fire resistance.

An improperly constructed or maintained refuse or laundry chute creates a potentially severe fire problem. For example, an ignition source may be dropped inadvertently or intentionally down the chute, igniting combustible materials at the bottom of the chute or at catch-points within the chute. A refuse or laundry chute can also become jammed, resulting in a large quantity of combustible material becoming lodged in the chute.

Grease Ducts

Typically, grease ducts are installed over deep-fat fryers and grills as part of an exhaust system for commercial cooking appliances. A grease duct travels vertically and carries grease vapors to the outside of the building, often utilizing in-line fans or fans on the roof. Proper insulation avoids dips or horizontal runs where grease may become trapped.

Some design applications include horizontal ducts. In these cases, a grease removal system is provided that minimizes the likelihood of grease-laden waste material collecting in the horizontal sections. The application, design, and protection required for grease ducts are specified in codes. Codes also

Chapter 4 • Building Systems **115**

Pipe Chase — Concealed vertical channel in which pipes and other utility conduits are housed. Pipe chases that are not properly protected can be major contributors to the vertical spread of smoke and fire in a building. *Also known as* Chase.

require that the grease duct be enclosed in fire-resistive construction, similar to the requirements for a shaft when penetrating rated floors or rated roofs.

Pipe Chases

A building may have one or more **pipe chases**, depending on building size and design **(Figure 4.32)**. A pipe chase contains piping needed for services including:

- Hot and cold potable water
- Drain lines
- Steam
- Hot and chilled water for heating and air-conditioning
- Sprinkler piping

Figure 4.32 Pipe chases may be a simple cut-out of the materials separating building stories.

As with any vertical opening in a building, pipe chases can spread smoke and fire to other floors of the building if not properly protected. Building codes specify shaft enclosure protection, typically requiring fire-resistive construction. The access openings must also be rated accordingly.

Although they are not required to be installed in a rated chase (shaft), plumbing pipes in one- and two-story residential and small commercial buildings of wood-frame construction typically form pathways in walls that are capable of spreading fire and smoke.

Plumbing fixtures drain into a vertical pipe connecting to the underground sewer pipe, which also extends above the roof to ventilate the system. This pipe typically travels through walls and horizontal layers and can serve as a pathway for fire and smoke if it does not fit tightly or is not firestopped at the penetrations.

Occasionally, buildings do not have pipe chases but instead use mechanical equipment rooms stacked one above the other on each floor. Pipes, electrical raceways, and other services pass through these rooms. The walls enclosing these rooms are then treated as shaft walls to separate the utility space from the rest of the building. Fire-rated horizontal separations may or may not exist between the mechanical rooms.

Heating, Ventilating, and Air Conditioning (HVAC) System — Mechanical system used to provide environmental control within a structure, and the equipment necessary to make it function; usually a single, integrated unit with a complex system of ducts throughout the building. *Also known as* Air-Handling System.

Air Handling Systems

The primary purpose of **heating, ventilating, and air conditioning (HVAC) systems** is to create and maintain a comfortable environment for occupants. The following functions can be delivered through one standalone system or individual component systems:

- Heating and cooling
- Humidifying and dehumidifying
- Filtering

- Expelling (exhausting) air
- Regulating intake (make-up) of outdoor air
- Recirculating indoor air

Depending on a building's age and complexity, an HVAC system may be simple or sophisticated. For example, a one-story convenience store may use a single rooftop unit for heating and air conditioning **(Figure 4.33)**. In a high-rise office building, the total HVAC system may be monitored and controlled by computers, and include:

- Hundreds of feet of ductwork
- Heating equipment
- Refrigeration equipment
- Motors and blowers

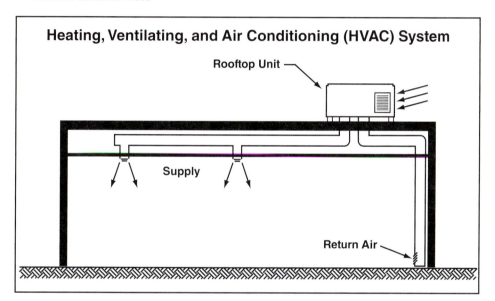

Figure 4.33 A simple air-handling unit may meet all of the requirements of a small building.

Wider accessibility of HVAC systems has had a major impact on overall building design. Today, many buildings have windows that do not open or no windows at all. The consequence has been near total dependence on the HVAC system to provide comfortable and livable conditions. In effect, the HVAC system in many complex buildings has become a life-support system. Disruptions in service are potentially life-threatening.

Historically, early forced-air systems provided only heat through a ducted system. Buildings included features like openable windows and rooftop **cupolas** to permit airflow through a building for ventilation and cooling **(Figure 4.34)**. Buildings were not airtight.

HVAC systems may incorporate natural ventilation features such as openable windows and vents in roofs. When available, these features can also be used to supplement the airflow in a building. This section is organized in order of complicated, modern systems through simple, low-technology components.

Cupola — A type of rooftop projection historically used for ventilation and lighting, and modernly added for aesthetics.

Figure 4.34 Modern cupolas are included on a building as a decorative element. *Courtesy of McKinney (TX) Fire Department.*

Chapter 4 • Building Systems **117**

HVAC System Components

Modern building codes require safety considerations to limit the possibility that contaminants will be spread throughout a building. The sections below explain the main system components of an HVAC system that work together to collect and deliver air to prescribed locations.

Outside Air Intakes

An outside air intake draws air from sources external to the building into the system. Air intakes must be positioned in a location that will allow unrestricted air flow **(Figure 4.35)**. Codes regulate the location of air intakes to minimize drawing in the following hazards:

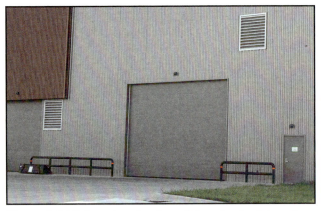

Figure 4.35 External vents allow air to enter the internal ventilation system under controlled conditions.

- Combustible, flammable, or toxic substances
- Vehicle exhaust
- Smoke from fires in nearby structures

Fans

Separate fans are generally used to draw supply air and to expel exhaust air. Some fans contain dual units or are reversible for use in both purposes. Fans move air throughout the system, but will also move contaminants that are introduced into the system. Duct detectors are typically provided for fans with capacities exceeding 2,000 cubic feet per minute (60 m^3/min), to stop these systems under fire conditions and minimize unwanted smoke movement.

Air Filtration

Air filtration systems are necessary to keep the air free of contaminants. Air can be cleaned with filters, with electrostatic equipment, or both. Filters should be made of approved materials to minimize their fire potential. A filter using liquid adhesives may present a combustible liquid hazard; the adhesive should be appropriately stored. Electrostatic equipment can present a significant electrical equipment hazard.

Figure 4.36 An air-cooled chiller removes the heat from ambient air and moves the cold air into an HVAC system.

Air Heating and Cooling Equipment

Many types of equipment are used to heat and cool the air circulated in buildings. These devices can be located almost anywhere in the structure, and the necessary fuels may also have variable locations. The particular hazards of each type of equipment and associated fuel must be addressed in the safeguards within the system and containment area. A best practice is to locate and note these items during preincident planning. Fuels used in fuel-fired heating equipment can include natural gas or oil. Other types of heating equipment use electricity or steam.

Air cooled chillers remove heat from a piped water system in a building that passes through fan-coil or other air-handling equipment **(Figure 4.36)**. The cooling equipment hazards are limited mainly to hazards associated with the refrigerant and the electrical equipment. Due to environmental concerns, some halogenated refrigerants have been prohibited. Some gases that may be used in their place, such as butane and propane, pose a greater hazard for firefighters. The use of flammable refrigerants warrants special awareness on the part of emergency responders.

Air Ducts

Air ducts are the distribution component of the HVAC system **(Figure 4.37)**. HVAC ducts frequently penetrate fire-rated assemblies. Building, mechanical, and fire codes contain many requirements for ducts, including allowable materials and the requirement for **smoke** and **fire dampers** to maintain the integrity of the fire-rated assemblies **(Figure 4.38)**.

Heated and/or cooled air may be provided without the use of ducted systems. In some cases, interstitial spaces are used as a **return-air plenum**. For example, the space between a suspended ceiling and roof deck, or under-floor spaces, may be utilized to provide supply air. This use of existing void space is less expensive than installing ducts to carry return air. Building codes regulate this use of interstitial spaces because improper implementation can result in dangerous egress conditions during a fire.

> **Return-Air Plenum** — Unoccupied space within a building through which air flows back to the heating, ventilating, and air-conditioning (HVAC) system; normally immediately above a ceiling and below an insulated roof or the floor above.

> **Smoke Damper** — Device that automatically restricts the flow of smoke through all or part of an air-handling system; usually activated by the building's fire alarm signaling system.

> **Fire Damper** — Device that automatically restricts the flow of air through all or part of an air-handling system; usually activated by the building's fire alarm signaling system or fusible links.

Figure 4.37 HVAC ductwork installed in a building delivers heated or chilled air throughout the building.

Figure 4.38 Fire dampers include fusible links and closing springs. *Courtesy of Gregory Havel, Burlington, WI.*

Exhaust System — Ventilation system designed to remove stale air, smoke, vapors, or other airborne contaminants from an area. *See* Heating, Ventilating, and Air-Conditioning (HVAC) System.

Forced-Air System — A building heating and cooling system that uses air as the heat transfer medium.

Simple Ventilation and Exhaust Systems

HVAC systems may be cooperative to or independent from simple ventilation or **exhaust systems**. An HVAC system conditions and delivers air to building occupants; a ventilation or exhaust system may only remove contaminated air. For example, toilet facilities that are vented separately are exhaust systems.

Forced-Air System

Many HVAC systems distribute conditioned air through the building from one or more mechanical equipment rooms via ductwork **(Figure 4.39)**. Such systems are generally known as **forced-air systems**. Systems that use extensive ducting are of great interest to fire protection engineers and firefighters because disadvantages include:

- Pathways for communication of heat and smoke through a building
- Penetrations of fire-rated assemblies that can destroy the integrity of the assembly
- Dedicated use of substantial amounts of space

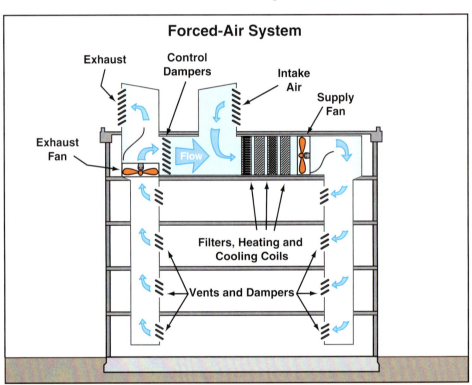

Figure 4.39 A forced-air HVAC system may be programmed to recirculate a portion of the air in a building as a function of efficiency.

Hydronic System — A building heating and cooling system that uses water as the heat-transfer medium.

Cooling Tower — Rooftop or independent unit that ejects waste heat into the atmosphere to lower the temperature in a system. Commonly used in HVAC systems.

Recirculation — Movement of air back into a ventilation system after being ejected.

The widely used NFPA® 90A, *Standard for the Installation of Air-Conditioning and Ventilating Systems*, contains requirements affecting horizontal and vertical HVAC ducts that penetrate a fire-rated assembly or a smoke barrier. In general, fire or smoke dampers may be enough. The local mechanical code may also regulate the operation of the dampers.

A forced-air HVAC system in a multistory building often includes vertical ducts and a mechanical room. With a few minor exceptions, the codes require that HVAC ducts be enclosed in a fire-rated shaft enclosure. For example, NFPA® 90A requires that the enclosure be 1-hour rated for buildings less than four stories in height and 2-hour fire rated for buildings four stories or greater.

Tall buildings may have more than one equipment room, with one room in the basement and the other at the top of the building. In very tall buildings, additional HVAC equipment rooms may also be located at intermediate levels. In these cases, the HVAC systems are divided into zones of several floors with each zone supplied from a separate equipment room. Placing the controls and intake/exhaust at the top of the building minimizes the obstructions to airflow. For example, congested urban settings may have more space available at the roof than at grade level. Some large **hydronic systems** have **cooling towers** staged on a building's roof. In contrast, an HVAC equipment room may be located solely in the basement of a building.

CAUTION
Modified HVAC systems may substantially change the weight of the system and the dead load on roof support systems.

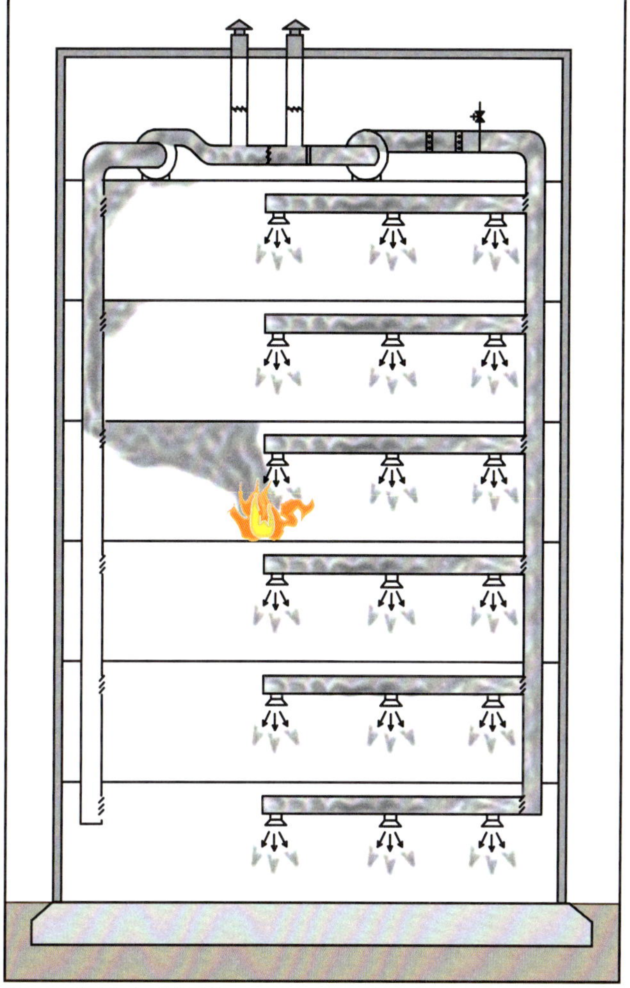

Most of the air flowing through the HVAC system can be **recirculated** through the building space. Air recirculation can reduce the amount of air that must be either heated or cooled to the desired building temperature, resulting in increased system efficiency. The control dampers are used to vary the airflow depending on the building needs. In large buildings, the HVAC system can be controlled through the use of temperature sensors connected to computers. The computers can adjust dampers, blower motors, and heating units to achieve the desired rate of airflow and temperature. Recirculation can be hazardous under fire conditions if products of combustion are drawn through the HVAC system and distributed throughout the building **(Figure 4.40)**. Without safety features, the system may spread contaminants from products of combustion or other sources throughout a building with great speed and efficiency.

Figure 4.40 An HVAC system operating in normal mode may draw the products of combustion into the ducts and transport them throughout the building.

Smoke Control Systems

The design of many modern buildings can make traditional ventilation methods difficult or impossible, especially in high rise construction. For example, some newer glazing types, such as **hurricane glazing**, may be very difficult to remove or ventilate. In these conditions, the HVAC system may be used in a **smoke control** capacity.

To prevent the recirculation of smoke through the HVAC system and to facilitate removal of the smoke, some types of HVAC systems can be switched from normal operating mode to **smoke control mode**. The transfer can be accomplished either automatically or manually, as described in the following sections.

Hurricane Glazing — Protective treatment for exterior windows designed to withstand hurricane conditions including high wind and impact.

Smoke Control — Strategic use of passive and active devices and systems to direct or stop the movement of smoke and other products of combustion.

Smoke Control Mode — Setting on an HVAC system or Fire Alarm Control Unit system that can be activated automatically or manually to initiate a programmed smoke control procedure.

NOTE: Refer to the IFSTA manual **Fire Protection, Detection, and Suppression Systems** for more information on smoke control systems.

An HVAC system operating in smoke control mode discharges smoke through the exhaust fan from the fire floor to the outside without returning air to the supply fan **(Figure 4.41)**. The continuance of supply of air to the non-fire floors creates a "pressure sandwich" of higher air pressure on floors above and below the fire floor(s), reducing the movement of smoke into those areas.

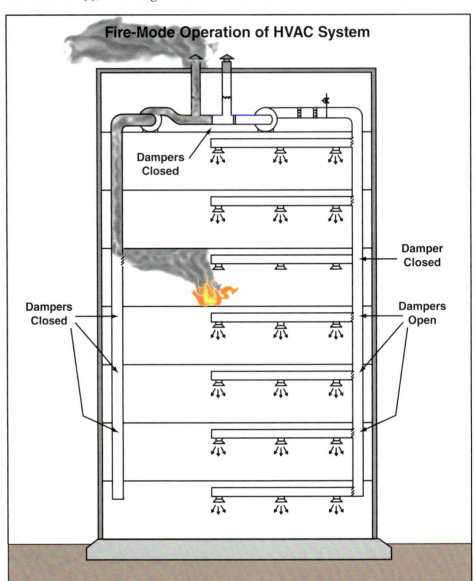

Figure 4.41 An HVAC system operating in the fire mode will exhaust smoke from the fire zone and supply fresh air to adjacent zones.

Air supply is restricted to the fire floor through the use of a damper, and continued to adjacent floors. Dampers can be opened or closed, depending on the location of the fire, to redirect the flow of air and to exhaust the smoke.

The system detectors must be carefully designed and placed to eliminate the possibility of a detector outside the fire area being activated first, which would result in the misdirection of the system with the wrong dampers being operated. Provision must also be made for a situation in which smoke detectors operate in more than one zone.

The design of a smoke control system requires extensive engineering analysis. Any equipment, such as fans and ducts, used to exhaust the products of combustion must be capable of withstanding the anticipated temperatures. Other factors the designer must anticipate include:

- Fire size
- Outside weather conditions
- Volume of a fire zone
- Maximum pressure differences across barriers, such as stairwell doors

Automatic Smoke Control

The transfer of an HVAC system to smoke control mode can be accomplished automatically when a system is coordinated to do so. Automatic initiation of fire operation in an HVAC system always takes priority over the normal system functions. The following systems can signal HVAC controls to transfer to smoke control mode:

- Smoke detectors
- Heat detectors
- Sprinkler waterflow switches

The primary advantage of an automatic system is the relatively fast activation, even when occupants are absent or asleep. A primary disadvantage of an automatic system is the number of elements that must be coordinated for maximum benefit, including:

- Fire alarm
- Automatic sprinkler
- HVAC zones

Manual pull stations accessible to the public should activate only the alarm system, not the smoke control system, to minimize the possibility of occupants seeing a fire but not operating a pull station until they have fled to another area of the building. Some occupancies, such as jails or hospitals, may require special accommodations, such as positioning the fire alarm system under control of the staff.

> **Firefighter's Smoke Control Station (FSCS)** — Interface between the smoke management system and the fire response forces

Manual Smoke Control

The transfer of an HVAC system to smoke control mode can be accomplished manually through controls provided for that purpose. When a system has both automatic and manual capability, the manual operations shall take priority over the automatic control.

The primary disadvantage of manual operation is its slower activation, compared to automatic operation. Manual activation usually occurs after arrival of the fire department and may not occur until late in the fire development when lives may already be in danger.

The system can be controlled from a dedicated control panel, the building's main control room, or a **firefighter's smoke control station (FSCS)** (**Figure 4.42**).

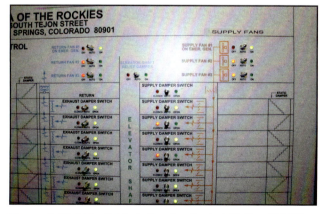

Figure 4.42 A Firefighter's Smoke Control Station (FSCS) is a control panel that simplifies controls of several components in a system. *Courtesy of Colorado Springs (CO) Fire Department.*

Figure 4.43 Theaters are required to have smoke vents above the stage. *Courtesy of Ed Prendergast.*

Figure 4.44 Smoke vents may operate manually or automatically.

Draft Curtains —
Noncombustible barriers or dividers hung from the ceiling in large open areas that are designed to minimize the mushrooming effect of heat and smoke and impede the flow of heat. *Also known as* Curtain Boards and Draft Stops.

The advantages to manual control include elimination of system disruption due to false alarms and more specific system control.

The FSCS should have complete system monitoring capability. Codes require status indicators and switches for all fans and dampers serving a smoke control function. The FSCS should also contain a diagram of the building that indicates the type and location of system components, such as fans and dampers.

Smoke and Heat Vents

Fire control and occupant safety are enhanced through venting the products of combustion to the outside through the shortest route possible. As discussed earlier in this section, vent openings may be placed on a roof to help remove air or contaminants from a building's HVAC system. Even in buildings without an HVAC system, roof ventilation openings are a simple and rapid means of ejecting products of combustion from inside the building. Built-in smoke and heat vents enable firefighters to make a faster and safer interior attack and dissipate some of the thermal energy of a fire. Without a means of venting the heat and smoke, firefighters could be forced to withdraw to a peripheral attack while the fire continued to burn in the interior.

Rooftop smoke and heat vents are typically required on the roofs of large-area buildings and in buildings with few windows including industrial, storage, and mercantile buildings **(Figure 4.43)**. Historically, smoke and heat vents were required in theaters over stages since the early part of the twentieth century.

Vent Types

Typical heat and smoke vents are often small-area hatchways with single- or double-leaf metal lids or plastic domes designed to open automatically or manually **(Figure 4.44)**. These hatchways often open a minimum of 4 feet (1.2 m) in either direction.

Draft curtains (curtain boards) may be used in conjunction with smoke vents to increase their effectiveness. The curtain boards reduce the dissipation of the heated air currents from a fire and increase the speed of operation of the vents **(Figure 4.45)**. The depth of a curtain board will vary depending on the nature of the hazards within an occupancy, but should not be less than twenty percent of the ceiling height. Curtain boards should be spaced so that they are not farther apart than eight times the ceiling height.

The size and spacing of smoke and heat vents depend on the floor-to-ceiling height of a building and the nature of the contents. NFPA® 204, *Standard for Smoke and Heat Venting*, and the International Fire Code (IFC), contains the design methodology for determining the required vent area. The method used to determine the vent area requires an analysis of the rate of heat release of the fuel, the ceiling height, and the depth of the curtain boards.

Vent Limitations

Smoke and heat vents are less effective when used in conjunction with sprinkler systems. When sprinklers operate, the discharge of the sprinklers cools the products of combustion (smoke and gases) and they lose their buoyancy. This loss of buoyancy reduces the natural tendency of the products of combustion to rise and escape through the roof vents. Thus, the roof vents in sprinklered buildings are not as effective as they are in nonsprinklered buildings. Ultimately, however, the removal of the products of combustion from the building must still be accomplished and the existence of roof vents facilitates this process. Roof vents in a sprinklered building may be of maximum value in removing products of combustion during the final or overhaul stages of a fire.

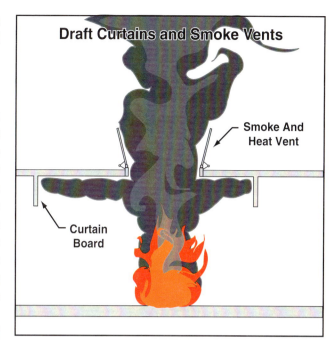

Figure 4.45 Curtain boards help funnel products of combustion toward a vent.

Vent Hazards

Personnel may encounter a number of vent hazards, whether from the materials used in the vents' construction or during the activation of vent features. Thermoplastic dome vents soften from the heat of a fire and fall out of their frame. Metal lid vents may be opened via spring-operated mechanisms triggered manually, or through automatic devices such as fusible links or detectors including smoke detectors. Oversensitive smoke detectors may allow vents to open under nonfire conditions. Firefighters manually activating these vents must ensure that they are operating the appropriate vents to prevent drawing the fire to other uninvolved areas.

> **CAUTION**
> Smoke vents are spring-loaded and can operate quickly. Firefighters manually opening vents must position themselves away from the hatch opening before operating them.

Smoke Towers

One style of smoke control for stairways is the use of a **smoke tower** separated from a building corridor by a vestibule that is open to the atmosphere **(Figure 4.46, p. 126)**. Smoke entering the vestibule from the corridor is exhausted to the atmosphere and the stairwell remains free of smoke. Smoke towers require the following expensive concessions:

- Location on the periphery of the floor plan
- Dedicated floor space in the building
- Corridor access to the stairwell

Smoke Tower — Fully enclosed escape stairway that exits directly onto a public way; these enclosures are either mechanically pressurized or they require the user to exit the building onto an outside balcony before entering the stairway. *Also known as* Smokeproof Enclosure *or* Smokeproof Stairway.

Figure 4.46 Similar to stairs and vestibules, smoke towers located at the periphery of buildings are used to keep smoke out of a means of egress.

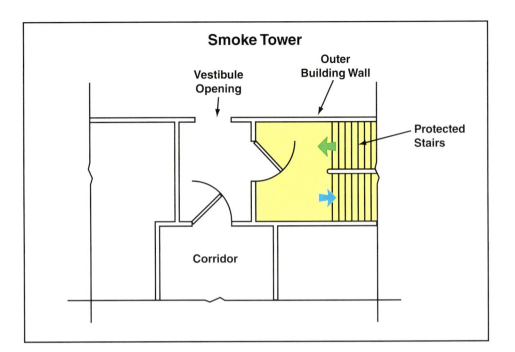

Pressurized Stairwells

A structural design that minimizes the use of space while still protecting stairways from the products of combustion is a pressurized stairwell. Blowers or fans provide a slightly greater pressure in the stairwell than the corridor to prevent the infiltration of smoke from the corridor into the stairwell.

Types of Pressurization Systems

The **single-injection system** uses a fan to supply air to a stairwell at a single point **(Figure 4.47)**. A limitation of the single-injection system is that if stairwell doors are opened at a point close to the air supply, all of the air pressure can flow directly out of the stairwell.

Multiple-injection systems use several discharge points along an air supply shaft running parallel to the stairwell from the supply fan **(Figure 4.48)**. Air discharge points into the stairwell are located at several points along the stairwell. This method provides a more uniform flow of air into the stairwell and negates the primary limitation of single injection systems.

> **Single-Injection System** — Stairwell pressurization system that uses one point of supply air; pressurization can be lost if the system becomes unsealed through the use of doors.

> **Multiple-Injection System** — Stairwell pressurization system that uses an air supply shaft that discharges supply air at a uniform rate along several points within the stairwell.

Calibration of Pressurization Systems

Stairwell pressurization systems require careful engineering analysis. The pressure in the stairwell must be high enough that it will prevent the flow of smoke into a stairwell, but low enough to allow occupant access into the stairwell.

> **Parameters for Pressurized Stairwells**
>
> NFPA® 92A, *Standard for Smoke-Control Systems Utilizing Barriers and Pressure Differences*, indicates the required minimum pressure difference, via water gauge, across a smoke barrier in a sprinklered building. A greater pressure difference may be necessary to compensate for the opening of doors. The designer of a stairwell system must work between narrow pressure limits to achieve an effective system.

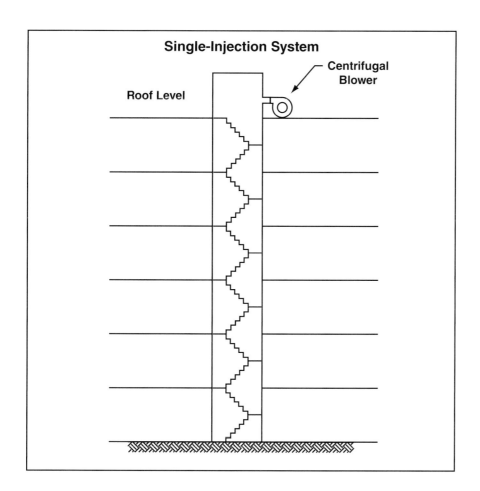

Figure 4.47 Stairwell pressurization using a single injection point for air can be effective under some conditions.

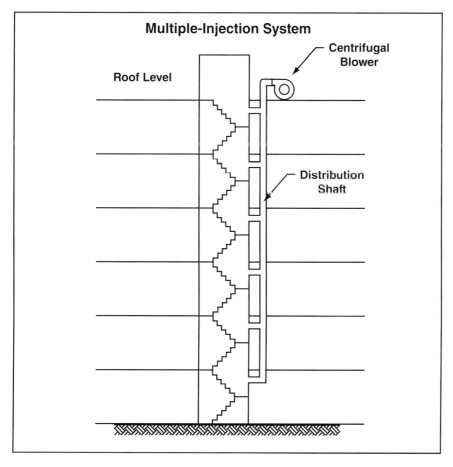

Figure 4.48 Stairwell pressurization using multiple injection points for air can be effective in a broad range of operations.

Chapter 4 • Building Systems

Compensated System — Stairwell pressurization system that can modulate the pressure in the stairwell in relation to the interior of the building, or vent excess pressure.

One calculation of that pressure is the number of doors that may be opened into a stairwell during building evacuation because the pressure loss from several doors open at a time requires a higher pressure to maintain a smoke-free atmosphere. In a **compensated system**, the airflow into the stairwell can be adjusted depending on the number of doors that may be open. The pressure in the stairwell may be modulated or vented.

Modulation uses input pressure sensors that compare the stairwell and the interior of the building. The system then adapts the fan components to reach the appropriate level of pressurization in the stairwell. Adjustments used in modulation can affect the following:

- Speed of the fan
- Inlet vanes
- Variable pitch fan blades
- Number of fans operating

Overpressure relief in a stairwell is accomplished through the use of dampers that open to the outside, relieving excess pressure in the stairwell. The simplest means of controlling the exhaust dampers is to include adjustable counterweights. The dampers open when the pressure in the stairwell is high enough to push the dampers open. A second type of damper uses motor-operated dampers that sense the pressure level and trigger a switch. This method is somewhat more complicated and therefore more costly.

Overpressure — Air pressure above normal or atmospheric pressure.

Electrical Equipment

Electrical equipment may be installed in dedicated rooms or vaults. High-voltage equipment is defined as operating at 600 volts or higher; low-voltage equipment operates at less than 600 volts. Codes may require fire-rated construction separations around some electrical equipment, as described in the following sections.

Transformers

Transformers convert high-voltage electricity from the electric utility service to an appropriate voltage for building systems use. Some dedicated transformers are used to supply special systems and equipment in industrial and commercial buildings.

Transformer — Device that uses coils and magnetic fields to increase (step-up) or decrease (step-down) incoming voltages.

Voltage Supply to Buildings

Voltage supplied to a structure may range as high as thousands of volts. The most common voltage delivered via transformers to medium and large buildings is carried via 3 phase 208/120 volt transformers. In Canada, 3 phase 600/347 volt transformers may supply medium and large buildings.

Rooms or vaults that contain electrical gear or transformers should be protected with sprinklers if the building has an automatic sprinkler system. In cases where power utility companies do not allow sprinkler protection for their equipment, the utilities may permit carbon dioxide detection systems.

Fires involving electrical equipment usually de-energize the equipment early in the event. Fire operations involving electrical rooms or vaults should use the same safety guidelines for operations involving any electrical source. Preincident planning can provide the information needed in an emergency to protect both fire personnel and to preserve property.

Transformers generate heat, and the built-in method of cooling the unit directly affects the hazard presented to emergency response personnel. The two most common cooling methods use air and oil. Transformers may be high or low voltage.

Air-Cooled Transformers

Air-cooled transformers, also called "dry" transformers, use the surrounding air to cool the unit through fins, heat sinks, and ventilation openings installed on the body of the transformer **(Figure 4.49)**. This type of transformer has similar hazards as other energized electrical equipment. Large transformers are usually set on the floor, while smaller units may be mounted on wall brackets or suspended from the roof or floor above. Most modern dry transformers are designed for use inside sprinklered spaces.

The electric utility supplies many buildings with 480/277-volt services, which can carry the same amount of energy in smaller wire and conduit when compared to traditional 120/240 volt services. The electricity is used at 480 volts by HVAC equipment, refrigeration, and other motors; and at 277 volts by light fixture ballasts. Buildings that commonly use this service include:

- Schools
- Medical facilities
- Strip malls
- Factories
- "Big box" stores

Figure 4.49 Electrical transformers generate heat; they must have a cooling solution in place to function safely and efficiently.

Dry transformers are located throughout the building to step down the voltage to 120-volts for use in resources such as:

- Office equipment
- Table lamps
- Household appliances

Oil-Cooled Transformers

Oil-cooled or oil-filled transformers contain oil to conduct heat away from the core and also to electrically insulate internal components from **arcing**. In addition to the hazard of energized electrical equipment, these transformers may be the source of a combustible liquid leak.

Because the oil also provides electrical insulation, it must have **dielectric** (non-conducting) properties. Newer oils are significantly less toxic than older types, and may also be less flammable. Older transformer cooling oils contain highly hazardous **Polychlorinated Biphenyls (PCB)** with excellent dielectric properties. Transformers containing PCBs are required to be labeled.

Arc — High-temperature luminous electric discharge across a gap or through a medium such as charred insulation.

Dielectric — Material that is a poor conductor of electricity, usually added to tools used to handle energized electrical wires or equipment.

Polychlorinated Biphenyl (PCB) — Toxic compound found in some older oil-filled electric transformers.

Chapter 4 • Building Systems **129**

Transformers are located in rooms or vaults that may be inside or outside the building. When transformers are inside the building, they are generally located at or near grade. However, they may also be located on upper levels in high-rise buildings. When transformers are inside, codes require that the transformer rooms or vaults be enclosed in 3-hour fire-rated construction if not protected by automatic sprinklers, or 1-hour fire-rated construction with sprinklers.

Emergency and Standby Power Supplies

Building codes or operational needs may indicate the type of emergency backup power supplies for building systems dependent on electric power. Backup systems may consist of **generators**, batteries, or a combination of both. Emergency backup generator systems are used in applications including:

- Buildings required to have smoke management systems; for example, high-rise buildings
- Occupancies required to maintain full-time access to power; for example, detention facilities
- Occupancies that require support for the facility's function; for example, telecommunications facilities

Generator — Device for generating auxiliary electrical power; generators are powered by gasoline or diesel engines and typically have 110- and/or 220-volt capacity outlets.

Generators

Emergency generators may be either permanent or portable, with the latter typically being used for small commercial or single-family residential properties. The following discussion will focus on permanent generators installed to meet code or major operational requirements.

Generators are typically engine-driven, using a gasoline, diesel, propane, or natural gas internal combustion engine. The size of the generator assigned will be determined by the amount of power needed to provide the desired services when the normal power fails. At a minimum, an occupancy should be supported by enough generator service to meet life safety systems plus the critical needs of the occupancy **(Figure 4.50)**. For example, a hospital requires power at all times for life-support and monitoring systems.

Figure 4.50 A generator is generally chosen by the amount of power needed. *Courtesy of McKinney (TX) Fire Department.*

Codes specify the minimum required fuel storage for diesel- or gasoline-driven generators. The amounts are stated in terms of the expected duration of operation which may vary from two to eight hours. Operational requirements for hospitals and other critical facilities, however, may be up to 48 hours or longer. Thus, for many facilities, operational needs will determine the fuel storage requirements. Fuel types and their storage systems and locations widely vary. Older installations may not meet current codes.

Fuel storage should be located separately from the generator. An exception to the fuel storage separation is a day tank located in the same room or mounted directly on the generator. Fire codes typically limit the tank to 60 gallons (230 L) for diesel fuel. Day tanks are usually kept full with fuel pumped directly from the main tank.

The emergency power supply system may include other components. Transfer switches may be required, by code, to be located in a protected room separate from the main electrical panel room for the building **(Figure 4.51)**. Buildings with fire control rooms should have a status panel and possibly a remote start/stop switch for the generator.

Emergency Power Batteries

Emergency power supplies that require batteries commonly use lead-acid type storage batteries or another, safer, type of battery in a **stationary storage battery system**. When located inside, the rooms should include fire-rated construction and sufficient ventilation. The areas containing the batteries are not usually diked or sealed to contain a liquid acid spill.

Figure 4.51 The transfer switch for a generator may be located in a separate area from the generator. *Courtesy of McKinney (TX) Fire Department.*

The presence of stationary storage battery systems should be documented during pre-fire incident planning. Battery storage is easy to overlook when assessing the hazards of the facility although large numbers of batteries may be found in dedicated rooms or even entire floors of a building. Cooperation with the building owner/operator will help ensure the safety of emergency operations in facilities with emergency battery power supplies.

In addition to the batteries used for the systems associated with the primary use of the building, types of battery systems found in and on buildings include:

- Small uninterruptible power supplies (UPS) containing lead-acid batteries, near fire alarm system control panels, under desks, or next to computers in many offices

- Battery charging room for battery-powered vehicles, such as storage, manufacturing, and golf clubhouses, in the building or on the property

- Cellular equipment with independent battery backup systems hosted on taller buildings

Stationary Storage Battery System — A system including a battery, a charger, and electrical equipment for a particular application. This type of system can include a lead-acid battery or a safer type of battery.

Chapter Summary

Building systems provide the ability for the occupants to efficiently and safely use the space in a comfortable environment. These same systems, however, create fire protection concerns. Many building systems, such as stairs, elevators, conveyors, vertical shafts, and utility chases, of necessity, must penetrate both vertical and horizontal fire-rated components.

Modern buildings rely extensively on HVAC systems to provide interior comfort. In large buildings these systems can become a means for communicating products of combustion through a building. Therefore, these systems must be designed to activate automatically or manually to prevent the spread of products of combustion.

HVAC systems also often include penetrations through fire rated barriers that can allow fire and smoke to spread throughout a building if the proper code provisions are not installed and maintained. The firefighter needs to be aware of the potential for fire and smoke spread due to building systems and not take anything for granted. Likewise, it is important for the firefighter to note any possible loss of the integrity of vertical building elements during company inspections.

Review Questions

1. Name types of stairs and their structural requirements.
2. What types of stairs are specifically indicated for egress?
3. What is the difference between moving stairs and moving walkways?
4. What are the differences between hydraulic and electric elevators?
5. Describe passenger safety devices found on elevators.
6. Describe emergency use of elevator access panels.
7. How do vertical shafts and utility chases contribute to fire development?
8. What are the functions of pipe chases in a building?
9. List the main system components of an HVAC system.
10. What are some fire safety concerns related to forced-air systems?
11. How can the HVAC system be used for smoke control?
12. What types of electrical equipment might a firefighter encounter in a structure?
13. Describe emergency and standby power supplies used for building systems.

Chapter Notes

1. Kear, Chris and Jerry Knapp. *New House Fire Hazard: Exploding Attic Stairs.* 08/28/2013 http://www.fireengineering.com/articles/2013/08/new-house-fire-hazard-exploding-attic-stairs.html?sponsored=firedynamics
2. Strakosch, George R. The Vertical Transportation Handbook, 3rd ed. John Wiley and Sons.
3. The American Society of Mechanical Engineers, ASME A17.1 – 2007/CSA B44-07, Safety Code for Elevators and Escalators.

Interior Finishes and Passive Fire Protection

Chapter Contents

Case History **137**	Fire Partitions 149
Interior Finishes **138**	Enclosure and Shaft Walls 149
Surface Burning Characteristics 139	Curtain Walls 150
Fire-Retardant Coatings 140	**Fire Doors** **152**
Testing Interior Finishes **141**	Fire Door Classifications 152
ASTM E-84 141	Fire Door Hardware and Features 158
NFPA® Interior Finish Tests 143	Fire Door Maintenance 162
Limitations of Test Findings 144	Fire Door Testing 162
Ceilings **145**	**Chapter Summary** **165**
Walls and Partitions **145**	**Review Questions** **165**
Compartmentation 145	**Chapter Notes** **165**
Fire Walls 146	

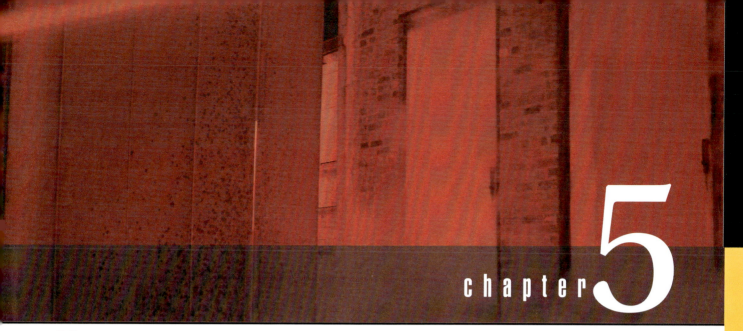

chapter 5

Key Terms

ASTM E-84 141	Louvers 162
Compartment 139	Mastics 140
Compartmentation 145	Metal-Clad Door 155
Criterion-Referenced Testing (CRT) 141	NFPA® 265 144
Curtain Wall 150	NFPA® 286 143
Door Closer 160	Nonload-Bearing Wall 151
Door Hold-Open Device 159	Overhead Door 154
Fire Area 146	Parapet Wall 148
Fire Door 152	Rated Assembly 146
Fire Flow 146	Rated Fire Door Assembly 153
Fire Partition 149	Self-Closing Door 160
Fire Wall 146	Shelter in Place 146
Flame Spread 139	Sliding Door 155
Flame Spread Rating 142	Smoke Developed Rating 142
Freestanding Walls 148	Steiner Tunnel 141
Fusible Link 154	Surface-Burning Characteristic 139
Glazing 161	Swinging Door 156
Hardware 158	Tied Walls 148
Interior Finish... 138	Tin-Clad Door 155
Intumescent Coating 140	Wired Glass 161
Listed 140	

Interior Finishes and Passive Fire Protection

FESHE Outcomes Addressed In This Chapter

Fire and Emergency Services Higher Education (FESHE) Outcomes: *Building Construction for Fire Protection*

1. Describe building construction as it relates to firefighter safety, buildings codes, fire prevention, code inspection, firefighting strategy, and tactics.
6. Differentiate between fire resistance, flame spread, and describe the testing procedures used to establish ratings for each.

Learning Objectives

After reading this chapter, students will be able to:

1. Describe how characteristics of interior finishes influence fire behavior.
2. Describe tests used for interior finishes.
3. Explain how ceilings can influence fire behavior.
4. Identify characteristics of fire walls and partitions.
5. Describe fire doors and how they limit fire damage.

Chapter 5
Interior Finishes and Passive Fire Protection

Case History

The interior finish of the Lame Horse nightclub in Perm, Russia contributed to both the ease of ignition and the acceleration of a fatal blaze on December 5, 2009. An illegal pyrotechnic firework used as part of a dance performance ignited the plastic sheeting and willow branches covering a low ceiling. In videos that were taken of the event, the dancers are still performing while the fire on the ceiling is fully involved above them. In the early stages of the fire, a crowd of over 300 individuals was in the process of evacuation when wooden decorations on the interior walls of the club ignited. The club license only allowed for 50 guests.

Of the 153 people who died as a result of the fire, 94 people died at the scene; the rest died in hospitals as a result of their injuries. Many were trampled because there were not enough exits to allow the people in the club to escape. Others died of exposure while lying on the pavement, waiting for ambulances in subzero temperatures.

In the aftermath of the fire, investigations revealed violations and corruption that resulted in multiple criminal charges, civil suits, and public officials being dismissed from their posts. The owners and management were found guilty of negligence and noncompliance with construction safety requirements. They were sentenced to prison for ignoring warnings about the interior finishes that led to the nightclub deaths. They were also found liable in civil suits for the victims and families of the deceased. The chief and all the deputies of the Perm Fire Safety Supervision Authority were dismissed for corruption, and the chief fire safety inspector was criminally charged for negligence on duty leading to fatalities. The tragedy led to increased activity and scrutiny from local Fire Safety Authorities across the country.

This catastrophe illustrates how the confluence of factors can contribute to an incident, and how lives can be saved when codes regulating the installation of interior finishes, building occupancy limits, and exit ways are followed and enforced.[1]

Early building codes focused primarily on the structure of the building, namely the construction materials and the structural system. Over time, more attention has been given to the fire behavior characteristics and layout of materials used for the interior finish.

This chapter explains the fire behavior relevance of the following topics:

- Interior Finishes
- Testing Interior Finishes
- Ceilings

- Walls and Partitions
- Fire Doors

Interior Finishes

> **Interior Finish** — Exposed interior surfaces of buildings, including fixed or movable walls and partitions, columns, and ceilings. Commonly refers to finish on walls and ceilings, but not floor coverings. *Also known as* Interior Lining.

The behavior of fire in buildings is influenced by a number of factors, including some not directly related to the basic construction or occupancy of a building. **Interior finishes** include the materials used for the exposed face of the walls and ceilings of a building, and are not limited to structural materials. Interior finishes can include:

- Plaster
- Gypsum wallboard
- Wood paneling
- Ceiling tiles
- Plastic
- Fiberboard
- Wall coverings including decorative furnishings, vegetation, and draperies

NOTE: In the international community, the term *interior lining* is used instead of *interior finish*.

Influential Interior Finishes Fires

Disastrous fires that have greatly influenced fire codes in the United States and proven that combustible interior finishes can contribute greatly to loss of life include:

- LaSalle Hotel fire in Chicago, Illinois in 1946 claimed 61 lives
- Beverly Hills Supper Club in Southgate, Kentucky in 1977 claimed 165 lives
- The Station Night Club fire in West Warwick, Rhode Island in 2003 claimed 100 lives

Other Common Interior Finishes and Trim

Movable partitions, such as those often used to subdivide a ballroom or banquet facility, are treated as interior finish. Other materials that do not present a continuous surface may be excluded from building code regulation. Surfaces include:

- Countertops
- Doors
- Window frames

Interior finishes may be classified as "trim" if they meet the following conditions:

- Do not exceed ten percent of the wall and ceiling area
- Distributed through the space
- Do not constitute a large continuous surface

Surface Burning Characteristics

Fire behavior is highly dynamic and is influenced by several thermal variables. **Flame spread** over a specific material can be measured and predicted in degrees known as the **surface-burning characteristics** of the material when evaluating the following:

- Composition, orientation, and thickness of the material **(Figure 5.1)**
- Ventilation
- Shape and size of a **compartment**
- Finish material on the ceiling or wall **(Figure 5.2)**

> **Flame Spread** — Movement of a flame away from the ignition source.
>
> **Surface-Burning Characteristic** — Speed at which flame will spread over the surface of a material.
>
> **Compartment** — Any enclosed space without internal fire barriers.

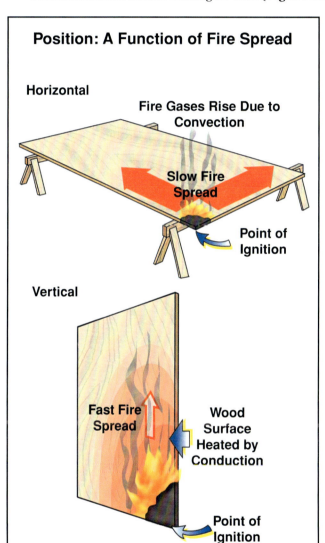

Figure 5.1 Orientation of a material will affect how it burns.

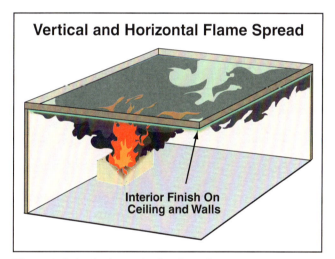

Figure 5.2 As the heat of a fire rises, flames can spread up walls and across the ceiling.

The most significant factor that determines a fuel's burn rate is the combination of the fuel and the available oxygen. Materials with substantial access to surrounding oxygen will burn more rapidly with a correspondingly higher heat release rate.

Another factor that can greatly affect a material's burning characteristic is the manner in which an interior finish is mounted. For example, a thin product ¼-inch (6.5 mm) or less will propagate flame more quickly when it is attached to studs with an air space behind the material than when it is attached directly to a more solid material such as gypsum board. Building codes therefore may require that materials with greater surface burning rates be installed over a noncombustible material.

Modern building codes also use material flame spread ratings to restrict the types of interior finish materials in some applications. Building codes generally allow an increase in the flame spread rating of interior finish materials in buildings equipped with an automatic sprinkler system[2].

NOTE: The numerical flame spread ratings will be addressed later in this chapter.

The first efforts at evaluating and controlling the combustibility of interior finish materials began after several disastrous hotel fires in the 1940s. The early investigations of the role of interior finish materials concentrated on evaluating the speed with which flame can spread over the surface of a material.

Thin Surface Treatments

Building codes usually exclude reference to surface treatments such as paint and wallpaper that are no thicker than 1/28 inch (1 mm). During a fire, thin materials may behave in a manner similar to the material to which they are attached because the heat is transmitted to the material beneath the surface material. In contrast, multiple layers of surface material, such as several layers of vinyl, act as an insulator and will contribute to the spread of fire.

Floor Coverings

Building codes separate floor coverings from wall and ceiling finishes. Floor coverings have increasingly developed as a factor in the development of fires, especially with the introduction of various deep-pile floor carpets. The testing of carpet as a floor covering is beyond the scope of this manual. Contact the manufacturer for information on a specific product.

NOTE: When carpet is used as a wall covering, it is tested as an interior finish. That test is described later in this chapter.

Fire-Retardant Coatings

The flame spread rating of some interior finishes, most notably wood materials, can be reduced through the use of properly applied fire retardant coatings. Coating products that have been tested and **listed** by a reputable laboratory have high effectiveness. Types of fire-retardant coatings available include:

- **Intumescent coatings**
- **Mastics**
- Gas-forming paints
- Cementitious and mineral fiber coatings

Types of coatings react to fire in unique ways. For example, intumescent paints expand upon exposure to heat and create a thick, puffy coating that insulates the wood surface from heat and excludes oxygen from the wood. Mastic coatings form a thick, noncombustible coating over the surface of the wood.

Listed — Refers to a device or material that has been tested by any of several testing laboratories (including the Underwriters' Laboratories Factory Mutual System) and certified as having met minimum criteria.

Intumescent Coating — Coating or paintlike product that expands when exposed to the heat of a fire; creates an insulating barrier that protects the material underneath.

Mastics — Heat resistant construction adhesive that bonds with most materials; can be used as a fire retardant coating.

Many code officials do not accept fire-retardant treatments for permanent applications due to the many variables of application, maintenance, and misuse. For example:

- Coatings must be applied at a specified rate of square feet per gallon (square meter per liter) and may require more than one coat.
- Treatments may require reapplication at specified intervals, especially when used in exterior applications or environments with high humidity.
- Fire-retardant coatings only protect the coated surface; they do not affect the untreated back side of a material.
- A material that is listed as a fire-retardant coating does not increase the fire resistance of structural components or assemblies unless it has also been tested and listed for use in a fire-resistive assembly.
- Because fire retardant coatings are easily applied, an attempt may be made to use them outside their listings as an alternative to other required fire protection.

> **CAUTION**
> Fire retardant coatings cannot be substituted for structural fire protection.

> **Criterion-Referenced Testing (CRT)** — Measurement of one component's tested performance against a set standard or criteria, not against similar components or assemblies. *Also known as* Criterion-Referenced Assessment.
>
> **ASTM E-84** — Standard test used to measure the surface burning characteristics of various materials. *Also known as* Steiner Tunnel Test *or* Tunnel Test.
>
> **Steiner Tunnel** — Test apparatus used in the determination of flame spread ratings; consists of a horizontal test furnace 25 feet (7.5 m) long, 17½ inches (440 mm) wide, and 12 inches (300 mm) high that is used to observe flame travel. A 5,000 Btu (5 000 kJ) flame is produced in the tunnel, and the extent of flame travel across the surface of the test material is observed through ports in the side of the furnace. Used with ASTM E-84.

Testing Interior Finishes

Criterion-referenced testing (CRT) procedures include standardized methodologies that are intended to control as many variables as possible and yield meaningful results. Several nationally recognized testing laboratories publish a list of materials that meet the fire testing requirements used in their facility.

Standardized fire test methods are carefully calibrated and quantified. Standardized testing methodologies allow researchers to evaluate materials that burn at different rates. Because of the wide potential for variety in the field, test results should be used as benchmarks, not guaranteed outcomes.

ASTM E-84

For the purposes of this manual, the standard test used for measuring the surface burning characteristics of interior finish materials is referred to as **ASTM E-84**. Because the ASTM E-84 test uses the **Steiner Tunnel**, other titles for this test include **(Figure 5.3)**:

- ASTM E-84 UL 723, *Test for Surface Burning Characteristics of Building Materials*
- The Steiner Tunnel Test
- The tunnel test

The ASTM E-84 test procedure is useful because it provides reproducible results and is a widely recognized standard. The limitations of the test have been recognized and efforts have been made to improve upon this method. Alternative testing methods are discussed later in this chapter.

Figure 5.3 A long furnace known as the Steiner Tunnel is used to conduct the ASTM E-84 test. *Courtesy of Underwriters Laboratories.*

Flame Spread Rating — (1) Measurement of the propagation of flame on the surface of materials or their assemblies as determined by recognized standard tests. (2) Numerical rating assigned to a material based on the speed and extent to which flame travels over its surface.

Smoke Developed Rating — The measure of the relative visual obscurity created during the testing process by a known material.

Flame Spread Ratings

Interior finishes are tested to derive several measures of a material's flammability including the **flame spread rating** and the **smoke developed rating**. The flame spread rating established by the ASTM E-84 test is a means of comparing the surface flammability of an unknown material to standard materials under controlled test conditions. Codes may indicate a maximum flame spread rating allowed in a building; building codes may also allow a building to include materials with a higher flame spread rating when the building is also equipped with an automatic sprinkler system.

The flame travel along the test material is compared to two standard materials: asbestos cement board is assigned a flame spread rating of 0, and red oak flooring is assigned a flame spread rating of 100. According to the test protocol, the flame will travel along the oak flooring 24 feet (7 m) in 5½ minutes. The flame spread of other materials during the test is compared to that of red oak. The higher the flame spread rating, the more rapidly flame will spread **(Table 5.1)**. Flame spread ratings over 200 are not permitted in occupancies, per Code.

**Table 5.1
Flame Spread Ratings
of Common Materials**

Rating	Example Material
0	Asbestos Cement Board
10-15	Gypsum Wallboard
15-25	Mineral Acoustic Tile
15-60	Treated Douglas Fir Plywood
100	Red Oak Flooring
171-260	Walnut-Faced Plywood
515 (approx.)	Veneered Woods

CAUTION
Asbestos is a known respiratory hazard. Components containing asbestos must be handled carefully in accordance with the AHJ.

The flame spread rating is NOT an absolute measure of the spread of fire travel. Differences between field applications and test conditions may result in different behavior in the field. For example, some materials will produce a fire hazard greater than indicated by the ASTM E-84 tests because of variations in the following:

- Room volume
- Room shape
- Fuel loading in the room

Floor Coverings

The flame spread rating developed in the ASTM E-84 test does not apply to floor coverings. In a case where a floor covering, such as carpeting, will be used for a floor or ceiling finish, the carpeting must meet the same flame spread criteria as other wall and ceiling finishes. Two tests that can evaluate the suitability of carpeting used in that way are the NFPA® 265 and NFPA® 286 tests, described later in this chapter.

NOTE: The Reference Radiant Panel Test ASTM D-2859 and NFPA® 253 are also established testing methodologies to determine the suitability of textile wall and ceiling coverings.

Smoke Developed Ratings

The smoke developed rating is a measure of the relative visual obscurity in an area because of the smoke generated by a burning material. The rating is determined through application of a photoelectric cell and a light source located at the end of the tunnel furnace during ASTM E-84 testing.

As with the flame spread rating, red oak is used as a standard testing material and is assigned a smoke developed rating of 100. Under test conditions, a material with a smoke developed rating of 200 produces smoke that is twice as visually obscuring as red oak. Codes do not allow a combination of materials that exceed a maximum smoke developed rating of 450.

The smoke developed rating has limited usability when a builder decides which materials to use. For example, the test does not detect or measure transparent products of combustion such as carbon monoxide. The test also does not measure other important smoke quality data, such as:

- Heat
- Irritation
- Toxicity
- Volatility

NFPA® Interior Finish Tests

A recently developed large-scale test is **NFPA® 286**, *Standard Methods of Fire Tests for Evaluating Contribution of Wall and Ceiling Interior Finish to Room Fire Growth*. In addition to more-closely simulating a room in an occupancy, this test has been developed to accommodate materials that may not remain in place during ASTM E-84 testing, such as plastic materials that may melt and drip.

NFPA® 286 — Large scale test used to evaluate the performance of textile wall coverings under fire conditions. Designed to accommodate materials that may not remain in place during ASTM E-84 testing. Also includes the capacity of attaching materials to the ceiling. Newer test, preceded by NFPA® 265. *Similar to ASTM E-84.*

Corner Tests

Considerable effort has been made over the years to develop test procedures that incorporate the size and shape of rooms in a building. These methods are collectively known as corner tests. Over time, the configurations have included more complexity, including variations in wall and ceiling dimensions. Early corner tests were conducted with a ceiling and two intersecting sidewalls.

NFPA® 265 — Large scale test used to evaluate the performance of textile wall coverings under fire conditions. Older test, succeeded by NFPA® 286. *Similar to* ASTM E-84.

The *International Building Code® (IBC)* allows interior finish materials to be tested in accordance with NFPA® 286 instead of ASTM E-84. However, the code then establishes specific acceptance criteria including:

- Flame spread to the ceiling of the test chamber must be noted
- The flame cannot spread to the outer extremity of the sample
- Flashover cannot occur
- Limitation of the peak rate of heat release below 800 kW
- Limitation of the maximum amount of smoke released

An older large-scale test developed for evaluating the fire performance of wall textile coverings is known as **NFPA® 265**, *Standard Methods of Fire Tests for Evaluating Room Fire Growth Contribution of Textile or Expanded Vinyl Wall Coverings on Full Height Panels and Walls*. The test was originally developed when carpet-like textiles began to be used as wall coverings.

Both the NFPA® 286 and NFPA® 265 tests use a room enclosure **(Figure 5.4)**. The material to be tested is placed on three of the walls; the surface of the wall containing the door opening is not covered. In the NFPA® 286 test, the material is also placed on the ceiling when it is intended to be used in that manner.

These tests do not provide a numerical test result such as the flame spread rating derived from ASTM E-84. Instead, the test material is judged either satisfactory or unsatisfactory depending on the extent of fire growth that occurs within the test room upon exposure to two different-size gas flames.

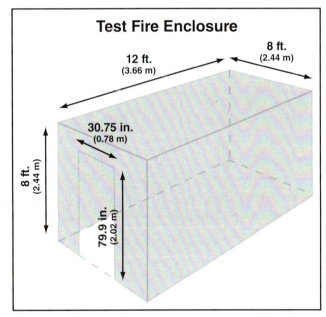

Figure 5.4 Room enclosures used in interior finish tests meet specific dimensions so the test can be reproducible.

Limitations of Test Findings

Although standardized fire test methods are carefully calibrated and quantified, the large variety of combinations of products used in most occupancies will limit the exact match between test results and conditions in those occupancies. Test results should be used as benchmarks, not guaranteed outcomes.

Another limitation of test findings is due to some material's unique features. The actual flame spread rating of materials is difficult to determine in the field because many materials are not labeled with their ratings, and the information may not be available without contacting the manufacturer of the exact item.

In cases where an estimate will suffice, characteristics of materials may be approximated from similar test ratings.

NOTE: Product specifications may be obtained from the manufacturer and verified during plan review.

The thickness of the test specimen has an effect on the flame spread rating because a thicker material has different thermal insulating properties than a thin material. Interior finishes must be tested in the thicknesses that will be used in practice. In the same way, the attachment method and materials must also match field practice.

Ceilings

In addition to the potential flame spread and smoke development features of ceiling materials, ceilings contribute to the void space in a building. In occupancies where ceilings are included, such as office and residential, ceilings serve the following functions:

- Aesthetic concealment of building utilities including piping and wiring
- Improved control of light diffusion and air circulation
- Change in interior décor, when added in older buildings

Ceiling materials can be attached directly to the underside of roof joists or trusses or they can be installed at a distance beneath the roof supports creating a considerable concealed space. The concealed space may disguise the type of roof structure above. The extent of fire development in roof spaces will be hidden by a ceiling.

Walls and Partitions

Floor, ceiling, and wall components will block fire to some degree, but not all components within a building are fire rated. The degree of fire resistance required of a wall or partition will depend on the purpose of the component. Building code requirements are changing and requirements for compartmentation are seen less often.

Any kind of rated assembly used as a fire wall must match the listed parameters of the assembly in order to be considered compliant. Governing organizations produce documents that guide assemblies, including the Underwriters Laboratory's (UL's) *Fire Resistance Directory* and the Gypsum Association publishes the *Fire Resistance Design Manual*. Listings specify details such as:

- Materials that can be used
- Allowable spacing of structural members
- Type, spacing, and nail/screw patterns of the fasteners

Compartmentation

Some degree of **compartmentation** is inherent in the enclosing walls of the architecture of a building. A building without divisions inside, though, can result in a rapid spread of fire horizontally and vertically through a building. Building codes contain explicit requirements for fire-rated walls and partitions

Compartmentation — Series of barriers designed to keep flames, smoke, and heat from spreading between spaces.

Figure 5.5 Fire-rated partitions are located in strategic areas of an occupancy.

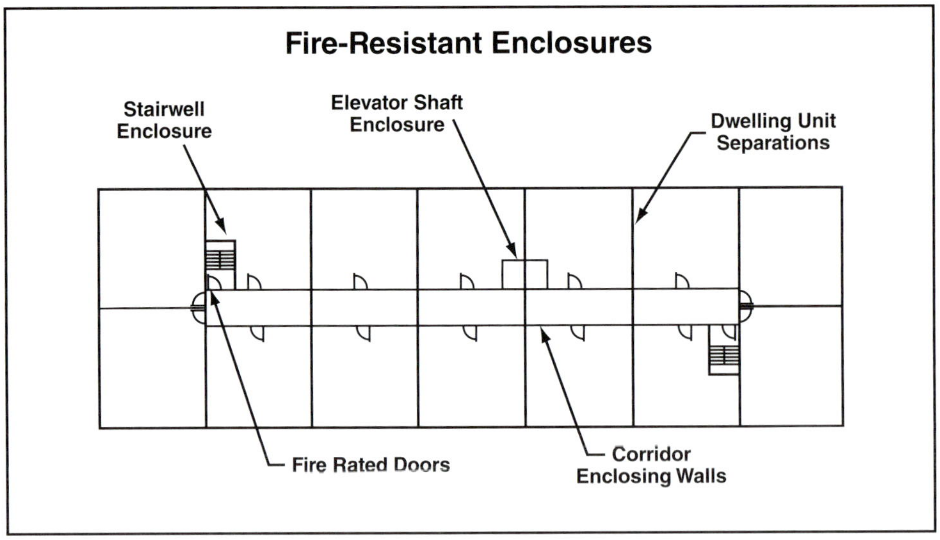

Fire-Resistant Enclosures

- Stairwell Enclosure
- Elevator Shaft Enclosure
- Dwelling Unit Separations
- Fire Rated Doors
- Corridor Enclosing Walls

> **Rated Assembly** — Assemblies of building components such as doors, walls, roofs, and other structural features that may be, because of the occupancy, required by code to have a minimum fire resistance rating from an independent testing agency. *Also known as* Labeled Assembly *and* Fire-Rated.

> **Shelter in Place** — Having occupants remain in a structure or vehicle in order to provide protection from a rapidly approaching hazard, such as a fire or hazardous gas cloud. *Opposite of* Evacuation. *Also known as* Protection-in-Place, Defending-in-Place, Sheltering, *and* Taking Refuge.

> **Fire Wall** — Fire-rated wall with a specified degree of fire resistance, built of fire-resistive materials and usually extending from the foundation up to and through the roof of a building, that is designed to limit the spread of a fire within a structure or between adjacent structures.

> **Fire Flow** — The amount of water required to extinguish a fire in a timely manner.

> **Fire Area** — One of a set of sections in a building separated from each other by fire-resistant partitions.

in various occupancies **(Figure 5.5)**. The fire-rated floor and ceiling assemblies required in building codes for multistory buildings provide structural fire resistance, and act to prevent vertical spread of fire.

Compartments enclosed with **rated assemblies** can provide areas of refuge for occupants when immediate or rapid evacuation is not possible. For example, model codes typically require rated assemblies to subdivide patient floors in a hospital so patients can be moved from the area of fire origin to a protected part of the floor. This concept of providing and using an area of refuge is referred to as *defending* or **sheltering in place**. High-rise building occupants are often able to shelter in place during a fire because of the fire-rated partitions, provided the intervening doors are closed **(Figure 5.6)**. Types of compartmentation, including walls and partitions, are described later in this chapter.

Fire Walls

Fire walls subdivide a building into smaller areas to limit the maximum spread of fire. One purpose of this subdivision is to maintain the thresholds for requirements of factors such as **fire flow** or allowable area. For example, fire walls could divide a 100,000 square foot (9 000 m^2) warehouse into four 25,000 square foot (2 250 m^2) **fire areas**.

Fire walls must have sufficient fire resistance and structural stability to serve as an absolute barrier to a fire and structural collapse on either side of the wall **(Figure 5.7)**. When a section of a building on one side of a fire wall becomes heavily involved, the fire wall is a natural line along which to establish a defense.

Containing a fire greatly reduces potential economic loss. Fire walls can separate functions within a building so that the loss of one area will not result in total loss of the facility.

Freestanding Walls

Freestanding walls are self-supporting with respect to vertical loads. Freestanding walls are also independent of the basic building frame, though the building frame may provide some horizontal support. Freestanding fire walls are usually found in buildings of Type III or V construction, although they may also be used in other types of construction including Type II. Freestanding walls must be designed to resist a lateral load of at least 5 pounds per square foot (0.25 kPa).

Tied Walls

Tied walls are erected at a column line in a building of steel-frame or concrete frame construction. In a steel-frame building, any steel members, such as columns, that may be incorporated into the fire wall must be provided with the same degree of fire resistance required for the fire wall itself. The structural framework must have sufficient strength to resist the lateral pull of the collapse of framework on either side.

Parapet Walls

Fire walls must extend beyond walls and roofs to prevent the radiant heat of flames on one side of a fire wall from igniting adjacent surfaces. By continuing the fire wall through the roof with a **parapet wall**, sufficient separation is achieved **(Figure 5.8)**. The parapet height above a combustible roof is determined by the building code and varies from 18 to 36 inches (450 to 900 mm). Some building codes contain exceptions that permit the elimination of parapets under certain conditions. For example, a fire wall can terminate at the underside of a noncombustible roof that has a covering of low combustibility (Class B).

Fire walls with parapets that are easily identifiable can be noted and incorporated into tactical fire fighting decisions. Firewalls without parapets are not readily identifiable from the outside of a building, particularly for fire walls with a 2-hour rating that can be constructed of materials other than masonry.

Fire Resistance Ratings of Fire Walls

The International Code Council allows fire walls with fire-resistive ratings of 2, 3, or 4 hours, depending on the occupancy. Historically, fire walls were required to have a fire-resistive rating of four hours[3].

The construction of the wall may use any listed assembly that meets the specified rating. 4-hour rated firewalls must be constructed of masonry or concrete; fire walls with lesser fire ratings can be constructed of other fire-resistive materials. Building codes may contain exceptions for fire wall specifications in wood-frame (Type V) buildings.

The *International Building Code® (IBC)* also permits

Figure 5.6 A protected opening in a nonsprinklered building can help contain a fire in an apartment and prevent the spread of fire into the adjacent corridor. *Courtesy of Ed Prendergast.*

Figure 5.7 A fire wall in a warehouse building isolated the protected area from the destruction seen on the other side of the wall. *Courtesy of Ed Prendergast.*

Figure 5.8 Rooftop projections show the location of a fire wall. *Courtesy of Dave Coombs.*

Freestanding Walls — Self-supporting fire walls independent of the structure's frame. Must resist a lateral load of 5 pounds per square foot (0.25 kPa).

Tied Walls — Fire walls connected to a line of columns or steel structural supports with the same degree of fire resistance. Must resist lateral collapse on either side of the structure.

Parapet Wall — Vertical extension of an exterior wall, and sometimes an interior fire wall, above the roofline of a building.

combustible structural members to be framed into a masonry or concrete fire wall from opposite sides provided there is a 4-inch (100 mm) separation between the ends of the structural members **(Figure 5.9)**.

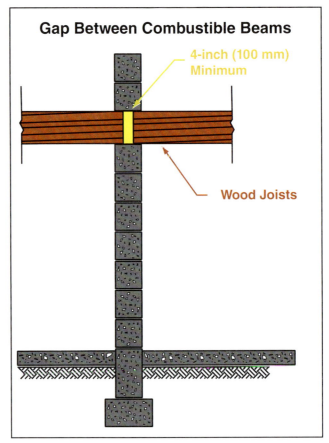

Figure 5.9 Combustible materials may be used in noncombustible construction, provided those materials are used according to minimum standards.

Negative Perception of Fire Walls

Fire walls are unpopular with designers for reasons including:

- Increase structural costs
- May interfere with the free movement of occupants or material
- Architecturally unattractive in occupancies where an expansive interior is desired

In some cases, developers may circumvent the requirements regarding fire walls by building free-standing structures with separate exteriors very near to each other. This technique is often used in densely populated neighborhoods of single-family residences. In structures as close as 18 inches (450 mm) apart, rated construction may take the place of the clearance space to prevent fire-spread from one structure to an adjacent exposure.

Building codes typically allow elimination of fire walls when a building is equipped with an automatic sprinkler system if it meets criteria for occupancy, height, water flow during fire conditions, and other code requirements. Types of facilities that may be constructed without fire walls include:

- Factories
- Warehouses
- Retail stores

> **CAUTION**
> Substituting one fire protection system for another may not provide an equivalent level of required fire protection.

Important Uses of Fire Walls

Firefighters should understand that not all acceptable fire code replacements are equivalent fire protection measures. Substitutions in fire protective systems may not yield equal solutions, even when they provide the required level of mandatory protection. For example, a significant distribution unit for K-Mart, a major retailer, replaced fire doors with a deluge system in order to broaden access to warehouse floor space. This change was permissible in Pennsylvania under the relevant codes.

When the building was exposed to a large-scale fire, aerosol cans stored in the warehouse exploded. The replacement deluge system was unable to contain or mitigate the exploding aerosol cans. If the building had still utilized fire-rated doors and partitions, then the explosions and ensuing fire could have been compartmentalized.

Fire Partitions

Fire partitions are interior walls that do not qualify as fire walls but are used to subdivide a floor or area of a building. Fire partitions are not required to extend continuously through a building. A fire partition is usually erected from a floor to the underside of the floor above.

Fire partitions are typically not required to have as much fire resistance as a fire wall. For example, partitions enclosing an exit corridor may have a 1-hour fire rating. Ratings required for partition walls can be reduced when a sprinkler system is installed.

The material chosen depends on the required fire resistance and the construction type of the building. Fire partitions can be constructed from a wide variety of materials including:

- Lath and plaster
- Gypsum wallboard
- Concrete block
- Combinations of materials

> **Fire Partition** — Fire barrier that extends from one floor to the bottom of the floor above or to the underside of a fire-rated ceiling assembly; provides a lower level of protection than a fire wall.

Enclosure and Shaft Walls

The construction of enclosure walls is similar to that of partition walls. The main difference between the two designations is in their function. The purpose of enclosure walls is to block the vertical spread of fire through a building's openings including:

Figure 5.10 Rated smoke enclosures should meet the expected conditions that they are intended to protect against. *Courtesy of Colorado Springs (CO) Fire Department.*

Figure 5.11 Like other vertical shafts, external light shafts can channel smoke and fire along an exposure. *Courtesy of Gregory Havel, Burlington, WI.*

Curtain Wall — Nonload-bearing exterior wall attached to the outside of a building with a rigid steel frame. Usually the front exterior wall of a building intended to provide a certain appearance.

- Stairwells
- Stairwell exit passageways
- Elevator shafts **(Figure 5.10)**
- Pipe chases

Enclosure walls are required to have a fire resistance rating of one or two hours depending on the height of the building. For example, stairwells in buildings four stories or lower are required to have a 1-hour rated enclosure. In buildings taller than four stories, stairwells are required to have 2-hour rated enclosures. Enclosure walls are usually non-load bearing, although load-bearing masonry stair enclosures are found in older mill buildings. The most common construction materials used for enclosure walls include:

- Gypsum board with steel or wood studs
- Lath and plaster
- Concrete block
- Hollow clay tile enclosure walls (older fire-resistive buildings)

Older buildings may still include shafts or interior courts to provide light and ventilation **(Figure 5.11)**. Windows from interior rooms open into a shaft to facilitate ventilation. Shafts could be provided in an individual building but were frequently provided between adjacent buildings. These shafts can provide a means of vertical communication of fire from window to window.

Curtain Walls

The development of the steel-framed high-rise building led to the existence of the **curtain wall**, a style of wall designed to separate the interior environment from the exterior environment. Modern curtain walls are frequently used in buildings with concrete frames.

NOTE: Refer to Chapter 10, Concrete Construction, for more information on concrete buildings.

Curtain walls serve the following functions:

- Resist environmental loads
- Control heat loss
- Limit noise transmission
- Limit solar radiation

Curtain walls are often constructed using a combination of materials. Newer types of curtain walls can be constructed with metal panels around core materials such as expanded paper honeycombs and compressed glass fiber. More common materials and combinations include:

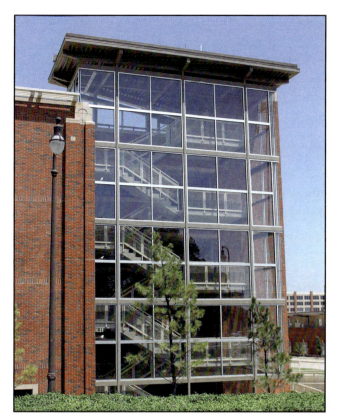

Figure 5.12 Curtain walls are nonload-bearing walls suspended by internal framing.

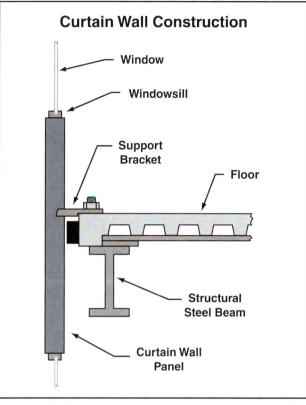

Figure 5.13 The support brackets in a typical curtain wall assembly are not usually continuous and therefore do not create an effective firestop.

- Glass and steel **(Figure 5.12)**
- Stainless steel
- Aluminum
- Lightweight concrete
- Plastic
- Fiberglass

Curtain walls are often **nonload-bearing**. Some curtain wall assemblies are noncombustible but have no fire resistance, such as those made of aluminum and glass. Building codes may require that exterior walls have some degree of fire resistance to reduce the communication of fire between buildings. The required fire resistance depends on the separation distance between buildings and the building occupancy.

Curtain walls are supported at the edge of each floor of the building and may have a gap between the edge of the floor and the curtain wall **(Figure 5.13)**. This opening may be several inches wide and can provide a path for fire spread up the inside of the curtain wall. Fire stops can be added to the edge of the floor to maintain the continuity of the fire-resistive barrier.

Nonfire-resistive curtain walls frequently extend from the floor to the ceiling of one level. When a room becomes heavily involved in fire, the flames may overlap the edge of a fire-resistive floor slab and expose the story above. A fire may also spread vertically up the outside of a building.

> **Nonload-Bearing Wall** — Wall, usually interior, that supports only its own weight. These walls can be breached or removed without compromising the structural integrity of the building. *Also known as* Nonbearing Wall.

Figure 5.14 A sliding metal fire door in an older mill-style building can be activated by a fusible link. *Courtesy of McKinney (TX) Fire Department.*

Fire Doors

Fire doors are the most common means for protecting openings through fire-rated walls. Fire doors can be found in industrial buildings dating back to the end of the nineteenth century **(Figure 5.14)**. As with other aspects of passive fire protection, fire doors are effective in limiting total fire damage when they are maintained and operated properly. Fire doors differ from ordinary or nonfire doors in their construction, hardware, and the extent to which they may be required to close automatically. Fire doors should be carefully noted during preincident surveys because they may be installed in unexpected areas.

Fire Door Classifications

A fire door is rated for its fire resistance in a manner somewhat similar to that used for fire-resistive structural assemblies. Fire doors are rated in increments of time from 20 minutes to 4 hours. The ½-hour and ⅓-hour doors are primarily used in smoke barriers and openings to corridors.

A fire door may also have a combination classification using a time rating and a letter indicating the type of opening. Historically, letters designated the type of opening, or in an older system, the door itself. Letter designations may still be encountered in older buildings. The letter designations are as follows:

Fire Door — Specially constructed, tested, and approved fire-rated assembly designed and installed to prevent fire spread by automatically sealing an opening in a fire wall to block the spread of fire.

Tactical Uses of Fire Doors

Fire doors provide a rated barrier that also functions as an opening in a fire wall. Firefighters can use this opening as a protected vantage point from which to attack the main body of fire. Fire doors will automatically close when activated and great care must be exercised when opening fire doors under these circumstances **(Figure 5.15)**.

When firefighters withdraw, fire doors must be closed. With fire doors closed, one or two handlines can be positioned to slow any fire spread around gaps including cracks in the structure or door edges. Preventing fire spread around fire doors can be accomplished with a minimum of personnel, freeing other firefighters to protect exposures or to attack the main body of fire.

Figure 5.15 Preincident surveys must include a note of fire safety systems used in less-common ways, such as an automatic fire door that covers an elevator door when activated.

- **Class A** – Openings in fire walls
- **Class B** – Openings in vertical shafts and openings in 2-hour rated partitions
- **Class C** – Openings between rooms and corridors having a fire resistance of 1-hour or less
- **Class D** – Openings in exterior walls subject to severe fire exposure from the outside of a building
- **Class E** – Openings in exterior walls subject to moderate or light exposure from the outside

Fire Door Requirements

To effectively block the spread of fire, the entire **rated fire door assembly** must have a degree of fire resistance similar to fire-rated walls. Lightly constructed panel doors or glass doors cannot act as a barrier to the high temperatures developed in a fire. Furthermore, the material of construction will affect the degree of fire resistance.

> **Rated Fire Door Assembly** — Door, frame, and hardware assembly that has a fire-resistive rating from an independent testing agency.

Fire door requirements are included in the following standards:

- NFPA® 1, *Uniform Fire Code*
- NFPA® 80, *Standard for Fire Doors and Other Opening Protectives*
- NFPA® 101, *Life Safety Code*
- NFPA® 5000, *Building Construction and Safety Code*

The above standards each contain a table in which the minimum fire protection rating is provided based upon the fire resistance rating of a component that was mandated within the Code. Codes typically require 3- or 4-hour rated doors in fire walls of greater than a 2-hour rating. Doors rated at 1½ hours are normally required for 2-hour rated vertical enclosures. 1-hour doors are used for 1-hour vertical shaft enclosures and exit enclosures.

Although the lower fire protection rating for a fire door as opposed to the surrounding fire wall may seem illogical, the rationale behind the discrepancy is explained this way: A fire door is only functional as a portal between spaces if it has a sufficient clear area on either side, as opposed to an interior fire wall which can be completely blocked without affecting its primary function of separating spaces. In other words, because a fire door will not have a high fuel load in its immediate proximity, it will not have to withstand the same extremity of conditions.

Some inconsistencies are built into the code in certain occupancies, and the fire official should be aware of them. For example, a code may permit an opening in a 2-hour stairwell enclosure to be protected with a 1½-hour fire door rather than a 2-hour door.

Other redundancies may also be built into the code. For example, a code may require two 3-hour fire doors to protect an opening in a 4-hour wall and not allow a 3-hour door to be used in combination with a 1½-hour door to satisfy the requirement. This redundancy can be viewed as a means for increasing the reliability of the protection for the wall opening because of the increased likelihood that at least one of the doors will close.

Fire doors are designed for use in specific types of settings. The four styles of fire doors identified in NFPA® 80 are described in the following sections.

Overhead Door — Door that opens and closes above a large opening, such as in a warehouse or garage, and is usually of the rolling, hinged-panel, or slab type. *Also known as* Rolling (Overhead) Door.

Fusible Link — Connecting link device that fuses or melts when exposed to fire temperatures; used to activate individual elements in active and passive fire suppression systems. Benefits include: inexpensive, rugged, easy to maintain. Disadvantages include: slower to activate than automated systems.

Rolling (Overhead) Doors

Rolling **(overhead) doors** are often installed in the following locations:

- Along corridors to protect convenience openings
- To protect an opening in a fire wall in an industrial occupancy **(Figure 5.16)**
- On one or both sides of a wall opening
- At an opening in a wall that separates buildings

Rolling (overhead) doors are constructed of interlocking steel slats with other operating components including:

- Releasing device
- Speed governor
- Counterbalance mechanism
- Wall guides

A rolling (overhead) door ordinarily closes under the force of gravity when a **fusible link** melts or a smoke detector releases the hold-open device. Motor-driven doors are also available **(Figure 5.17)**. One architectural advantage of a rolling (overhead) fire door is that it is relatively inconspicuous and unobtrusive.

Rolling doors should never be used in a path of egress. Without another means of egress available, the overhead door may create a dangerous dead-end corridor when it closes. In addition, a door that closes after firefighters have passed through it can cause the following hazards:

- Disorient firefighters who do not realize that the door closed the corridor behind them
- Trap firefighters in the fire area
- Cut off firefighter's escape path
- Restrict water through pinched hoselines

Overhead doors can also create a dangerous condition for firefighters who may not be able to see the door's tracks on each side of an opening through heavy smoke. Firefighters should take precautions to ensure that they will not be struck in case the door suddenly closes.

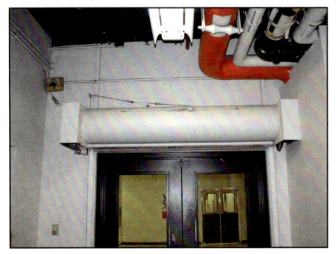

Figure 5.16 Overhead fire doors are commonly used to protect large openings.

Figure 5.17 Overhead fire doors that are operated with a motor may be more quickly and easily opened and closed than overhead doors that are activated with a fusible link. *Courtesy of Ed Prendergast.*

Rolling Overhead Doors

Firefighters should attempt to secure an overhead rolling door in the open position before proceeding through it. Common tools, such as pike poles or vice grips, can block the channel to help prevent the door from closing on firefighters or equipment, including hoses.

Horizontal Sliding Fire Doors

Horizontal **sliding fire doors** are often found in older industrial buildings. These doors are usually held open with a fusible link. When the link is activated, the door slides into position along a track either by gravity or by the force of a counterweight **(Figure 5.18)**.

Most horizontal sliding doors are **metal-clad** or **tin-clad doors** with a wood core that provides insulation, covered in sheet metal that protects the wood from the fire. Because wood undergoes thermal decomposition when exposed to heat, a hole is usually provided in the sheet metal to vent the gases of decomposition **(Figure 5.19)**. Metals used often include:

- Steel
- Galvanized sheet metal
- Terneplate

Sliding Door — Door that opens and closes by sliding across its opening, usually on rollers.

Metal-Clad Door — Wood core door protected with galvanized sheet metal steel or other heavy metal exterior. *Also known as* Kalamein Door.

Tin-Clad Door — Similar to a metal-clad door, except covered with a lighter-gauge metal, often an alloy of tin and lead.

Figure 5.18 Sliding fire doors may provide first responders a strategic vantage when open, and a means to separate themselves from the hazard when closed.

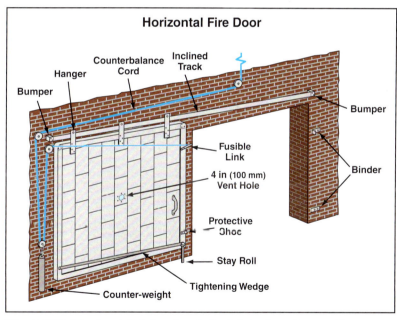

Figure 5.19 A horizontal sliding door is likely to be found in an older building.

Swinging Door — Door that opens and closes by swinging from one side of its opening, usually on hinges. *Also known as* Hinged Door.

Swinging Fire Doors

Swinging fire doors commonly protect stairwell enclosures and corridors. Swinging fire doors are available with ratings from 20 minutes to 3 hours. Just as with sliding doors, swinging doors can be constructed from a variety of materials, including the metal-clad wood style **(Figure 5.20)**. Many companies in the U.S. produce listed swinging fire doors, so a large variety of them are available.

Although a swinging fire door has the disadvantage of requiring a clear space around the door to ensure closure, it is a good choice where the door is frequently in the closed position and provision must be made for pedestrian traffic. In some cases, standard architectural practice cannot address the needs of a space. For example, it may be necessary to provide a fire door on either side of a wall. In this case, the swinging doors must swing in the direction of exit travel **(Figure 5.21)**. To meet this requirement, a vestibule with fire-resistive construction can be built between the two fire doors.

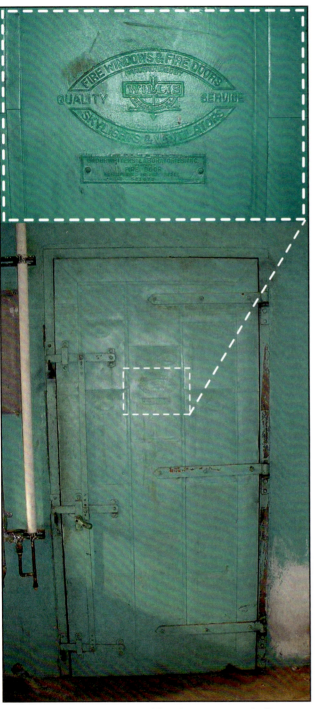

Figure 5.20 Older metal clad fire doors may not indicate an hourly rating despite the indication of successful UL testing. *Courtesy of Gregory Havel, Burlington, WI.*

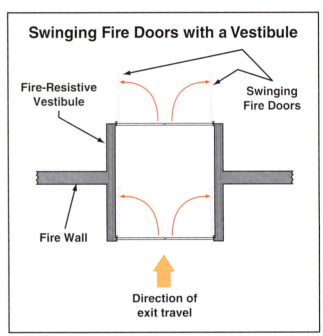

Figure 5.21 When a firewall must be penetrated, the use of a vestibule and two sets of doors may provide the necessary degree of protection.

A pair of fire doors may be installed to close off a corridor at a fire wall, with one door swinging in each direction to accommodate exit travel in both directions. These vestibules are used in locations including:

- Health care facilities
- Apartment buildings
- Schools

Figure 5.22 Special-purpose horizontally sliding accordion or folding fire door assemblies may be used where a fixed wall is not desired. *Courtesy of Ed Prendergast.*

Special Fire Doors

The code identifies parameters for special-purpose fire doors that can be used in applications including:

- Freight and passenger elevators
- Service counter openings
- Security (bullet-resisting)
- Dumbwaiters
- Chute openings

Other types of special-purpose fire doors include horizontally sliding accordion or folding doors. Both types of doors are motor driven and require electrical power for operation. A signal from a smoke detector or fire alarm system initiates the door closing. A battery powers the motor when the regular power supply is interrupted.

Horizontal sliding accordion or folding doors are frequently used where a fire-rated partition is required and the designer does not wish to provide a fixed wall to create an unobstructed floor plan **(Figure 5.22)**. For example, these types of doors are used in a corridor separation in the lobby of a health care facility.

Hardware — General term for small pieces of equipment made of metal, including ancillary equipment affixed to another medium to aid the use of the primary tool. Fire door hardware includes: door knobs, hinges, and door closure devices.

Fire Door Hardware and Features

For a fire door to effectively block the spread of fire, it must remain closed and attached to the fire wall under fire conditions. Therefore, a fire door must be equipped with **hardware** that securely latches the door closed under the stresses of fire exposure. In addition, when fire doors are installed in a frame, the frame must also withstand exposure to a fire. The testing of fire doors includes the frames as well as the hardware **(Figure 5.23)**. All components must be listed by a testing laboratory for compatibility.

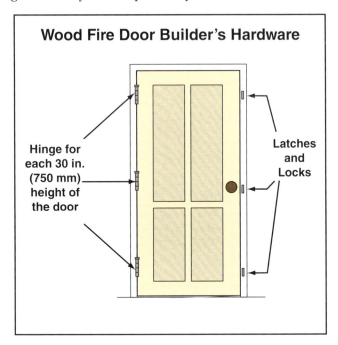

Figure 5.23 (left) When testing the rating for a fire door assembly, all of the components of the door's hardware are included in the test.

Figure 5.24 (above) Builder's hardware for a wooden fire door is often shipped separately from the door itself.

Wood swinging fire doors include hardware that can also be referred to as "builder's hardware" or "fire door hardware." Builder's hardware can be shipped to a job site separately from the fire doors and includes **(Figure 5.24)**:

- Hinges
- Locks and latches
- Bolts
- Closers

Metal- and tin-clad sliding and swinging fire doors are normally shipped with the requisite hardware. Hardware components may include **(Figure 5.25)**:

- Hinges
- Vent holes (tin-clad doors only)
- Adjustable spring

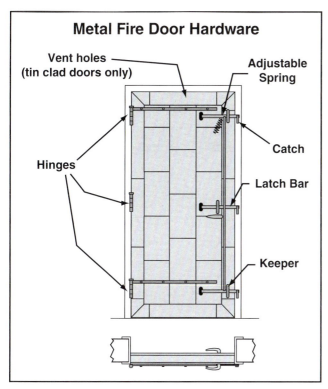

Figure 5.25 Hardware for a steel fire door is often shipped already assembled on the door.

- Catch
- Latch bar
- Keeper

Fire Door Closing Devices

To perform its function of containing a fire, a fire door must be closed when a fire occurs. However, during non-fire conditions, fire doors must often remain open and/or useable to allow pedestrian traffic. Tools and combinations of tools that retain a door's functionality both as a fire barrier and portal through a partition are explained below and include:

- Door holders
- Door closers
- Door operators

A **door hold-open device** (door holder) can be used with swinging, sliding, or rolling fire doors. The use of a door holder with a fire door is useful in areas with a large volume of traffic such as school stair enclosures **(Figure 5.26)**. When fire doors are held open under non-fire conditions, the doors are less likely to be otherwise secured in an open position.

Electromagnetic door holders may be released as part of the programmed response during fire alarm activation. This system activates more quickly than fusible link door closers and can be tested easily.

Figure 5.26 Electromagnetic door holders retain a swinging door in its open position until released.

Door Hold-Open Device — Mechanical device that holds a door open and releases it upon a signal. Mechanism may be a fusible link that releases under fire conditions, or an electromagnet connected to a smoke detector. *Also known as* Door Holder.

Chapter 5 • Interior Finishes and Passive Fire Protection **159**

Figure 5.27 A typical self-closing swinging fire door mechanism found on stairway doors helps ensure that enclosure doors will reset to their appropriate position when not in use.

Door Closer — Mechanical device that closes a door. *Also known as* Self-Closing Door.

Self-Closing Door — Door equipped with a door closer.

Door closers can be used with sliding or swinging fire doors **(Figure 5.27)**. When used with a door hold-open device, the door will close automatically when signaled. Devices that react to smoke or a rise in temperature activate quickly and can be reset easily. Fusible link door closers are generally incorporated on doors that only close during a fire event.

Limitations of smoke detectors include:

- Higher cost compared to fusible links
- Requires periodic cleaning
- Must be positioned properly with respect to ventilation

A **self-closing door** is normally closed, and will return to the closed position using a spring hinge when opened and released. Self-closing door closers are used for applications including stairwell doors and doors that separate hotel rooms from corridors.

Door operators open and close a door for normal use; often used with sliding fire doors mounted on a level or inclined track **(Figure 5.28)**. Under fire conditions, a fusible link disconnects the door from the operator and allows the door to close using a spring-powered door closer or a system of suspended weights.

Figure 5.28 Sliding doors mounted on a level or inclined track may be operated by electronic controls.

Glazing

Glazing can be used in partitions and fire doors where visibility is desired and a fire rating is required **(Figure 5.29)**. Examples of locations where glazing may be used include fire doors to stair enclosures and partition walls in health care facilities.

> **Glazing** — Glass or thermoplastic panel in a wall or other barrier that allows light to pass through.
>
> **Wired Glass** — Flat sheet glass containing an embedded wire mesh that increases its resistance to breakage and penetration; installed to increase interior illumination without compromising fire resistance and security. May be transparent or translucent.

Figure 5.29 Recent advances in fire-rated glazing can eliminate the need for reinforcing wires.

The first type of fire-rated glazing available was **wired glass**, a sheet of glass in which a steel wire net has been embedded **(Figure 5.30)**. The steel net distributes the heat throughout the glass and helps hold the glass in place. Wired glass will crack when exposed to a fire but will remain in place until the wire begins to soften and fall out.

Modern fire-rated glazing does not include embedded steel wire. These products can provide higher hourly fire ratings than wired glass. Wireless fire-rated glazing is somewhat more visually appealing and can be used as windows or sidelights in fire-rated walls as well as in fire doors. Some fire-rated glazings are impact-resistant and can be used for security purposes.

Fire doors are the most common application of fire-rated glazing. Doors with ratings up to 3 hours can be equipped with glazing. NFPA® 80 requires that each piece of glazing installed in a fire door include a listing mark that remains visible after installation. If the door manufacturer does not provide the glazing then a glazing contractor may install it at the job site.

Figure 5.30 At one time, glazing required the addition of wires to provide the required fire resistance in a fire door.

Restrictions regulate the allowable area of glass in fire doors. For example, fire doors with ratings of 1-3 hours can have glass panels up to 100 square inches (64 500 mm^2) in area per door. Fire doors with ratings

Chapter 5 • Interior Finishes and Passive Fire Protection

of ¾ hour can have a total glass area consistent with their listing, below a stated maximum area. Fire doors with ratings of ½ or ⅓ hour can have fire-rated glass up to the maximum area to which they were tested.

Louvers

Louvers may be installed in a fire door to permit ventilation while the door is closed under normal conditions, such as in the case of a furnace room enclosure. The louvers in a fire door must automatically close under fire conditions. Usually, the mechanism of closing louvers is the release of a fusible link.

Louvers cannot be arbitrarily installed in fire doors. Only fire doors that are listed for the installation of louvers can have louvers installed. For example, swinging fire doors with ratings up to 1½ hours can be equipped with louvers. The door manufacturer may not produce the louvers, and testing laboratories may list them separately.

> **Louvers** — A series of horizontal slats that are angled to permit easy ventilation in one direction of flow and restricted ventilation in the opposite direction. Louvers are commonly used in applications where the restrictive side blocks sunshine, rain, or products of combustion.

Fire Door Maintenance

For compartmentation to be effective, the doors protecting the openings must operate correctly and close under fire conditions. Proper fire door operation requires that the doors be properly maintained. NFPA® 80 contains extensive information on fire doors including best practices for the following:

- Inspection
- Testing
- Maintenance

Failure of fire doors to close properly is a common occurrence in fire conditions. A door will be likely to fail when the following components are damaged:

- The door closer
- The door itself
- Door guides

Overhead fire doors are especially subject to damage. The closing mechanisms on overhead doors are more complicated and typically more inconspicuous than those on swinging doors.

> **CAUTION**
> Any fire door can fail and become nonoperational during a fire. Fire fighting tactics should include resources to accommodate a door fixed in a closed or open position.

Fire Door Testing

Fire doors are tested in accordance with the procedures contained in NFPA® 252, *Standard Methods of Fire Tests of Door Assemblies*; also designated ASTM E-152. The test procedure uses a furnace to expose the fire doors to the same time-and-temperature curve used to establish the fire resistance rating of structural assemblies **(Figure 5.31)**. The conditions for passing the test for door assemblies are not as rigid as is required for fire-rated walls.

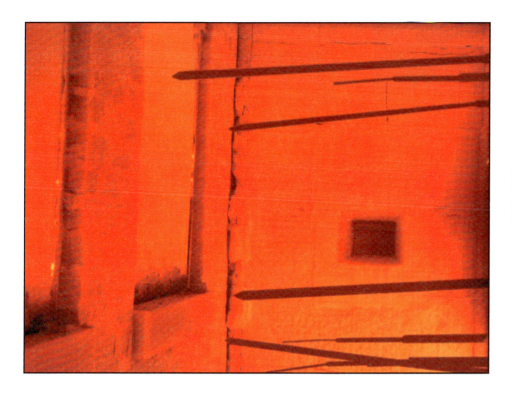

Figure 5.31 The ASTM E-152 test subjects a wooden fire door and its assembled hardware to a test fire controlled by a furnace.

Criterion Referenced Testing

Many of the same laboratories that test interior finishes and building materials also test fire doors. Several nationally recognized testing laboratories publish a list of fire doors that meet their particular criterion-referenced fire testing requirements. During fire door testing, the following two criteria for acceptability are described below.

For fire doors, the primary criterion for acceptability is that the fire door must remain securely in its frame during the flame test. Parameters include:

- Some warping of the door is permitted.
- Intermittent passage of flames is permitted after the first 30 minutes of the test **(Figure 5.32)**.
- Surface temperature rise is not regulated on the unexposed side of the door for most of the doors tested. In fact, metal doors may glow red from the heat of the test fire.

The fact that fire doors are allowed to get very hot reinforces the importance of keeping combustibles away from the immediate vicinity of fire doors in fire walls when they are kept permanently closed. If an opening through a fire wall is no longer needed for passage, the opening should be filled in with construction materials to the equivalent of the fire resistance rating of the wall.

The second criterion for acceptability is that the fire door assembly must remain in place when subjected to a hose stream immediately following the fire test

Figure 5.32 During fire door testing, intermittent flames may pass the door assembly after 30 minutes have elapsed.

Figure 5.33 Immediately after the furnace test, fire doors must remain in place when impacted with a stream from a fire hose.

Figure 5.34 The manufacture and testing label for a swinging fire door is placed on the edge of the door. *Courtesy of Ed Prendergast.*

(Figure 5.33). The use of a hose stream subjects the door assembly to cooling and the impact forces that may accompany fire fighting. Doors with a 1/3-hour rating may not be subjected to the hose test depending on their intended application.

Marking Rated Fire Doors

Fire doors that pass a testing process are marked with a label or plate on the top or on the hinge side of the door that indicates information including **(Figure 5.34)**:

- Door type
- Hourly rating
- Identifying symbol of the testing laboratory

Although the door's rating information can help building and fire inspectors while determining the opening's protection, the information cannot protect against limitations including:

- The presence of a rated door and frame assembly does NOT indicate that the surrounding wall is also rated.

- Damage, removal, or disguising of labels may give the appearance of a lower fire rating.
- Counterfeit laboratory labels give false information.

Chapter Summary

Interior finishes contribute substantially to the surface flammability of a structure. Because of their significance in fire load, interior finishes are tested and classified, and their application is regulated via building codes.

In addition to controlling interior finishes, passive controls including compartmentation are provided in buildings to slow or prevent the spread of fire and smoke. Elements such as fire walls, partitions, and other enclosures are specified in building codes. Fire doors that protect openings in fire-rated walls must also be sufficiently rated and maintained.

Review Questions

1. How do characteristics of interior finishes influence fire behavior?
2. What tests are used to determine surface burning characteristics of interior finishes?
3. What are some limitations of tests for interior finishes?
4. How can ceilings influence fire behavior?
5. What are the different types of fire walls?
6. What are the differences between fire partitions, enclosure walls, and curtain walls?
7. Describe the four styles of fire doors.
8. What is the function of fire door hardware?
9. What two criteria must fire doors meet for acceptability?

Chapter Notes

1. "A look at past deadly nightclub fires," Associated Press, http://www.cbsnews.com/8301-201_162-57566065/a-look-at-past-deadly-nightclub-fires/.
2. International Fire Code 2009, Table 803.3, http://publiccodes.cyberregs.com/icod/ifc/2009/icod_ifc_2009_8_par012.htm.
3. *International Building Code®*, Chapter 7, Table 706.4, http://www2.iccsafe.org/cs/committeeArea/pdf_file/BU_03_06_06.pdf.

Foundations

Chapter Contents

Case History **169**	Stone 174
Soil Properties **169**	Wood 174
Types of Foundations **170**	EPS 174
Shallow Foundations 171	**Building Settlement** **175**
Deep Foundations 172	**Shoring and Underpinning** **176**
Foundation Walls **174**	**Chapter Summary** **177**
Concrete and Mortared Masonry 174	**Review Questions** **177**

chapter 6

Key Terms

Caisson 174	Masonry 174
Column Footing 171	Mat Slab Foundation 172
Expanded Polystyrene (EPS) 174	Mortar 174
Floating Foundation 172	Pier 173
Footing 171	Piles 173
Foundation Wall 174	Settlement 175
Frost Line 170	Shoring 176
Grillage Footing 171	Soil Property 170
Heaving 175	Stratum 170
Insulated Concrete Form (ICF) Construction 175	Underpinning 176
Lateral Displacement 175	Wall Footing 171
	Water Table... 170

FESHE Outcomes Addressed In This Chapter

Fire and Emergency Services Higher Education (FESHE) Outcomes: *Building Construction for Fire Protection*

1. Describe building construction as it relates to firefighter safety, buildings codes, fire prevention, code inspection, firefighting strategy, and tactics.
4. Explain the different loads and stresses that are placed on a building and their interrelationships.
5. Identify the function of each principle structural component.
8. Identify the indicators of potential structural failure as they relate to firefighter safety.

Foundations

Learning Objectives

After reading this chapter, students will be able to:

1. Explain how soil properties influence building foundation types.
2. Identify types and components of building foundations.
3. Describe types of foundation walls.
4. Explain the symptoms and causes of building settlement.
5. Recognize uses of shoring and underpinning.

Chapter 6
Foundations

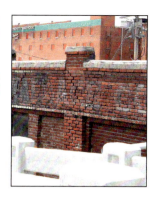

Case History

On June 29, 2009, a high-rise building in Shanghai, China collapsed, killing one person. The cause of the collapse was attributed to a pressure difference on two sides of the structure, exerting 3,000 tons of force on the foundation, causing it to shift and weakening the concrete piles. The conditions were worsened by several days of heavy rain which saturated the soil below the building and eroded the supporting soil on the pit side.

A primary contributing factor to the collapse was the improper placement of pits and spoil piles. Construction was in the process to dig an underground garage on one side of the building. The spoil pile was placed near the other side of the building. At the time of the collapse, the pit was 15 feet (4.5 m) deep, and the spoil pile was 30 feet (10 m) high. Investigations indicated that the building's foundations and materials complied with the AHJ.

The function of a foundation is to transfer a building's weight to the ground. Although foundations are not a primary consideration for firefighters, the failure of a foundation can create or aggravate structural problems within the building above. This chapter provides a brief overview of factors involved in foundations through the following topics:

- Soil properties
- Types of foundations
- Foundation walls
- Building settlement
- Shoring and underpinning

Soil Properties

Types of soils on which a building is constructed may range from loose sand at one end of the texture spectrum to solid granite at the other. **Soil properties** influence the type of foundation, and therefore the type of building, that can be built at a given location. For example, bedrock is able to support significantly more weight than sandy clay.

NOTE: A full discussion of soil analysis is beyond the scope of this manual. For more information, refer to the IFSTA manual **Fire Service Technical Search and Rescue**.

Soil Property — Physical qualities of the materials at the surface of the earth. Affects a building's foundation and size. Influential variables include texture, structure, density, porosity, and consistency.

Water Table — The highest level of ground water saturation of subsurface materials. Influential variables include the season, soil properties, and topography.

Frost Line — Common depth at which ground water in soil will freeze. Influential variables include climate, soil properties, and nearby heat sources.

Stratum — Sheet-like layer of rock or earth; numerous other layers, each with different characteristics, are typically found above and below. *Plural:* Strata.

Soil may not have the same consistency at different depths or even within a given location. Because the soil properties at a site must be known before a building's supports can be planned, a soil assessment will often be taken to observe and measure the soil's qualities and other important factors including the **water table** and **frost line**. Two strategies used to assess soil are *test pits* and *test borings*.

Test pits may reach a depth up to 8 feet (2.5 m). The use of a test pit permits the **strata** (layers) of the soil to be observed and measured **(Figure 6.1)**. Depending on the soil type, the level of the water table may also be determined.

Test borings are used when a test pit may not reach deep enough. A test boring can provide information on the bearing capacity of soil through the use of a small-bore tube and a driving hammer. The number of impacts required to reach a given distance will provide information about the soil strata. The soil collected in the tube can also provide information about the water table and soil samples. Usually a number of test borings will be taken across a given site to provide an overview of conditions.

Figure 6.1 Soil type varies by depth, as well as by location. Types of soil are important because undisturbed bedrock can support significantly more weight than sandy clay.

Types of Foundations

The size of the structure will influence the required depth of the foundation. For example, a small garage or shed may only require a shallow foundation. In contrast, a high-rise building requires a foundation that extends deep into the ground. Several other factors that influence the type and depth of the foundation include:

- Soil conditions at the site
- The type of building
- The building's intended structure and contents
- Lateral forces (seismic and wind)
- Working space requirements
- Influence on adjacent exposures
- Building codes and regulations

Shallow Foundations

A shallow foundation transfers the weight of the building directly to the soil at the base of the building **(Figure 6.2)**. Shallow foundations usually use reinforced concrete **footings** to transmit the building's load to the soil in a limited amount of space. The increased area of the footing reduces the compressive stress on the soil. Footings are carefully compacted to prevent excessive settling.

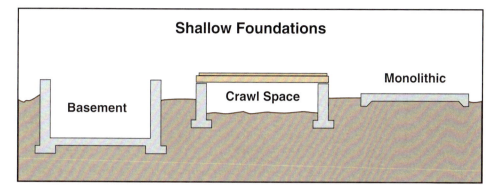

Figure 6.2 Shallow foundations often include a wider area at the base of the wall to distribute loads.

Footing — Part of the building in contact with the bearing soil. Footings are thicker (deeper) than the column or foundation wall and are often embedded below the surface of the soil to rest on bedrock.

Concrete footings may be constructed in several ways including:

- Increased thickness of a floor slab at its edges (known as a *monolithic floor*)
- A thick and wide strip of concrete under full story-high walls that create a full or partial basement
- A thick and wide strip of concrete under a wall that supports a raised floor with a crawl space

Specialized types of footings are matched to the loads supported above them:

- **Wall footing** – Continuous strip of concrete that supports a wall. This type of footing equals the full length of the wall, and is wider and deeper at the base to distribute the load **(Figure 6.3)**.

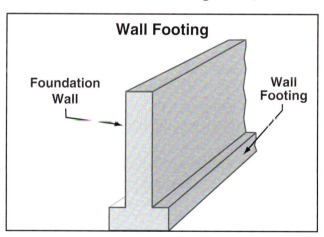

Figure 6.3 A wall footing is a stretch of concrete that extends continuously beneath the length of a wall.

Wall Footing — Type of shallow foundation that includes a wide, thick area to distribute the weight of a wall on the bearing soil. *Also known as* Strip Footing.

Column Footing — Square pad of concrete that supports a column. Footings of decorative columns are often above the bearing surface.

Grillage Footing — Footing consisting of layers of beams placed at right angles to each other and usually encased in concrete.

- **Column footings** – A square pad of concrete that supports a column; often reinforced, and limited to a relatively small load.
- **Grillage footings** – Parallel structural beams (often steel), arranged in multiple layers at right angles to each other, and usually encased in concrete **(Figure 6.4, p. 172)**. Similar to a column footing but designed to transmit loads over a wider area.

Chapter 6 • Foundations **171**

Figure 6.4 A grillage footing can be designed to transmit vertical loads to the footing.

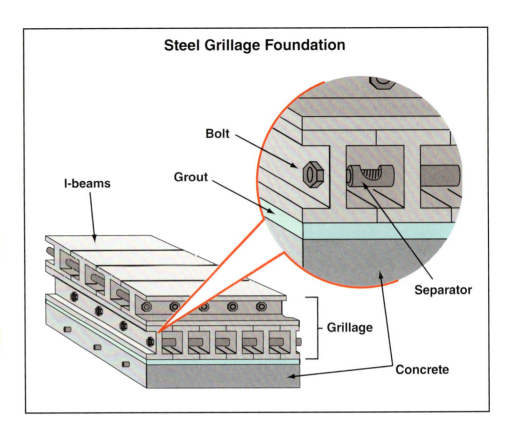

Mat Slab Foundation — Thick slab beneath the entire area of a building; thicker and more reinforced than a simple slab-on-grade foundation.

Floating Foundation — Shallow foundation type; the supported building "floats" as the supporting earth contracts and expands with the seasons.

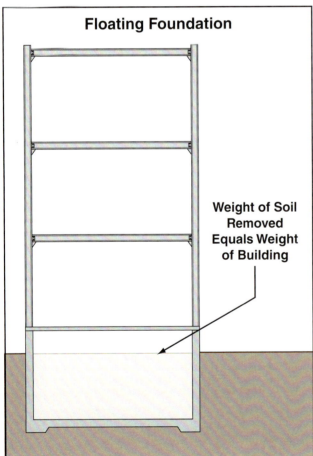

Figure 6.5 A floating foundation is designed to support a building that weighs the same as the soil removed, in an effort to minimize the building's settling.

When the load-bearing capacity of the soil is not able to bear a heavy weight, the footing must be large enough to spread out the weight of the building. Simple slabs may be only one foot thick. Other types of slab foundations that serve specific purposes include:

- **Mat slab foundation** – A thick slab beneath the entire area of a building. A mat may be several feet thick and heavily reinforced.

- **Floating foundations** – The weight of the soil removed is equal to the weight of the building. The total weight supported at each soil layer beneath the building remains the same before and after excavation (**Figure 6.5**). Constructed in the same way as a mat slab foundation.

NOTE: The weight of one story of soil can equal five to eight stories of a building, depending on the density of the soil and the construction features of the building.

Deep Foundations

Deep foundations are more costly than shallow foundations, so they are used only where shallow foundation cannot be used. Deep foundations take the form of **piles** or **piers** that penetrate the layers of soil directly under a building to reach soil or rock that can support the weight of the building (**Figure 6.6**).

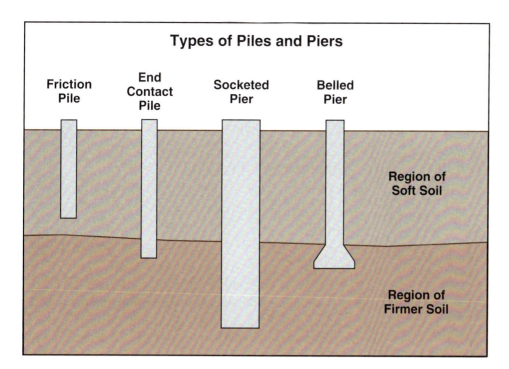

Figure 6.6 Deep foundations can be constructed in long supports known as piles or piers.

Piles — Deep foundation type that uses beams used to support loads. Develop load-carrying ability either through friction with the surrounding soil or by being driven into contact with rock or a load-bearing soil layer.

Pier — Deep foundation type that uses beams mounted on concrete wedges/blocks to support loads. *Also known as* Caissons *and* Belled Piers.

When a structure is intended to be built on a steep slope, such as beachfront or the side of a canyon, the foundation must be specially constructed to account for the slope. The steeper the slope is, the more critical the foundation design becomes. When the ground slope angle is severe, piles or piers are placed in the more dense lower soils. These deep elements act as vertical cantilevers to resist the lateral force of the building **(Figure 6.7)**. The vertical elements are connected with a tie beam.

Piles
Piles are driven into the ground and support a load by transferring the load either through friction with the surrounding soil, or through contact with rock or other stable soil layer. Materials used for beams include steel and precast concrete. Timber piles have been used for centuries and still may be used to support light loads. Factors that limit the use of timber piles include the possibility of decay and the length of available trees.

Piers
Post-and-pier foundations are a system of upright posts mounted to wedge-shaped concrete piers that transfer the weight of the structure to the ground. Construction of piers begins with drilling or digging a shaft, and then filling it with concrete. Then the post is attached to the top of the pier. When a pier is designed with a footing, it is known as a "belled" pier.

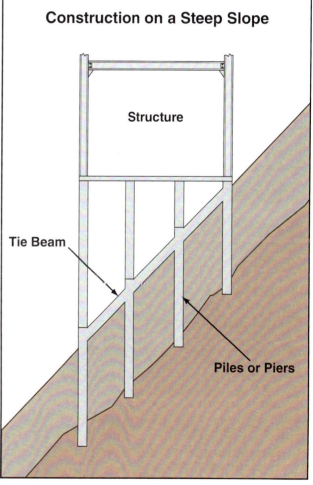

Figure 6.7 On a steep slope, piles or piers are driven into bedrock. The vertical elements are connected with a tie beam to resist the lateral force of the building.

Chapter 6 • Foundations

Caisson — Protective sleeve used to keep water out of an excavation for a pier.

Piers are sometimes referred to as **caissons**. More accurately, the caisson is the sleeve used to protect the excavation for the pier.

Foundation Walls

Foundation walls connect to the foundation and footer and encase a basement. Types of foundation walls are described in the following sections **(Figure 6.8)**.

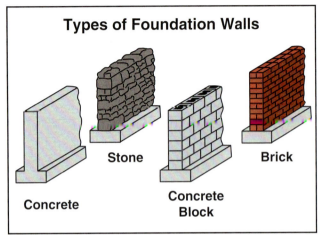

Figure 6.8 Foundation walls can be constructed with a wide range of materials to suit the needs of the structure and the soil composition of the land.

Concrete and Mortared Masonry

Concrete and **masonry** (brick or concrete block) secured with **mortar** are the materials most commonly used for foundation walls. These materials are durable against hazards associated with longterm exposure, including moisture and insects.

Concrete and mortared masonry foundation walls may develop visible cracks over time, but these cracks usually do not significantly affect the ability of the wall to support or distribute a load. However, any change in size or extension of cracks or fissures should be noted. Any vertical or horizontal misalignment along the length of a crack in a foundation wall indicates a movement or shift in the structure, which may indicate a change in the alignment of loads on structural components.

Stone

Not all stone masonry construction includes mortar. A distinguishing aspect of stone construction is the careful craftsmanship that may not require the use of any bonding mortar or cement: the stones are shaped or placed to form tight-fitting connections. Stone basement walls are usually found only in older buildings.

Foundation Wall — Vertical element of a foundation; rests on the foundation footers. May be full-story height as in a basement, or partial height. Materials often include poured concrete, or mortar elements such as block, brick, or stone.

Masonry — Bricks, blocks, stones, and unreinforced and reinforced concrete products.

Mortar — Cement-like liquid material that hardens and bonds individual masonry units into a solid mass.

Expanded Polystyrene (EPS) — Closed-cell foam used for a growing number of purposes including building insulation. Properties include rigidity, low weight, and formability.

Wood

Wood may be used in foundation walls in light frame construction or where the walls must be highly insulated. Wood foundations can be constructed at the same time as wood-frame buildings to save money. The wood must be treated with preservatives to resist decay.

NOTE: Chapter 7 includes information regarding wood construction.

EPS

Expanded polystyrene (EPS) can be used as a component of foundation walls. It may be placed on the outside of below-grade walls for insulation. Depending on its chemical composition, EPS may add to the fire load of a building. EPS must also be protected from UV light because sunlight will damage it. To protect EPS from fire and UV light, products such as stucco or drywall can easily be affixed to the outside surface of EPS.

Hollow EPS blocks can be filled with concrete to create **insulated concrete form (ICF) construction** **(Figure 6.9)**. ICF construction can be used for applications including:

- Foundation
- Above and below grade walls
- Other structural applications

EPS helps conserve cost and energy in the following ways:

- Conserves heat in cold weather
- Reduces the energy needed for air conditioning in warm weather
- Foundations limit the transfer of heat to the surrounding soil
- May be used in areas with a shallower frost line

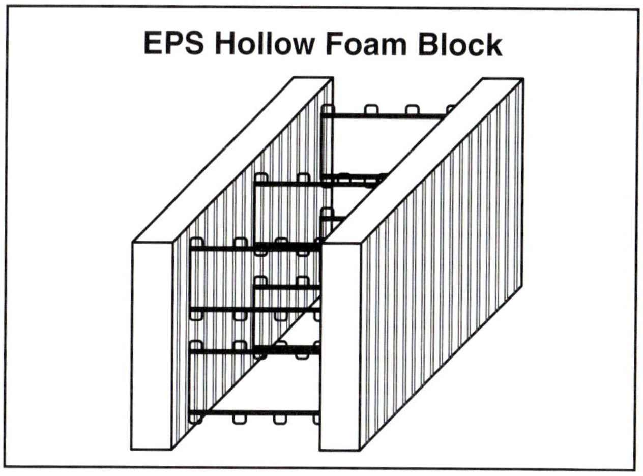

Figure 6.9 Hollow polystyrene blocks can connect together and be filled with concrete to provide insulation in a basement or other structural applications.

Building Settlement

After buildings are constructed, they will often shift to some degree. Settlement of foundations is the most frequent type of building movement, and all buildings are subject to some degree of settlement. Types of movement include:

- **Settlement** – Downward movement
- **Heaving** – Upward movement
- **Lateral displacement** – Outward movement

The effects of shifts may range from a creaking noise and no damage, to significant structural damage. Supports that shift or settle will alter the forces on the structural members above the foundation of the building. These altered load patterns may hasten structural collapse under fire conditions. Symptoms of settlement include:

- Distorted building frame
- Sloped floors
- Cracked walls and glass **(Figure 6.10)**
- Improperly working doors and windows
- Damaged building utilities and systems

> **Insulated Concrete Form (ICF) Construction** — Construction technique that uses hollow foam blocks with predetermined sizes and shapes. The blocks lock together and are filled with concrete to form structural supports.
>
> **Settlement** — Downward deformation of a building's structural elements. *Also known as* Settling.
>
> **Heaving** — Upward deformation of a building's structural elements
>
> **Lateral Displacement** — Sideways deformation of a building's structural elements

Figure 6.10 A settling or uneven foundation can cause structural instability all the way up to the roof level.

Settlement of a foundation can be either uniform or differential. Uniform settlement results in parts of a foundation settling at the same rate and minimal misalignment between structural members. Differential settlement can result in significant misalignment of structural members **(Figure 6.11)**. Causes of differential settlement include:

- Nonuniform soil conditions under the foundation
- Footings of different sizes
- Footings placed at different elevations
- Unequal loads on footings

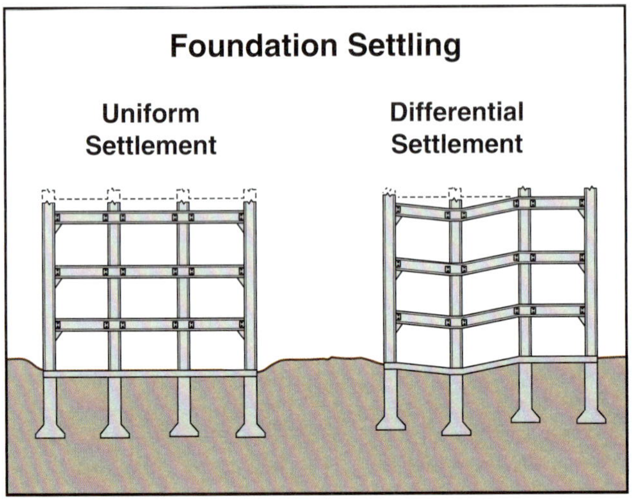

Figure 6.11 Differential settlement produces distortion between building components.

Shoring and Underpinning

Shoring is frequently necessary to support the structure until **underpinning** can be put into place **(Figure 6.12)**. For the purposes of this manual, *shoring* refers to temporary supports and *underpinning* refers to permanent supports.

Underpinning an existing foundation may be necessary because of changes over time including:

- Excessive settlement
- Increased load on a foundation
- Excavation on adjacent property
- Erosion of soil from under or around the foundation

The placement of shoring and underpinning components is difficult and often dangerous work. For example, when preparing to support a basement, an area must be excavated to place components. The necessary excavation work is often completed in an area with a limited amount of space, so it must be completed with small tools instead of excavation equipment.

If a collapse occurs in connection with shoring and underpinning work, the fire department typically is called upon to conduct a rescue operation. Such rescue operations always require significant caution and coordination.

NOTE: Refer to the IFSTA **Fire Service Technical Search and Rescue** manual for more information about shoring operations and structural collapse rescue techniques.

Shoring — General term used for lengths of timber, screw jacks, hydraulic and pneumatic jacks, and other devices that can be used as temporary support for formwork or structural components or used to hold sheeting against trench walls. Individual supports are called shores, cross braces, and struts.

Underpinning — The use of permanent supports to strengthening an existing foundation.

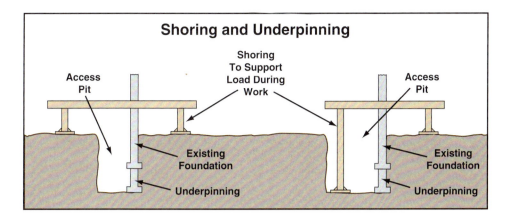

Figure 6.12 An existing wall may be supported with shores while permanent underpinning is placed.

Chapter Summary

Although foundations are normally not a significant factor in fire fighting, they do affect overall structural stability. Because soil conditions vary in different locations, engineers will use different types of foundations. Foundations can be shallow or deep depending on the soil properties and the building design. Foundations may also occasionally need to be reinforced through shoring and underpinning. Accidents involving shoring and underpinning may involve the fire department in rescue operations.

Review Questions

1. What two strategies are used to assess soil properties?
2. What factors influence the type and depth of a foundation?
3. What materials may be used in the construction of foundation walls?
4. What are the symptoms of settlement?
5. What different purposes do shoring and underpinning serve?
6. What changes in a building foundation may necessitate underpinning?

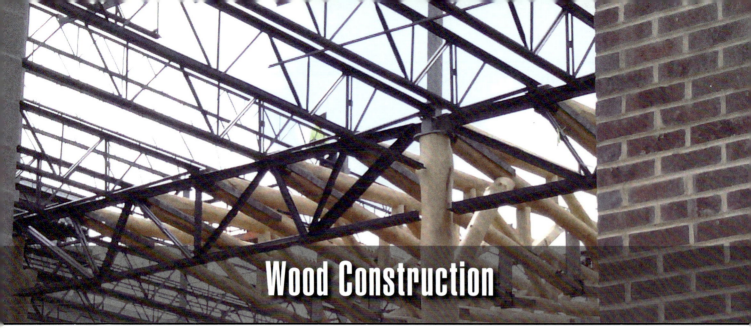

Wood Construction

Chapter Contents

Case History **181**	Ignition-Resistant Construction 200
Material Properties of Wood and	Calculating Structural Endurance under Fire Conditions .. 201
** Manufactured Components** **181**	**Wood Structural Systems** **202**
Solid Lumber 182	Light Wood Framing 203
Engineered Wood 183	Heavy Timber Framing 205
Panels 187	Post and Beam Framing 208
Firestopping 189	Box Beams and I-Beams 208
Exterior Wall Materials 190	Trusses 209
Brick or Stone Veneer 193	**Structural Collapse of Wood**
Interior Finish Materials 194	** Construction** **210**
Manufactured Components 194	**Chapter Summary** **211**
Quality Control of Lumber 195	**Review Questions** **211**
Combustion Properties of Wood 196	**Chapter Notes** **211**

chapter 7

Key Terms

Balloon-Frame Construction 203	Manufactured Components 194
Butt Joint 184	Nominal Dimension of Lumber 182
Cladding 192	Nonveneered Panel 188
Composite Panels 189	Oriented Strand Board (OSB) 188
Dimensional Lumber 182	Particleboard 188
Engineered Wood 183	Platform Frame Construction 204
Exterior Insulation and Finish Systems (EIFS) 191	Plywood 187
Finger Joint 185	Polyurethane 189
Glue-Laminated Beam 184	Polyvinyl Chloride (PVC) 187
Grain 183	Pyrolysis 197
Hygroscopic 200	R-Value 189
Ignition Source 197	Scarf Joint 185
I-Joist 208	Specific Gravity 183
Laminated Wood 184	Structural Insulated Panel (SIP) 189
Ledger Board 203	Surface-To-Mass Ratio 198
Lumber 195	Thermoplastic 187
	Veneered Walls 193

Chapter 7 • Wood Construction 179

Wood Construction

FESHE Outcomes Addressed In This Chapter

Fire and Emergency Services Higher Education (FESHE) Outcomes: *Building Construction for Fire Protection*

1. Describe building construction as it relates to firefighter safety, building codes, fire prevention, code inspection, firefighting strategy, and tactics.
2. Classify major types of building construction in accordance with a local/model building code.
3. Analyze the hazards and tactical considerations associated with the various types of building construction.
4. Explain the different loads and stresses that are placed on a building and their interrelationships.
5. Identify the function of each principle structural component in typical building design.
8. Identify the indicators of potential structural failure as they relate to firefighter safety.

Learning Objectives

After reading this chapter, students will be able to:

1. Describe materials used in wood construction.
2. Recognize combustion properties of wood.
3. Describe ignition-resistant construction.
4. Recognize the importance of calculating structural endurance under fire conditions.
5. Describe various types of wood structural systems.
6. Identify forces that may undermine the structural integrity of wood construction.

Chapter 7
Wood Construction

Case History

In spring 2010, a fire started at the rear of a single-family ranch-style house, and burned through to the attic. Initial attack was made through the front door. The crew progressed through the structure toward the rear of the house to attack fire spread in the attic. The second firefighter on the line stepped out of the structure onto a deck twelve feet above grade, without properly sounding the deck. He broke through the decking, and the nozzleman quickly pulled his partner back up onto the deck and into the structure.

This incident did not cause any fatalities or serious injuries, but easily could have escalated. Critical information was not communicated efficiently at this incident. For example, indoor crews were informed directly that the fire had originated at the back deck, but new incoming crews were not informed. Also, not all teams knew that the area below the deck had some fire spread.

Firefighters must maintain situational awareness, and watch out for each other. In fire conditions, wood quickly loses structural stability and can no longer support heavy loads such as firefighters navigating a structure.

Source: NEAR-MISS EVENT, NO INJURY OR DAMAGE #10-0000725

Wood has been used as a basic construction material for centuries and continues to be a fundamental structural material. Wood is used in a wide variety of building applications in all localities. This chapter includes the following topics:

- Material properties of wood and manufactured components
- Wood structural systems
- Structural collapse of wood construction

Material Properties of Wood and Manufactured Components

Wood has a unique position among building materials. It is cheap to produce and renewable; most of its manufacture occurs in nature. Types of wood used in construction are typically softwoods including:

Dimensional Lumber — Lumber with standard, nominal measurements for use in building construction. Dimensional lumber is also available in rough, green components with actual dimensions that match the nominal dimensions.

Nominal Dimension of Lumber — Actual dimensions of processed lumber do not match the nominal dimensions, within defined parameters. Historically, the two sets of dimensions were identical.

- Pine
- Fir
- Spruce

Some disadvantages to wood are related to the natural growth of a tree and include:

- Wood is never dimensionally true.
- Weather conditions can affect the size and shape of wood.
- Wood does not shrink or swell uniformly.
- Intrinsic defects include knots, knotholes, decay, insect damage, splits, and warping.
- Wood strength varies significantly with species, grade, age, and growth rate of the tree.
- Wood strength changes over time after components are placed in use.

Solid Lumber

Solid lumber includes **dimensional lumber**, boards, and timbers. The standard measurements of dimensional lumber match the stated measurements. Dimensional lumber is available in lengths from 8 to 24 feet (2.5 to 7 m) in 2-foot (600 mm) increments. The practice of matching standard and stated measurements is not followed for finished boards and timbers, which are typically described in **nominal dimensions** (Table 7.1).

Table 7.1 Dimensions of Softwood Lumber Products	
Nominal Size in inches (mm)	**Actual Dimension in inches (mm)**
2 in x 4 in (50 mm x 100 mm)	1½ in x 3½ in (38 mm x 89 mm)
4 in x 4 in (100 mm x 100 mm)	3½ in x 3 9/16 in (89 mm x 90.5 mm)
6 in x 6 in (150 mm x 105 mm)	5½ in x 5 5/8 in (140 mm x 143 mm)
2 in x 6 in (50 mm x 150 mm)	1½ in x 5 5/8 in (38 mm x 143 mm)
2 in x 8 in (50 mm x 200 mm)	1½ in x 7¼ in (38 mm x 185 mm)

Nominal and Dimensional Lumber

The difference between nominal and dimensional measurements arises because of the process of cutting a log into rough lumber, smoothing it, and shrinkage while drying. The dimensions of a piece of rough lumber will be reduced to a standard size in the finishing process. Advances in modern technology allow rough lumber to be rough-cut closer to the actual finished (nominal) size than historically possible.

Solid wood has a useful tensile strength comparable to some types of steel on the basis of strength to unit weight. Defects in wood, however, greatly reduce this comparison, so the standard tensile strength of wood is considered about 700 psi (4 900 kPa).

NOTE: The tensile strength of steel is explained in Chapter 9.

Moisture content is a significant factor in wood strength. As moisture leaves wood (naturally or through drying) after the tree is cut, the wood begins to decrease (shrink) in size and increase in strength. The moisture content of lumber can be controlled to any level; most structural lumber has 19 percent or less. Moisture is expressed in terms of **specific gravity**.

Another factor that affects wood strength is load direction: wood is stronger parallel to the **grain** than against the grain **(Figure 7.1)**. For example, the allowable compressive strength parallel to the grain varies from 325 to 1,700 psi (2 300 to 12 000 kPa) for commercially available grades and species of framing lumber. The difference between these measurements represents a variance of a factor of five. Other factors that will contribute to component strength include the type (material, shape, and size) of fasteners and applied position in respect to the grain of the wood.

> **Specific Gravity** — Mass (weight) of a substance compared to the weight of an equal volume of water at a given temperature. A specific gravity less than 1 indicates a substance lighter than water; a specific gravity greater than 1 indicates a substance heavier than water.

> **Grain** — Direction of growth of a tree. Loads aligned perpendicular to the grain are more sturdily supported; lumber will split more easily when cut parallel to the grain.

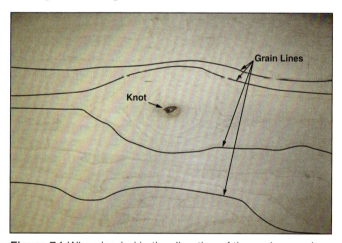

Figure 7.1 When loaded in the direction of the grain, wood strength is comparable to steel; defects in the grain can undermine that strength.

Figure 7.2 Engineered wood products take many forms and have properties unique to the materials and production method.

Engineered Wood

Engineered wood components are produced from a combination of wood particles and a bonding agent **(Figure 7.2)**. Components are rated according to the amount of weight they can carry once complete. Engineered wood products provide the advantages of strength and cost efficiency.

> **Engineered Wood** — A material manufactured by bonding pieces of wood with glue or resin to form finished shapes.

The disadvantages to engineered wood products include quick and unpredictable failure in fire conditions when unprotected. The most common types of engineered wood products are described in the following sections.

Engineered Wood Construction Terminology

Engineered wood components may be used interchangeably with their solid-dimension counterparts. Because of the increasing prevalence and usability of engineered components, light-wood construction and heavy timber construction are likely to include engineered wood materials. Construction using only engineered materials is known as an *engineered structural system*.

Lightweight construction is a term coined in the 1950s to refer to milled (light-wood) lumber in contrast to heavy timber. This term is becoming obsolete with the decrease of structures framed solely with solid-dimension wood.

> **Laminated Wood** — Material made of wood strips and resin, shaped, and bonded with heat and/or pressure.
>
> **Glue-Laminated Beam** — (1) Wooden structural member composed of many relatively short pieces of lumber glued and laminated together under pressure to form a long, extremely strong beam. (2) Term used to describe wood members produced by joining small, flat strips of wood together with glue. *Also known as* Glued-Laminated Beam *or* Glulam Beam.

Laminated Wood

Laminated wood products are made of flat strips of wood joined with glue **(Figure 7.3)**. Beams constructed in this way are known as **glue-laminated beams**. In addition to beams, laminated structural products can be formed into sizes and shapes that are not available from solid pieces cut from logs, including curves or varying cross sections **(Figure 7.4)**.

Figure 7.3 (left) Glulam beams are produced using flat strips of wood plus adhesive.

Figure 7.4 (above) Curved glulam beams can be manufactured in the particular curve intended for the purpose, as opposed to bending and shaping nominal lumber.

> **Butt Joint** — Connection between two parts made by simply securing end surfaces together without additional shaping at the ends; a simple but weak joint.

When necessary, short pieces of lumber can be joined to obtain the required length during the manufacturing process. Standard lumber or laminated members can be secured end-to-end using a number of techniques **(Figure 7.5)**. The **butt joint** is easy to produce but cannot be used where tensile stresses will be transmitted along the length of the beam. **Scarf** and **finger joints** can be used to transmit tensile stresses. The thickness of finished beams ranges from ¾ inch to 2 inches (19 to 50 mm). Finished beams may have depths ranging from 3 to 75 inches (75 to 1 900 mm) and lengths up to 100 feet (30 m). Laminated components may have comparable structural integrity to solid-wood components, under fire conditions, when protected.

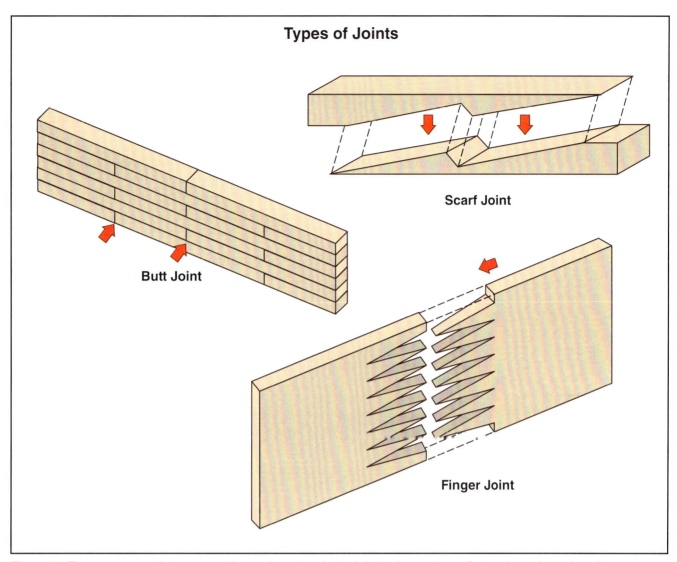

Figure 7.5 Three common joints are used in wood construction to join lumber and manufactured wood members into a required length beam.

Glulam Beams

Glulam beams are used frequently in heavy timber construction where greater length components are required **(Figure 7.6)**. Glulam beams react similarly to solid timbers under fire conditions. Current research indicates that the heat of a fire has essentially no effect on the adhesives that are used in contemporary glulam beams[1].

Scarf Joint — Connection between two parts made by the cutting of overlapping mating parts and securing them by glue or fasteners so that the joint is not enlarged and the patterns are complementary.

Finger Joint — Connection between two parts made by cutting complementary mating parts, and then securing the joint with glue.

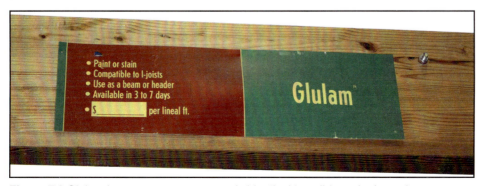

Figure 7.6 Glulam beams may appear nearly identical to solid nominal members.

> **CAUTION**
> All materials may fail when subjected to high enough temperatures over a long enough time.

Structural Composite Lumber

Because of increased efficiency in the process of harvesting and processing lumber, new products have been developed that use more materials that had historically been considered waste. One group of products, known as *structural composite lumber (SCL)*, use the outer fibers of a log as well as the inner portions traditionally used.

Laminated veneer lumber (LVL) uses sheets of veneer peeled from the outer portion of a log. These sheets of veneer are laminated in parallel alignment. LVL is used in I-joists and beam sections that are 1 3/4 to 3½ inches thick (45 to 90 mm) **(Figure 7.7)**.

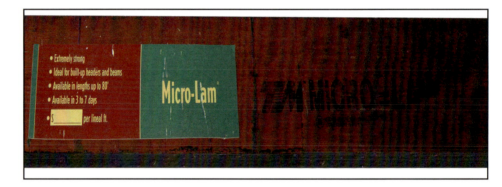

Figure 7.7 Laminated veneer lumber (LVL) beams feature a smooth face suitable for finishing work.

Parallel strand lumber (PSL) is made from veneers that are not as uniform as those used in LVL. These veneers produce odd-shaped strands that are coated with an adhesive and cured under pressure. PSL can be produced in standard sizes ranging from 2 to 8 feet in length (0.6 to 2.5 m). PSL is the strongest of the three SCL products and can be used for heavily loaded columns and long spans **(Figure 7.8)**.

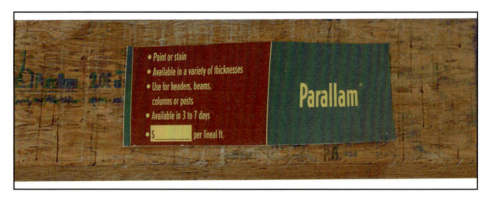

Figure 7.8 Parallel strand lumber (PSL) beams are created from smaller pieces of wood oriented in the same direction.

Laminated strand lumber (LSL) is made with long strands of wood up to 12 inches (300 mm) in length. The strands are bonded with a resin in a steam pressing process. LSL is typically used for short-span beams and columns.

Thermoplastic Composite Lumber

Thermoplastic composite lumber is a wood-like product made from wood fiber and polyethylene or **polyvinyl chloride (PVC)**, developed as an alternative to preservative-treated lumber. It is manufactured as boards in sizes comparable to sawn lumber and in various shapes as architectural trim. Thermoplastic composite lumber is not intended to be used in the structural framing of a building.

Thermoplastic composite lumber is primarily used in the construction of outside decks and railings **(Figure 7.9)**. Its main advantage is its resistance to weathering. Thermoplastic composite lumber is a combustible product with a flame spread rating of 80. Decks constructed of thermoplastic composite lumber may look at first glance like wood but under fire conditions will melt like plastic. These types of decks also burn black and sooty, unlike wood.

Figure 7.9 Thermoplastic composite lumber looks much like ordinary lumber but will behave like plastic under fire conditions. *Courtesy of Donny Howard.*

Panels

Wood panel products differ greatly from solid dimensional lumber. The available styles of wood panel products change over time because of available technology, especially in regard to composite types. Nonveneered components should not be trusted to maintain structural integrity if exposed to fire conditions. The following sections describe common wood panel products.

Plywood

Plywood panels are made up of several thin layers (veneers) rotary-sliced from rotating logs and glued together. Plywood is produced in standard sheets measuring 4 feet by 8 feet (1.2 m x 2.5 m). The direction of the grain of adjacent veneers is aligned at right angles to each other **(Figure 7.10)**. The grain of exterior veneers is oriented in the long dimension of the sheet. Plywood is used for applications including:

- Sheathing
- Concrete formwork
- Webs of composite beams
- Hulls of ships

> **Thermoplastic** — Plastic that softens with an increase of temperature and hardens with a decrease of temperature but does not undergo any chemical change. Synthetic material made from the polymerization of organic compounds that become soft when heated and hard when cooled.
>
> **Polyvinyl Chloride (PVC)** — Synthetic chemical used in the manufacture of plastics and single-ply membrane roofs.
>
> **Plywood** — Wood sheet product made from several thin veneer layers that are sliced from logs and glued together.

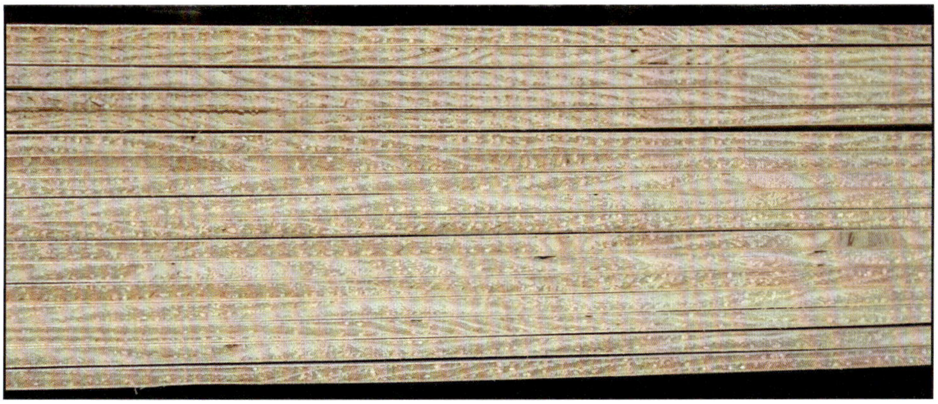

Figure 7.10 Plywood panels are used for many structural purposes, including the sheathing over a wood-frame building.

Nonveneered Panel — Lightweight wood construction panel manufactured from wood chips, strands, wafers, or sawdust and a bonding agent such as glue or resin. Used as sheathing, reinforcement of structural elements, and sub-flooring. Includes OSB, particleboard, waferboard.

Oriented Strand Board (OSB) — Wooden structural panel formed by gluing and compressing wood strands together under pressure. This material has largely replaced plywood and planking in applications including roof decks, walls, and subfloors.

Nonveneered Panels

Nonveneered panels are made of engineered wood formed into sheets using resin, heat, and/or pressure. Each type of nonveneered panel is formed from a different size and shape of wood piece as described below:

- Oriented strand board
- Particleboard
- Waferboard

Oriented strand board (OSB) uses long, strand-like wood particles compressed and glued into three to five layers **(Figure 7.11)**. The strands are oriented in the same direction in each layer, similar to the grain in the veneer layers in plywood. Because the direction of the strands is controlled, OSB panels are stronger and stiffer than waferboard or particleboard. OSB is widely used for sheathing and subflooring in wood-frame buildings.

Figure 7.11 Oriented strand board (OSB) is commonly used for sheathing.

Particleboard is not generally used for structural applications, although it may be used in lateral-force-resisting diaphragms. Because it can be manufactured in large sheets, particleboard is used for flooring in manufactured and mobile homes. Particleboard is made from wood particles bonded with synthetic resins under heat and pressure **(Figure 7.12)**. Individual wood particles can range in size from 1 inch (25 mm) to very fine. Particleboard panels may be single layer or multilayer. Particleboard can be manufactured in sizes up to 8 by 40 feet (2.5 x 12 m).

Particleboard — Wooden structural panel formed from wood particles and synthetic resins. *Also known as* Flakeboard, Chipboard, *or* Shavings board.

Figure 7.12 Particleboard is often used in protected applications to prevent it from soaking up available water and losing structural integrity.

Waferboard is similar to particleboard but uses larger wafer-like pieces of wood. OSB has almost entirely replaced waferboard for structural purposes.

Composite Panels

Composite panels serve several functions including insulation and structural support. Composite panels consist of a face and back panel of plywood or OSB bonded to a central core material. The core can be made of a variety of materials such as reconstituted fiber, paper honeycomb, or plastic foam.

One type of composite panel, the **structural insulated panel (SIP)**, consists of outer wood panels (usually OSB) with a plastic foam core between the panels **(Figure 7.13)**. The plastic foam is usually expanded polystyrene. New developments include the use of foams such as expanded **polyurethane** instead of polystyrene to increase fire resistance.

SIPs are manufactured under factory-controlled conditions and can be fabricated to fit nearly any building design. SIPs can be used to increase energy efficiency. The inner core can be up to 1 foot (300 mm) thick for large **R-values**. Special features can include precut holes for electrical and plumbing risers and preinstalled electrical outlets and conduits. Once in place, the inner surface of the SIP can be covered with wallboard and the outer surface covered with a siding. Therefore, construction with SIPs is difficult to identify as such without a preincident survey or opening the wall **(Figure 7.14)**.

Studs are not used with this system, and the SIPs are bonded directly together. In terms of structural collapse, these systems are as stable as the glues that hold the assemblies together. SIP systems are solid and resist fire spread especially when fire resistive sheeting and/or foam core are used.

> **Composite Panels** — Produced with parallel external face veneers bonded to a core of reconstituted fibers. *Also known as* Sandwich Panel.
>
> **Structural Insulated Panel (SIP)** — A composite panel used in structural applications; made of plastic foam between two outer wood panels, often oriented strand board (OSB).
>
> **Polyurethane** — A polymer formed by reacting an isocyanate with a polyol; used in many applications including floating insulating foams and floating ropes.
>
> **R-Value** — A measure of the ability of a material to insulate. Used in structural engineering and construction. Insulators with higher R-values are more effective.

Figure 7.13 One type of composite panel is constructed with a plastic foam core and OSB outer layers. *Courtesy of Ed Prendergast.*

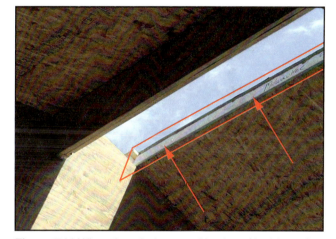

Figure 7.14 When the missing panel is placed in this roof assembly, the structural insulation roof panels will not be identifiable over the laminated wood arches. *Courtesy of Gregory Havel, Burlington, WI.*

Firestopping

To prevent the rapid spread of fire through the concealed spaces within combustible construction, building codes require fire stopping or fireblocking. Materials used for firestopping include:

- 2-inch (50 mm) nominal lumber
- Gypsum board

- Cement fiber board
- Batts or blankets of mineral wool, glass fiber, or other approved materials

The placement of firestopping is also specified in codes. Locations where firestopping is required include:

- Within stud walls at the ceiling and floor levels **(Figure 7.15)**
- At the connection points between vertical stud wall spaces and horizontal spaces
- Between stair stringers
- Behind fascia and other architectural features

In a platform-frame building, the plate installed on the top of the studs provides a fire stop that will block the spread of fire between floors within the walls. In balloon-frame buildings, however, firestopping must be provided in addition to the structural members.

Building codes require draftstopping in attic spaces with combustible construction. The draft stops can be constructed of materials including gypsum board, wood structural panels, 1-inch (25 mm) nominal lumber, or cement fiberboard **(Figure 7.16)**. The usual requirement is for the attic space to be subdivided into areas of 3,000 square feet (280 m^2).

Figure 7.15 Firestopping can be accomplished by placing nominal lumber horizontally to help stop vertical fire spread. *Courtesy of Dave Coombs.*

Exterior Wall Materials

In addition to the structural framing, the exterior walls of a wood-frame building include materials that provide resistance to environmental and pest infiltration. These *siding* materials may be chosen for their functional qualities or for aesthetic reasons. The underlayer components used with sidings may be chosen simply for their compatibility with the chosen siding.

Sheathing

Sheathing is a layer of material installed outside of the studs to provide structural stability, insulation, and an underlayer for the siding. The most common sheathings are plywood, OSB, particleboard, or exterior gypsum sheathing.

Building Wrap

A layer of building wrap between the sheathing and the siding acts as a vapor barrier **(Figure 7.17)**. The wrap reduces the infiltration of moisture and air. Modern synthetic building wraps are much more fire resistant than the felt or tar paper used in older installations.

Figure 7.16 Gypsum board can be used to block direct access to void spaces. *Courtesy of McKinney (TX) Fire Department.*

Figure 7.17 Building wraps are added over the sheathing and under the external siding, to prevent moisture damage to the frame and sheathing.

Figure 7.18 Commonly used sheathing materials include gypsum board and a protective insulation barrier.

Foam Insulation

Exterior insulation and finishing systems (EIFS) are used to increase the insulative properties of a building. Because foam insulation is combustible and because flame spreads rapidly over its surface, building codes impose stringent regulations on its use. Typically, a code will require that foam insulation include a facing that serves as a thermal barrier, such as gypsum wallboard, to prevent or slow surface ignition of the foam **(Figure 7.18)**.

The use of a combustible insulation does somewhat increase the possibility of a fire starting within the wall; for example, from an electrical malfunction igniting the insulation. The extent to which foam insulation will increase fire spread within a wood-framed wall depends on the existence of air space between the foam and the wall surface. If the space is completely filled with the foam, the fire has to burn upward through the material and will progress much more slowly than if it has easy access to large quantities of air. Fire fighting tactics require that the wall be opened and the insulating material thoroughly checked.

> **Exterior Insulation and Finish Systems (EIFS)** — Exterior cladding or covering systems composed of an adhesively or mechanically fastened foam insulation board, reinforcing mesh, a base coat, and an outer finish coat. *Also known as* Synthetic Stucco.

NOTE: Void spaces are discussed earlier in this chapter.

Noncombustible materials used for insulation include:

- Glass wool and rock wool in the form of batts or blankets with combustible paper or foil coverings
- Fiberglass **(Figure 7.19)**
- Some older vermiculite and batt insulation that may contain asbestos

Insulation can also take the form of loose-fill material including:

- Granulated rock wool
- Mineral wool and glass wool, either blown into stud spaces or manually packed
- Cellulose fiber and shredded wood, treated with water-soluble salts to reduce combustibility (fire in this material will slowly smolder).

Figure 7.19 Fiberglass batts, covered with either paper or foil, are commonly used to provide insulation in stud spaces. *Courtesy of McKinney (TX) Fire Department.*

Solid-fill foam insulations are applied as soft foam that hardens after application. The foam is treated with flame retardants before application. This style of insulation is gaining popularity and is referred to as "building icing" because of its appearance. Two types of solid-fill foam insulations are urea formaldehyde foam and polyurethane foam[2].

Siding Materials

Siding provides the exterior **cladding** of a wood-frame building. Sidings provide weather protection and can contribute to the appearance of a building. Some siding materials are noncombustible; other materials are combustible. Materials used for siding include:

- Aluminum
- Asphalt siding/shingles
- Cement board
- Plywood
- Stone
- Stucco
- Wood boards **(Figure 7.20)**
- Wood shingles
- Vinyl **(Figure 7.21)**

Cladding — Exterior finish or skin.

Figure 7.20 Wood shingles shed rainwater and provide a specific appearance to a building when used as exterior siding. *Courtesy of Ed Prendergast.*

Figure 7.21 Vinyl siding is a type of cladding known for its longevity.

The combustibility of a siding material can affect fire behavior by allowing exterior fire travel or ignition due to an exposure fire. When a building is remodeled, new siding material is frequently applied over the existing siding. Older buildings, therefore, may have multiple layers of siding.

Asbestos Components

Asbestos was commonly used in the U.S. from the 1930s until the 1970s. Asbestos is not commonly used in the U.S. today because it is known to cause respiratory ailments. Asbestos can be found modernly in a wide variety of building products including:

- Siding
- Insulation
- Construction adhesives
- Dry wall compound
- Electrical equipment
- Heating equipment
- Floor tile
- Ceiling tile

Asbestos sidings may be covered with another siding or remain exposed. The hazardous nature of asbestos can cause problems during overhaul. In these cases, environmental officials must be notified, per the AHJ.

In addition to respiratory hazards, asbestos fibers are also difficult to remove from contaminated clothing and other resources. Any activity near or affecting asbestos products must include proper PPE and decontamination procedures. All appropriate precautions must be exercised while in proximity to components that may potentially contain asbestos. The AHJ may require contaminated resources to be discarded after use. For additional information, refer to NFPA® 1851, *Standard of Selection, Care, and Maintenance of Protective Ensembles, Structural Fire Fighting and Proximity Fire Fighting.*

Veneered Walls — Walls with a surface layer of attractive material laid over a base of a common material.

Brick or Stone Veneer

A wood-frame building may be provided with an exterior brick or stone **veneer** to provide the architectural styling of those materials with the lower cost of wood construction. From the outside of the building, it can be difficult for a firefighter to visually determine whether brick work is structural or aesthetic. For example, the common indicators presented by the alignment of brick placement may not be used in bearing walls, and may be mimicked in veneer walls **(Figure 7.22)**.

Veneers must be tied to the wood frame wall at intervals of 16 inches (400 mm). Over time, the metal ties may corrode. A brick or stone veneer alone does not significantly affect fire behavior in a wood-frame building, but it does add to the thermal insulating value of the wall.

Fire spread can also occur in open spaces between the veneer and the building wrap. Under fire conditions, the external layer of a brick or stone veneer building protects the wood frame from external exposure. Veneer adds little structural support.

NOTE: See Chapter 8 for more information on brick construction.

Figure 7.22 Brick veneer applied to a wood frame will give the appearance of noncombustible construction. *Courtesy of Ed Prendergast.*

Interior Finish Materials

The interior walls of wood-frame buildings can be left exposed with no interior finish, as is done in small buildings such as garages or sheds. Such buildings are classified as Type V-B (wood frame, unprotected). When the structural framing of a wood-frame building, including the floor and roof construction, is provided with protection to achieve a 1-hour fire resistance, the building can be classified as Type V-A (wood frame, protected). If a wood-frame building is equipped with an automatic sprinkler system, the codes may permit the elimination of the 1-hour structural fire resistance. Additionally, a code may permit the elimination of the structural fire resistance for roof members located more than 20 feet (6 m) above the floor level.

Figure 7.23 Gypsum board provides a measure of fire resistance. *Courtesy of Gregory Havel, Burlington, WI.*

In most occupancies, an interior finish is provided to enhance appearance and provide a measure of thermal insulation. The interior of a wood-frame building can be finished using a number of materials including ordinary plywood or OSB.

As indicated in the firestopping section earlier in this chapter, gypsum board or plaster are commonly used where a specified degree of fire resistance is required. A typical means of adding or increasing fire resistance is through the use of 5/8 inch (15.5 mm) gypsum board attached to the studs and ceiling joists **(Figure 7.23)**. Several specific methods for utilizing gypsum board are listed in the *Underwriters Laboratories Fire Resistance Directory*. Plaster is not often used in modern construction because it requires a relatively large amount of labor.

During overhaul, firefighters can usually breach gypsum board easily. Opening the wall aids firefighters in locating fire travel in light wood-frame construction. Some occupancies, such as schools and correctional facilities, may use gypsum board produced with a fiberglass mesh to resist impact as a building hardening measure. Impact-resistant gypsum board is indistinguishable from ordinary gypsum board, but will prove more difficult to penetrate with hand tools.

Innovation with Dangerous Implication

As discussed throughout this manual, innovations intended to reduce costs and improve efficiency often do so at the cost of safe fire fighting operations. In addition to impact-resistant gypsum boards, for example, a new type of acoustic board adds a steel sheet between two drywall panels. This addition is intended to improve the speech intelligibility or other sound qualities of a space. Unintended consequences in fire conditions include increased difficulty in forcible entry, extinguishment, and overhaul.

Manufactured Components — Structural elements constructed in a factory and shipped to the construction site.

Manufactured Components

Manufactured components are prefabricated and shipped to the construction site for placement. Manufacturing items at a distance from the job site permits greater quality control and more efficient use of materials than assembling them at the construction site. Materials used as manufactured components include:

- Adhesives
- Dimensional lumber
- Metal fasteners
- Panels

> **Lumber** — Lengths of wood prepared for use in construction; items are graded for strength and appearance.

Quality Control of Lumber

To control some variables of wood, **lumber** can be graded (evaluated) for both structural strength and appearance **(Figure 7.24)**. Lumber with a higher grade is more costly. In a given structure, only a few critical columns or beams may require a high structural grade. Less expensive, lower grade materials may be specified in some applications as a cost-cutting measure.

Wood panel products are also graded for their structural use and their exposure durability **(Figure 7.25)**. A grade stamp on the back of a structural panel indicates its intended structural application and its suitability for exposure to water. Span ratings are different for roof sheathing and subflooring because roof supports are often spaced wider apart than floor supports.

Figure 7.24 Lumber grading stamps may simply indicate the quality of the finished product.

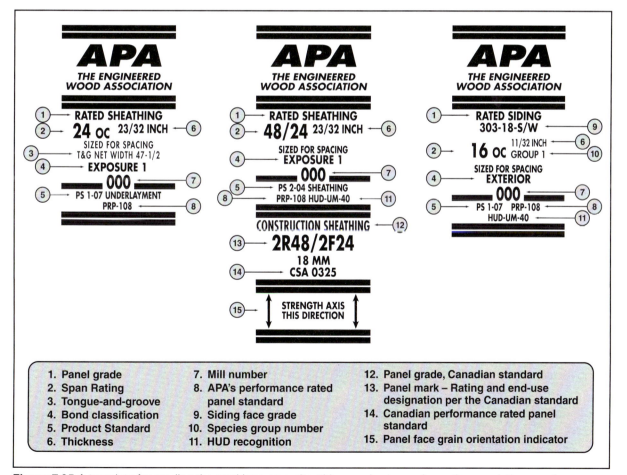

Figure 7.25 A template for reading the markings on a sheathing grade stamp shows three variations on the presentation of information. *Source: American Plywood Association.*

Combustion Properties of Wood

One serious and fundamental drawback to wood as a building material is its combustibility. Despite the numerous advantages of using wood as a construction material, the structural members provide a large amount of fuel for combustion. The relative hazard of a combustible material, such as wood, is a function of several variables, described in the following sections.

Life Safety and Fire Fighting Tactic Research

Wood construction has long been known to present a fire hazard because the support system itself contributes to the fire load. With numerous changes in component dimensions, materials, and applications, the range of topics available in the subject of wood construction have increased substantially. Changing collapse time frames is particularly relevant in wood construction buildings. To quantify the implications of these changes, several agencies and organizations have published results of tests and studies on a range of topics to inform first responders of trends and hazards in the job.

Organizations that produce tested and quantified studies with discrete results include:

- Underwriters Laboratory (UL) – Uses hands-on research to gather data on fire attack tactics that have changed as building technology changes[3].
- National Institute for Occupational Safety and Health (NIOSH) – Alert on the dangers of lightweight wood construction[4].
- National Institute of Standards and Technology (NIST) – Test burns including simulated living environments to inform the current research on topics such as the amount of time between the ignition and full development of fires[5].

Reports and findings from actual fire service experience, and recommendations for future safety:

- NFPA® online publication – Information on the failure rates of dimensional lumber to lightweight and engineered lumber[6]. This information is essential in evaluating "how buildings come down."
- NFPA® Fire Analysis and Research Department – Twenty percent of firefighter fatalities between 1997 and 2006 can be attributed to structural collapse[7].
- Near Miss and Line of Duty Death (LODD) reports – Hazards of the job and to help promote safe practices.
- Firefighter Nation – One example of a trade publication that includes collections of critical information such as collapse times for different types of construction[8] and tactical considerations[9].

Ignition Temperature

Generally speaking, materials with relatively low ignition temperatures are easier to ignite than materials with high ignition temperatures. Many factors influence the burning of wood, and ignition temperatures are difficult to measure accurately because of variability in the following:

- Density of the wood
- Size and form of the wood

- Moisture content (humidity)
- Rate of heating
- Nature of the heating source
- Air supply

Ignition of wood occurs when an **ignition source** of sufficient intensity is applied to the wood. The ignition source, such as a flame, must produce enough heat to raise the temperature of the wood to a point where **pyrolysis** begins. Pyrolysis is the thermal decomposition of wood and begins at a temperature somewhere below approximately 392°F (200°C).

The initial products of pyrolysis are the release of water retained in the wood and carbon dioxide. Because these two products are noncombustible, the ignition process is reversible if the ignition source is removed. As the temperature of wood is increased, additional products are combustible and increase in quantity. Eventually, a point is reached where the chemical process is self-sustaining and produces flame.

Ignition Source — Mechanism or initial energy source employed to initiate combustion, such as a spark that provides a means for the initiation of self-sustained combustion.

Pyrolysis — Thermal or chemical decomposition of a solid material by heating, generally resulting in the lowered ignition temperature of the material; the pre-ignition combustion phase of burning during which heat energy is absorbed by the fuel, which in turn gives off flammable tars, pitches, and gases; often precedes combustion. Pyrolysis of wood releases combustible gases and leaves a charred surface. *Also known as* Pyrolysis Process *or* Sublimation.

Pyrolysis and Ignition Temperatures

Some evidence indicates that pyrolysis and ignition can occur at temperatures lower than normally required if the wood is subjected to a temperature higher than ambient but lower than the ignition temperature. For example, wood framing in a wall close to a stove chimney may not ignite for years, but may eventually ignite after exposure to heat at a temperature below the original ignition temperature.

Heat of Combustion

The heat of combustion of a fuel is the total amount of thermal energy that can be released if the fuel is completely burned. The heat of combustion is measured in British Thermal Units (Btu) per pound or kilojoules per gram (kJ/g). Heat of combustion is significant because the output from each wood component can be substantial.

When an item is burned thoroughly, the thermal energy released during the fire can be calculated as the weight of the item multiplied by the heat of combustion. This number is considered theoretical because most fires do not consume all items completely. The heat of combustion is used as a baseline for calculating the full potential of a fire. For example, the thermal energy potentially available in wood frame structures with many tons (tonnes) of wood is large. In contrast, the potential thermal energy available from a similar fire-resistive or noncombustible building is limited.

CAUTION
Many variables affect fire conditions. No single variable can reliably predict fire behavior or intensity.

Surface-To-Mass Ratio — Relationship between the available surface area of the fuel and the mass of the fuel; used to predict the rate of fire consumption of combustible material.

Surface Area and Mass

Flaming combustion takes place at the surface of the material where the gaseous products of pyrolysis can combine with the surrounding air **(Figure 7.26)**. Greater surface area for a given mass of wood permits a more rapid combining of fuel vapors and air for combustion and, therefore, an overall greater rate of burning. The **surface-to-mass ratio** of wood has great significance in fire fighting **(Figure 7.27)**. For example, heavy timber components burn slowly and can retain their structural integrity longer than light-frame structural lumber members.

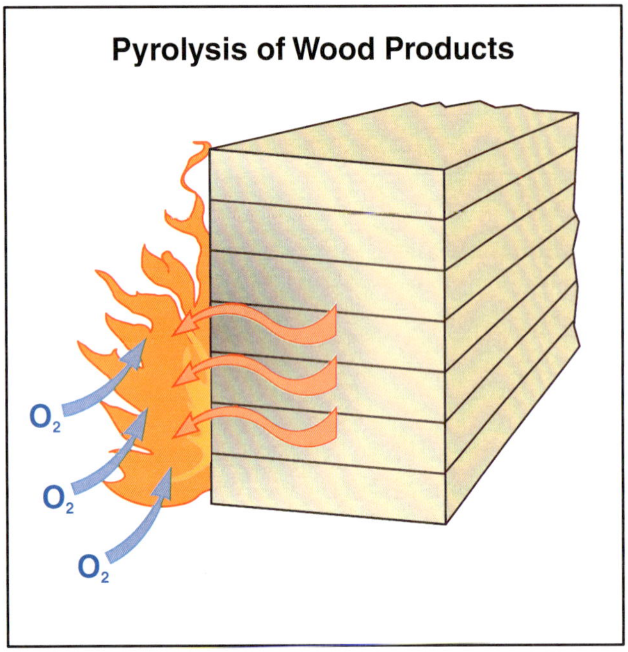

Fire-Retardant Treatment of Wood

Wood can be treated with a fire retardant to greatly reduce its combustibility **(Figure 7.28)**. Treated wood resists ignition and has higher fire endurance when compared with nontreated wood, but is not classified as fire-resistive.

Building codes permit the use of fire-retardant treated wood for certain applications in Type I (fire-resistive) and Type II (noncombustible) construction. For example, the *International Building Code® (IBC)* allows fire-retardant treated wood in nonload-bearing partitions where the required fire resistance is two hours or less.

The two main methods of fire-retardant treatment are surface coating and pressure impregnation. Surface coating is used primarily to reduce the flame spread rating of wood **(Figure 7.29)**. Pressure impregnation of wood affects the whole component, and is permanent when used under proper conditions.

Figure 7.26 Flaming combustion occurs at the surface of wood products as the fuel products of pyrolysis evolve from the wood and combine with oxygen in the air.

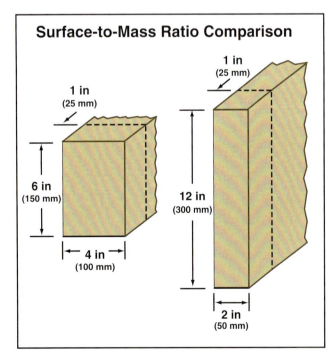

Figure 7.27 The piece of wood on the right, with a higher surface-to-mass ratio, would fail in a fire before the one on the left, despite the fact that they have the same mass.

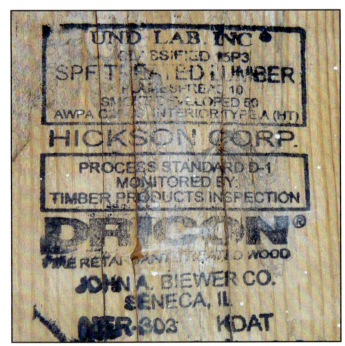

Figure 7.28 A full stamp used on fire-retardant wood can include significant information such as the manufacturer and any applicable ratings. *Courtesy of Gregory Havel, Burlington, WI.*

Pressure Impregnation of Wood Process

Pressure impregnation of wood is completed using the following steps:

- Wood is placed in a large vacuum cylinder.
- The vacuum draws air out of the cells of the wood.
- A solution containing the fire-retardant chemical is introduced into the cylinder and the cylinder is pressurized.
- The pressure forces the fire-retardant chemicals into the cells of the wood.

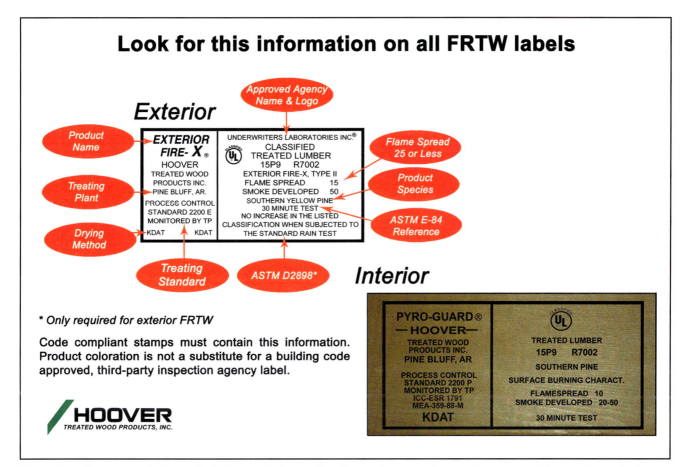

Figure 7.29 Some manufacturers include a guide for reading the markings used on lumber treated with specific products. *Courtesy of Hoover Wood Products.*

Most fire-retardant chemicals operate by accelerating the formation of charring in the wood when the wood is exposed to heat. The charring reduces the formation of volatile gases in the wood and slows flaming combustion. The chemical reaction of the fire retardant is intended to occur at lower temperatures than are developed in fire conditions.

Disadvantages and limitations to fire-retardant treatments include:

- Water soluble chemicals are not approved for use in applications exposed to uncontrolled or high humidity.

Chapter 7 • Wood Construction

- Compliance with approved usage cannot be proven after application.
- Fire-retardant treatment reduces wood strength; allowable stresses must be matched to the values indicated after treatment.

New fire-retardant treatments and wood products are continually under development. A number of fire-retardant chemicals are available; most fire-retardant products are proprietary and their exact formulations are not available. The fire-retardant treatments most commonly used are combinations of inorganic or organic salts. Any of the following chemicals may be used in the treatment:

- Ammonium phosphate
- Ammonium sulfate
- Boric acid
- Zinc chloride
- Sodium dichromate
- Borax

Hygroscopic — Ability of a substance to absorb moisture from the air.

Fire-retardant treatments used in the 1980s were somewhat **hygroscopic**. In some cases, for example in attic spaces, fire-retardant treated plywood reacted with the moisture in the air when exposed to elevated temperature and became brittle and crumbly. After three to five years, the roofs sagged unevenly.

Figure 7.30 Exposed wood floor construction in a residential basement will not protect the subflooring, engineered I-beams, and small-diameter steel column under fire conditions. *Courtesy of Ed Prendergast.*

Void Spaces

Void spaces can result in many square feet (square meters) of combustible surface area near large volumes of air. Combustible voids inherent in lightweight and engineered construction provide paths for the rapid spread of fire through a structure. Fire-resistive finishes will delay the entrance of fire into the void spaces, as long as they are uncompromised. Once the framing members are exposed to a fire, rapid failure of the structural system must be anticipated. Where truss joists are used in floor construction, fire may spread parallel to and perpendicular to the truss joists. Firefighters may not be able to determine the full extent of fire.

Frequently, especially in residential construction, the flooring will consist of plywood or OSB subflooring with a carpet or tile floor surface. The thin subflooring will fail within minutes when exposed to significant fire. A further area of concern is the possible existence of an unfinished ceiling over a basement space, where firestopping or other barriers may not be intact **(Figure 7.30)**.

Ignition-Resistant Construction

As urban development encroaches into rustic wildland areas, fires in highly flammable vegetation can rapidly engulf and destroy structures **(Figure 7.31)**. Light wood-frame construction is especially vulnerable. Wildland/urban interface development, and its vulnerability to wildland fires, has been particularly serious in the western part of the United States. To protect property in these areas, jurisdictions may adopt codes that require buildings to be ignition-resistant. For example, the International Code Council publishes the *International Wildland-Urban Interface Code.*

Ignition-resistant construction is different from fire-resistive construction.

For example, unprotected steel components will resist ignition but may not have high resistance against fire. Applicable requirements for ignition-resistant construction may include:

- Fire-resistant roof coverings to protect against flaming embers (Chapter 11).
- An exterior wall that is either noncombustible or that has a 1-hour fire-resistive rating when exposed from the outside.
- Limitation on the size of attic and under-floor vents and their protection with corrosion-resistant screens.

The specific requirements for ignition-resistant construction will vary with the severity of the hazard in a given area. Factors used to evaluate the hazard severity in a given location include:

- Ground slope
- Clear space around property
- Water supply
- Climate

Figure 7.31 Structures built in an urban/wildland interface without a defensible space around them are in special danger of destruction due to fire. *Courtesy of Dave Coombs.*

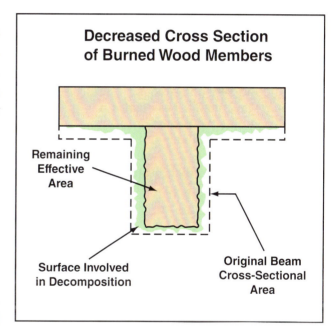

Figure 7.32 The cross-sectional area of a wood member gradually decreases as it burns.

Calculating Structural Endurance under Fire Conditions

Because they are more massive and have a lower surface-to-mass ratio, heavy timbers display greater structural endurance under fire conditions than members used in light-frame construction. The integrity of a wood structural member deteriorates as the wood is consumed unless it is somehow protected, as explained earlier in this chapter.

Wood that is allowed to burn through will gradually lose mass and stability until it can no longer support the applied loads **(Figure 7.32)**. The fire resistance of heavy timber columns and beams has been tested with the standard ASTM E-119 fire, and equations have been developed to estimate the reactions. For example, one test is used for beams exposed to fire on three sides. This equation is applicable to timber members with nominal dimensions 6 inches (150 mm) or greater. A different equation is used for components exposed to fire on four sides or for columns.

The structural integrity of heavy timber framing in an actual fire situation must always be viewed conservatively because the numerical values needed for an analytical solution are simply not available in the course of an incident.

Equations are primarily used for analytical purposes ahead of an incident. An engineer designing heavy timber construction will account for factors including:

- Likelihood of the collapse of roof or floor decks
- Methods used to join the joists, beams, and columns **(Figure 7.33)**
- Integrity of timber connections under fire conditions
- Suitability of protection of connectors

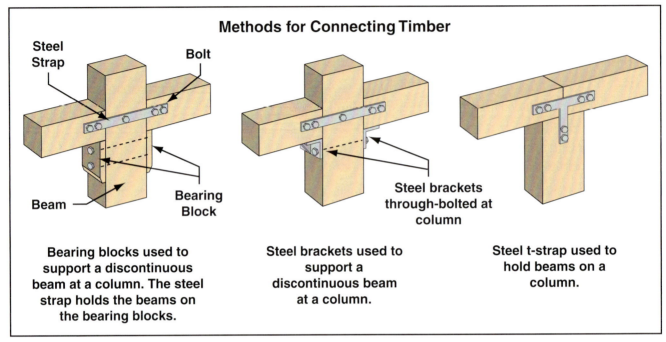

Figure 7.33 Timber members may be connected using metal fasteners.

Wood Structural Systems

Wood is so commonly used in frame structural systems that "frame buildings" are generally understood to be constructed of wood even though other similar structures are constructed of steel and concrete.

NOTE: Steel construction is discussed in Chapter 9; concrete construction is discussed in Chapter 10.

The wood framing systems most frequently encountered can be broadly classified into two basic types: light-wood framing and heavy timber framing. These framing systems may be supported with beams or trusses. Other wood construction types that may be encountered include:

- Pole construction
- Log construction
- Prefabricated panel construction

Smaller wood-frame structures, such as private garages and single-family dwellings, may be constructed using only carpentry techniques. Large or custom-designed wood structures require engineering analysis. Because of labor costs and limitations in the basic strength of wood, most wood-frame buildings do not exceed three stories. In contrast, engineered wood structures can be built several stories high.

Light Wood Framing

Light wood framing uses nominal lumber that is 2-inch (50 mm) at its smallest dimension. The walls are formed by attaching panels to studs that are spaced according to the dimensions of the uprights and the required stability. The floors are supported by solid joists, truss joists, or wood I-joists. Inclined roofs are supported by light trusses (rafters).

Balloon Framing

In **balloon frame construction**, the exterior wall studs are continuous from the foundation to the roof **(Figure 7.34)**. Joists that support the second floor rest on **ledger boards** recessed into the vertical studs.

The vertical combustible spaces between the studs in balloon frame construction provide a channel for the rapid travel of fire between building levels. Unlike timber framing, light wood framing is usually not left exposed. The framing is usually covered with an interior finish of plaster or drywall. The interior finish will act to slow the spread of fire into the stud spaces; however, a fire may penetrate the interior finish through penetrations for electrical fixtures, plumbing, or heating.

A fire in a balloon frame building can be difficult to control. Once fire originates in or enters the stud space, it can readily travel from the vertical cavity into the floor joists and into the attic space **(Figure 7.35)**. For example, fire issuing from an attic may give arriving firefighters the impression that the fire originated in the attic when it may have originated in the basement and traveled through the stud wall.

> **Balloon Frame Construction** — Type of structural framing used in some single-story and multistory wood frame buildings; studs are continuous from the foundation to the roof, and there may be no fire stops between the studs.
>
> **Ledger Board** — Horizontal framework member, especially one attached to a beam side that supports the joists. *Also known as* Ribbon Board.

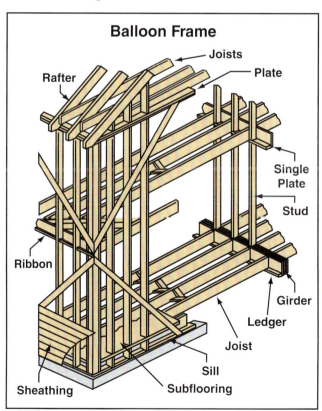

Figure 7.34 Balloon frame construction features open void spaces that may span from the foundation to the attic.

Figure 7.35 A balloon frame house is often built with channels in that can contribute to fire spread. *Courtesy of Wil Dane.*

Platform Frame Construction — (1) Type of framing in which each floor is built as a separate platform, and the studs are not continuous beyond each floor. *Also known as* Western Frame Construction. (2) A construction method in which a floor assembly creates an individual platform that rest on the foundation. Wall assemblies the height of one story are placed on this platform and a second platform rests on top of the wall unit. Each platform creates fire stops at each floor level restricting the spread of fire within the wall cavity.

Shrinkage in lumber occurs to a greater degree in the cross-sectional dimensions than in its length. The continuous studs of balloon framing have the advantage of minimizing the effects of lumber shrinkage that can occur over time as the lumber dries and loses its moisture content. As dried lumber is more commonly used in modern structures, however, the advantages of balloon framing have diminished.

Historically, *balloon frame* refers to the fragile appearance of the thin, closely spaced studs compared to the more massive members used in the earlier timber construction style. Balloon framing has not been widely used since the 1920s, although many balloon frame buildings remain.

Platform Framing

In **platform framing** (also sometimes known as *Western framing*), the exterior wall vertical studs are not continuous to the second floor **(Figure 7.36)**. The first floor is constructed as a platform upon which the exterior vertical studs are erected. The second floor is also constructed as a platform and the second floor studs are erected on the second floor.

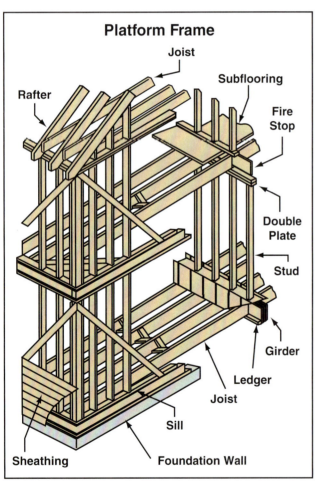

Figure 7.36 Platform frame construction includes independent construction platforms for each level.

Construction of Platform Framing

The construction of a platform frame building begins with the following steps:

Step 1: Attach a wood sill to the foundation, usually with bolts.

Step 2: Attach a header and floor joists or trusses to the sill.

Step 3: Attach subflooring to the floor joists to form a floor deck.

The first floor wall framing with a top and bottom plate is usually laid out horizontally on the floor deck and then raised into its vertical position. When the first floor walls are in position and braced, the second floor joists are erected on the top plates of the first floor walls.

From a construction standpoint, platform frame buildings are easier to erect than balloon frame buildings. This type of construction uses shorter, more easily handled lengths of lumber **(Figure 7.37)**. The flooring of each story can be used as a platform on which to work while erecting additional walls and partitions.

Platform framing is more prone to shrinkage than balloon framing because platform framing makes use of more horizontal members in its frame than a balloon frame building **(Figure 7.38)**. The shrinkage can produce greater vertical movement at different points. This vertical movement can cause undesirable effects such as cracking of plaster and misalignment of door and window openings. Modern use of kiln-dried lumber minimizes this effect.

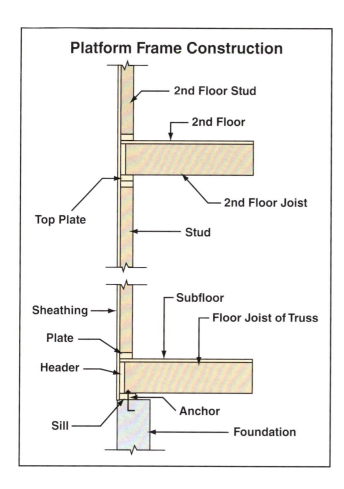

Figure 7.37 (left) A wall in platform frame construction includes fire stops at each level.

Figure 7.38 (above) Platform-frame building has studs that are not continuous from floor to floor. *Courtesy of Ed Prendergast.*

Heavy Timber Framing

Type IV, Heavy Timber (mill) construction, is characterized by heavy wooden structural interior supports with a masonry exterior **(Figure 7.39)**. Type IV construction is more similar to Type III (exterior protected) than Type V (wood frame), but is included here because of the wooden components.

NOTE: Masonry walls and construction are discussed in Chapter 8.

Figure 7.39 Heavy-timber framing uses columns not less than 8 inches by 8 inches thick (200 mm x 200 mm). *Courtesy of Vermont Timber Works.*

Identifiable features of heavy timber framing include:
- Trusses or beams can be used to support the roof.
- The exterior walls are nonload-bearing panels with an exterior siding that may include any of several materials including corrugated sheet metal.

- Internal support columns are not less than 8 x 8 inches (200 x 200 mm) and the beams (except roof beams) are not less than 6 x 10 inches (150 x 250 mm) **(Figure 7.40)**.

Figure 7.40 Atypical heavy-timber framing may use whole trees, stripped of their bark, as structural components. *Courtesy of Scott Strassburg.*

Heavy Timber and Mill Construction

Heavy timber and mill construction are separate styles but share innovations. Modern heavy timber construction is a descendent (evolution) of mill construction. Because of their similarities, references to these styles are often used as interchangeable. Building codes include both styles in the language for Type IV construction.

Historically, heavy timber construction evolved from hand-hewn wooden timbers that were painstakingly cut from logs. Until the development of water-powered sawmills in the 19th century, the production of individual boards was a slow and laborious procedure.

The mill construction design was an improvement on the original heavy timber design in the attempt to create a style of building that would provide the greatest resistance to fire loss. Strategies included the use of only large-dimension timber and masonry exterior, and eliminating all void spaces. The absence of concealed spaces in mill construction is a significant advantage because firefighters can easily access all fire areas. Mill construction was used extensively in factories, mills, and warehouses in the 19th and early 20th centuries. Many old buildings of this type remain in use.

The advantages of mill construction can be significantly lessened when a mill building undergoes a change of occupancy. Many older mill-style buildings have been converted to residential occupancies, which results in the subdivision of floor space into residential units. These divisions can lead to the creation of concealed spaces when partitions and ceilings are installed in individual units.

Codes specify unique characteristics that differentiate Type IV (heavy timber) mill construction from Type III (exterior protected) masonry construction. As indicated in this chapter, the two primary differences between these construction types are:

- Type IV (heavy timber) has thicker dimensions of (solid or laminated) wood structural members
- Type IV (heavy timber) does not allow combustible concealed spaces

Other differences between the two construction types are specified in the codes. For example, codes indicate unique dimensions, attachment joints, and materials used in flooring and roofing surfaces for Type IV and Type III construction. Laminated members may also be used with dimensions that are slightly different from the wood members.

The fire resistance requirements for the structural elements of Type IV construction are posted by the *International Building Code® (IBC)* (**Table 7.2**). Many of the structural components are not given a fire resistance rating; instead, minimum dimensions are specified.

Table 7.2
Fire-Resistance Requirements for Mill Construction

Building Element	Fire Resistance in Hours
Structural Frame (Columns and beams, girders, trusses, and spandrels connected to the columns.)	HT
Bearing Walls Exterior Interior	 2 1 or HT
Nonbearing exterior walls and partitions	0 to 3 depending on occupancy and separation distance
Nonbearing interior walls and partitions	See below
Floor construction	HT
Roof Construction	HT

Members designated HT (Heavy Timber) are required to have minimum dimensions not less than the following:

Nominal Dimensions for Sawn Lumber

	Width, inches (mm)	Depth
Columns		
Supporting Floors	8 (203)	8 (203)
Supporting Roofs	6 (152)	8 (203)
Floor Framing	6 (152)	10 (254)
Roof Framing	4 (102)	6 (152)

Source: International Code Council, 2006 *International Building Code®*, Table 601 and Table 602.4

Figure 7.41 Post and beam framing is heavier than light-frame construction but lighter than timber construction. *Courtesy of Ed Prendergast.*

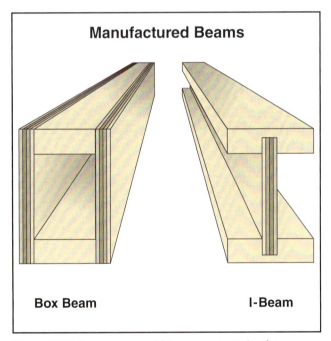

Figure 7.42 Box beams and I-beams are made of a variety of materials arranged strategically for a determined purpose.

I-Joist — Engineered wood joists with an "I" shaped cross section. Commonly used in modern roof and floor construction.

Post and Beam Framing

Post and beam framing is a form of wood-frame construction with columns (posts) and beams that use dimensions smaller than those used in heavy timber framing but greater than those used in light-frame construction. Structural members are spaced according to the loads they are rated to support **(Figure 7.41)**.

The posts and beams used in the framing create square or rectangular shapes that must be braced using diagonal bracing or the use of wall panels. In both heavy timber framing and post and beam framing, the interior wood surface is usually left exposed. The exposed wood framing eliminates combustible voids. Architecturally, the exposed surface of the wood creates an attractive, rustic finish.

Post and beam construction was once fairly common; it has enjoyed some resurgence and is frequently used in rustic-style dwellings and small storage buildings. This style of construction is usually more labor intensive than light-frame construction.

Box Beams and I-Beams

Box beams and I-beams can be manufactured in several ways **(Figure 7.42)**. The vertical webs can use a range of thicknesses of plywood, laminated veneer lumber, or oriented strand board.

The flanges of the I-beam can be made of laminated veneer lumber or solid wood lumber. The flanges resist common bending stresses, and the web provides shear resistance. Wood I-beams are frequently used for floor joists and rafters in the framing of roofs.

The replacement of dimensional lumber with engineered wood products is becoming more common because the components are economical, resource efficient, and can be custom-built with few application limitations. Engineered wooden joists, known as **I-joists**, are constructed of three engineered wood components that are bonded together to form an I-shaped cross-section. An I-joist consists of top and bottom flanges of a range of widths bonded to webs with a range of depths.

Engineered I-joists have many structural and economic advantages over conventional wood joists. I-joists are increasingly common in floor supports in residential and non-residential occupancies. A primary safety limitation of engineered wood systems is the possibility of swift collapse under fire conditions, especially if void spaces are not protected by a non-combustible covering or sprinkler system.

Trusses

Light-frame trusses have become popular for roof framing where the spans are small or moderate. Light wood frame trusses use a series of 2-inch (50 mm) nominal members that align in the same plane. The relatively slender wood members used to construct the truss will fail earlier in a fire than the thicker components used in heavy timber trusses.

Connectors between light wood frame truss members can include metal toothed plates driven into the wood members, or nailed plywood gusset plates **(Figure 7.43)**. Wood and steel behave differently when exposed to the heat of a fire. Some authorities have theorized that the thermal expansion of the steel teeth of the metal connectors can cause the teeth to work loose from the wood and result in early failure. Steel connectors that are able to reflect some thermal radiation may offset this tendency. In light wood frame construction, nails, staples, or screws may be adequate.

Heavy timber trusses use members up to 8 or 10 inches (200 to 250 mm). In current practice, heavy timber trusses are used mainly for their appearance. Heavy timber trusses were once common before the mainstream use of steel, and many remain in use.

The most common style of connector between heavy timber members are steel gusset plates with through-bolts. Other styles include special brackets, and the bearing of one member directly on another **(Figure 7.44)**. Designers must plan connections that accommodate the forces that transfer from one member to another. The following sections describe types of connections that may be used.

In modern construction, mortise and tenon joints are used only in rare cases where the designer desires an artistic or quaint appearance **(Figure 7.45)**. In this method, one timber member is cut to fit into a recess in a mating member. This method of joining members is highly labor intensive and, therefore, costly. Older timber construction may use a mortise and tenon joint as a matter of course.

With a split-ring connector, a bolt with a thrust washer is run through the split ring to hold the members together **(Figure 7.46, p. 210)**. The split-ring connector provides a larger bearing surface for the transfer of load between the two members. A wood truss can use split-rings at the connection points. A split-ring truss uses a short circular piece of steel within and between two adjacent wood members to transfer the load between the members **(Figure 7.47, p. 210)**.

Figure 7.43 Gusset plates are steel connectors used on trusses. *Courtesy of Colorado Springs (CO) Fire Department.*

Figure 7.44 A heavy-timber joint can be assembled with through-bolts, brackets, and direct support. *Courtesy of Ed Prendergast.*

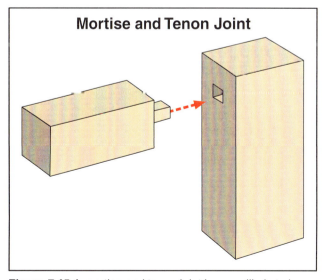

Figure 7.45 A mortise and tenon joint is more likely to be found in older construction than newer, because this type of joint is relatively labor-intensive to construct.

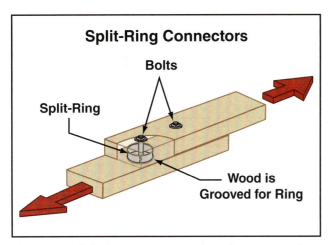

Figure 7.46 Split-ring connectors reduce the stress on the bolts.

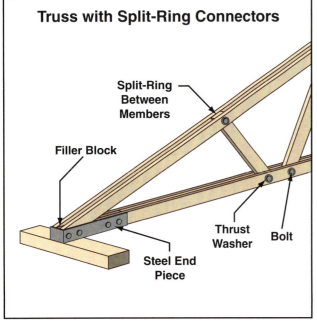

Figure 7.47 Wood trusses use split-rings to increase the longevity of the structural support.

Simply using screws or bolts to connect wood members has a serious limitation: steel screws and bolts are stronger than wood. This type of connection tends to concentrate the load application to the wood member over the surface area of the screw or bolt. The result is deformation of the wood at the point of application and an inefficient use of the wood.

Failure of Unprotected Engineered Truss Components

On August 13, 2006, a 55-year-old Wisconsin firefighter was killed and another was injured when they both fell into the basement of a single-family dwelling. The fire occurred in a two-story, seven-year-old single family residence of ordinary construction. The floor system in the structure consisted of wood trusses and engineered wood I-beams. The compartment with the origin of the fire was unfinished, and the wood supports were unprotected.

Seven minutes after firefighters arrived on site, two firefighters were directed to conduct a primary search of the first floor. They were forced to go to their knees due to heavy smoke conditions. As they crawled forward, they heard a loud crack and then both fell through the floor into the basement. This portion of the basement immediately became engulfed in fire. One firefighter was able to shield herself from the fire and reach safety. The Incident Commander activated a Rapid Intervention Team (RIT) for the second firefighter, but rescue efforts were unsuccessful and the body of the deceased firefighter was recovered the next day.

Lesson Learned: Unfinished basement ceilings are commonly encountered in residential construction. Early failure of unprotected wood floor trusses must be anticipated whenever there is an indication of significant fire.

Source: NIOSH

Structural Collapse of Wood Construction

Structural collapse may occur regardless of fire. Structures with light and engineered materials are the most common types of buildings in most jurisdictions, and they have a high potential for sudden, catastrophic structural failure. Furthermore, this type of construction is often disguised as other construction types, and may not be immediately identifiable without pre-incident planning. Heavy timber construction has a lower potential for catastrophic failure, and often manifests significant warning signs ahead of collapse.

Wood is uniquely vulnerable to deterioration from several causes including insects, decay, and shrinkage. In addition, wood structures are subject to the same forces that affect buildings constructed from other materials, such as settling, erosion, and weathering. All of these forces can undermine the structural stability of a wood-frame building. Indications of the deterioration of a wood-frame building are often readily apparent from the outside **(Figure 7.48)**. Firefighters must maintain situational awareness of building conditions, and approach any building showing exterior signs of deterioration with caution.

Figure 7.48 Wood buildings frequently show indications of deterioration from age and weather.

Chapter Summary

The distinguishing characteristic of a wood-frame building is that the basic structural system is combustible. The fundamental combustibility of wood contributes fuel to a fire that occurs in a wood-frame building. In addition, the structural integrity of the wood framing members is lost as the wood is consumed, and structural failure will occur. The trend toward lighter weight, more precisely engineered assemblies, increases the speed at which they can fail during a fire.

Wood-frame buildings, especially light wood-frame buildings, have numerous concealed spaces within the walls, attics, and floor spaces. These concealed spaces provide an avenue for the spread of fire. The concealed spaces must be opened in the course of fire fighting to check for extension of fire. In addition, the concealed spaces contain heating ducts, electrical wiring, plumbing, cooking exhausts, and chimneys. These building components give rise to the possibility of fires originating within the concealed spaces.

Review Questions

1. List disadvantages of wood construction.
2. List various types of exterior wall materials used in wood construction.
3. What variables influence the combustibility of wood?
4. What is the difference between ignition-resistant and fire-resistive construction?
5. What are the two basic types of wood framing?
6. What forces may undermine the stability of a wood frame building?

Chapter Notes

1. "Superior Fire Resistance," *American Institute of Timber Construction*, 2003, http://www.aitc-glulam.org/shopcart/Pdf/superior%20fire%20resistance.pdf.
2. Spray Polyurethane Foam Alliance, http://www.sprayfoam.org/index.php?page_id=38.

3. "Innovating Fire Attack Tactics," *New Science: Fire Safety Article*, Summer 2013, http://www.ul.com/global/documents/newscience/article/firesafety/NS_FS_Article_Fire_Attack_Tactics.pdf.

4. "Preventing Injuries and Deaths of Fire Fighters Due to Truss System Failures," DHHS (NIOSH) Publication Number 2005-132, http://www.cdc.gov/niosh/docs/2005-132/.

5. National Institute of Standards and Technology, http://www.nist.gov/.

6. Earls, Alan R, "Lightweight Construction," *NFPA® Journal*, July/August 2009, http://www.nfpa.org/newsandpublications/nfpa-journal/2009/july-august-2009/features/lightweight-construction.

7. U.S. fire Administration, http://apps.usfa.fema.gov/firefighter-fatalities/.

8. Dalton, James M, et al, "Collapse Time for Different Assemblies," *Fire Rescue Magazine*, http://my.firefighternation.com/profiles/blogs/collapse-time-for-different?q=profiles/blogs/collapse-time-for-different.

9. Dalton, James M, et al, "Tactical Considerations for Firefighting Operations in Lightweight Construction," Fire Rescue Magazine, http://my.firefighternation.com/profiles/blogs/tactical-considerations-for.

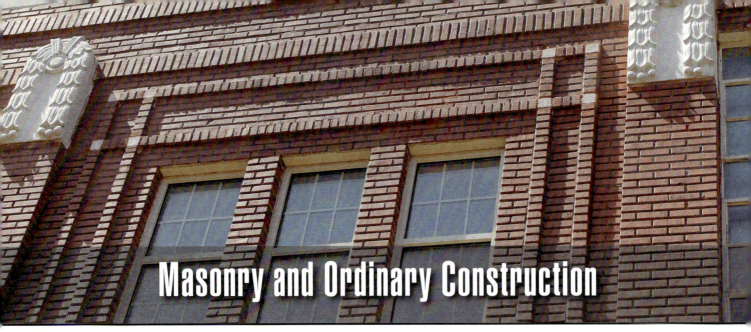

Masonry and Ordinary Construction

Chapter Contents

Case History 217	Construction of Masonry Walls 223
Material Properties of Masonry Construction 217	Interior Framing 227
	Openings in Masonry Walls 228
Stone 219	Parapets 229
Bricks 219	False Fronts and Voids 230
Concrete Blocks 220	**Structural Failure of Masonry Construction** 230
Other Masonry Units 220	
Mortar 221	Collapse of Masonry Construction 230
Fire Resistance of Masonry Walls 221	Tie Rods and Bearing Plates 232
Features and Functions of Masonry Structures 221	Nonfire-Related Deterioration 233
	Chapter Summary 235
Code Classification of Masonry Buildings 222	**Review Questions** 235

chapter 8

Key Terms

Buttress 227	Fire Cut 228
Concrete Block Brick Faced (CBBF) 227	Grout 227
	Lintel 228
Corbel 228	Pilaster 227
Corbelling 228	Portland Cement 220
Cornice 230	Spalling 220
Course 225	Wythe 223
Facade 230	
Fascia 230	

FESHE Outcomes Addressed In This Chapter

Fire and Emergency Services Higher Education (FESHE) Outcomes: *Building Construction for Fire Protection*

1. Describe building construction as it relates to firefighter safety, buildings codes, fire prevention, code inspection, firefighting strategy, and tactics.
2. Classify major types of building construction in accordance with a local/model building code.
3. Analyze the hazards and tactical considerations associated with the various types of building construction.
4. Explain the different loads and stresses that are placed on a building and their interrelationships.
5. Identify the function of each principle structural component in typical building design.
8. Identify the indicators of potential structural failure as they relate to firefighter safety.

Masonry and Ordinary Construction

Learning Objectives

After reading this chapter, students will be able to:

1. Describe properties of masonry construction components.
2. Explain how masonry structures are classified in building codes.
3. Describe features and functions of masonry structures.
4. Identify causes of structural failure of masonry construction.

Chapter 8
Masonry and Ordinary Construction

Case History

In October 2003, the Tropicana Casino parking garage in Atlantic City, NJ collapsed during construction, killing four construction workers and killing 21 others. Other renovation work on the Casino had shown signs of trouble from the beginning, including an earlier collapse in 2002. Investigation into the collapse of the parking garage showed several deficiencies in construction materials and oversight, including:

- Reports of damaged pole shores and cracked structural supports were ignored.
- Sufficient shores were not placed.
- Sufficient reinforcing steel was not placed.
- The concrete had not finished curing before shores were completely removed.
- The intervals between concrete pours were significantly truncated from standard practice.
- The structural engineer allowed plans to continue even though they were flawed.

The catastrophic collapse of this parking garage led to a $101 million settlement. The cause was ruled to be completely preventable, and no significant environmental factors contributed to the timing, severity, or life hazard of the collapse.

Masonry is one of the oldest and simplest building materials; its use dates back thousands of years. Masonry has its origin in the simple piling up of stones found in fields. Over the centuries, the technique has evolved into stacking shaped masonry units on top of one another and bonding them into solid, sometimes intricate, barriers. Masonry remains a commonly used construction material today, and many different types of buildings are constructed using masonry. This chapter will describe the following topics:

- Material properties of masonry construction
- Features and functions of masonry structures
- Structural failure of masonry construction

Material Properties of Masonry Construction

Several types of masonry components may be found in structures. Each has benefits and limitations based on their properties, dimensions, and application. The primary benefit of masonry components is their durability and inherent resistance to weather, fire, and insects.

Figure 8.1 Mortar used in masonry walls decays at a different rate than brick or stone. Some types of damage can be easily repaired. *Courtesy of Ed Prendergast.*

Drawbacks to masonry construction include long-term deterioration of mortar joints, and the labor-intensiveness of laying individual units by hand **(Figure 8.1)**. Masonry units have no significant tensile strength. In their structural application, they are used to support compressive loads **(Table 8.1)**. In practice, masonry construction must limit the applied stresses to account for the weaker mortar joints and to provide a factor of safety. The density of masonry units varies depending on the specific type **(Table 8.2)**.

Table 8.1
Ultimate Compressive Strengths for Masonry

Type	Compressive Strength
Brick	2,000 to 20,000 psi (14 000 kPa to 140 000 kPa)
Concrete Masonry Units	1500 to 6000 psi (10 000 kPa to 41 000 kPa)
Limestone	2,600 to 21,000 psi (18 000 kPa to 145 000 kPa)
Granite	15,600 to 30,800 psi (108 000 kPa to 212 000 kPa)
Sandstone	4,000 to 28,000 psi (2 800 kPa to 193 000 kPa)

Table 8.2
Density of Masonry Materials

Type	Density
Brick	100 to 140 lb/cu ft (1,600 – 2,240 kg/cu m)
Concrete Masonry Unit	75 to 135 lb/cu ft (1,200 – 2,160 kg/cu m)
Limestone	130 to 170 lb/cu ft (2,080 – 2,720 kg/cu m)
Granite	165 to 170 lb/cu ft (2,640 – 2,720 kg/cu m)
Sandstone	140 to 165 lb/cu ft (2,240 – 2,640 kg/ cu m)

Stone

Stone masonry consists of rock pieces that have been removed from a quarry and cut to the size and shape desired **(Figure 8.2)**. Stone may be laid with or without mortar to form walls similar to brick or concrete block. Stone is also used as an exterior veneer attached by supports to the structural frame of the building. The most common types of stone used in construction include:

- Limestone
- Sandstone and brownstone
- Granite
- Marble
- Slate

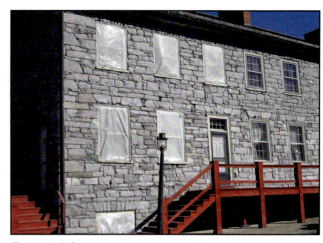

Figure 8.2 Stone masonry is one of the most durable building materials. *Courtesy of Ed Prendergast.*

Bricks

Bricks are produced from a variety of locally available clays and shales **(Figure 8.3)**. The hardness of brick is dependent on the materials used in its composition. Bricks are produced in a number of sizes. For most brick sizes, three courses (horizontal layers) of brick plus the intervening mortar joints equals a height of 8 inches (200 mm).

Figure 8.3 Brick construction often uses clays that are locally sourced.

Brick Manufacture

Two methods for shaping bricks are:

- Placing moist clay in molds, removing them from the molds, and then drying the bricks.
- Extruding moist clay through a rectangular die and using a cutter to slice bricks into the desired size.

The bricks are then fired in a kiln at temperatures as high as 2,400° F (1 300° C). This intense heat converts them to a ceramic material. The firing process takes 40 to 150 hours.

Figure 8.4 Steel roof beams may be supported by a masonry bearing wall. *Courtesy of Ed Prendergast.*

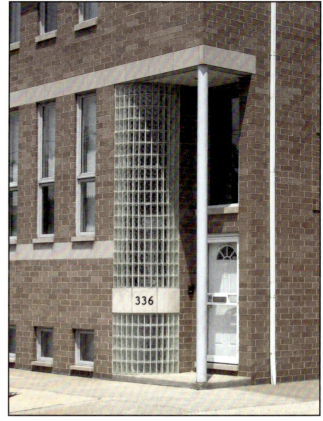

Figure 8.5 Glass block can be used in a structural masonry wall. *Courtesy of Ed Prendergast.*

> **Portland Cement** — Most commonly used cement, consisting chiefly of calcium and aluminum silicate. It is mixed with water to form mortar, a paste that hardens, and is therefore known as a hydraulic cement.

> **Spalling** — Expansion of excess moisture within masonry materials resulting in tensile forces within the material, and causing it to break apart. The expansion causes sections of the material's surface to disintegrate, resulting in pitting or chipping of the material's surface.

Concrete Blocks

Hollow concrete blocks are the most common concrete masonry units (CMUs). Hollow concrete blocks are produced in a number of sizes and shapes; the most common is the nominal 8 x 8 x 16 inch (200 x 200 x 400 mm) block **(Figure 8.4)**. Hollow blocks may be filled with cement or other material for added strength.

Concrete masonry units can also be produced as bricks or as solid blocks. Concrete blocks are larger than bricks and are therefore somewhat more economical to use because they each take the place of several bricks.

NOTE: See Chapter 10 for more information about concrete and its manufacture.

Other Masonry Units

Clay tile blocks and gypsum blocks were once widely used for the construction of interior partitions. Their use has diminished in modern practice although they can still be found in many buildings. Similarly, fired clay tile, known as *structural terra cotta*, was once popular for decorative effects and may still be found in older buildings.

Structural glazed tile is still frequently used where a smooth, easily cleaned surface is desired, such as in shower rooms, institutional kitchens, or corridors. Glass block is available in many textures and is architecturally popular for both interior partitions and exterior applications **(Figure 8.5)**. Glass block is also frequently used to fill in windows in existing buildings.

Mortar

Mortar is an inherent part of most (but not all) masonry construction. The primary function of mortar is to bond individual masonry units into a solid mass. Mortar also serves to cushion the rough surfaces of the masonry units, permitting uniform transmission of the compressive load from unit to unit. Mortar provides a seal between masonry units and is important in the final appearance of a masonry wall.

Because the mortar must bear the same weight of the masonry wall, its compressive strength is as important as that of the masonry units. The mortar joints are often the weakest part of the wall **(Figure 8.6)**. Mortar is available in five basic types with compressive strengths ranging from 75 psi (525 kPa) to 2,500 psi (17 500 kPa). The use of master streams during a fire can weaken mortar, either from the pressure of the stream or from the flushing effect of the water.

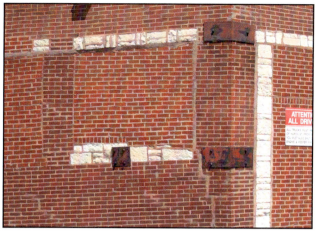

Figure 8.6 A masonry wall is most likely to show damage along the mortar when the foundation shifts. Note that this wall has been repaired.

Most mortar is produced from a mixture of **portland cement**, hydrated lime, sand, and water. The portland cement functions as the bonding agent. Until the 1890s, mortar was commonly produced with lime as the bonding agent instead of portland cement. Today, sand-lime mortar is found only in historic buildings. Because of the differences in properties between portland cement mortar and sand-lime mortar, older masonry construction with sand-lime mortar must be repaired with sand-lime mortar.

Fire Resistance of Masonry Walls

A well-constructed masonry wall that has not been undermined or weakened is usually the last structural component to fail in a wood-joisted building. The fire resistance of a masonry wall depends on the type of masonry units used and the thickness of the wall. For example, walls constructed with fire-rated concrete masonry units or bricks can have fire-resistance ratings of two to four hours or more. In contrast, nonfire-rated masonry may have little fire resistance and may **spall** and crumble when exposed to a fire or extensive weathering **(Figure 8.7)**.

Figure 8.7 Extensive weathering on masonry units can look similar to fire damage.

Features and Functions of Masonry Structures

Masonry structures may remain intact for many centuries. Masonry can be used for a variety of purposes in architecture including primarily decorative functions such as a masonry fence or stonework trim. Precast concrete slabs may be used in a floor or roof system with masonry walls. In this case, the applied load can be distributed uniformly along the masonry wall. Masonry is most relevant to firefighters when it is used in walls.

Figure 8.8 In traditional masonry construction, the masonry walls support wood floor and roof joists. *Courtesy of Ed Prendergast.*

Figure 8.9 Wood truss construction has prominently replaced earlier construction methods. *Courtesy of McKinney (TX) Fire Department.*

Code Classification of Masonry Buildings

The code classification of buildings with masonry components depends on the fire resistance of the joists, beams, and rafters that span the exterior load-bearing walls and interior columns, and transfer the live loads of the building to those walls and columns. The traditional and most basic masonry structure includes exterior load-bearing masonry walls that support the interior wood floors and roof constructed of wood joists and rafters **(Figure 8.8)**. This type of construction was so commonplace in the 19th and earlier part of the 20th century that it bears the designation "ordinary construction." Ordinary construction is also known as "masonry, wood-joisted" construction. In modern practice truss joists and wood roof trusses are often used in place of the traditional solid joists and rafters **(Figure 8.9)**.

Buildings of ordinary construction, as explained above, are classified as Type III (exterior protected) in the building codes. Depending on the type of interior construction, buildings with masonry exterior walls can also be Type I (fire-resistive) or Type II (protected noncombustible).

Classifying Buildings with Masonry Exterior Walls

A building with masonry exterior walls cannot be assumed to meet any single classification based on a simple evaluation of the exterior. Material combinations that affect classification include:

- Type III (exterior protected) construction may be subclassified as Type III-A or Type III-B depending on the degree of fire resistance provided to the structural members.

- Buildings with masonry exterior walls and noncombustible interior framing can be Type I-A or I-B if the interior framing members are protected with fire-retardant materials as required by the building code.

- Masonry buildings supported by unprotected steel structural framing are classified as Type II-B construction.

Construction of Masonry Walls

Masonry exterior walls are found in both fire-resistive and nonfire-resistive buildings with a variety of interior structural framing systems including unprotected steel, protected steel, and wood. The weight that a wall can support will depend on the width of the wall and whether it is reinforced or nonreinforced.

Nonload-Bearing Masonry Walls

Masonry can be used for nonload-bearing curtain walls or partitions. Some masonry materials, such as gypsum block and lightweight concrete block, are limited to use in nonload-bearing partition walls. In some cases, masonry veneer walls may be used in combination with a steel-frame multistory design to give the appearance of a masonry bearing wall **(Figure 8.10)**. Stone masonry is often used as an architectural veneer.

Figure 8.10 Brick veneers are very common, and may disguise the construction type of the structure.

Load-Bearing Masonry Walls

Masonry can be used to construct load-bearing walls that provide the basic structural support for a building. In modern practice, materials used in the most commonly encountered load-bearing masonry walls include:

- Brick
- Concrete block
- Combination of brick and block

In an ordinary nonreinforced load-bearing wall, the strength and stability of the wall are derived from the weight of the masonry and horizontal bonding of each **wythe** of wall to other wall components. Horizontal bonding can be

Wythe — Single vertical column of masonry units in a wall; usually brick or concrete block.

accomplished with strategic placement of bricks or with corrosion-resistant metal ties between wythes.

The simplest brick wall consists of a single wythe. Multiple wythes are normally provided to supply the necessary strength and stability in a masonry wall. A nonreinforced bearing wall must have adequate thickness to keep the compressive stresses within acceptable limits and to provide lateral stability **(Figure 8.11)**.

The height of the building and the method of construction used will affect the thickness of a masonry wall. Walls that provide the structural support for multistory buildings must be greater in thickness than those supporting single-story buildings because masonry units in the lower portions of a wall must support the dead load weight of the upper portion of the wall **(Figure 8.12)**.

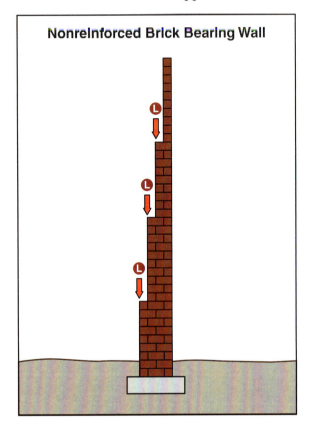

Figure 8.11 (left) When a masonry wall supports a multistory structure, the wall is constructed thicker at the base to handle the increasing load and to provide stability.

Figure 8.12 (above) The Monadnock building in Chicago has masonry bearing walls 6 feet (2 meters) thick at the base of the building. *Courtesy of Ed Prendergast.*

Limitations of Nonreinforced Masonry Construction

In contemporary practice, when a building will be more than three or four stories tall, the use of a steel or concrete structural frame is usually more economical than erecting a nonreinforced masonry bearing wall. Tall masonry structures are generally impractical or more costly than alternative designs unless the masonry is reinforced with steel.

Nonreinforced masonry walls are usually limited to a maximum height of six stories. These types of walls are more commonly found in structures built during the early part of the 20th century. For example, the Monadnock building in Chicago, Illinois was constructed to a height of 16 stories in 1893 using masonry exterior load-bearing walls. To support the weight of the building, the walls at the base are 6 feet (2 m) thick.

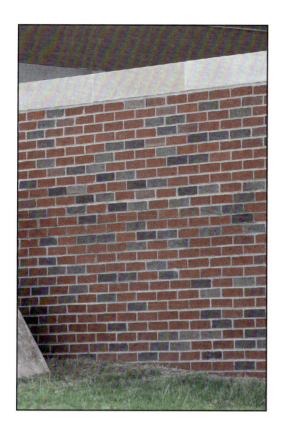

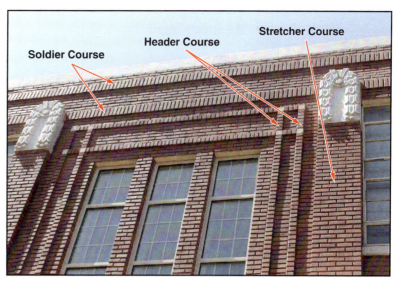

Figure 8.13 (left) A course is a horizontal layer of bricks in any alignment.

Figure 8.14 (above) In addition to visual interest, stretcher, soldier, and header courses serve specific reinforcement purposes in the wall.

In brick and concrete block construction, masonry units are laid side by side in a horizontal layer known as a **course** (**Figure 8.13**). Strategic brick and block placement is used for strength or appearance (**Figure 8.14**):

- A *stretcher course* has bricks placed end-to-end (**Figure 8.15**)
- A *soldier course* has bricks placed vertically on end
- A *header course* has bricks placed with the end facing out

The existence of header courses in a wall is one way to identify the method of construction of a masonry wall. Header courses are used alternating with other types of courses to provide a stronger horizontal bond between two wythes.

Course — Horizontal layer of individual masonry units.

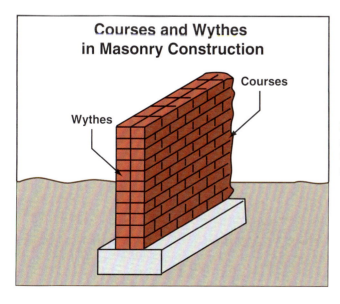

Figure 8.15 Wythes and courses are the two most basic facets of brick structures.

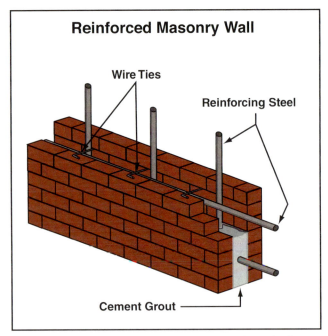

Figure 8.16 Reinforcement may be invisible from the face of the brick wall with concrete block and steel supports between parallel brick wythes.

Reinforced Masonry Walls

A masonry wall that is reinforced with steel can have a reduced thickness. For example, load-bearing masonry walls may be constructed to a height of ten stories or more with a wall thickness of only 12 inches (300 mm) when using reinforced masonry.

Masonry walls are reinforced to support the weight of a taller building or to provide stability against lateral forces. A common support for masonry walls is a series of vertical steel rods placed between two adjacent wythes of brick wall.

In **concrete block brick faced (CBBF)** masonry construction, a brick wythe is commonly used in combination with a concrete block wythe. Metal tie rods may be placed between the brick wythe and the concrete block wythe in a CBBF wall for reinforcement **(Figure 8.16)**. The cavity between the wythes is then filled with **grout**. Metal ties are frequently attached directly to metal or wood studs for masonry curtain walls.

A *cavity wall* is an exterior brick wall constructed with a vertical cavity between the exterior wythe and the interior wythe. The cavity prevents water seepage through the mortar joints to the interior of the building and increases the thermal insulating value of the wall. The placement of metal ties in a cavity wall is especially important because the use of a brick header course usually is not practical. In contrast, concrete block walls are reinforced with steel rods in the openings in the individual blocks and the openings are filled with grout.

The reinforcement of masonry walls can take other forms and can include architectural features, such as:

- **Buttresses** (Figure 8.17)
- Flying buttresses
- **Pilasters** (Figure 8.18)

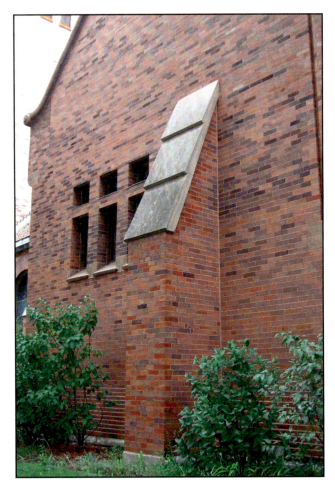

Figure 8.17 Buttresses provide lateral support without requiring extra thickness in the bearing wall. *Courtesy of Ed Prendergast.*

Figure 8.18 Structural pilasters indicate the presence of a lateral beam.

Figure 8.19 Steel beams or trusses can be used as interior framing to support curtain walls over masonry construction.

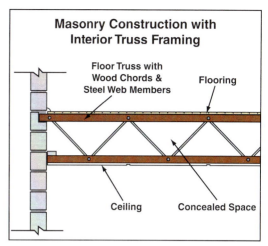

Figure 8.20 Regardless of the exterior construction material, concealed void spaces may exist in a structure that uses protected trusses.

Interior Framing

As indicated earlier in this chapter, the presence of an exterior masonry wall does not prove that a building is made of "ordinary" construction. The interior structural framing in masonry buildings includes columns of materials that transfer the loads to the exterior bearing walls. Before the 20th century, construction could include cast iron columns. More modern masonry buildings have interior framing systems using materials including:

- Masonry columns or interior bearing walls
- Steel beams or trusses
- Wood

Both protected and unprotected steel interior framing can be used with masonry bearing walls; therefore, masonry walls can be encountered in both fire-resistive and nonfire-resistive buildings **(Figure 8.19)**. The interior framing of a wood-joisted building will be finished with plaster, drywall, or other interior finish materials to provide required fire resistance. Therefore, wood-joisted masonry construction will have concealed combustible voids similar to wood-frame construction **(Figure 8.20)**. Fire spread through floor and ceiling spaces should be anticipated just as with wood-frame construction, especially where truss joists are used.

> **CAUTION**
> First responders must always be on the alert for early collapse involving any trusses.

In many applications such as residential and small commercial buildings, wood joists or beams simply rest on the masonry wall in an indentation known as a *beam pocket*. The beam pocket is several inches deep to provide an adequate bearing surface for the beam. A metal strap may be provided to function as a horizontal tie between the masonry and the end of the beam.

Concrete Block Brick Faced (CBBF) — Wall construction system that includes one wythe of concrete blocks with a brick wythe attached to the outside. See Course, Header Course, and Wythe.

Grout — A mixture of cement, aggregate, and water that hardens over time; used to embed reinforcement materials in masonry walls. Similar to mortar.

Buttress — Structure projecting from a wall, designed to receive lateral pressure action at a particular point. Flying buttresses include a gap between the lower part of the support and the structure.

Pilaster — Rectangular masonry pillar that extends from the face of a wall to provide additional support for the wall. Decorative pilasters may not provide any support.

Fire Cut — Angled cut made at the end of a wood joist or wood beam that rests in a masonry wall to allow the beam to fall away freely from the wall in case of failure of the beam. This helps prevent the beam from acting as a lever to push against the masonry.

The end of a wood joist or beam will be cut at a slight angle. This angle is known as a **fire cut** (Figure 8.21). The purpose of a fire cut is to allow the beam to fall away freely from a wall in the case of structural collapse without acting as a lever to push against the masonry. However, fire cuts in joists do not completely preclude the collapse of a masonry wall.

When a beam transmits a large vertical load to a masonry wall, the wall may be increased in thickness at the point of support with a pilaster to reduce the compressive stresses in the masonry. Wood roof trusses in commercial buildings, for example, are frequently supported on pilasters.

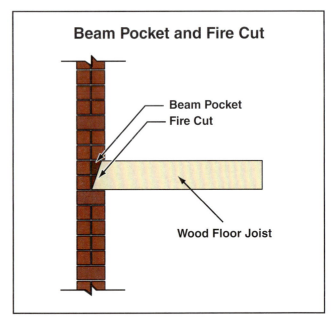

Figure 8.21 A fire cut in a horizontal support will cause the support to fail vertically in a predictable direction, in contrast to exerting a lateral force on the supporting wall.

Lintel — Support for masonry over an opening; usually made of steel angles or other rolled shapes, singularly or in combination.

Corbel — Bracket or ledge made of stone, wood, brick, or other building material projecting from the face of a wall or column used to support a beam, cornice, or arch.

Corbelling — Use of a corbel to provide additional support for an arch.

Openings in Masonry Walls

As with other types of walls, openings must be provided in masonry walls for doors and windows. Adequately supporting the weight of the masonry units over these openings poses a design problem because the mortar joints between the individual bricks or blocks provide little tensile support. Masonry over an opening is supported by the use of a **lintel**, arch, or **corbel** (Figure 8.22). Lintels are the most common method of supporting loads over openings in masonry walls, followed by arches. **Corbelling** is used to improve the aesthetics of an arch.

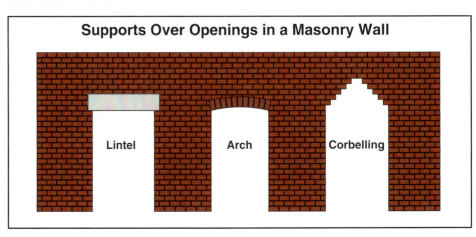

Figure 8.22 Strategic support-addition and material-removal strategies create a secure opening in a masonry wall.

A lintel is a beam over an opening in a masonry wall. Materials used in lintels include steel, reinforced concrete, or reinforced masonry. Wood lintels are not commonly used in modern construction because they shrink over time.

When designing lintels, engineers do not intend for the lintel beam to support the complete weight of the masonry wall above the lintel. A lintel beam is required to support only the weight of a triangular section immediately above the lintel. This limitation in weight occurs due to a certain amount of arching between the masonry units above the lintel **(Figure 8.23)**. However, if the height of the wall above the opening is shorter than the height of the triangular section, the lintel is engineered to support the entire weight of the masonry above the opening.

A beam and column system may be added at the grade level as needed to support the weight of masonry wall **(Figure 8.24)**. The weight of many tons of masonry is transmitted through the horizontal beams and columns to the foundation.

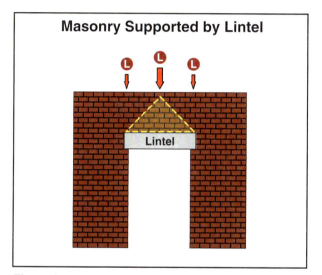

Figure 8.23 A lintel is designed to support the portion of the masonry wall over an opening, as indicated by the shaded triangle.

Figure 8.24 Masonry can be supported with beams and columns instead of other masonry wythes.

Parapets

A parapet is an extension of a masonry or steel wall that projects above the roof 1 foot (300 mm) or more. Parapets usually do not have lateral support. The purpose of a parapet on an exterior wall can be both aesthetic and functional. Parapets are found on exterior masonry walls and fire walls of buildings with combustible roofs **(Figure 8.25)**. A parapet may also provide a barrier to prevent fire spread between closely spaced buildings. Artificial parapets made of exterior insulation and finishing system (EIFS) materials with no fire resistance may be included in a building's structure for aesthetic purposes, but these may be indistinguishable from masonry parapets.

Parapets on the fronts of buildings are especially significant during fire fighting operations because the following forces can cause a parapet wall to lose structural integrity:

Figure 8.25 Parapets can serve fire barrier functions or simply change the silhouette of a rooftop. *Courtesy of McKinney (TX) Fire Department.*

- Exposure to high wind, particularly if erosion of the mortar joints or other deterioration has occurred
- Roof collapse during the course of a fire
- Impact from aerial ladders, especially when forcefully extended or retracted
- Force of master streams

False Fronts and Voids

A masonry building is sometimes provided with a decorative false front or **facade** through renovation or the original design. A false front can create a combustible void that is not normally encountered with masonry walls. For example, a mansard-style **fascia** forms a **cornice** beyond the building wall that creates a concealed space through which a fire can travel **(Figure 8.26)**.

Figure 8.26 Some types of construction include concealed spaces that may protect an avenue for fire spread.

Fascia — (1) Flat horizontal or vertical board located at the outer face of a cornice. (2) Broad flat surface over a storefront or below a cornice.

Cornice — Concealed space near the eave of a building; usually overhanging the area adjacent to exterior walls.

Facade — Fascia added to some buildings with flat roofs to create the appearance of a mansard roof. *Also known as* False Roof *or* Fascia.

Structural Failure of Masonry Construction

Although inherently resistive to fire, masonry construction affects fire behavior in profound ways:

- Some deterioration of concrete masonry units (CMU) can occur because of exposure to fire conditions.
- False fronts (fascia) and some construction materials may not be protected along void spaces.
- Combustible outcrops of roofs and fasciae change the dynamics of fire resistance in masonry in some types of buildings, such as heavy timber construction.

Building codes usually require less clearance between buildings with masonry or other fire-resistive exterior walls than between buildings with combustible exteriors. The exterior fire-resistive walls of masonry construction tend to reduce fire spread between structures. Of course, any openings or void spaces in a fire-resistive wall can create an exposure problem.

Collapse of Masonry Construction

Simply stated, buildings collapse when supports fail. Every building may fall in a unique way depending on a number of factors. Understanding the mechanisms of building collapse and considering different combinations of factors will affect how first responders arrange apparatus and other resources at an incident **(Figure 8.27)**.

Establishing Collapse Control Zones

Collapse zones are typically at least 1.5 times the height of the building all around the building's perimeter. When staging at a structural collapse incident, the safest location for apparatus is in line with the angle formed by a building's corners. Debris may travel a significant distance, depending on the mechanism of collapse.

Figure 8.27 Collapse zone calculations are intended to provide a guideline during incident response, but may not be enforceable in a densely built area.

Collapse of masonry walls often occurs when interior wood framing fails. A masonry wall may collapse partially or completely. Factors that affect a building's structural integrity include:

- Collapsing interior floor or roof members can exert horizontal forces against a wall and push the wall outward. Horizontal forces create tensile forces that mortar joints cannot resist.
- The collapse of interior framing removes interior bracing for the wall and the wall may be simply pushed out from the building.
- Steel within a reinforced wall can withstand some tensile stress, making collapse less likely.

In general, wherever masonry walls intersect, they will support and reinforce each other. Such walls also provide lateral support. Because intersecting masonry walls support each other, the corners of the building or other points of intersection, such as stairwells or elevator shafts, will be the strongest points in a masonry structure.

Identification of Reinforced Masonry Walls
Reinforced and nonreinforced masonry walls may look identical from a building's exterior. Preincident plans may include information on whether a wall is reinforced and what type of reinforcement is used.

Masonry Wall Breaching

Masonry walls are inherently difficult to breach, but newer reinforcing and security measures can make it even more difficult to enter these types of structures. Caution must be exercised while breaching masonry walls because of the possible presence of utilities or the disruption of load bearing walls. Local and regional jurisdictions may indicate proper procedures for this tactic.

In some cases, breaching is the best option available. For example, breaching a masonry wall may be essential to access a trapped victim and accommodate hoselines or other extinguishing methods. Two considerations should be followed to ensure the maximum stability of the masonry. First, search for a weak point in the mortar or concrete, and work in a triangle shape from that point until the breach is large enough for the purpose. Second, maintain a corbelling shape to serve as a guide for choosing bricks that are likely to be safe to remove.

Tie Rods and Bearing Plates

A masonry wall that bulges or leans outward will tend to pull away from the interior framing. One way to stabilize a masonry structure under normal conditions is to extend a series of steel tie rods inside the building through the masonry walls parallel to the joists, and secure them in place outside the wall with bearing plates or structural washers. The tie rod usually has a turnbuckle to adjust the tension in the rod **(Figure 8.28)**.

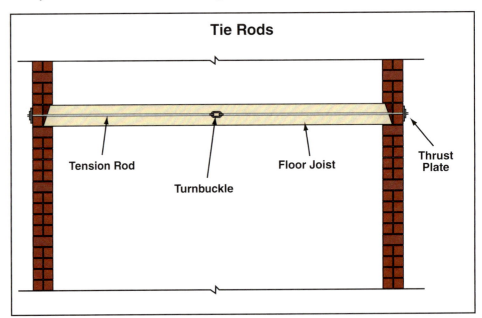

Figure 8.28 Tie rods are commonly used to reinforce a masonry wall.

Bearing plates can take several forms, and are usually easily visible on the outside of a building. Some are intended to be architecturally decorative and can be in the shape of stars. Occasionally, items similar to these stars are placed on masonry walls for purely ornamental purposes.

The presence of tie rods and bearing plates does not necessarily mean that a building has undergone repair; the tie rods may have been part of the

Figure 8.29 Bearing plates may be a part of an original structural design, or may be added as the result of a repair; they may be functional and/or decorative.

original construction **(Figure 8.29)**. Designers intentionally used tie rods to reinforce the structures in the early 19th century when masonry buildings began to be constructed more than one story in height and needed to support greater loads.

One potential problem with the use of tie rods is that the steel rods can become heated under fire conditions and stretch, weakening the walls. Firefighters should be most concerned about tie rods used to repair a wall rather than where they are part of the original construction. It is usually possible to differentiate between repairs and original construction. The bearing plates used where repairs have been undertaken are likely to be:

- Less compatible with the architecture of the building. Steel channels may be used.
- Not uniformly positioned on a wall **(Figure 8.30)**.
- Found in conjunction with other repairs.

Nonfire-Related Deterioration

Deterioration of masonry walls is normally a slow process that takes place over many years. Old buildings sometimes collapse without warning or apparent reason. Regardless of the reason for deterioration, even a relatively small section of masonry wall can cause significant damage when it fails. Masonry walls may be repaired when deterioration has occurred **(Figure 8.31, p. 234)**. When the repair work is completed competently, the stability of a structure will be restored. If the repairs are not made properly, however, the walls may remain unstable.

Figure 8.30 A building that has undergone repairs may have bearing plates that are not decorative, and irregularly spaced.

Figure 8.31 Correct repair of a masonry wall will restore full functionality to a damaged structure. *Courtesy of Ed Prendergast.*

Figure 8.32 Stone masonry veneers may pull away from their anchors for a number of reasons including fire damage and simple weathering. Notice that the building has also been braced at the second-floor level. *Courtesy of Ed Prendergast.*

Masonry walls can deteriorate from several causes, including:

- Erosion of the mortar or reinforcing steel as a result of exposure to the elements, including tensile stresses from the freeze/thaw cycle of weather **(Figure 8.32)**.
- Shifts in the foundation can cause cracks and misalignment of supports.
- Wooden interior members can rot and shift from long-term exposure to moisture.

Despite the exceptional stability of masonry construction, total collapse is possible. Deterioration from any cause will contribute to structural failure under fire conditions. Some factors that determine fire behavior in a masonry structure are obvious and can be detected by visual observation. Others are subtle and not likely to be detected during the course of a fire.

Indicators of Masonry Wall Structural Failure
Cracks in masonry walls must be monitored for change and growth during emergency operations. Indicators of imminent collapse include changes in the alignment of cracks. In the case of a fire, the increased presence of light shining through the wall is a clear indicator. Total collapse of a masonry building is possible if the structure becomes heavily involved in fire.

Chapter Summary

Masonry construction is encountered in several applications. The oldest form of masonry construction is ordinary construction with masonry bearing walls and interior wood framing. These structures are classified as Type III in the building codes. Mill buildings, also known as heavy-timber buildings, are masonry buildings constructed with heavy-timber interior framing and the codes classify them as Type IV construction. Masonry veneer construction can be used with other framing systems. All types of buildings can have masonry exteriors.

Masonry itself is noncombustible and inherently fire-resistive, so masonry walls reduce fire spread between structures. Combustible interior framing can collapse, however, and masonry walls can and will fail under heavy fire conditions. The interior combustible framing also contributes to the fuel load. Masonry walls can deteriorate with age from several causes. Firefighters should view any sign of masonry deterioration as reason to proceed with caution.

Review Questions

1. What are some of the benefits of masonry construction components?
2. What are some types of masonry components?
3. How are masonry buildings classified in building codes?
4. What building structures use masonry components aesthetically rather than structurally?
5. Why must firefighters understand the mechanism of building collapse as it relates to masonry construction?
6. What are some common reasons that masonry structures fail?

Steel Construction

Chapter Contents

Case History 239
Material Properties of Steel and Iron 240
Steel Ductility 241
Steel Expansion and Deterioration 242
Fire Protection of Steel 243
Steel-Framed Structures 246
Beam and Girder Frames 247
Steel Trusses 248
Gabled Rigid Frames 249

Steel Arches 249
Steel Suspension Systems 250
Steel Columns 250
Floor Systems in Steel-Framed Buildings 251
Code Modifications 251
Collapse of Steel Structures 252
Chapter Summary 253
Review Questions 253

chapter 9

Key Terms

Alloy 240	Rolling 241
Calcination 244	Slenderness Ratio 250
Calcined 244	Spray-Applied Fire Resistive
Cold Rolled Steel (CRS) 241	Material (SRFM) 243
Corrugated 251	Steel 240
Ductility 241	Unprotected Steel 242
Membrane Ceiling 245	

FESHE Outcomes Addressed In This Chapter

Fire and Emergency Services Higher Education (FESHE) Outcomes: *Building Construction for Fire Protection*

1. Describe building construction as it relates to firefighter safety, buildings codes, fire prevention, code inspection, firefighting strategy, and tactics.
2. Classify major types of building construction in accordance with a local/model building code.
3. Analyze the hazards and tactical considerations associated with the various types of building construction.
5. Identify the function of each principle structural component in typical building design.
8. Identify the indicators of potential structural failure as they relate to firefighter safety.

Steel Construction

Learning Objectives

After reading this chapter, students will be able to:

1. Describe the material properties of steel.
2. Describe methods used to protect steel construction building elements during a fire.
3. Explain how steel is used in the construction of structural framework.
4. Identify common reasons for collapse of steel structures.

Chapter 9
Steel Construction

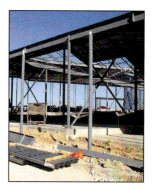

Case History

In May 2013, fire crews responded to a reported fire in an auto body shop. Upon arrival, heavy smoke and fire was showing, with employees still trying to remove vehicles from the shop area. The incident itself seemed to go extremely well, with safeguards in place and teams coordinating effectively. Five minutes into the interior fire attack, the safety officer reported that a steel beam supporting a corrugated roof appeared to have twisted. Crews were immediately ordered out of the building. When the Incident Commander evaluated the time of fire, he realized that the crews should have been out of the building much sooner than they were, and only the vigilance of the Safety Officer prevented injuries or worse.

An understanding of building construction is critical to understanding how fire will affect a structure. While the Incident Commander made note of the construction type, the IC did not make initial decisions based on an understanding of steel construction exposed to heavy fire conditions. Specifically understanding the effects of fire on steel, including the time steel is exposed to heavy fire conditions, is critical to understanding what would happen during this incident.

Source: National Firefighter Near-Miss Reporting System. Report Number: 13-0000324

Steel beams and trusses have largely replaced wood beams and trusses in commercial structures. Steel is used in applications varying from heavy beams and columns to door frames and nails. The development of steel structural framing at the end of the 19th century permitted the construction of high-rise buildings in the 20th century. Steel framing is found in buildings of all heights and is used in both fire-resistive and non-fire resistive buildings.

The firefighter must understand that the behavior of steel under fire conditions depends on the mass of the steel and the degree of fire resistance provided. This chapter discusses the following topics:

- Material properties of steel and iron
- Steel-framed structures
- Collapse of steel structures

Material Properties of Steel and Iron

The primary two metals **alloyed** in **steel** are iron and carbon. Common structural steel has less than three tenths of one percent carbon. In contrast, cast iron has a carbon content of three to four percent **(Figure 9.1)**. The higher carbon content of cast iron makes the material hard but brittle.

Figure 9.1 Though new construction will not include cast-iron fascia, they may still be found in many older cities. *Courtesy of Ed Prendergast.*

> ### Cast Iron
> Because cast iron is a brittle material, it tends to fail by fracturing from impact loading rather than by yielding as in the case of steel. Cast iron has been completely displaced by steel in modern structural applications. Cast iron columns and staircases can still be found in older buildings. Cast iron was used in buildings in structural framing before the turn of the 20th century. Some structures were built with complete cast iron fronts. Firefighters should consider the way the cast iron fronts are attached to the structures. Failure of these attachment points often lead to the collapse of the cast iron front.

Alloy — Substance or mixture composed of two or more metals (or a metal and nonmetallic elements) fused to and dissolved into each other to enhance the properties or usefulness of the base metal.

Steel — An alloy of iron and carbon; proportions and additional elements affect the characteristics of the finished material. Used widely in the construction of buildings and other infrastructure.

The basic properties of steel include:

- Strongest of the common building materials
- Non-rotting, resistant to aging, and dimensionally stable
- Consistent quality from controlled industrial manufacturing process
- Relatively expensive, but strength and other qualities enable it to be used in smaller quantities than other materials

One inherent disadvantage of steel is the tendency to rust when exposed to air and moisture. Ways steel can be protected from the formation of rust include:

- Painting the surface with a rust-inhibiting paint
- Coating the material with zinc and aluminum
- Adding alloy elements that resist rust

During the alloying process, elements are combined to produce an end result that can be used for a specific purpose. The following elements added to steel will alter the composition of the material and contribute and increase specific attributes:

- Molybdenum – Strength
- Vanadium – Strength and toughness
- Manganese – Resistance of steel to abrasion

Steel Ductility

The lower carbon content of steel, compared to cast iron, results in a material that is **ductile** rather than brittle. The ductility of steel also allows it to be shaped by **rolling**, as opposed to molding like concrete or cutting like wood and stone. This attribute enables steel to be rolled into a variety of shapes **(Figure 9.2)**. The rolling process consists of repeatedly passing ingots of steel heated to 2,200°F (1 200°C) between large rollers until the intended shape is achieved.

Cold rolled steel (CRS) is used for members that have a thin cross-section, such as floor and roof decking and wall studs. The CRS studs can be used either for interior non-load bearing partitions or for exterior bearing walls.

One common structural steel is ASTM A36 which includes manganese, carbon, and silicon. The ductility of this steel can be illustrated by comparing the stress exerted on the steel against the resulting deformation known as the *strain* **(Figure 9.3)**. When the stress and strain for different types of steel are plotted, the resulting curve for A36 steel is initially steep and straight. When the *yield point stress* is reached (approximately 36,000 psi [250 000 kPa]), the steel undergoes a pronounced deformation. Finally, the steel breaks at the *ultimate stress*.

Figure 9.2 Steel can be formed into many shapes. *Courtesy of McKinney (TX) Fire Department.*

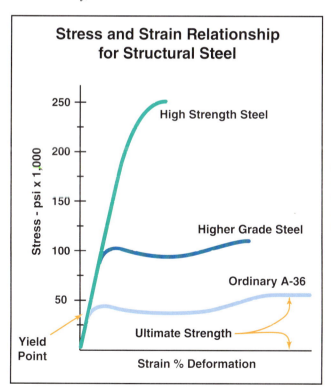

Figure 9.3 The strength characteristics of different types of steel will affect the maximum allowable stress for each type.

> **Ductility** — A measure of a metal's ability to be drawn, hammered thin, or rolled into shapes without breaking. The high ductility of steel makes it very versatile for use in constructing buildings.
>
> **Rolling** — Process of forming metal stock into shapes including sheets by passing thick bars of metal through a pair of rollers. Cold rolling occurs at temperatures above recrystallization temperature.
>
> **Cold Rolled Steel (CRS)** — Commercial and drawing steels; shaped after cooling below its recrystallization temperature by being passed through a series of rollers to reduce the thickness incrementally.

Steel alloys with higher yield points have less ductility. For example, steels for special application including bridge strands have tensile strengths as high as 300,000 psi (2 100 000 kPa) but have very little ductility.

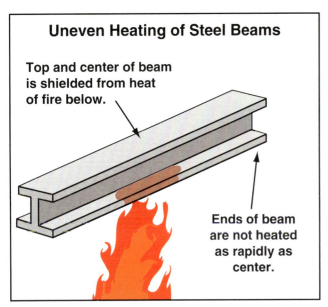

Figure 9.4 The uneven heating of a steel beam will change the stresses within the beam.

Figure 9.5 The mass of steel components will affect how quickly and in what ways they fail under fire conditions. *Courtesy of Colorado Springs (CO) Fire Department.*

Unprotected Steel — Steel structural members that are not protected against exposure to heat.

Steel Expansion and Deterioration

Steel expands as it is heated. The amount of expansion for slender members, such as beams and columns, can be determined through a property known as the *linear coefficient of thermal expansion*. The amount of expansion, and other factors such as any restraints on the beam, are important to know because steel components unable to push their lateral constraints will weaken, bow or buckle, and fail, which may create several points of failure.

The heating of steel or other materials does not occur uniformly during fire incidents. For example, the bottom of a beam is often heated more by the fire than the top or the ends **(Figure 9.4)**. Therefore, the resulting yielding and deformation is not uniform over the length of the beam.

An important factor of steel use is the support system used with a beam. For example, an unrestrained steel beam 20 feet (6 m) long can expand 1.4 inches (35 mm), significantly pushing at lateral constraints. On the other hand, individual steel members that are rigidly welded or bolted into a large structural system are better able to resist failure than if they are simply supported. The end restraint provided by rigid connections exerts a resistance to the deformation of individual members.

The deterioration of steel strength at elevated temperatures is the characteristic most significant to the fire service. Many variables often combine at a fire scene, and account for the different types of distortion or failure that are observed in fire scenes. The speed of failure depends on several factors, including:

- Type of steel
- Mass of the steel members **(Figure 9.5)**
- Load supported by the steel
- Type of connections used to join the steel members
- Intensity of the exposing fire

Steel is a good conductor of heat because it is a heavy material, having a density of around 490 pounds per cubic feet (7 850 kg/m^3). Heavy steel beams and girders frequently remain in place under severe fire exposure. A significant amount of heat is required to raise the temperature of heavy steel structural members.

Unprotected steel structural members with less mass require less heat to reach the failure temperature. Members such as bar joists or slender trusses can be expected to fail early when exposed to an intense enough fire. Alternatively, in a structure with a light fuel load, unprotected steel may not fail if the fire does not supply enough thermal energy. Structure fires typically do not generate temperatures hot enough to melt steel; however, some fires do create temperatures in excess of 1,200°F (650°C), which is hot enough to weaken steel to its yield point **(Figure 9.6)**.

Yielding and thermal expansion take place simultaneously; however, the tendency for steel to yield and, therefore, to bend or buckle is the more significant concern in most fire situations. The load that steel members are supporting affects the behavior of steel because the loads produce the stresses in the steel. Steel with lower stresses must be heated to a higher temperature for the yield point to be reached.

The loss of steel strength because of increased temperature is often not a sudden occurrence; rather, the steel loses its strength gradually as its temperature increases. In more extreme situations, a sharp increase in temperature may cause steel components to fail suddenly.

In a structural fire, a large amount of energy is radiated away from the seat of the fire and moves upward where it disperses in the atmosphere. Therefore, the fire would have to generate a large amount of heat above the theoretical minimum amount required to raise the temperature of the beam to 1,000°F (540°C).

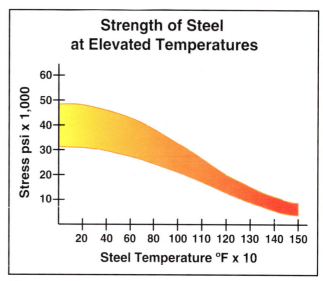

Figure 9.6 The strength of structural steel may change depending on the severity of temperature increase.

Fire Protection of Steel

No matter its mass, steel is ultimately not inherently fire-resistive. If exposed to high enough heat long enough, steel will fail. Steel used in fire-resistive buildings must meet minimum heat resistance ratings. The usual way to protect steel from the heat of a fire is to add an insulating material.

In older buildings, the steel framework was encased in brick or ordinary concrete. A steel column encased in 3 inches (75 mm) of concrete with a siliceous aggregate would have a fire resistance of four hours. This method is effective, but increases the weight and cost of a structure. Structural designers prefer to use lighter-weight materials for the protection of steel.

Some insulating materials are applied by spraying. Others may be applied in a coating or in sheets. Lightweight concrete can also be used.

Spray-Applied Materials

Spray-applied fire-resistive materials (SFRM) are efficient and inexpensive. The most commonly used SFRMs are mineral fiber or expanded aggregate coatings such as vermiculite and perlite. The degree of fire resistance provided will depend not only on the material but also on the thickness of the application.

Because of the variety of SFRMs available, it can be difficult to ensure that the applied material meets the specifications of the design documents. Furthermore, for an SFRM to be effective, proper installation procedures must be followed, in accordance with the manufacturer's listing and recommendations. For example, the surface to which the SFRM is applied must be clean of oil, dirt, loose paint, and any other substance that would prevent good adhesion. Also, hangers and supports must be installed before application of the SFRM because hangers and supports added after the fact may require that fireproofing material is removed, which limits the effectiveness of the remaining material.

> **Spray-Applied Fire Resistive Material (SRFM)** — Coating used to increase the fire resistance rating of structural components. Materials commonly include mineral fiber or aggregates such as vermiculite and perlite.

Most fire-insulating materials can be applied in specific thicknesses to achieve different fire-resistance ratings. The applied fireproofing can vary from 7/8 to 1 7/8 inches (22 to 47 mm) to produce a fire-resistive rating of one to four hours. After application, identification of the type of fireproofing material and verification of the applied thickness may be impossible **(Figure 9.7)**.

Low-density mineral fiber materials are relatively soft and can be easily dislodged from the steel. Low-density fiber materials are not suitable for exterior use. More durable mineral fiber products with densities greater than 20 lb/ft^3 (320 kg/m^3) can endure conditions of limited weather exposure and higher humidity such as might exist in parking facilities. High-density SFRMs that use magnesium oxychloride have densities ranging from 40 to 80 lb/ft^3 (640 to 1 300 kg/m^3).

Figure 9.7 Sprayed-on insulating material is difficult to regulate after application.

NOTE: Asbestos has not been used in SRFMs since the 1970s.

Cementitious

Cementitious materials have densities ranging from 15 to 50 lb/ft^3 (240 to 800 kg/m^3). Cementitious materials are produced in various formulations. Ingredients can include:

- Portland cement
- Gypsum
- Perlite
- Vermiculite

NOTE: Some manufacturers of cementitous cement add magnesium oxychloride, or oxysulfate, calcium aluminate, phosphate, or ammonium sulfate.

Gypsum

Gypsum can be used as an insulating material either in the form of flat boards or a plaster. Gypsum board consists of a core of **calcined** gypsum, starch, water, and other additives that are sandwiched between two paper faces **(Figure 9.8)**. Gypsum board is available as *regular* or *type X*. Regular gypsum board has no special additives to enhance its fire resistance, although it will provide some degree of fire protection. Type X gypsum board contains additives to increase its fire resistance and is usually required where a specified fire resistance is desired.

The value of gypsum as an insulating material arises in part from the water that is chemically combined within the material. Gypsum includes approximately 20 percent entrapped water. This water content enhances gypsum's performance as a fire-insulating material. The water turns to steam upon exposure to fire and, in doing so, absorbs the heat. This process is known as **calcination**. Once the moisture has been driven off, the remaining gypsum will act as an insulating material.

> **Calcined** — Process that heats a substance to a high temperature but below the melting or fusing point, causing loss of moisture, reduction or oxidation, and decomposition of carbonates and other compounds.

> **Calcination** — Process of driving free and chemically bound water out of gypsum; also describes chemical and physical changes to the gypsum component itself.

Figure 9.8 Gypsum board is often used to cover the interior of lightweight construction to provide a measure of fire resistance.

Gypsum can be used to protect both columns and beams, providing fire resistance ratings from one to four hours. Gypsum board is used in multiple layers to attain higher fire resistance ratings.

NOTE: For more information about construction systems and materials and their ratings, consult the UL Fire Resistance Directory.

Intumescent and Mastic Coatings

Intumescent materials undergo a chemical reaction when exposed to the heat of a fire. An intumescent coating will char, foam, and expand when heated. The coating material will expand to fifteen to thirty times its original volume. The expanded coating then acts as an insulating material to protect the steel.

Intumescent coatings are applied as paint. They have an applied thickness of 0.03 to 0.4 inches (0.75 to 10 mm) which is less than the thickness of the spray-applied materials. Because they have the appearance of paint, it can be difficult to visually establish that a fire-resistive coating has been applied to steel components.

Membrane Ceiling — Usually refers to a suspended, insulating ceiling tile system.

Mastic coatings function in a manner similar to intumescent coatings except they are based on more complex organic materials and their reaction to heat is more complex. Both intumescent and mastic coatings are relatively expensive. Their advantages include lighter weight, durable surfaces, and good adhesion. In addition they are frequently the most aesthetically attractive.

Membrane Ceilings

A commonly used method of protecting a steel floor or roof assembly is the **membrane ceiling**. A membrane ceiling consists of a ceiling material suspended from the supports for the floor or ceiling above. The most common method is to use mineral tiles in a steel framework suspended by wires **(Figure 9.9)**. The mineral tiles are

Figure 9.9 Acoustic tile used in dropped ceilings provides a measure of fire resistance to the steel framework above.

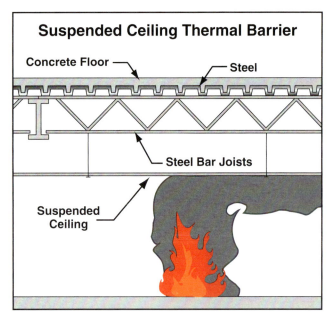

Figure 9.10 A suspended ceiling protects roof framing systems.

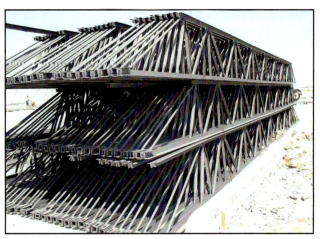

Figure 9.11 Lightweight steel trusses, here shown packaged for transport, are commonly used to support roofs. *Courtesy of McKinney (TX) Fire Department.*

Figure 9.12 Steel frames can support many types of exterior finish, including corrugated plastic sheeting.

a lightweight insulating material and usually contain perforations for acoustical applications. Gypsum panels are also used for membrane ceilings.

The ceiling material acts as a thermal barrier to protect the steel that supports the floor or ceiling above **(Figure 9.10)**. They are frequently used in steel framing systems that make use of the open web joists described earlier. The use of a membrane ceiling can provide a floor and ceiling assembly or a ceiling and roof assembly with a fire rating of one to three hours depending on the specific details of the installation.

Ceiling materials are never rated independently. A ceiling is always rated as part of a floor and ceiling assembly, so it is not accurate to speak of the fire resistance of a ceiling alone. Because the membrane ceiling forms an integral part of a fire-rated assembly, it follows that any removal or penetration of the ceiling material reduces or even eliminates the fire resistance of the total assembly.

The fire-rated membrane floor and ceiling assemblies are listed by the testing laboratories as a total assembly. All the specific details of the assembly must be adhered to in its installation. Deviation from the laboratory specifications will affect the fire rating of the assembly.

Membrane ceilings are popular partly because building utilities such as electrical wiring, automatic sprinkler piping, and ventilation ducts can be concealed above the ceiling. Penetration of membrane ceilings is frequently necessary for lighting fixtures and ventilation diffusers. When a floor and ceiling assembly is rated, any such penetrations must be provided for in the testing. It may be necessary to provide additional insulation on the back of lighting fixtures and to equip ventilation ducts with fire dampers so fire does not penetrate through the opening.

Steel-Framed Structures

The basic method by which steel is used in the design of buildings is the construction of a structural framework that supports the floors, roof, and exterior walls. Several different techniques can be used to construct a steel frame. Steel structural shapes can be used to construct a frame of columns, beams, and girders. Steel also can be used in heavy or lightweight trusses to support roofs and floors **(Figure 9.11)**. Rigid frames and arches can be constructed from steel. Steel cables or rods can be used to support roofs. Cold-rolled steel studs are being used to construct exterior walls.

Because steel is a strong but dense material, it is not efficient to use it in the form of solid slabs or panels as is done with other materials such as wood or concrete. Steel in sheet form, however, is used for applications such as floor decking and exterior curtain walls. The exterior envelope of a steel-frame building can consist of concrete, masonry, or glass **(Figure 9.12)**.

Beam and Girder Frames

The design of the connections in steel-frame buildings is important for two reasons. First, the connection of a beam to a column transfers the loads between members. Second, connections determine the rigidity of the basic structure. Some structural rigidity must be provided to resist wind load and other lateral forces that cause the distortion of the building. In a structure with a large beam and girder frame made of repeating sections, the adjacent sections of the frame tend to be mutually supporting. These adjacent sections provide a degree of redundancy to the overall system that reinforces the structure's strength. Beam and girder steel frames can be classified as rigid, simple, or semi-rigid.

Beams and columns in steel-frame buildings are connected by bolting or welding. Riveting was used in the first half of the 20th century, but is not practical to use today.

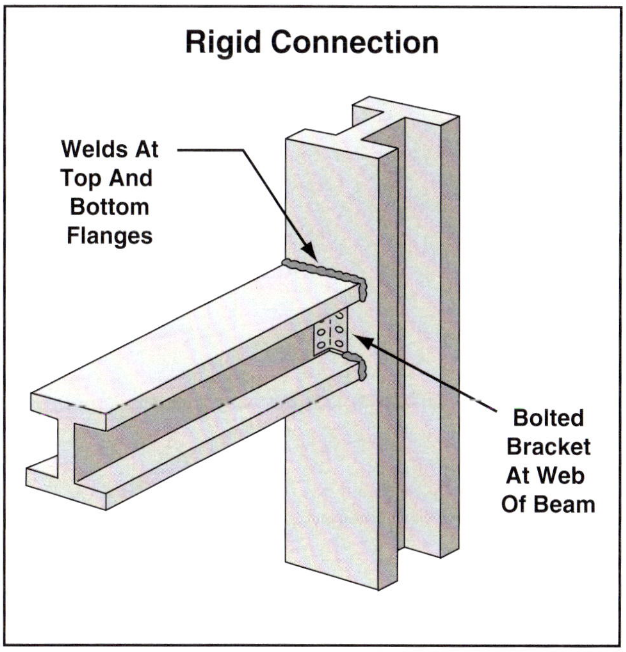

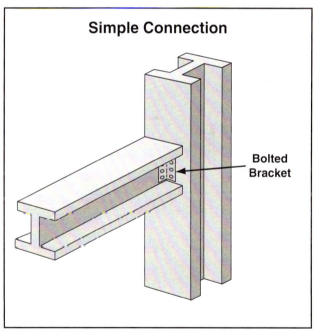

Figure 9.13 A rigidly designed beam and column connection often includes both bolts and welded joints.

Figure 9.14 A simple connection may use a bolted bracket that can support a vertical force but not lateral movement.

Rigid Frame

The connections between the beams and the columns in a rigid frame system are designed to resist the bending forces resulting from the supported loads and lateral forces **(Figure 9.13)**. Within this connection type, sufficient rigidity exists between the beam and the column so that no change occurs in the angle between the beam and the column as the loads are applied.

Simple Frame

The joints in a simple frame are designed primarily to support a vertical force. A degree of angular change between beams and columns can occur if some form of diagonal bracing is not provided **(Figure 9.14)**. Steel beams and trusses are frequently supported by a masonry wall. These designs are also examples of simply supported systems.

Semi-Rigid Frame

The connections in a semi-rigid frame are not completely rigid but possess enough rigidity to provide some diagonal support to the structure. When rigid connections are not used, lateral stability for a frame must be provided through the use of diagonal bracing or shear panels **(Figure 9.15, p. 248)**. Shear panels are reinforced walls located between columns and beams to brace them laterally. Ideally a shear wall should be continuous from the foundation of a building to the highest story at which it is needed.

Figure 9.15 Lateral bracing may be combined with rigid panels to resist lateral movement. *Courtesy of Colorado Springs (CO) Fire Department.*

Steel Trusses

Steel trusses provide a structural member that can carry loads across greater spans more economically than beams can. Steel trusses can be fabricated in a variety of shapes to meet specific applications. They are frequently used in three-dimensional space frames, in which case they are known as *delta trusses* because the cross-section resembles the Greek letter Delta (Δ) **(Figure 9.16)**. Two commonly encountered applications of the basic steel truss are the *joist girder* and the *open web joist*. Joist girders are heavy steel trusses used to take the place of steel beams as part of the primary structural frame **(Figure 9.17)**.

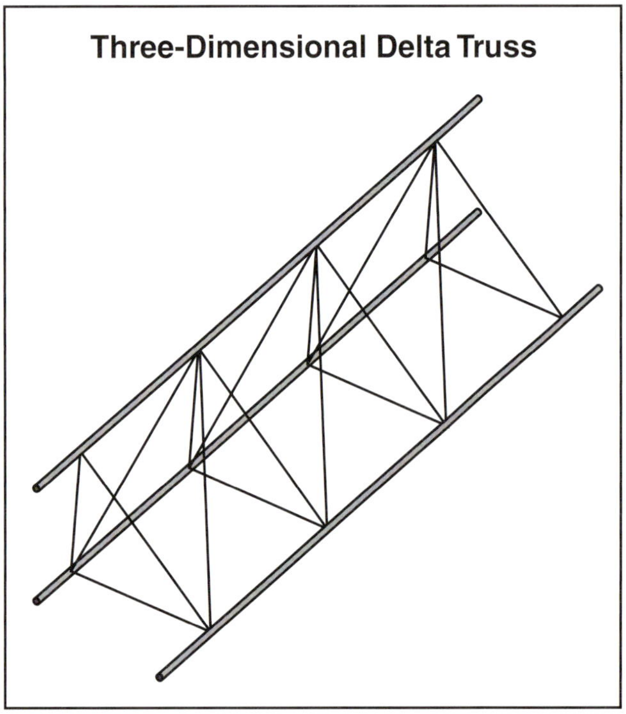

Figure 9.16 A three-dimensional Delta truss, known as a space frame, is one type of open-web steel structural support.

Figure 9.17 A steel joist girder is used in place of a heavy steel beam to support a roof.

Open web joists are mass produced and are available with depths of up to 6 feet (2 m) and span up to 144 feet (45 m). However, they are more frequently found with depths less than 2 feet (600 mm) and spans of 40 feet (12 m) **(Figure 9.18)**. The top and bottom chords of a web joist can be made from two angles, two bars, or a T-shaped member. The diagonal members can be made from flat bars welded to the top and bottom chords or they can be a continuous round bar bent back and forth and welded to the chords. When round bars are used for the diagonal members, the open web truss is known as a *bar joist* **(Figure 9.19)**.

Bar joists are frequently used in closely spaced configurations for the support of floors or roof decks. Bar joists are frequently supported on a masonry wall to support a roof. In multistory buildings, they are supported by the steel framing beams and are used for the support of the floor decks.

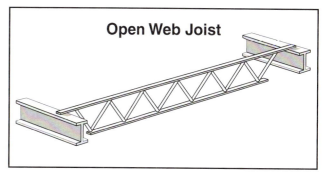

Figure 9.18 A series of open-web joists may be spaced closely together to provide support for a floor.

Figure 9.19 When bar joists are used to support a roof deck, they may be spaced farther apart according to the anticipated loads. *Courtesy of Ed Prendergast.*

Gabled Rigid Frames

Steel rigid-frame buildings with inclined (or gabled) roofs are widely used for the construction of one-story industrial buildings, farm buildings, and a variety of other applications **(Figure 9.20)**. The inclined top members of the one-story rigid frame configuration allow an increase in interior clear space. Steel rigid frames usually are used for spans from 40 to 200 feet (12 to 60 m) and are fabricated by welding or bolting together steel shapes and plates.

The top of the rigid frame is known as the crown and the points where the inclined members intersect the vertical members are known as the knees. The crown and the knees are designed as rigid joints with no rotation between members. The vertical members may be rigidly connected to the foundations depending on anticipated wind loads.

Gable roof rigid-frame structures must be braced diagonally for structural rigidity. This brace is built with diagonal cross-members in the plane of the roof and in the vertical plane of the walls between the rigid frame sections.

Figure 9.20 The construction of a steel rigid-frame building with a gabled roof starts with the frame. *Courtesy of Ed Prendergast.*

Steel Arches

Steel arches are used to support roofs on buildings where large unobstructed floors are needed, such as gymnasiums and convention halls. Steel arches can be constructed to span distances in excess of 300 feet (100 m).

Steel arches can be designed as either girder arches or trussed arches. A girder arch is constructed as a solid arch that may be built up from angles and

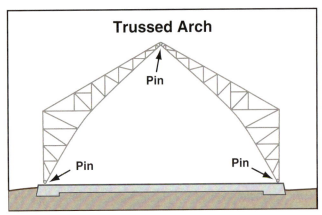

Figure 9.21 A hinged truss steel arch can include pins at strategic points to allow the frame to move slightly.

Figure 9.22 One style of support for a cantilever roof includes upright rods and cables. *Courtesy of Ed Prendergast.*

Figure 9.23 The size, reinforcement, material, and shape of a structural support will all affect its ability to maintain a load.

> **Slenderness Ratio** — Comparison of the height or length of a structural component and the width/thickness of the component. Used to determine the load that can be supported by the component; lower ratios indicate higher are more stable.

webs with a cross section similar to that of a beam. A trussed arch is built using truss shapes (**Figure 9.21**). The pin connections allow for slight movement between the two halves due to settling or temperature change.

Steel Suspension Systems

Steel can be used in slender components such as rods and cables. Drawing steel bars through a die to produce wire greatly increases the strength of the steel. Wire for use in bridge cables can have strengths as high as 300,000 psi (2 100 000 kPa). Such slender supports easily buckle under compression forces and therefore are limited to the support of tension forces.

Steel rods and cables are sometimes used in suspension systems to support roofs. Suspension roof systems can provide large unobstructed areas similar to arches without the reduction in vertical clearance at the sides of a building that occurs with an arch. As with arches, applications include sports complexes and convention halls. Steel suspension systems make some unique designs possible (**Figure 9.22**).

Steel Columns

Types of steel columns can range from simple single-piece cylindrical pipes to complex tower assemblies. The most common column cross-sections are:

- Hollow cylinder
- Rectangular tube
- Wide flange shape similar to the cross section of an I-beam

Steel columns can be disproportionately thin compared to their length because of the high compressive strength of steel. Thin steel columns are more likely to buckle than thicker columns made with other materials, even though the compressive strength of steel is higher. Engineers must plan safeguards to prevent buckling or weakening from exposure to high temperatures.

The possibility of buckling in an individual column is a function of its length, its cross-section, and the method by which the column is supported at its top and bottom (**Figure 9.23**). A property of a given column, known as its **slenderness ratio**, is used in combination with the condition of the column end to determine the load that can be safely supported without buckling.

The slenderness ratio compares the unbraced length of a column to the shape and area of its cross-section. The higher the numerical value of the slenderness ratio, the more likely it is that buckling will occur. In general, columns used for structural support in buildings should not have a slenderness ratio greater than 120.

In evaluating a given design, the significance of the slenderness ratio is modified by the manner in which the ends are attached to the rest of the structure. Columns that are erected so they cannot rotate at their ends have fewer tendencies to buckle than columns that are free to rotate at their ends **(Figure 9.24)**. For example, a round steel column that is simply resting on a concrete footing has low resistance to rotation at its ends and subsequent buckling. In contrast, a wide flange column with rigid connections at each end has a large resistance to rotation and buckling.

The investigation of a structural collapse under any circumstance must include an evaluation of any columns and their means of support. A beam that is simply supported by a column may become dislodged and fall off the supporting column if the column shifts or buckles.

Floor Systems in Steel-Framed Buildings

Steel structural components can be used to support floors in multistory buildings. The most common configurations are described in the following sections.

Open-Web Joists

A common floor design in steel-frame buildings uses a lightweight concrete with a minimum thickness of 2 inches (50 mm) supported by **corrugated** steel decking. The corrugated steel is, in turn, supported by open-web steel joists **(Figure 9.25)**. The steel joists can be supported by steel beams or directly supported on a masonry wall. The open web joists can also be used to support precast concrete panels or wood decking.

Steel Beams and Light-Gauge Steel Joists

Where floor loads or spans dictate, steel beams are used to support flooring instead of the lighter open-web joists. Light-gauge steel joists are also sometimes used to support flooring **(Figure 9.26)**. The light-gauge joists are produced from cold-rolled steel and are available in several cross-sections. Like the open-web steel joists, the light-gauge joists can be used to support metal decks or wood panel flooring systems. The steel joists are produced with depths of 6 to 12 inches (150 to 300 mm) and can be spaced 16 to 48 inches apart (400 to 1 200 mm) depending on the span and the load to be supported.

Code Modifications

Protected steel is one of the two common materials used in fire-resistive construction. The other material is reinforced concrete, which will be discussed in

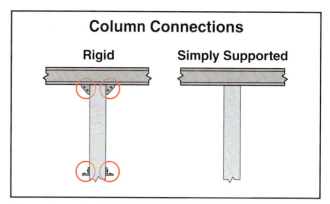

Figure 9.24 A column with rigid connections (left) will withstand buckling and twisting/rotating better than a simply supported column (right).

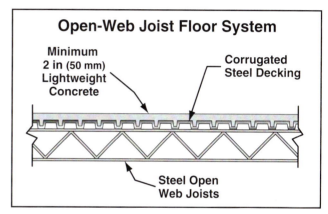

Figure 9.25 Lightweight floor systems can include construction materials including steel and concrete, arranged in slabs and trusses.

Corrugated — Formed into ridges or grooves; serrated.

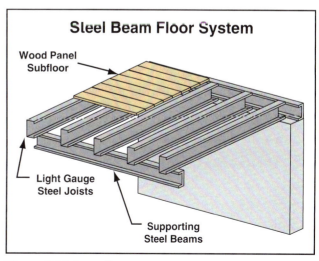

Figure 9.26 Some floor systems include steel beams and wood subflooring.

Chapter 10. Building codes specify the degree of fire resistance required for various structural members, and they also allow exceptions under certain circumstances. For example, the fire-resistance rating may be eliminated for roof construction located more than 20 feet (6 m) above the floor below for some occupancies. Another example is the allowed reduction of the required fire resistance when an automatic sprinkler system is provided that is not otherwise required by the provisions of the code.

As a consequence of these code provisions, firefighters may encounter unprotected steel structural members in buildings that are classified under the building code as fire-resistive. Proper preincident planning is necessary to help avoid making tactical decisions based on incomplete information.

Collapse of Steel Structures

Steel trusses that are constructed with slender components, and simply supported on a bearing wall or beam, can easily fail and collapse under fire conditions. As in the case of steel beams, failure will not occur unless the trusses are exposed to fire conditions.

The light-gauge steel sheeting used in floor systems and in roofs has a large surface area compared to its mass (large surface area to mass ratio). It will heat rapidly under fire conditions. Therefore, unprotected, light-gauge steel sheeting may fail structurally although it will not melt.

Connection types and their relative strength in fire conditions will influence the overall strength of steel structures. The following three connection types increase the mass at the point of connection to make it the last item to fail within a structural system.

The rigid connections used in the beam and girder type of frame have a greater mass of steel at the point of connection than do simple connections. Therefore, it takes much more heat to cause rigid connections to fail than it does in the less-massive simple connections. Rigid connections are frequently found intact after a fire even after other parts of a frame have failed. In contrast, a simply supported beam may fail under fire conditions as loads shift.

Figure 9.27 Steel gusset plates provide strength and additional mass at the joints. *Courtesy of McKinney (TX) Fire Department.*

Steel connections, both in the case of rigid connections used with beam and girder frames and heavy trusses, frequently use a steel web known as a *gusset plate* **(Figure 9.27)**. The primary purpose of a gusset plate is to strengthen the connection, and increase the steel mass at the connection, decreasing the possibility of failure.

In gabled rigid-frame structures, the knee joint between the roof and the wall will be the strongest part of the frame and the last part to fail **(Figure 9.28)**. This connection has greater mass than other similar places. The knee joint helps transfer the roof load to the vertical members.

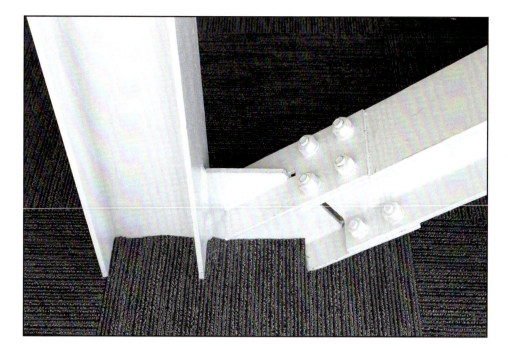

Figure 9.28 Some kinds of joints are stronger than the beams they connect.

Chapter Summary

Steel is a durable and noncombustible building material. Its strength permits it to be used for the framework in high-rise buildings. Steel can be used in columns, beams, and trusses. Steel trusses and beams can span greater distances than other materials. Steel, however, is affected by the heat of a fire. Steel members will lose a large percentage of their strength at the temperatures encountered in fires and can fail. The extent of failure that may occur will depend on the mass of the steel member. If steel is to be used in a fire-resistive building it must be protected and several methods are available to achieve this protection.

Review Questions

1. What are some advantages and disadvantages of using steel as a construction material?
2. What can be done to protect steel construction elements from fire?
3. How can steel be used in building construction to provide structural stability?
4. What can cause steel structures to collapse during fire conditions?
5. How do connection types influence the overall strength of steel structures?

Concrete Construction

Chapter Contents

- Case History 257
- **Material Properties of Concrete** 257
  - Reinforced Concrete 259
  - Applications of Concrete 263
  - Quality Control of Concrete 264
  - Fire Resistance of Concrete Construction ... 266
- **Concrete Framing Systems** 267
  - Flat-Slab Concrete Frames 267
  - Slab and Beam Framing 268
  - Waffle Construction 268
  - Concrete Plus Structural Steel 268
  - Precast Concrete 268
- **Chapter Summary** 272
- **Review Questions** 272
- **Chapter Notes** 272

chapter 10

Key Terms

Admixture 258	Precast Concrete 263
Aggregate 258	Prestressing 261
Cast-in-Place Concrete 263	Pretensioned Reinforcement
Cement 258	(Concrete) 262
Concrete 258	Reinforced Concrete 259
Flat Plate 266	Reinforcing Bars (Rebar) 259
Flat-Slab Concrete Frame 266	Slump Test 265
Heat of Hydration 264	Superplasticizer 258
Posttensioned Reinforcement	Tilt-Up Construction 271
(Concrete) 262	Two-Way Slab Construction 268

FESHE Outcomes Addressed In This Chapter

Fire and Emergency Services Higher Education (FESHE) Outcomes: *Building Construction for Fire Protection*

1. Describe building construction as it relates to firefighter safety, building codes, fire prevention, code inspection, firefighting strategy, and tactics.

2. Classify major types of building construction in accordance with a local/model building code.

3. Analyze the hazards and tactical considerations associated with the various types of building construction.

5. Identify the function of each principle structural component in typical building design.

8. Identify the indicators of potential structural failure as they relate to firefighter safety.

Chapter 10 • Concrete Construction **255**

Concrete Construction

Learning Objectives

After reading this chapter, students will be able to:

1. Identify material properties of concrete.
2. Differentiate between precast and cast-in-place concrete.
3. Determine factors that affect the finished quality of concrete.
4. Recognize factors that influence fire resistance in concrete construction.
5. Describe types of concrete framing systems.

Chapter 10
Concrete Construction

Case History

In March 2010, a fire department conducted a live fire training evolution in an acquired concrete block building. This old building had been used for storage in the city for several years. The structure was configured as a room and contents fire, and companies were tasked to practice extinguishment techniques. Between evolutions, the concrete ceiling partially collapsed due to the continued exposure to heat and fire. No one was inside the building at the time of the partial collapse.

An understanding of building construction is critical to understanding how fire will affect a structure. The wear on the building from the size and number of fires during this training evolution should have been taken into consideration. The team that set up the evolutions thought that concrete construction, with concrete floors and ceilings, should have been able to withstand these types and number of fires. A better understanding of how fire affects concrete would have helped predict what would happen during this training evolution.

Source: National Firefighter Near-Miss Reporting System, Report Number: 10-0000389

Like masonry, concrete does not burn. Concrete also resists insects and the effects of contact with soil. Concrete can be placed in forms to create a variety of architectural shapes. Concrete has many applications in building construction. This chapter includes information on the following aspects of concrete construction:

- Material properties of concrete
- Concrete framing systems

Material Properties of Concrete

Concrete is the hardened form of **cement** produced from portland cement, coarse and fine **aggregates**, and water **(Figure 10.1, p. 258)**. The aggregates are inert mineral ingredients that reduce the amount of cement that would otherwise be needed. Coarse aggregates include gravel or stone; fine aggregates include sand. Aggregates make up a large percentage of the total volume of concrete. The addition of water to the other ingredients forms a paste that coats and bonds the aggregate.

Figure 10.1 After curing, concrete can endure weathering for many decades, even when shaped into intricate designs.

Concrete — Strong, hard building material produced from a mixture of portland cement and an aggregate filler/binder to which water is added to form a slurry that sets into a rigid building material.

Cement — Any adhesive material or variety of materials which can be made into a paste with adhesive and cohesive properties to bond inert aggregate materials into a solid mass by chemical hardening. For example, portland cement is combined with sand and/or other aggregates and water to produce mortar or concrete.

Aggregate — Particulate material used in construction to provide a stable bedding or reinforce a composition material. Used as an extender in concrete. Can be graded into coarse and fine grain sizes and material types including sand, gravel, stone, etc.

Admixture — Ingredients or chemicals added to concrete mix to produce concrete with specific characteristics.

Superplasticizer — Admixture used with concrete or mortar mix to make it workable, pliable, and soft while using relatively little water.

In addition to the variance possible from the standard ingredients in concrete, **admixtures** can help tailor a batch of concrete for specific functions. Types of admixtures and their purposes include:

- Shale or clinker – Reduce the density of the concrete
- **Superplasticizers** – Produce a mixture that flows more freely
- Coloring – Added for aesthetic or safety reasons, such as indicating buried electrical cables

Types of Concrete

Specialized types of concrete include:

- Ordinary stone concrete
- Structural lightweight concrete
- Insulating lightweight concrete
- Gypsum concrete
- High early-strength concrete
- Expansive concrete
- Water-permeable concrete

Concrete structural elements usually retain their integrity and concrete slabs and walls act as good fire barriers. Concrete is widely used in fire-resistive (Type I) construction. The primary advantages of concrete include:

- Produced from locally available and low cost raw materials
- Fundamentally noncombustible
- Performs well under mild to moderate fire conditions
- Good insulating properties

Reinforced Concrete

Like masonry, concrete is strong in compression but weaker in tension. The ultimate compressive strength can range from 2,500 to 6,000 psi (17 500 to 42 000 kPa). The allowable stress used in design work will be reduced by a safety factor.

Because concrete is weak in tension, it cannot be used alone where tensile forces occur in a structure. Depending on the load the concrete will support, reinforcements may be added. **Reinforced concrete** includes components added to the concrete before it hardens to resist tensile forces. Reinforcing components can include steel **reinforcing bars (rebar)**, wire mesh, or fiberglass additives.

In some structural designs, such as an arch, the forces are primarily compressive. In these cases concrete could, theoretically, be used without reinforcing. The following sections discuss reinforcement techniques.

Ordinary Reinforcing

Ordinary reinforcing uses steel bars placed in the formwork, and wet concrete is placed in the formwork around the bars **(Figure 10.2)**. The design engineer must specify the number of reinforcing bars to be used, their size (diameter), and the depth of concrete cover around the bars.

The concrete must be properly compacted as it is placed in the forms to completely surround the reinforcing bars (rebar) and to avoid cavities in the hardened concrete. Mechanical vibrators are used to ensure that the wet concrete fills all the spaces within the formwork. The concrete then is permitted to cure. When the concrete has hardened, it adheres to the reinforcing bars because of textural shaping on the surface of the bars.

> **Reinforced Concrete** — Concrete that is internally fortified with steel reinforcement bars or mesh placed within the concrete before it hardens. Reinforcement allows the concrete to resist tensile forces.

> **Reinforcing Bars (Rebar)** — Steel bars placed in concrete forms before the cement is poured. When the concrete sets (hardens), the rebar within it adds considerable strength and reinforcement.

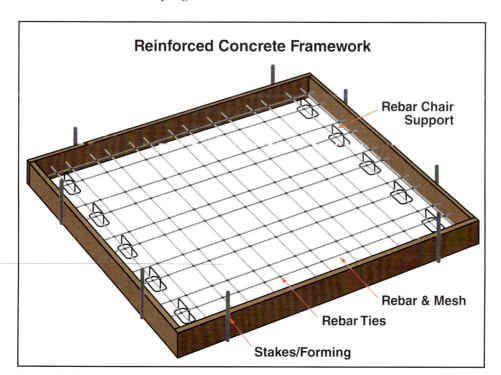

Figure 10.2 Reinforced concrete uses a planned grid of structural reinforcing materials to provide lateral and tensile support.

Rebar Reference
Rebar sizes are commonly referred to by a standardized number instead of the actual diameter[1]. For example, the diameter of #3 rebar is 0.375 inches (9.5 mm). The largest size listed is #18, and measures 2.257 inches (57 mm). The most commonly used size is #5 (0.625 inches [16 mm]).

The actual tensile and compressive forces developed within structural components are complex. For example, the fundamental tensile and compressive forces are not uniform throughout a beam. A concrete rigid frame requires an extensive placement of reinforcing steel (**Figure 10.3**).

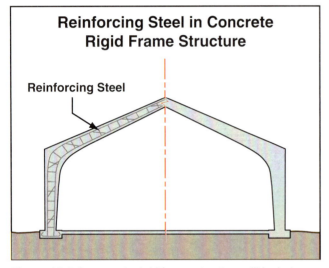

Figure 10.3 A concrete rigid frame structure will include reinforcing steel arranged in a strategic pattern.

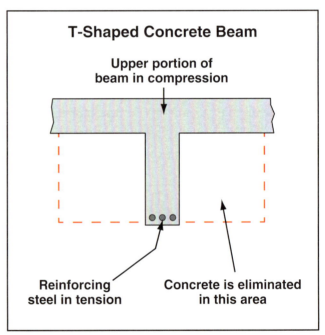

Figure 10.4 A tee-shaped concrete beam is a more efficient and lightweight design than an unshaped beam.

Concrete beams are frequently cast in the shape of a tee (**Figure 10.4**). The wider area at the top of the tee permits the concrete to support a greater load. At the same time, the removal of concrete below the top area reduces the dead load that would result with a simple rectangular beam. Reinforcing steel is placed in the bottom of the tee to resist the tensile force.

Although the primary function of placing reinforcing steel in concrete is to resist tensile forces, the steel can also be used to support some of the compressive forces. Vertical reinforcing bars are known as *stirrups* and are provided to resist the diagonal tension. The steel bars support some of the compressive load and also resist bending forces in the column from such sources as wind load and settling (**Figure 10.5**).

The compressive forces in a column can be great enough to cause the steel reinforcing bars to buckle even though they are embedded in the concrete. To avoid possible buckling, lateral reinforcing is provided around the vertical bars.

Figure 10.5 Vertical reinforcing bars in a concrete column allow the column to withstand a wider range of conditions. *Courtesy of Ed Prendergast.*

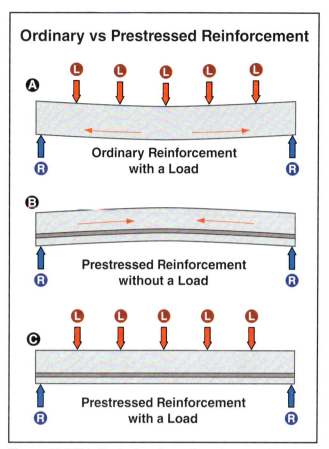

Figure 10.6 This illustration shows three images of a concrete beam. A) The load causes downward deflection. B) Prestressed reinforcing steel deflects the beam upward. C) When the load is applied to the prestressed beam, the tensile and compressive forces equalize and deflection disappears.

Ordinary reinforcing is a fundamental and useful construction method, but it has inherent limitations. When a concrete beam or floor slab supports a load, the concrete in the part of the beam in tension is essentially doing no work.

Prestressing Reinforcing

The technique of **prestressing** is a more efficient use of concrete than ordinary reinforcing. This technique tightens (preloads) the reinforcing steel, adding compressive stresses to the surrounding concrete. The compressive stresses counteract the tensile stresses from the applied load **(Figure 10.6)**. Two common methods of prestressing concrete are pretensioning and posttensioning, as explained below.

Regardless of any tension, reinforcing steel should not be cut during fire fighting operations unless it is necessary to rescue trapped victims. Cutting through reinforcing steel with a saw or torch is particularly dangerous in posttensioned concrete because the steel is not bonded to the concrete. The steel strands are stretched like giant rubber bands. If they are cut, they are likely to spring out of the concrete, injuring emergency responders. Releasing the posttensioned element may also lead to the failure of the concrete structural element, resulting in total or partial collapse.

Prestressing — Stress introduced to the concrete before the load is applied; accomplished by tensioning reinforcing bars before the concrete is poured.

> **CAUTION**
> Posttensioned reinforcing steel can recoil with violent force and destroy surrounding supports.

The prestressing process requires large loads to be applied to the concrete along the axis of the beam. These loads can result in compressing (shortening) the concrete over time. The steel may also slowly stretch in length. This stretching may result in a reduction of the compressive force and a possible loss of load-carrying capacity. To compensate for this loss, the forces that are initially applied during the prestressing process are slightly higher than the forces needed to support the intended concrete and applied loads. The strength of the reinforcing steel used in concrete is essential to the strength of a reinforced concrete component.

Pretensioning. **Pretensioned reinforcement (concrete)** uses steel strands (cables) stretched between anchors producing a tensile force in the steel. Concrete is then placed around the steel strands and allowed to harden. After the concrete has hardened sufficiently, the force applied to the steel strands is released.

As the force is released, the strands exert a compressive force in the concrete. When the steel strands are released, the concrete member usually takes on a slight upward deflection. As loads are applied to the pretensioned member, the deflection usually disappears and the member becomes flat.

Posttensioning. **Posttensioned reinforcement (concrete)** uses reinforcing steel cables that are not tensioned until after the concrete has hardened to a certain strength **(Figure 10.7)**. The forces that are produced in the posttensioning process remain locked in the steel for the life of the assembly.

Pretensioned Reinforcement (Concrete) — Concrete reinforcement method. Steel strands are stretched, producing a tensile force in the steel. Concrete is then placed around the steel strands and allowed to harden.

Posttensioned Reinforcement (Concrete) — Concrete reinforcement method. Reinforcing steel strands in the concrete are tensioned after the concrete has hardened.

Figure 10.7 Posttensioning strands in a concrete slab project from the slab until secured after the concrete fully cures. *Courtesy of McKinney (TX) FD.*

Technique for Posttensioning Concrete

Reinforcing strands are placed in a formwork and covered with grease or plastic tubing to prevent binding with the concrete. When the concrete has hardened, the strands are anchored against one end of the concrete member and a jack is positioned at the other end. The jack is used to apply tensile force to stretch the steel and result in a compressive force in the concrete. The pulled end of the reinforcing strand is anchored to the concrete and the jack is removed. The reinforcing cables are trimmed to the edge of the concrete and grouted.

> **Precast Concrete** — Method of building construction where the concrete building member is poured and set according to specification in a controlled environment and is then shipped to the construction site for use.
>
> **Cast-in-Place Concrete** — Common type of concrete construction. Refers to concrete that is poured into forms as a liquid and assumes the shape of the form in the position and location it will be used.

Collapse of Prestressed Concrete

Prestressed concrete systems may be more vulnerable to failure than ordinary reinforced concrete. The systems use reinforcing cables and rods made of high-strength steels that can yield at temperatures as low as 752°F (400°C). Therefore for the same depth of cover (insulation), a prestressed assembly will fail sooner than a conventional reinforced assembly.

Applications of Concrete

One differentiation in concrete applications is where it is cast and used. **Precast concrete** is placed in forms and cured at a plant away from the job site. Precast concrete structural members are then transported to the job.

Cast-in-place concrete is placed into forms at the building site as a wet mass and hardens in prepared forms **(Figure 10.8)**. Cast-in-place concrete permits the designer to cast the concrete in a wide variety of shapes. This type of concrete does not develop its design strength until after it has been placed in the location where it will be used. Most cast-in-place concrete is proportioned at bulk plants and then mixed in a mixing truck en route to the job site. The wet concrete is then transported from the truck to the formwork, either via buckets or pumping.

Figure 10.8 Cast-in-place concrete must be handled correctly for the intended end result. *Courtesy of McKinney (TX) FD.*

Both cast-in-place and precast concrete buildings can achieve the fire-resistance ratings required by building codes. Cast-in-place concrete buildings have a structural advantage over precast buildings because the nature of the construction of cast-in-place provides an inherent continuity in intersecting members. This continuity results in a fundamentally greater structural rigidity for cast-in-place buildings.

Regardless of where the concrete is cast, concrete in almost all structural applications is reinforced with steel **(Figure 10.9)**. Common applications for concrete include:

- Pavement
- Foundations
- Columns

Figure 10.9 Concrete is used for many functions, including structural and aesthetic applications. *Courtesy of McKinney (TX) FD.*

- Floors
- Walls
- Concrete masonry units (CMU)

Quality Control of Concrete

Great care must be exercised in the mixing, placing, and curing of concrete to ensure good quality. For example, if the concrete is vibrated excessively as it is placed in the forms, heavy coarse aggregates will settle at the bottom of the mixture and the water and cement will rise to the top.

Several factors affect the finished quality of concrete. The basic materials, including aggregates, may have a range of quality and features. For example, using sand from an ocean beach introduces salt into the concrete. Over time, the salt will corrode and deteriorate any reinforcing steel.

During the curing process, concrete will shrink slightly. The hardness of concrete is a function of time in days. Theoretically, properly cured concrete continues to harden indefinitely at a gradual rate; normal design strength is reached after 28 days.

Improper curing methods will also negatively affect the strength and finished surface of concrete. Poor-quality concrete will not attain its desired strength upon hardening or will otherwise be defective. Concrete of poor structural quality will break apart under fire conditions. The quality of concrete must be tested to ensure the suitability of the mixture for the purpose.

Water-to-Cement Ratio

The single most important factor in determining the ultimate strength of concrete is the water-to-cement ratio. Water reacts with the cement powder in the hydration process. An amount of water greater than required for curing is added to the concrete mix to increase its workability as it is placed in the forms. Some of this excess moisture evaporates and leaves microscopic voids in the hardened concrete; a portion of the excess moisture remains locked in the concrete. If too much water has been used in the mix, the final product will not achieve its desired strength.

Hydration

Hardening of concrete involves a chemical process known as *hydration*, in which water combines with the particles of cement to form a microscopic gel. As the concrete hardens, this gel releases **heat of hydration**.

Concrete initially hardens fairly quickly but then begins to harden more slowly. Proper curing requires that the concrete be kept moist until it reaches its desired strength. The moist curing of concrete produces a stronger concrete **(Figure 10.10)**.

> **Heat of Hydration** — During the hardening of concrete, heat is given off by the chemical process.

Temperature

In addition to maintaining proper moisture, concrete in the process of curing must be maintained at the correct temperature, ideally between 50° and 70°F (10° and 21°C). Concrete cured at or above 100°F (37°C) will not reach its proper strength. Concrete cured near freezing temperatures will harden more slowly.

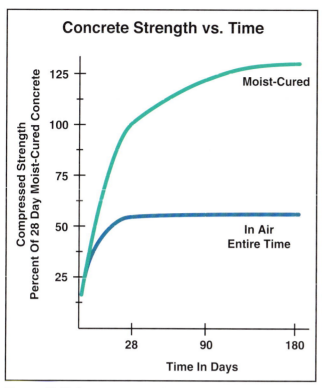

Figure 10.10 Concrete strength and cure time are closely related to the moisture levels maintained during curing.

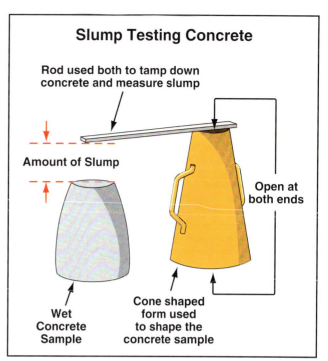

Figure 10.11 The slump in a concrete sample will indicate several features of the batch, including the moisture levels.

Temperature Control Strategies

During hot weather, concrete can be cooled with cold water, or can use chilled water in the mixing process. In cold weather, concrete can be protected with a heated enclosure. In massive concrete structures, the heat of hydration generated can adversely affect the final strength of the concrete. One strategy to minimize complications is to pour concrete in batches and allow each to cure to a certain strength before adding the next layer.

Concrete Quality Tests

The **slump test** uses a standard-sized cone-shaped mold and a sample of wet concrete. The purpose of this test is to check the moisture content of a batch of concrete, as indicated by the amount that the concrete settles (slumps) after it is removed from the test mold **(Figure 10.11)**. Concrete with high moisture content has greater slump than dryer concrete. Concrete with slump considered excessive by the structural engineer may be rejected.

Compression testing is a separate test that uses small test cylinders of a concrete batch to determine the compression strength of that batch. This method is accurate but has the disadvantage of requiring that the concrete be permitted to harden before the results are known. This test would be costly in both money and time if the concrete were ultimately found to be unsatisfactory.

Slump Test — Method of evaluating the moisture content of wet concrete by measuring the amount that a small, cone-shaped sample of the concrete slumps after it is removed from a standard-sized test mold.

Fire Resistance of Concrete Construction

Concrete structural systems can have fire-resistance ratings from one to four hours. The fire resistance of a concrete assembly is affected by such variables as the following:

- Concrete density
- Concrete thickness
- Concrete quality
- Supported load
- Depth of concrete cover over the reinforcing bars

NOTE: Although the steel used in reinforced concrete is not fire-resistive, the concrete surrounding the steel acts as insulation to protect it from the heat of the fire.

Some types of concrete are better insulators than others. For example, structural lightweight concrete has a lower density than ordinary concrete and has a lower thermal conductivity, and therefore acts as a better insulator against the heat of a fire than ordinary concrete of comparable thickness.

NOTE: Structural lightweight concrete is not used for load-bearing applications.

The fire resistance of concrete assemblies are sometimes compromised in ways including:

- Non-resistive members supporting concrete floor slabs or walls panels
- Precast wall panels horizontally braced with exposed steel roof beams **(Figure 10.12)**
- Openings in concrete slabs or walls without a rated assembly protecting the opening
- Force of an explosion **(Figure 10.13)**

> **Flat-Slab Concrete Frame** — Construction technique using concrete slabs supported by concrete columns.

> **Flat Plate** — Plain floor slab about 8 inches (200 mm) thick that rests on columns spaced up to 22 feet (6.5 m) apart and depends on diagonal and orthogonal patterns of reinforcing bars for structural support because the slab lacks beams; simplest and most economical floor system.

Figure 10.12 Steel trusses can serve both to hold precast concrete walls in place and function as floor or ceiling supports. *Courtesy of Dave Coombs.*

Figure 10.13 San Juan, Puerto Rico, November 22, 1996: Task Force members began performing search and rescue operations inside the Humberto Vidal Building following a gas mainline explosion. *FEMA News Photo.*

Spalling

The primary cause of spalling is the expansion of the moisture within concrete when heated or frozen. The expansion of the water as steam or ice creates tensile forces within the concrete. Because concrete has little resistance to tension, small pieces of the concrete break off. Spalling structurally weakens the concrete and exposes the reinforcing steel to the fire **(Figure 10.14)**.

The extent of spalling depends on the amount of moisture in the concrete and the length of time the concrete has been in place. New concrete that has not completely cured will spall more severely when exposed to a fire. The severity of spalling also depends on the duration and intensity of the components' exposure to fire.

Heat Sink Effect

Because concrete has relatively good insulating properties, it tends to retain the heat of an exposing fire and release it slowly, in an effect referred to as the *heat sink effect*. The heat released from the concrete is not enough to reignite combustibles, but will sustain high temperatures for a significant amount of time if not cooled. Firefighters must be aware of the concrete features that are a factor of conditions inside a structure during overhaul.

Concrete Framing Systems

Large cast-in-place structures cannot be cast in one operation. Construction joints unavoidably occur between successive pours. To transfer loads and stresses from one component to the next, the reinforcement steel will overlap the joints **(Figure 10.15)**. Concrete buildings are constructed with structural systems that use bearing walls formed from cast-in-place concrete. However, a more typical design is to construct a concrete frame. The following sections describe common cast-in-place structural systems.

Flat-Slab Concrete Frames

The **flat-slab concrete frame** is a simple system that consists of a concrete slab with concrete columns for support. The slab of concrete ranges in thickness from 6 to 12 inches (150 to 300 mm). Shear stresses develop in the concrete where the slab intersects the supporting columns. In a building that will support heavy live loads, the area around the columns is reinforced with additional concrete in the form of drop panels or mushroom capitals. If the building will support light loads, this additional reinforcing is not necessary. The system then is known as a **flat plate**.

Figure 10.14 Spalling may expose and weaken reinforcing steel, and cause failure of structural elements. *Courtesy of Ed Prendergast.*

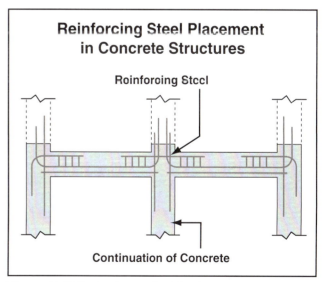

Figure 10.15 Redundancy of reinforcing steel rods in weaker places, such as intersections of slabs and columns, will provide continuity of strength between successive concrete pours.

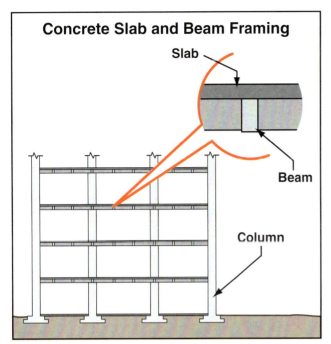

Figure 10.16 Slab and beam framing is a system of horizontal and vertical concrete components.

Figure 10.17 Waffle construction features shallower sections to reduce the weight of the slab, plus thicker, reinforced sections to maintain strength.

> **Two-Way Slab Construction** — Concrete construction framework type that uses reinforcing steel placed on the bottom of the framework that provides reinforcement in two directions. *Also known as* Waffle Construction.

Slab and Beam Framing

A slab and beam frame consists of a concrete slab supported by concrete beams **(Figure 10.16)**. This framing system is extremely lightweight and is best suited for buildings with light floor loads. Slabs in this type of construction can be as thin as 2 inches (50 mm). The concrete beams must be closely spaced in order to provide adequate support to the thin slab. This spacing often gives an appearance similar to wood joists and is sometimes referred to as *concrete joist construction*. Slab and beam systems are often highly susceptible to fire damage because of the thinness of the slab. Fireproofing of some sort is often necessary, especially when specific fire ratings must be achieved. When the concrete beams run mainly in one direction, the framing is known as a *one-way reinforced slab*.

Waffle Construction

Slab and beam concrete framing featuring concrete beams running in two directions is known as a **two-way slab construction**. Two-way slab construction is known as *waffle construction* because of the waffle-like pattern of the bottom of the concrete slab **(Figure 10.17)**. The pattern results from the placement of square forms over which the wet concrete is placed.

Waffle construction (two-way framing system) is used where spans are short and floor loadings are high. This design provides a thicker slab while eliminating the weight of unnecessary concrete in the bottom half of the slab. Reinforcing steel placed in the bottom of the formwork provides reinforcement in two directions.

Concrete Plus Structural Steel

Structural steel beams can replace concrete beams to support a poured concrete slab. If the assembly is intended for a Type I (fire-resistive) building, the steel must be provided with some form of fireproofing, as described in Chapter 9.

Precast Concrete

As noted earlier, precast concrete may be produced at a precasting plant some distance from the work site. Other precast components, such as tilt-up panels, are cast at the site and moved into position. The precast structural shapes, including slabs, wall panels, and columns, are transported to the needed location and hoisted into position **(Figure 10.18)**.

Figure 10.18 Large precast concrete wall sections can be lifted into place using heavy machinery. *Courtesy of McKinney (TX) FD.*

Figure 10.19 Precast concrete slabs may be engineered with foam insulation in the core for efficient on-site construction. *Courtesy of Gregory Havel, Burlington, WI.*

Advantages and Disadvantages

Advantages to using precast concrete include:

- Higher degree of quality control possible than with cast-in-place concrete:
  — Precasting forms can be located under a shelter.
  — Ingredients can be finely controlled for quality.
  — Mixing and pouring the concrete can be more mechanized and efficient.
- Work can proceed more quickly at the job site:
  — Construction and removal of on-site forms and frameworks is unnecessary.
  — Work can proceed immediately because concrete is already hardened.
- Precast concrete sandwich panels can be produced using a polystyrene core to improve the insulating properties of the precast concrete **(Figure 10.19)**.

A major disadvantage to using precast concrete is the need to transport the finished components to the job site. Transportation cost and limitations affect the dimensions of the shapes that can be precast.

Precast concrete buildings can be built using whole precast modular units but it is more common to assemble precast parts into a framework for a building. Therefore, from a construction standpoint, precast concrete structures have more in common with steel-framed buildings than with cast-in-place concrete buildings.

NOTE: Precasting concrete became a common practice after World War II.

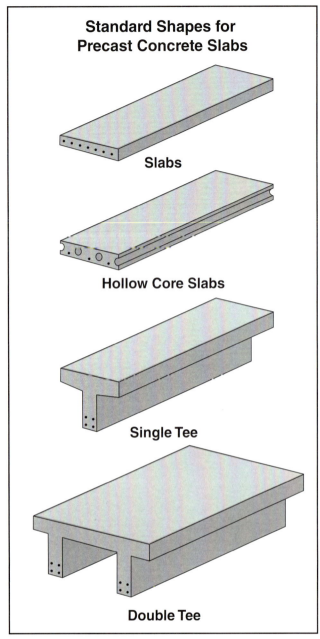

Figure 10.20 Standard shapes commonly used with precast concrete include slabs and tees.

Precast concrete slabs for floor systems can be cast in standard shapes that include solid slabs, hollow-core slabs, single tee slabs, and double tee slabs **(Figure 10.20)**. Solid slabs are used for short spans up to approximately 30 feet (9 m), while the tee slabs can be used for spans up to 120 feet (35 m).

Tilt-Up Construction

Tilt-up construction is a common form of construction used with precast concrete. In tilt-up construction, reinforced wall panels are cast at the job site in horizontal casting beds. After the concrete has cured, a crane tilts the wall panels up into the vertical position. Temporary bracing is provided until the roof supports or other permanent horizontal bracing is provided.

Tilt-up walls can be several stories in height. Tilt-up walls can support several types of roof including timber beams, precast slabs, steel beams, and steel trusses **(Figure 10.21)**. This style of construction requires that the roof assembly maintain structural integrity; failure of the roof can result in failure of the wall from outward horizontal forces.

Precast Connections

In a precast concrete structure, the connections between the individual components are a critical aspect of structural engineering. Precast construction has less continuity along the same span than cast-in-place frames.

A variety of techniques, such as bolting, welding, and posttensioning can be used to connect precast structural components to each other. In the simplest of precast designs, precast slabs simply rest on a bearing wall or column. Simple designs of this type are not inherently rigid and the slabs need to be laterally "tied" together to resist horizontal forces **(Figure 10.22)**.

Figure 10.21 Tilt-up structures often include structural steel elements including roof trusses. *Courtesy McKinney (TX) FD.*

Figure 10.22 Connections between precast concrete sections can include welded or bolted fasteners. *Courtesy of McKinney (TX) FD.*

Precast Parking Garages

Precast concrete is commonly used in the construction of parking garages. The floor loads and the span lengths make a precast structural system a practical choice. The precast columns and beams are typically left exposed. As indicated earlier in this chapter, precast products may be either pretensioned or posttensioned.

Precast parking facilities perform well structurally under fire conditions. For example, a fire in a parking garage in Chicago, Illinois involving 11 automobiles caused only minor damage to the structure.

Tilt-Up Construction — Type of construction in which concrete wall sections (slabs) are cast on the concrete floor of the building, then tilted up into the vertical position. *Also known as* Tilt-Slab Construction.

Identification of Concrete Systems

Concrete frame structures often have nonbearing curtain walls at their exterior. A curtain wall tends to conceal the structural details of a building and makes it difficult to make an accurate visual identification of the structural system. The choice of materials used in a curtain wall may be influenced by architectural style, thermal insulation properties, and cost. Materials may include:

- Aluminum
- Glass
- Steel panels
- Masonry

Because the exterior walls may be nonload-bearing, the type of reinforcement within the concrete may be difficult to identify. Frequently, the only warning firefighters have about the reinforcement type is a familiarity with prevailing construction methods in their jurisdictions and the results from preincident surveys.

Examples of details that are difficult to determine after construction is completed include:

- Ordinary reinforcing versus posttensioned reinforcing
- Cast-in-place concrete versus precast concrete
- Stucco and exterior insulation finish systems (EIFS) versus concrete **(Figure 10.23)**

Figure 10.23 Exterior finish Insulation systems can give the appearance of concrete construction regardless of the material used for the frame of the building – in this case, wood. *Courtesy of Ed Prendergast.*

Supports for precast beams may include corbels (brackets) cast into the columns. Another type of support for precast beams includes a short steel beam cast into the poured column. The precast beams are secured to the column through the use of steel angles cast into the columns or through the use of posttensioned steel cables.

Chapter Summary

Concrete is a noncombustible building material that is strong in compression but weak in tension; therefore, it must be combined with reinforcing materials. Several methods of reinforcing concrete include ordinary reinforcing and prestressing. The specific method used to reinforce a concrete structure cannot be identified visually. Therefore, reinforcing bars should not be cut unless it is necessary for rescue purposes.

Concrete structures are built from either cast-in-place or precast concrete. Precast concrete buildings are assembled in a manner similar to steel structures. Cast–in-place structures have greater inherent rigidity than precast structures.

Reinforced concrete structures generally perform well under fire conditions. The quality of the concrete affects the fire resistance. Spalling of concrete will result in failure of the reinforcing bars and failure of the structural assembly.

Review Questions

1. How is concrete produced?
2. Why might prestressed concrete systems be more vulnerable to failure than ordinary reinforced concrete?
3. Compare and contrast precast concrete and cast-in-place concrete.
4. What factors affect the quality of concrete?
5. What factors influence the fire resistance of concrete assemblies?
6. What are some examples of concrete framing systems?

Chapter Notes

1. "Rebar chart," United States Concrete, http://unitedstatesconcrete.com/rebar_chart.html.

Roofs

Chapter Contents

Case History 277
Roofs and Fire Fighting 278
Architectural Styles of Roofs 279
   Flat Roofs 279
   Pitched Roofs 279
   Curved Roofs 281
   Dormers 283
Roof Support Systems 283
   Flat Roof Support 283
   Conventional Roof Framing 285
   Pre-Engineered Roof Framing 287
   Arches 289
Roof Decks 289
   Function of the Roof Deck 289
   Roof Deck Materials 290

Roof Coverings 291
   Flat Roof Coverings 292
   Pitched Roof Coverings 294
   Fire Ratings of Roof Coverings 298
   Rain Roofs 299
Green Design Roofs 300
   Photovoltaic Roofs 301
   Vegetative Roof Systems 302
Roof Openings 303
   Penthouses 303
   Skylights 303
Chapter Summary 304
Review Questions 304
Chapter Notes 304

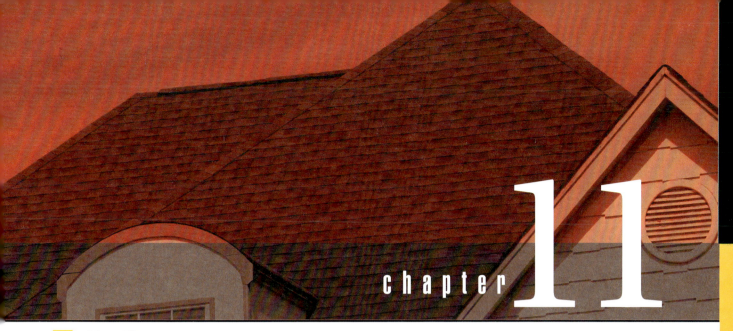

chapter 11

Key Terms

Clean Energy 301	Lamella Arch 282
Collar Tie 285	Nailability 290
Common Truss 287	Photovoltaic (PV) System 301
Conventionally Framed Roofs 285	Purlin 289
Green Design 300	Rafter 285
Green Roof 302	Rafter Tie 285
Inverted Truss 285	Ridge Board 285
Joists 283	Roll Roofing 289

FESHE Outcomes Addressed In This Chapter

Fire and Emergency Services Higher Education (FESHE) Outcomes: *Building Construction for Fire Protection*

1. Describe building construction as it relates to firefighter safety, building codes, fire prevention, code inspection, firefighting strategy, and tactics.
4. Explain the different loads and stresses that are placed on a building and their interrelationships.
5. Identify the function of each principle structural component in typical building design.
8. Identify indicators of potential structural failure as they relate to firefighter safety.

Roofs

Learning Objectives

After reading this chapter, students will be able to:

1. Explain the role roofs play in structural fire fighting.
2. Describe major architectural styles of roofs.
3. Identify types of roof support systems.
4. Describe the function of roof decks.
5. Identify materials used to construct roof decks.
6. Distinguish among types of roof coverings.
7. Identify types of green design roofs.
8. Recognize how roof openings can be used in fire fighting operations.

Chapter 11
Roofs

Case History

In 2002, the Hayman Fire burned 137,000 acres in the forests near Colorado Springs, Colorado. This fire started about two years after Colorado Springs Fire Department launched their Wildfire Mitigation program, which was designed to educate homeowners on the risks of wildfire. Knowing that wood roofs pose an extremely high risk of ignition during wildfires, and the fact that a large percentage of homes in our wildland urban interface neighborhoods had wood roofs, the fire department felt the time was right to proactively address the issue of wood roofs in the community.

Fire department staff studied the fire and the performance of various construction materials, including roofing products. The goal was to determine the contributing factors of the home ignitions, especially where those factors related to wildland fires. In the years before the fire, the department had conducted evaluations on 36,000 properties to determine existing attributes such as roofing and siding materials. The data from the evaluations allowed the researchers to accurately report the construction materials for each of the homes damaged or destroyed in the fire.

A task force was created including members from the fire department, building department, housing industry, community advocates, and homeowners. This task force researched various fires where wood roofing had been a direct contributor in the ignition of homes. The group also conducted extensive research on roofing materials, testing procedures, and rating systems of various roofing products and systems.

The findings concluded that 72% of the homes that burned had wood roofs, wood siding, or both. The findings also showed that burning brands and embers were responsible for 54% of the total number of home ignitions. Homes with Class A roofing products had a much higher survival rate. The conclusions from the study validated the department's concern over the risk of wood roofing materials and their vulnerability to wildfires.

The end result was the passage of a local ordinance requiring Class A roofs (assemblies) on all residential properties, and specifically excluding wood roofing materials. The ordinance did not require retrofits of existing roofs. Instead, it required that all new roofs or re-roofs comply with the Class A requirements. From the passing of the ordinance in 2002, through May of 2012, 55,000 roof replacements were permitted.

Roofs function as the primary sheltering element for the interior of a building, and the significance of roofs in fire protection and fire fighting operations has long been recognized. A number of critical fire fighting operations are conducted from roofs. Roofs constructed of combustible materials, however, can contribute to the problem. For example, the combustibility of thatched roofs was one of the first fire hazards addressed in the fire regulations adopted in colonial America. In modern times, combustible wood shake shingles that allow fires to travel from building to building are still a problem in some communities. Today, more roofs are being used as part of green design with solar panels and even gardens. Solar panels in particular represent a new element of safety hazard during emergency operations. Topics described in this chapter include:

- Roofs and fire fighting
- Architectural styles of roofs
- Roof support systems
- Roof decks
- Roof coverings
- Green design Roofs
- Roof openings

Roofs and Fire Fighting

A roof is a waterproof covering for a building. That fact can limit the penetration of streams from ladder pipes and platform apparatus from above into the seat of the fire. Furthermore, if the roof collapses into a structure, it will form a waterproof covering over buried fire.

Roofs play an important role in structural fire fighting. Firefighters work on roofs to ventilate heat and the products of combustion from within the structure. Sometimes, a roof may be used as a vantage point for attacking a fire involving a neighboring structure. And, of course, firefighters work beneath a roof whenever they are inside a building. For these reasons, firefighters must be familiar with all aspects of roof construction including such functional aspects as the use of a roof to support ventilation equipment. Several fundamental safety points regarding roofs include:

- Roofs are usually not as strong as floors because they are typically designed to support lighter live loads.
- Many types of roof construction have inherent concealed spaces between the ceiling and the roof deck, making it difficult to determine the extent to which a fire has developed overhead.
- Over time, loads may be added to roofs for which they were not originally designed **(Figure 11.1)**.

Roofs are subject to wear and deterioration from the elements. They are often repaired or renovated along with other parts of a building. A roof can wind up with several layers of roofing materials, again making it difficult for firefighters to determine the extent of fire or to perform ventilation.

Figure 11.1 Roofs can become overloaded over time if more and larger air conditioning units and equipment are added.

Architectural Styles of Roofs

From a fire fighting standpoint, the roofs of buildings can be classified into three styles: flat, pitched, and curved. Each of these are addressed below with a discussion of the fire fighting strategies and life safety aspects.

Flat Roofs

Flat roofs are found on all types of buildings including large-area warehouses, factories, shopping centers, schools, and numerous other applications **(Figure 11.2)**. It is possible to construct a roof that is completely horizontal, but this design presents a drainage problem. If the roof is not constructed with a method for drainage, pools of water will form, which leads to early deterioration. Therefore, many flat roofs are provided with a slight slope, typically from front to rear to facilitate drainage. Many large buildings have roofs sloped toward drains in the center of the roof. These roof drains may have the capacity to handle a heavy rainfall, but not the water from a master stream. Firefighters must remember that these streams may overload the roof structure and cause it to collapse.

Flat roofs are the easiest roofs on which firefighters can work. However, they can provide a false sense of security and are not without potential dangers. In darkness, a firefighter can step off the edge of a roof or stumble over a low parapet. Firefighters can also fall through an opening in a roof such as an opened roof hatch or skylight, or hole that has been cut for ventilation.

Pitched Roofs

Care must be taken when interacting with any roof, but especially on steep roof pitches and slick roofing materials. A pitched roof is designed to shed water and snow **(Figure 11.3)**. The pitch of a roof presents a major hazard to firefighters because the steepness of the roof results in a lack of secure footing. This hazard is increased when the roof is wet or covered with ice but also exists when the roof is dry because of the loose or granular texture of some roof coverings. Loose or broken pieces of roof tiles can also slide off a pitched roof and create a hazard to firefighters on the ground.

The inclined surfaces of pitched roofs may be categorized into low slope roofs and medium to high slope roofs. Low slope roofs have a slope of up to 3/12, meaning for each 12 units of horizontal dimension the roof slopes upward 3 units **(Figure 11.4)**. Medium to high

Figure 11.2 Flat roofs are commonly constructed over large buildings.

Figure 11.3 Steeply pitched roofs may not provide stable footing for work that must be done at the level of the roof. *Courtesy of Chris E. Mickal, NOFD Photo Unit.*

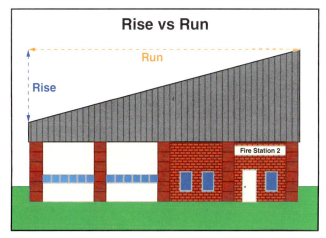

Figure 11.4 Rise and run are the two metrics used to numerically indicate the pitch of a roof.

Figure 11.5 Medium and high-pitched roofs are too steep for firefighters to work on them safely. *Courtesy of McKinney (TX) FD.*

slope roofs have slopes of 4/12 to 12/12 **(Figure 11.5)**. (A slope of 12/12 equates to a 45-degree angle.) Some structures, including churches and mansions, have roofs with slopes of 18/12 or greater — too steep to work from a roof ladder. Aerial apparatus or ground ladders are a safer alternative.

Climate, function, and aesthetic considerations determine the design of pitched roofs. The simplest pitched roof is the shed roof that slopes in only one direction. Several commonly encountered pitched roof styles include **(Figure 11.6)**:

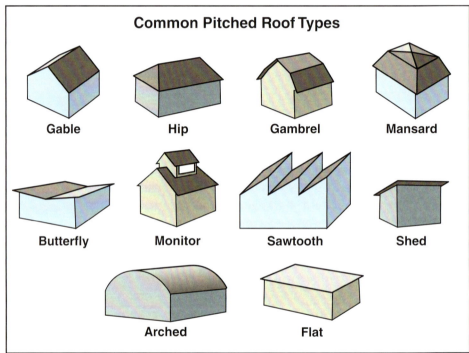

Figure 11.6 Common pitched roof types each have unique features that make them ideal for some applications.

- **Gable roofs** - Common roof style that consists of two inclined surfaces that meet at their high side to form a "ridge."

- **Hip roof** - Style that slopes in four directions and has a degree of slope similar to the gable roof.

- **Gambrel roofs** - Slope in two directions, but there will be a break in the slope on each side. The space under gambrel roofs can be used as an attic or living space.

- **Mansard roof** - Has a break in the slope of the roof on all four sides. A mansard roof constructed with a flat deck is sometimes known as a *modern mansard* or *deck roof*. The mansard style roof forms a projection beyond the building wall that creates a concealed space through which a fire can travel **(Figure 11.7)**. A false mansard front is sometimes added to the front of a flat-roofed building as an architectural detail. Firefighters may be exposed to danger while working under these structures, which can collapse in large sections.

Figure 11.7 A mansard-style structure includes a fascia over the building wall that may conceal a void space.

- **Butterfly roof** - Roof style that slopes in two directions — basically two shed roofs that meet at their low eaves.
- **Monitor roof** - Style designed to provide light and ventilation. Monitor roofs were once commonly used on factory buildings. A raised central section of the roof extends several feet above the surrounding roof surface. The vertical sides of this monitor section, which are normally openable windows, are known as "clerestories."
- **Sawtooth roofs** – A style also once commonly used on industrial buildings for light and ventilation. Ideally, the glass vertical sections should face north because the northern light is more constant during the day and the glare of the sun can be avoided.

NOTE: Modern ventilation and lighting systems have largely eliminated the need for monitor and sawtooth roofs.

Curved Roofs

Curved roof surfaces take their form from the structural system used to support them. Curved roofs are most frequently supported by arches and bowstring trusses. A dome roof can be used to cover a circular area **(Figure 11.8)**. A dome can be thought of as an arch rotated 360 degrees on its top point (keystone).

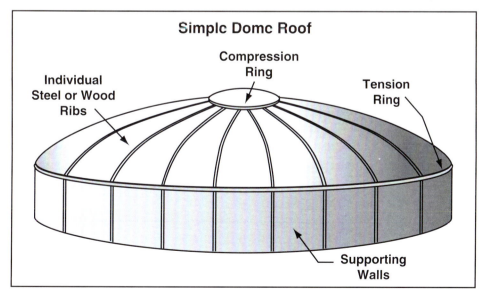

Figure 11.8 Circular roofs are often constructed as a series of half arches that connect at a central point.

The structural forces of a dome roof are similar to those of an arch. However, the forces in a dome are exerted around a complete circle instead of just one plane. More architecturally spectacular curved roofs can be created using "lamella" arches or geodesic domes.

NOTE: Arches were discussed in Chapter 3.

Lamella Arch

The **lamella arch** is a special form of roof constructed from short pieces of material known as *lamellas* **(Figure 11.9)**. Lamellas are most commonly made of wood, and vary in thickness from 2 x 8 inches (50 x 200 mm) to 3 x 16 inches (75 x 400 mm) and in lengths varying from 8 to 14 feet (2.5 to 4 m). The short lamellas are bolted together in a diagonal pattern with a special plate known as a *lamella washer*. The curvature of the lamella arch results from the beveling

> **Lamella Arch** — Arched roof structure composed of a series of intersecting, skewed arches, made up of relatively short, straight members; two members are bolted, riveted, or welded to a third piece at its center.

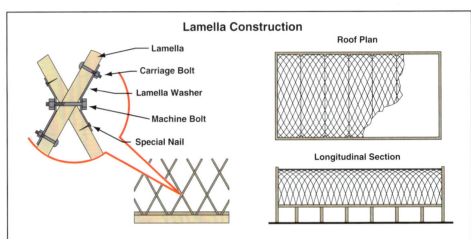

Figure 11.9 The compression and tension rings in a lamella dome are the most important factors in the structural integrity of the dome.

(inclining) of the ends of the individual lamellas. Lamellas can form a dome as well as an arch. If the compression or tension rings in a lamella dome are damaged to the point of failure, the entire structure will fail. Both rings are required for this design to remain sound. Roofs of this type have been used for occupancies including:

- Gymnasiums
- Exhibitions halls
- Auditoriums

Geodesic Domes

A geodesic dome is created using spherical triangulation. That is, triangles are arranged in three dimensions to form a nearly spherical surface **(Figure 11.10)**. A geodesic dome can be constructed with materials including:

- Wood
- Steel
- Concrete
- Plywood
- Bamboo
- Aluminum

Figure 11.10 Geodesic domes are constructed by strategically arranging triangle-shaped materials.

Dormers

A dormer is frequently provided in buildings with pitched roofs to increase the available living space in an attic **(Figure 11.11)**. False dormers are also used as decorative elements, but the false impression of increased living space may create challenges for fire departments when determining the need for ventilation and search and rescue operations **(Figure 11.12)**.

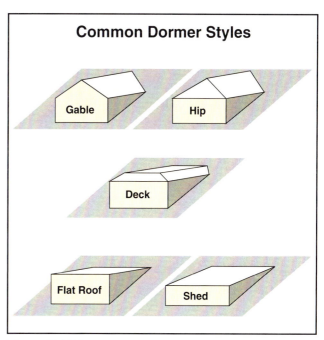

Figure 11.11 Several styles of dormers are commonly used in pitched roofs.

Figure 11.12 Dormers are designed to create extra living space and allow natural light into a structure.

Roof Support Systems

As a tactical factor, firefighters must be able to identify the type of supports and materials used in roof construction. Different types of roof support systems will react differently in fire and collapse conditions.

Flat Roof Support

Flat roofs may be supported by open-web steel **joists** and steel beams **(Figure 11.13)**. The simplest system of flat roof support uses ordinary wood joists supported at either end by load-bearing walls. The wood joists function as beams to support the roof deck just as floor beams support a floor system. Solid or laminated beams and columns may be used to support the wood roof joists.

Joists — Horizontal structural members used to support a ceiling or floor. Drywall materials are nailed or screwed to the ceiling joists, and the subfloor is nailed or screwed to the floor joists.

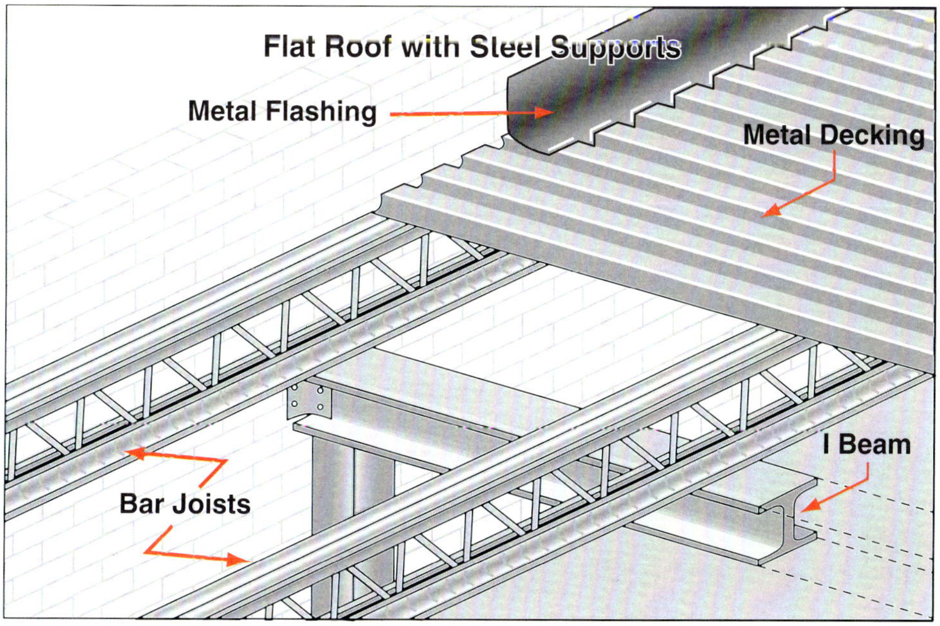

Figure 11.13 One type of flat roof structural system includes steel beams supporting steel joists.

The traditional wood-joisted roof uses solid wood joists that tend to lose their strength gradually as they burn. This loss of strength results in the roofs becoming soft or "spongy" before failure, especially with a wood plank roof deck.

Although the softening or sagging of a roof is an obvious indication of structural failure, it should not be mistaken as being the only sign of imminent collapse. The relatively thin plywood or oriented strand board used for roof sheathing can fail quickly without prior warning. Firefighters should view any indication of advanced or heavy fire development as a warning sign that the roof is weakening.

WARNING
Roof support systems can fail without warning under fire conditions.

Box Beams and I-Beams

In modern practice, box beams and I-beams manufactured from plywood and wood truss joists are often used to support flat roofs **(Figure 11.14)**. Although these beams provide adequate strength, the thin web portion of plywood I-beams renders them susceptible to early failure in a fire. The relatively slender component pieces of truss joists are also susceptible to early failure during a fire.

In addition, the open web design of truss joists also permits the rapid spread of fire in directions perpendicular to the truss joist instead of simply along the long dimension of the member. Depending on the fuel load within an occupancy, unprotected lightweight open-web joists can be expected to fail quickly in a fire.

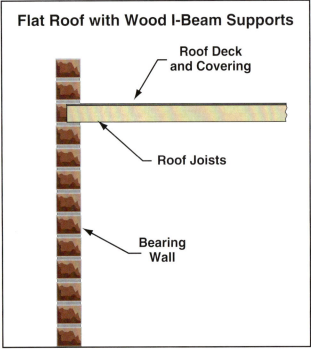

Figure 11.14 Simple flat roofs may be constructed with wood beams shaped for the purpose.

CAUTION
Unprotected lightweight open-web joists of any material should be expected to fail quickly in a fire.

Under certain conditions, building codes will allow the omission of structural fire proofing from roof supports in Type I construction. For example, fireproofing can be omitted from roof supports when the roof is located more than 20 feet (6 m) above the floor in an assembly occupancy. Therefore, unprotected steel roof supports may be encountered in a building in which the main structural supports are fire-resistive.

Because roofs are designed for lighter live loads than floors are, it is not unusual for modern flat roofs to deflect or vibrate noticeably as personnel walk across them. Nonetheless, flat roofs usually must be designed to support the weight of at least a few workers so they can be accessed safely for maintenance purposes. Therefore, deflection or vibration under the weight of firefighters may not signal imminent failure. However, the deflection and vibration are an indication of lightweight roof construction, and firefighters should view such construction cautiously.

Inverted Roofs

A variation of the flat roof is a type known as the inverted roof. Inverted roofs use **inverted trusses** that differ from conventional roofs primarily in the location of their main roof beams. In a conventional roof system, the main joists are located at the final roof level directly supporting the roof deck. A ceiling is attached to the underside of the joists or, more commonly, suspended below the joists. With the inverted roof, the main joists are located at the level of the ceiling and a framework is constructed above the main joists to support the roof deck. From the outside, the inverted roof looks like any other flat roof. The design of the inverted roof creates a concealed space that may be several feet in height between the ceiling and the roof deck.

Conventional Roof Framing

Conventionally framed roofs use inclined members to support some types of pitched roofs that are built on site utilizing dimensional lumber **(Figure 11.15)**. Construction of this type of roofing system is becoming less common as a construction technique because this type of construction has higher requirements than prefabricated framing systems in the following categories:

- Knowledge and skills of construction crews
- Cost of materials
- Time needed for construction

Conventional framing components include:

- **Rafters**
- **Ridge boards**
- **Collar ties**
- Ceiling joists and **rafter ties**

> **Inverted Truss** — Truss support system that is constructed with a deep triangular portion projecting down instead of up, and the portions of a standard truss are under compression instead of tension.
>
> **Conventionally Framed Roofs** — Roofing system constructed on site; often uses dimensional lumber and nails/screws but can also use preengineered components.
>
> **Rafter** — Inclined beam that supports a roof, runs parallel to the slope of the roof, and to which the roof decking is attached.
>
> **Ridge Board** — Highest horizontal member in a pitched roof to which the upper ends of the rafters attach. *Also known as* Ridgepole.
>
> **Collar Tie** — Horizontal roof framing member in the top third of the framing system; braces the roof framing against the uplift of wind.
>
> **Rafter Tie** — Horizontal roof framing member at the bottom of the roof framing system; helps keep walls from spreading due to the weight of the roof.

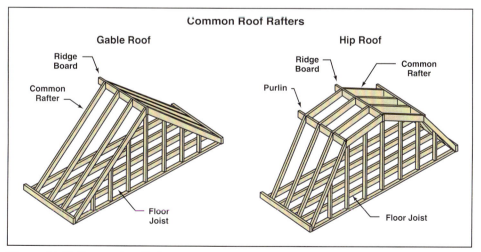

Figure 11.15 Conventionally framed pitched roofs are commonly constructed on site.

Figure 11.16 The roofing structural supports of a pitched roof place an outward load against the wall supports. *Courtesy of Wil Dane.*

These types of supports are used with many types of roofs. Even primarily pre-engineered roof systems include some conventionally framed portions. The most common roof types constructed with conventional framing include:

- Shed
- Gable
- Hip
- Gambrel
- Mansard

The basic design of a raftered roof results in an outward thrust against the walls, similar to the action of an arch **(Figure 11.16)**. Ceiling or attic floor joists resist the outward thrust of the rafters. If these joists are damaged or destroyed in a fire, the roof can push out against the walls. If the architect desires to leave the underside of the roof exposed without joists, a structural ridge beam must be used to support the rafters **(Figure 11.17)**.

Conventional roof framing is constructed using substantial materials. Fasteners common to this type of roof structure include:

- Nails and screws at connection points
- Heavy bolts or brackets in heavy timber construction
- Architectural hardware for exposed beams

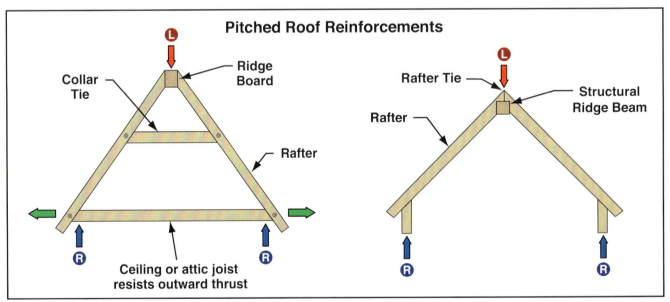

Figure 11.17 The removal of one type of structural support in a roofing system necessitates the addition of a different type of support that will counteract the same forces.

Rafters are commonly made of wood, although steel beams and steel trusses can be found in contemporary commercial construction. Supports are often substantial, with the ridge beam typically one size larger than the rafter. Wood rafters vary in size from 2 x 4 inches (50 x 100 mm) to 2 x 14 inches (50 x 350 mm). They can be spaced from 12 to 24 inches apart (300 to 600 mm), depending on the span and design load. The failure of one or two supports causes the roof deck to give more than in places where the decking is more solid. The corresponding spongy texture of partially supported decking is an indication to firefighters that the rest of the decking should not be trusted.

Pre-Engineered Roof Framing

Pre-engineered roof framing, also known as roof trusses, are a common roof support system. Trusses use less material and are lighter than a comparable beam or joist for an equal span. The reduced mass of their components and the interdependence of those components make them vulnerable to early failure under fire conditions **(Figure 11.18)**.

> **Common Truss** — Truss structure with the chords and diagonal members arranged in parallel planes. *Also known as Monoplane Truss.*

Several types of roof trusses may be used to support roofs. A **common truss** is arranged with all of the chords and diagonal members in the same plane **(Figure 11.19)**. This configuration is typical of lightweight trusses.

NOTE: Common types of trusses are illustrated in Chapter 3 of this manual.

Figure 11.18 Roof trusses are often significantly lighter in weight than the supporting walls. *Courtesy of Ed Prendergast.*

Figure 11.19 Common truss systems align all the structural chords and diagonal members in the same plane. *Courtesy of McKinney (TX) FD.*

As discussed in Chapter 3, lightweight wood trusses are commonly used in many types of structures. The joints used in trusses often are connected using gang-nail type gusset plates **(Figure 11.20)**. In trusses of this type, the individual members would be wooden 2 x 4 (50 x 100 mm) or 2 x 6 (50 x 150 mm) and individual trusses would be spaced 2 to 4 feet (0.6 to 1.2 m) apart center to center. Where a heavier truss system is needed, multiple wood components or steel trusses may be used together.

Void spaces in truss roof construction are large because of the unblocked distance between the top chord and bottom chord and internal supports of truss systems. When fighting a fire in a building with structural truss components, the AHJ should consider prioritizing defensive fire suppression operations.

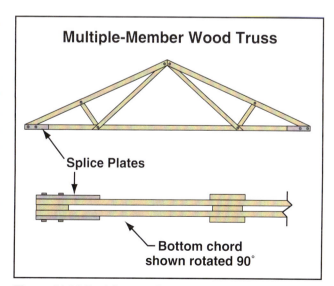

Figure 11.20 Each intersection within each truss is connected using a gusset plate.

Bowstring Trusses

Bowstring trusses, which use a curved top chord, were once commonly used for roofs, and many remain in use **(Figure 11.21)**. This assembly uses split-ring connectors at all joints, except the heel plates located at the ends of the truss **(Figure 11.22)**. The two elements work together to maintain structural stability. In simple terms, the top chord (bow) tries to straighten out and the bottom chord (string) maintains the shape of the top chord through tension.

The failure of any single element of a bowstring truss will lead to catastrophic failure. A failed wood bowstring truss may only partially fall out of place, with some of the supports remaining in tension against the supporting wall. This pressure creates an outward horizontal force against the wall that can result in collapse of the wall. Modern construction techniques, including steel trusses, have replaced the need for bowstring trusses for large covered open areas.

Figure 11.21 A bowstring truss is identifiable by its distinctive curved roof.

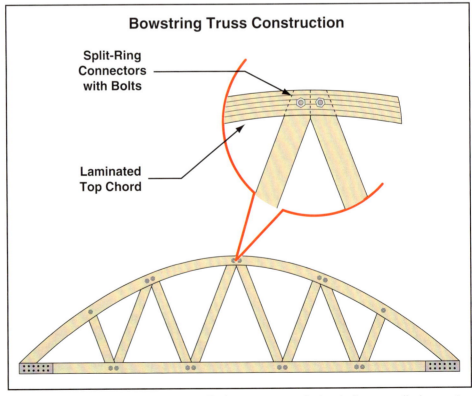

Figure 11.22 Bowstring trusses use split-ring connectors instead of gang-nailed gussets at most of the intersections within the truss.

Wood and Steel Trusses

Roof trusses are fabricated from steel as well as wood. Fink and Pratt trusses are the most common types used for pitched roofs. Both wood and steel trusses are usually fabricated elsewhere and shipped to the job site. If a truss is too large to be transported as one unit, it can be moved in sections and connected in the field.

Arches

Arches will often behave true to their construction materials in fire conditions. Materials used in arches include:

- Masonry
- Laminated wood
- Steel

NOTE: The basic structural principles of an arch were described in Chapter 3.

A complicating factor may include the use of a steel tie rod between the two ends of the arc in an arch-supported roof to resist the outward thrust. Failure of the tie rods will permit the arches to spread outward and the roof will collapse. The tie rods extend through the interior of the building and are usually unprotected.

> **Roll Roofing** — Roof covering made of flexible material that may be applied to the roof deck as a continuous sheet. Commonly used on shallow pitch roofs.
>
> **Purlin** — Horizontal member between trusses that support the roof.

Roof Decks

Roof decks serve several purposes including separating the structure from the effects of weather and supporting the weight of the materials used to weatherproof the structure. During fire suppression responses, the incident analysis must account for the support system of the roof and the structural integrity of that support.

Function of the Roof Deck

The deck of a roof is the portion of roof construction to which the roof covering or **roll roofing** material is applied **(Figure 11.23)**. Through the deck, the loads on the roof are transmitted to the roof supporting members. The components of roof decks include sheathing, roof planks or slabs, and **purlins**. Sometimes, as in concrete deck roofs, the roof deck serves as the roof support. In other

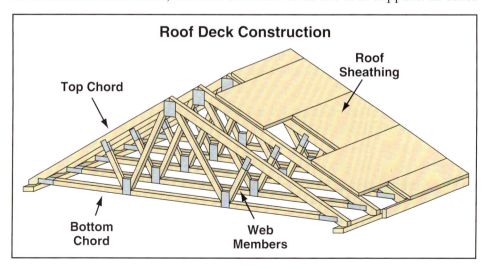

Figure 11.23 Roof decks are added to the outermost surface of the roof. Figure 11.15 includes purlins, a structural feature of some roofs that may be an additional anchor point for decking.

cases, the roof covering and the deck are the same. Corrugated steel decking is frequently used in applications where it serves as both the deck and the exterior roof covering **(Figure 11.24)**.

A roof deck must be stiff enough that it does not deflect excessively under anticipated loads. From a construction standpoint, the deck material should be clean and smooth so that any insulation or roof covering can be attached.

Figure 11.24 Where a roof's purpose does not include significant thermal insulation, corrugated steel may be used as both decking and roof finish material. *Courtesy of McKinney (TX) FD.*

Roof Deck Materials

Materials used in the construction of roof decks include:

- Plywood
- Wood planks
- Corrugated steel
- Precast gypsum or concrete planks
- Poured gypsum
- Poured concrete
- Cement planks containing wood fiber

Wood panel decking may have a thickness of ½ inch (13 mm) on supports 24 inches (600 mm) on center. Wood planks will have a minimum 1-inch (25 mm) nominal thickness.

Corrugated steel used in roof decking ranges from 29 gauge, the thinnest, to 12 gauge, the thickest. The overall depth varies from ¾ to 2 inches (19 to 50 mm). Corrugated steel decking can be used with a sheet of flat steel welded to the bottom to form cellar decking. The attached flat steel increases the stiffness of the deck.

Gypsum has the advantage of being **nailable**. Precast concrete can also be made nailable with the inclusion of an appropriate aggregate. Cast-in-place concrete decks are not nailable. When cast-in-place concrete is used as a roof deck, the roof must be attachable to the deck. This attachment may be accommodated with wood nailing strips imbedded in the concrete at intervals of 3 feet (1 m), or similar strips drilled and anchored, or placed between rigid insulation panels if rigid insulation is used.

> **Nailability** — Property of a material that allows it to accept a fastener, such as a nail. Nailable materials include wood, gypsum, and some thin metals.

The usual practice in a multistory building with a flat roof is to use the same structural system for the roof and the floors because it is more economical. Therefore, a building with wood-joisted floors will usually have a wood-joisted roof system, and a steel-framed building will have a steel roof. Exceptions to this general rule may exist, especially where an additional story has been added to an older building. If a building has been fire damaged and the roof is replaced, a roof structure different from the original may be installed. As a result, firefighters may encounter unusual combinations of floor and roof construction. An example would be steel bar joists supporting a steel deck roof in a building with wood-joisted or heavy-timber floor construction.

Roof Coverings

The roof covering provides the water-resistant barrier for the roof system. The type of roof covering used depends on the form of the roof structure, the slope of the roof, the local climate, and the appearance desired. Some other factors that affect the choice of roof covering include:

- Maintenance requirements
- Durability
- Wind resistance
- Fire resistance

Examples of conditions roofing materials must resist include:

- Punctures from hail
- Corrosion from fog, salt air, smoke, and other pollutants
- Expansion and contraction from roof-top temperatures that can range from over 100°F (38°C) in the summer and below 0°F (-18°C) in the winter

Given the wide range of considerations, it is not surprising that a large number of roof covering materials and systems are in use. A roof covering can consist of a single layer of material as in a corrugated steel roof. More typically, it can consist of several layers of material used in combination. Furthermore, as roofs are repaired and resurfaced over time, firefighters may encounter more than one layer and type of roof covering on a given roof.

Layers of Roofs

New roofing materials are sometimes added over an existing roof for the following reasons:

- Repair sections of damage
- Update the roofing materials at a minimum of cost and disruption
- Cheaper and faster than replacing the entire roof covering

The primary concern with layered roofs is the extra thickness of the roofing materials that will impede progress during ventilation and access operations. When the materials are not consistent through all of the layers, the ventilation team may have to call for extra resources during the process.

NOTE: Adding layers to roofs should not be confused with the construction of a rain roof over an existing roof. Rain roofs are discussed later in this chapter.

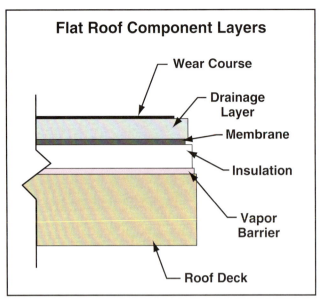

Figure 11.25 Flat roofs often include several layers of materials each intended to mitigate specific conditions.

Flat Roof Coverings

Because flat roofs drain more slowly than pitched roofs, they usually require more complex roof covering assemblies than pitched roofs. In addition to the roof decking previously described, a flat roof usually consists of several component layers, explained in the following sections **(Figure 11.25)**.

Vapor Barrier

The vapor barrier is designed to reduce the diffusion of interior moisture into the insulation layer. It is used in climates where significant temperature fluctuations are common. Vapor barriers consist of a continuous sheet of material resistant to the passage of water vapor including:

- Plastic
- Aluminum foil
- Kraft paper laminated with asphalt
- Asphalt saturated roofing felt

Thermal Insulation

The thermal insulation reduces heat loss through the roof. In addition to resisting the flow of heat, the insulation should have resistance to mechanical damage such as gouging, moisture decay, and fire. Insulation can be poured or rigid. Poured insulation materials can be portland cement or gypsum. Several rigid insulation materials are in use and are listed in **Table 11.1**.

Roofing Membrane

The membrane used under a roof consists of waterproof material that keeps out rain and snow from the interior of the building. The three general categories of membranes used are *built-up membranes, single-ply membranes,* and *fluid-applied membranes.*

Built-Up Membranes. Built-up membranes use several overlapping layers of roofing felt saturated with a bituminous material that may be either tar or asphalt. The layers of roofing felt are cemented together with hot bituminous roofing cement **(Figure 11.26)**. The roofing felt usually is supplied in rolls 3 feet (1 m) wide. The number of layers of roofing felt used varies, but four layers is a common design. The more layers of felt used, the more durable the resulting roof will be. Built-up roofs usually last for 20 years if the manufacturer's specifications are followed.

Single-Ply Membranes. A single-ply membrane roof consists of a single membrane laid in sheets on the roof deck. The membrane material comes in sheets 10 or 20 feet wide (3 or 6 m) and up to 200 feet long (60 m). The membranes are thin, typically 0.03 to 0.10 inches thick

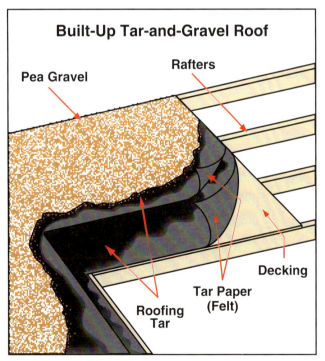

Figure 11.26 Built-up membrane roofs use materials intended to insulate, waterproof, and provide long-term durability.

Table 11.1
A Comparison Of Various Rigid-Roof Insulating Materials

Insulating Material	Composition
Cellulose Fiberboard	A rigid, low-density board of wood or sugar cane fibers with a binder
Glass Fiberboard	A rigid, low-density board of glass fibers and a binder
Polystyrene Foam Board	A flammable rigid foam of polystyrene plastic
Polyurethane Foam Board	A flammable rigid foam of polyurethane sometimes faced with felt
Polyisocyanurate Foam Board	A rigid foam of polyisocyanurate sometimes with glass fiber reinforcing and best when combined with materials to increase fire resistance
Cellular Glass Board	A fire-resistant rigid foam of glass
Perlite Board	Fire-resistant granules of expanded volcanic glass and a binder pressed into a rigid board
Lightweight fill with Asphaltic Binder	Lightweight mineral aggregate with asphaltic binder
Composite Insulating Boards	Layers of foam plastic and other materials such as perlite board and glass fiberboard

(0.75 to 2.5 mm). Single-ply membranes are made from several materials. The most common is a synthetic rubber material, ethylene propylene diene monomer (EPDM). Other materials include polyvinyl chloride (PVC) and chlorinated polyethylene (CPE). The single-ply materials can be stretched and consequently will accommodate shifting in a building. They can be applied over decks in new buildings and over existing roofs. The single-ply membranes are attached to the roof by means of adhesives, gravel ballast, or mechanical fasteners. Using a propane torch to heat the underside of the membrane as it is unrolled will cause it to adhere to the roof. This process has resulted in roof-covering fires that spread rapidly across the entire roof. The burning material liquefies and can drop down through holes in the roof decking onto the contents below.

Fluid-Applied Membranes. Fluid-applied membranes are useful for buildings with curved roof surfaces such as domes that would be difficult to cover with other materials. The material is applied as a liquid and allowed to cure. Usually several coatings are applied. The materials used include:

- Neoprene
- Silicone
- Polyurethane
- Butyl rubber

Drainage Layer

The drainage layer permits the free movement of rain water to the roof drains. Depending on the membrane material used, the drainage layer can be the ballast layer in a single-ply roofing system, a drainage fabric, or the aggregate used in a built-up roofing system.

Wear Course

The wear course protects the roof from mechanical abrasion. It can consist of the aggregate in a built-up roofing system or gravel ballast. Built-up roofs that use gravel as the wear course are commonly known as *tar and gravel roofs*. When a gravel surface is used for the wear course, it also increases the resistance of the roof to fire spread from adjacent buildings. Roofs used for pedestrian traffic may use deck pavers for the wear course.

Pitched Roof Coverings

Firefighters must understand the common types of coverings and their effect on fire fighting strategy and life safety. For example, some types of roof coverings create conditions that may allow fire to spread from one place to another.

The roof coverings used on pitched roofs function differently from those used on flat roofs. Water immediately drains from a pitched roof, which minimizes the possibility of it pooling on the roof and working through seams in the roof covering. The coverings used on a pitched roof must be secured to the roof deck or roof support. Materials may be shaped to resemble other roof coverings such as wood shingles. These include porcelainized aluminum, mineral-based materials, and composite materials.

NOTE: Thatch, which consists of bundles of reeds, grasses, or leaves, technically is also a covering for pitched roofs. In North America, its use is limited to a few special situations such as for decorative effect.

The most common types of roof coverings, and their performance under fire conditions, are described in the following sections. Two broad categories of roof coverings used on pitched roofs are shingles and metal roof coverings.

Asphalt Shingles and Tiles

Shingles and tiles are small overlapping units that are relatively easy to handle. Their small size allows for movement between individual units caused by thermal expansion and shifting of the building structural system. Shingles, shakes, and tiles are available in a wide variety of types and uses **(Figure 11.27)**.

Asphalt shingles are usually installed over an *underlayment*, which is a layer of roofing felt or synthetic covering. The underlayment serves as a cushion and provides protection from wind-driven rain. Shingles and tile roof coverings are sometimes applied over a deteriorated existing roof.

NOTE: Slate tiles have preset nail holes. The proper installation technique is to have the head of the nail just touching the slate so that the slate hangs from the nail.

Modern asphalt shingles are fiberglass based. A mineral aggregate is embedded in the top surface to act as a wearing surface and to provide color **(Figure 11.28)**. Asphalt shingles are available in several sizes but the most common size is 12 x 36 inches (300 x 900 mm).

Figure 11.27 Applications of roofing tiles, shakes, and shingles vary somewhat based on the specific features of the materials and surface to which they are affixed. *Courtesy of McKinney (TX) FD.*

Figure 11.28 Similarly to built-up membrane roofs, asphalt shingles are small pieces of fiberglass coated with asphalt and embedded with inert mineral (rock) material for durability. *Courtesy of McKinney (TX) FD.*

Figure 11.29 Shake shingles used as exterior siding present similar fire exposure hazards as shake roofs.

Asphalt shingles are fundamentally combustible. They tend to drip and run under fire conditions and produce a characteristic heavy black smoke. Asphalt shingles used for roofs are typically produced with a grit surface that reduces their ease of ignition and permits their use under the provisions of building codes. Historically, asphalt shingles were produced from heavy sheets of asphalt-impregnated felt made from rag, paper, or wool fiber.

Wood Shingles and Shakes

Some roof coverings, such as wood and asphalt shingles, are used for siding as well as for roofs. When used as siding, they can become subject to the heat of an exposing fire **(Figure 11.29)**.

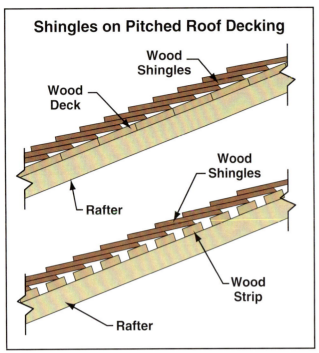

Figure 11.30 Roof tiles and shingles are arranged to provide maximum water displacement and durability.

The difference between wood shingles and shakes is in their method of production. Wood shingles are thin, tapered slabs of wood that are sawn from pieces of a tree trunk. Shakes are manually or machine split from the wood and are thicker than shingles. Wood shingles and shakes used in North America are made from red cedar, white cedar, or redwood because of the resistance of these woods to decay.

Shingles and tiles are usually attached to the roof with corrosion-resistant nails. Wood shingles are installed with an overlap so only one-third of the surface of the shingle is actually exposed to the weather. Wood shingles can be nailed to a conventional solid deck or to an open deck consisting of wood strips attached to the roof rafters **(Figure 11.30)**. This latter method of construction can produce earlier failure of the roof in the instance of an attic fire.

Wood shingles and shakes can be pressure-impregnated with a fire-retardant solution to reduce their combustibility and to meet model code requirements. Pressure-impregnation of wood shingles and shakes may or may not remain effective after exposure to the elements. As such, many jurisdictions disallow the use of wood shingles because the base material is not fire resistant in its own right.

Fire-retardant shingles and shakes are shipped to the job site with a paper label identifying them. Once in place, however, identification of treated shingles or shakes can be difficult. Painting or staining shingles or shakes can reduce the effectiveness of any fire treatment, especially if oil-based materials are used.

Wood roof shingles and shakes are popular architecturally because they produce a rustic appearance and may be more resistant to wind damage than asphalt shingles. Their disadvantage is that they pose a serious fire potential. Burning brands from an exposing fire can easily ignite them. Once ignited, they can produce embers that spread fire to other roofs. In some parts of the country, they have contributed to fires involving entire neighborhoods. For these reasons, some jurisdictions have prohibited their use.

Clay, Slate, and Cement Tiles

Clay, slate, and cement tiles are noncombustible and produce fire-resistant roof coverings that have excellent resistance to flying brands. Flying brands, however, can be blown under tiles such as the Spanish tiles that do not lie flat, and ignite the roof deck **(Figure 11.31)**. Operational problems that tiles may create include:

- Tiles can become loose and fall from a roof as the deck burns away and nails lose their grip or as firefighters conduct ventilation operations.
- The surface can become slippery, posing a serious fall hazard. Proper equipment and caution should be used at all times.
- The thin pieces of slate are brittle and may have sharp edges.

Figure 11.31 Clay tiles do not burn, but they may cover combustible void spaces.

Slate. Slate is produced from hard rock that has a tendency to split along one plane **(Figure 11.32)**. This characteristic permits roofing slate to be produced in smooth sheets as thin as 1/16 inches (1.5 mm) although it may be as thick as 1½ inches (40 mm). Slate is a durable material and can have a life expectancy of 150 years. Slate is also a heavy material, weighing 8 to 36 pounds per square foot (45 to 200 kg/m²). Therefore, roof framing and decking that is heavier than normal may be required if slate is to be used.

Clay Tile. Clay tile is a dense, hard, and nonabsorbent material and can be used for flat or curved tiles. The curved clay tiles are known as "mission" tiles and are used in genuine and imitation Spanish-style architecture. The clay tiles are shaped in molds and fired in kilns, as they have been for thousands of years.

Concrete Tiles. Concrete tiles are made from portland cement, aggregate, and water. Concrete tiles are frequently made to look like clay tile, slate, or even wood in color and texture. A major advantage of concrete tiles over wood tiles is their greater longevity.

Metal Roof Coverings

Metal roof coverings may be used as corrugated or flat sheets **(Figure 11.33)**. Aluminum and steel sheets are corrugated to increase the strength of the material; corrugated aluminum or steel are primarily used on industrial and agricultural buildings. Metal roofs are also found on many residential and commercial buildings. Metal roof coverings may use several materials including:

Figure 11.32 Slate tiles are noncombustible, but they may create a hazardous environment if their connection to the roof fails. *Courtesy of McKinney (TX) FD.*

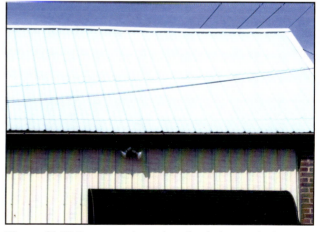

Figure 11.33 Corrugated metal roofing is increasingly common in a wide range of occupancy types. *Courtesy of Ed Prendergast.*

- Galvanized or painted sheet metal
- Copper
- Zinc
- Aluminum
- Lead

NOTE: Galvanic corrosion occurs when some types of dissimilar metals are in contact. Construction practices to avoid that corrosion may include using nails of the same metal as the sheeting, or using insulation between the nails and sheeting.

Corrugated roofing sheets are generally stiff enough to be installed without decking **(Figure 11.34)**. Roof beams or purlins support the corrugated roofing sheets.

Figure 11.34 Corrugated metal roofing may be installed without decking or insulation. *Courtesy of McKinney (TX) FD.*

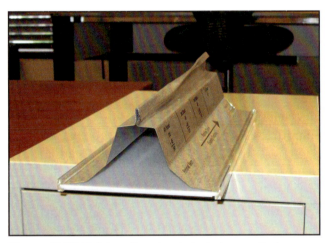

Figure 11.35 Metal roofing sheets include a vertical ridge at the seam where the edges are crimped together. *Courtesy of Sturzenbecker Construction Company, Inc.*

Flat roofing sheets are nailed to a deck beneath. A layer of roofing felt is placed on the metal deck beneath the metal sheets. When wood decking is used, the roofing felt increases the fire resistance of the roof because it acts as an insulating layer and protects the wood deck against the heat of external exposing fires. The individual flat sheets of metal roofing are joined at seams and crimped watertight. The seams stand up vertically at the joint between adjacent sheets and make the metal panel roof readily identifiable **(Figure 11.35)**.

CAUTION
Visible roofing materials may not indicate the structural supports underneath.

Fire Ratings of Roof Coverings

Building codes impose restrictions on the combustibility of roofs of certain buildings, occupancies, or locations within a community. Test procedures contained in NFPA® 256, *Standard Methods of Fire Tests of Roof Coverings*, also designated ASTM E-108, evaluate the fire hazards of specific roof coverings. The test simulates several fire exposure conditions for fires originating outside a building. The standard does not evaluate the fire resistance of the structural system supporting a roof or the fire resistance of the roof itself with respect to a fire originating within a building.

In the test, samples of roof coverings are attached to a wooden deck measuring 3 feet 4 inches by 4 feet 4 inches (1 m x 1.3 m). The samples are then subjected to the required test procedures. In order to be a third-party listed product, materials are subject to six separate test procedures including:

- Intermittent flame exposure test
- Burning brand test
- Flying brand test
- Rain test
- Weathering test
- Spread of flame test

The individual test procedures may be repeated from two to fifteen times on different samples depending on the specific material being tested. For example, fifteen samples of wood shakes or shingles may be subjected to the weathering test while another material may be subjected to the burning brand test twice. In addition, if the properties of a specific roof covering material are subject to variation, more than the minimum number of tests contained in NFPA® 256 may be required.

Roof coverings that pass the required test procedures are classified A, B, or C. The three classifications are based on the severity of fire the material can withstand:

- Class A roof coverings are effective against a severe fire exposure.
- Class B roof coverings are effective against a moderate fire exposure.
- Class C roof coverings are effective against a light fire exposure.

Building codes use these three classifications to control the flammability of roofs. Therefore, certain types of construction, such as fire-resistive buildings, may be required to have a Class A or B roof covering. A building code may also use the classifications to restrict the flammability of roofs on buildings in congested areas such as a downtown area. In other parts of a community, roof coverings may be used that do not pass the test procedures and are unclassified.

Laboratories that test roof coverings, such as Underwriters Laboratories, publish a list of roof coverings that have passed NFPA® 256 with their classifications in a manner similar to that of fire-resistance ratings described in Chapter 2.

Rain Roofs

A roof is a building's first line of defense against the elements. As such, roofs deteriorate over the years from exposure to wind, snow, and rain. Reasons rain roofs may be installed over existing roofs include:

- To cover deteriorated roofing elements
- To change the profile of a building
- To update architectural design/appearance

- Cost-effective compared to replacing the original roof
- Less disruptive to the operations within a building, as compared to replacing the existing roof

Rain roofs can be constructed of any material over any material, and can take any shape, regardless of the preexisting construction **(Figure 11.36)**. Often the new rain roof will have a steeper pitch than the original. Preplanning may be critical in order to identify this type of construction.

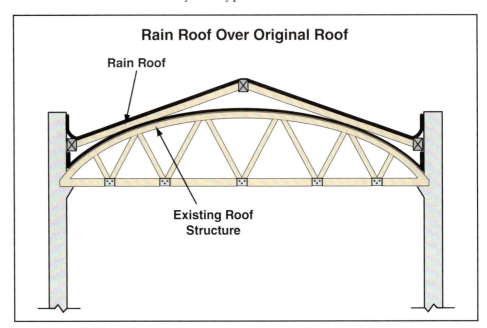

Figure 11.36 Unpredictable voids may be created when a rain roof is installed over an older roof.

A rain roof presents some special difficulties for the firefighter, including:

- When products of combustion enter the void space, they can be difficult to detect, access, and extinguish.
- The existence of two separate roofs can also impede rapid and effective ventilation.
- Small spaces between the two roofs can create an entrapment hazard for firefighters.
- The rain roof may not be structurally solid enough to support the weight of fire fighting operations.

Green Design Roofs

One manifestation of the increased interest in environmental protection has been the development of a variety of **green design** roofs. The greatest benefit to this style of roof is the increased energy efficiency of the building. In addition to the photovoltaic and vegetative types explained below, green design roofs may include reflective systems known as "cool roofs" and intentionally enhanced biodiversity known as "brown roofs."

Green Design — Term used to describe the incorporation of such environmental principles as energy efficiency and environmentally friendly building materials into design and construction.

A significant hazard that many of these systems share is the increased weight from the added elements. In buildings that include these loads as an original plan for the structure, the supports will have been designed for the weight. When added after the fact, the structural supports may not be adequate. Under fire conditions, the increased load can hasten structural failure, particularly if the roof is combustible. The systems can also interfere with ventilation practices and indicators of fire location and spread.

Photovoltaic Roofs

A **photovoltaic (PV) system** (solar) produces reliable, **clean energy** that can be used in a wide range of applications, including within a building's systems. The collection of photovoltaic energy is a rapidly developing field. Although photovoltaic technology or applications are not commonly used throughout North America at the time of this writing, several jurisdictions have already seen significant increases in the prevalence of this technology. Each jurisdiction must research the specific systems relevant to an area, develop appropriate response tactics, and train response personnel.

Photovoltaic (PV) System — An arrangement of components that convey electrical power to an energy system by converting solar energy into direct current (DC) electricity.

Clean Energy — Energy sources that meet the needs of current consumers without compromising future resources. *Also known as* Sustainable Energy.

> **CAUTION**
> Firefighters may find rooftop photovoltaic applications on many structures, regardless of the occupancy, roof type, or pitch.

Photovoltaic cells are typically shaped as panels and shingles, and can be installed on top of a roof or embedded in the roof covering **(Figure 11.37)**. Recent updates in solar energy applications have increased the overall prevalence and cost-efficiency of photovoltaic systems in residential applications. In fact, current photovoltaic shingles cost-match more traditional types of shingles. Some solar shingles are designed as a standalone roofing system and are durable enough to be walked on. Photovoltaic systems now include elements with a wide range of shapes, sizes, and thickness. For example, new technology in this field includes the development of photovoltaic paints. The hazards of photovoltaic systems are explained below.

Figure 11.37 Solar panels should always be treated as though they are energized, even if conditions indicate that they may not be. *Courtesy of McKinney (TX) FD.*

Solar Cell Terminology

A single unit of a solar energy collector is referred to as a "cell." A series of solar cells arranged in a self-contained unit are referred to as a "panel" or "module." Individual cells may also be connected in series, as is common with solar shingles. A system of solar panels or shingles is called an "array."

The energy feed from photovoltaic cells cannot be isolated or shut off. Even when electric power to the building is shut off and the cells are isolated from the building's electrical system, the cells continue to store and generate electric power. These systems should be handled with the same care as any other electrical system: all wiring and conduits must be assumed to be live.

Figure 11.38 Solar panels may not be readily visible in low-visibility conditions. *Courtesy of McKinney (TX) FD.*

Although not common, PV systems can transfer an electrical charge to metal roofing materials if the supports and other components are compromised.

Photovoltaic cells may not be readily identifiable on flat roofs or in low light, adverse weather, or during fireground operations **(Figure 11.38)**. For example, one type of solar panel is designed to be rolled out as a sheet on a flat membrane roof. In low light, it may look like a maintenance walkway. Further, as firefighters pause operations to assess PV elements, the fire continues to spread and develop. Where the entire roof is covered with panels, space for rooftop access, travel, and ventilation may be unavailable. Raised panels may create a significant traction, tripping, and falling hazard. Raised panels may also include void spaces.

PV technology is continuing to develop, and the utilities are becoming more commonly available, also meaning that incidents involving these materials are becoming more prevalent[1]. Model codes and other authorities continue to propose and add parameters regarding photovoltaic applications, including:

Green Roof — Roof of a building that is partially or completely covered with vegetation and a growing medium, planted over waterproof roofing elements. Term can also indicate the presence of green design technology including photovoltaic systems and reflective surfaces.

- Clear space along the edges and ridge of a roof
- Clear aisle space between arrays with certain dimensions
- Minimum visibility requirements of photovoltaic components
- Uniform labeling of structures with photovoltaic related materials
- External shut-off switches to reduce or eliminate electrocution danger
- Capability for rapid shut-down of PV systems on buildings

Vegetative Roof Systems

A **green roof** can take several forms, ranging from the use of potted plants and flower boxes to a layer of earth with growing plants covering a large area of a roof **(Figure 11.39)**. Rooftop gardens can be developed on existing roofs and in new construction. Benefits to this addition include the increased insulation between the building and its environment, and the increase in air quality due to the oxygen-carbon dioxide exchange of growing plants, particularly in urban areas.

A rooftop garden constitutes a dead load on the roof structural system, which must be capable of supporting the load. The depth of soil required for a garden can range from a few inches (millimeters) to a few feet (meters). Depending on the depth of the soil, the dead load can vary from 20 pounds per square foot to 150 pounds per square foot (110 to 830 kg/m^2). In new construction, the structural engineer can provide for this load in the structural plans just as is done for snow loads. When a garden is planned for an existing roof, the existing structural system must be analyzed to ensure its adequacy. Another primary hazard of vegetative roofs is the added fire load if the vegetation is not properly hydrated, or if fertilizers are improperly stored[2].

Figure 11.39 A six-story parking garage is immediately under this park. *Courtesy of Ed Prendergast.*

Roof Openings

A roof may be built with breaches in its continuity for a number of reasons, such as for penthouses, skylights, and roof ventilation openings. These roof openings are normally provided for purposes other than fire protection, but they can be used in the course of fire fighting for roof access or ventilation.

Penthouses

Penthouses are small structures erected on the main roof of a building. Penthouses are constructed for several purposes such as a stairway enclosure, elevator machinery enclosure, mechanical equipment storage, or additional living space **(Figure 11.40)**. When a stairwell is provided with a rooftop penthouse, firefighters can gain rapid access to the roof from inside the building to combat fires at the roof level.

Figure 11.40 Penthouses on a roof may house several functions including utilities and additional living space. *Courtesy of McKinney (TX) FD.*

Although some means of access to a roof must always be provided for maintenance purposes, the access may not be readily apparent and may entail climbing up ladders through roof hatches. Products of combustion can travel in these spaces. However, when the roof is beyond the reach of ladders, firefighters must locate a route to the roof. Elevator and mechanical equipment may not be directly accessible from the inside of a building and must be accessed from the roof.

Skylights

The primary purpose of skylights is to provide natural lighting to the interior of a building. They can be located to serve only the top story of a building or they may be located over the top of an atrium, stairwell, or light shaft **(Figure 11.41)**. Building codes restrict the materials used in skylights to plastic, wired glass, or tempered glass **(Figure 11.42)**.

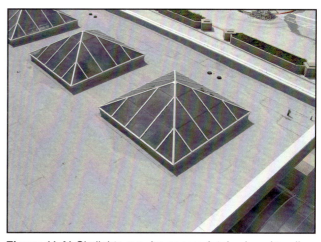

Figure 11.41 Skylights may be appropriately placed to allow for easier ventilation of a roof. *Courtesy of McKinney (TX) FD.*

Skylights are sometimes equipped with operable glass panes to facilitate normal building ventilation. Though skylights usually do not have provision for automatic venting, most can be opened to provide a rapid means of ventilating heat and smoke.

Skylights can be spring-loaded or manually operated using a cable inside or releasing a catch outside **(Figure 11.43, p. 304)**. Skylights may also be equipped with photovoltaic strips for electronic operation. If no other options are available, the glass in a skylight can be broken or the skylight housing can be pried up and pushed aside.

Figure 11.42 Materials used in skylights are too weak to stand on, and may be difficult to see in low visibility operations. *Courtesy of McKinney (TX) FD.*

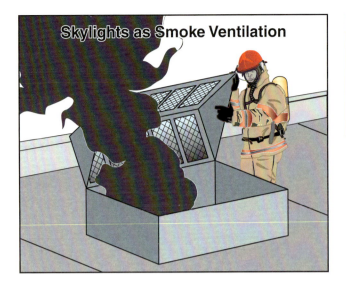

CAUTION
Skylights that also serve as smoke and heat ventilation openings use a fusible link and may open with great force and without warning under fire conditions.

Figure 11.43 Some skylights may be engineered to open automatically or with the use of tools.

Chapter Summary

Roofs can be constructed in a variety of styles for architectural, functional, and environmental reasons. Roofs can also have several types of coverings. The combustibility of a roof can affect fire spread. The structural system of a roof often creates concealed spaces that are difficult to evaluate, access, and control. A roof typically is not designed to support the same amount of live load as a floor; consequently, firefighters should always observe roofs carefully. Some newer types of roofs may include unknown hazards. Because roofs include many hazards, careful preincident planning is necessary.

Review Questions

1. Why must firefighters be familiar with all aspects of roof construction?
2. What are three architectural styles of roofs?
3. What roof support systems are used in roof construction?
4. What materials are used in the construction of roof decks?
5. How do roof coverings affect fire fighting strategies and life safety?
6. What are the hazards associated with green design roofs?
7. How can roof openings be used in fire fighting operations?

Chapter Notes

1. Duval, Bob, "Perfect Storm," NFPA® Journal, January-February 2014, http://www.nfpa.org/newsandpublications/nfpa-journal/2014/january-february-2014/features/perfect-storm.
2. Durso, Fred, "Easy Being Green," NFPA® Journal, November-December 2012, http://www.nfpa.org/newsandpublications/nfpa-journal/2012/november-december-2012/features/easy-being-green.

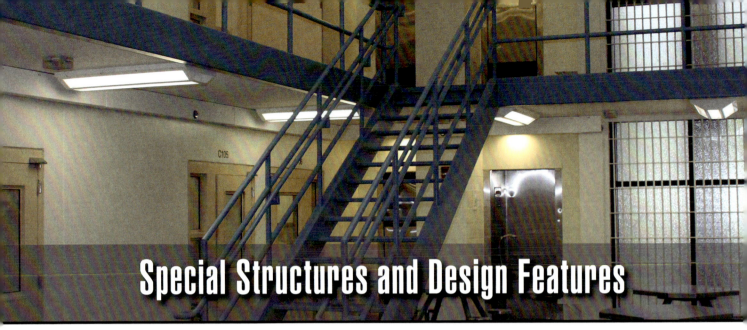

Special Structures and Design Features

Chapter Contents

Case History **309**	Covered Mall Buildings 328
High-Rise Buildings **310**	Detention and Correctional Facilities 330
Early versus Modern High-Rise Buildings 311	**Special Features within Buildings** **332**
High-Rise Construction Type 313	Atriums 332
Fire Protection Systems in High-Rise Buildings ... 314	Explosion Venting of Buildings 334
Fire Extension in High-Rise Buildings 318	Areas of Refuge 337
Emergency Use of Elevators in High-Rise Buildings ... 319	Rack Storage 337
Limited or Controlled Access Buildings .. **322**	**Chapter Summary** **340**
Underground Buildings 322	**Review Questions** **340**
Membrane Structures 325	**Chapter Notes** **340**
Cable- and Frame-Membrane Structures 327	

chapter 12

Key Terms

Air-Inflated Structure 326	Institutional Sprinklers.......................... 330
Air-Supported Structure 326	Phase I Operation 320
Atrium 332	Phase II Operation 321
Cable Membrane Structure................... 327	Pressure-Reducing Valve 315
Frame Membrane Structure.................. 327	Shunt Trip 319
High-Rise Building 310	Standpipe System 315

FESHE Outcomes Addressed In This Chapter

Fire and Emergency Services Higher Education (FESHE) Outcomes: *Building Construction for Fire Protection*

1. Describe building construction as it relates to firefighter safety, buildings codes, fire prevention, code inspection, firefighting strategy, and tactics.

5. Identify the function of each principle structural component in typical building design.

7. Classify occupancy designations of the building code.

8. Identify the indicators of potential structural failure as they relate to firefighter safety.

Special Structures and Design Features

Learning Objectives

After reading this chapter, students will be able to:

1. Describe the characteristics of high-rise buildings and their impact on fire fighting tactics.
2. Explain the emergency use of elevators in high-rise buildings during a fire event.
3. Identify characteristics of limited or controlled access buildings.
4. Recognize characteristics of atriums.
5. Describe the characteristics of explosion venting in buildings.
6. Identify the need for areas of refuge within a structure.
7. Identify fire protection hazards that rack storage can create.

Chapter 12
Special Structures and Design Features

Case History

On October 17, 2003 a fire broke out in the Cook County Administration Building in Chicago, Illinois. The fire originated in a storage room on the 12th floor of the building. This fire resulted in severe fire damage to the fire floor with smoke and heat damage to surrounding floors, and a loss of six lives. The victims of this fire were found in a stairwell several floors above the fire floor.

This building is a 37 story structure with one level below grade, constructed of reinforced cast-in-place concrete with concrete and glass panel walls. At the time of the fire, the building was only partially sprinklered; the fire floor was not sprinklered. The fire damaged about a third of the 18,000 square foot (1 600 m^2) floor.

Compartmentation served a limited role in containing the fire, though the solid core doors and gypsum board partition walls did help. Unfortunately, the partition walls did not extend to the underside of the deck, simply terminating at the dropped ceiling. The dropped ceiling assembly and lack of full height walls were major contributing factors to the ultimate spread of smoke and fire gasses throughout the building.

Smoke and heat travelled via unprotected openings for mechanical equipment and other equipment to cause damage on floors other than that where the fire occurred. The stairwell also contributed to fire spread, and was the location where six lives were lost.

Damage to surrounding floors was limited. This was due, in part, to the fire resistive construction of the building. No structural damage was reported. Had all openings been protected, the fire damage and life loss would have been minimized.

Previous chapters have explained basic building construction design, materials, building services, life safety systems, and fire behavior. This chapter addresses special structures and design features in some jurisdictions, including:

- High-Rise Buildings
- Limited or Controlled Access Buildings
- Special Features within Buildings

High-Rise Buildings

High-Rise Building — Building that requires fire fighting on levels above the reach of the department's equipment. *Also known as* High-Rise.

Model building codes define a **high-rise building** as being more than 75 feet (20 m) in height. The fire protection definition is more practical: any building with occupied stories beyond the effective reach of fire equipment located at the street level **(Figure 12.1)**.

Figure 12.1 Practically speaking, the reach of fire equipment defines high rises for first responders.

Defining a High-Rise

The height at which a building becomes classified as a high-rise varies from jurisdiction to jurisdiction. A high-rise building may be defined as exceeding 80 or 100 feet in height (25 or 30 m) at the roof. Other jurisdictions may define a high-rise building as exceeding 50 feet (15 m) or 5 stories in height because of limitations in fire fighting resources.

No matter how a high-rise building is defined, increases in building height create special protection problems, and the safety of occupants and firefighters become increasingly dependent on the safety features of the building itself. As the firefighter becomes more dependent on built-in features, preincident planning becomes an even more important factor of fireground operations. Specific challenges of high-rise buildings include:

- Exterior access is not possible at heights beyond the reach of aerial equipment.
- Access to the staging and fire floors takes more time.
- Incidents with more resources and personnel require more coordination.
- Larger buildings contain a greater number of occupants and activities, increasing the probability of emergency response calls.

In the early part of the 20th century, high-rise buildings existed primarily in large cities. Within fifty years, high-rises began to be constructed in many medium-sized communities. Today, tall buildings may be constructed in almost any community **(Figure 12.2)**. Early high-rise buildings still stand in many communities, and they are different in many significant respects from modern buildings.

NOTE: Fire protection systems in high-rise buildings are described later in this chapter.

Early versus Modern High-Rise Buildings

Two developments that made high-rise buildings possible and practical at the end of the 19th century were the use of steel-frame construction and elevators. These innovations made the following limitations obsolete:

- Height limitations of masonry and wood construction
- Unpredictability and brittleness of cast iron
- Difficulty of access to high-level floors without mechanical assistance

Figure 12.2 Many communities of all sizes include one or more high rise buildings.

High-Rise Construction Height

The most significant and obvious feature of modern high-rise buildings is their height. Buildings exceeding 60 stories have become commonplace. The taller buildings have larger populations, making evacuation under fire conditions more difficult and time consuming **(Figure 12.3)**.

The earliest high-rise buildings were rarely more than 10 or 12 stories. In the 1920s and 1930s, several buildings were constructed exceeding 40 stories. For example, New York's Empire State building was constructed in 1930 and has 102 stories.

Occupancy and Use

Modern buildings may be used for many individual purposes, including:

Figure 12.3 As a general rule, larger buildings have larger occupancies.

- Assembly
- Institutional
- Mercantile
- Educational

Newer high-rise buildings often have multiple occupancies; for example, the same building may contain a garage, a hotel, and offices **(Figure 12.4, p.312)**. Early high-rise buildings were usually limited to residential or office use.

Ventilation and Vertical Enclosures

Buildings with modern HVAC systems are designed to use the system for ventilation, and are often constructed without operable windows **(Figure 12.5, p.312)**. The enclosure of stairwells and elevator shafts reduces the flow of combustion products. During emergency operations, the fire department

Figure 12.4 The exterior of a building may not indicate the types of occupancies or activities inside.

Figure 12.5 Modern HVAC systems are intended to serve all air-flow purposes of buildings with closed ventilation systems.

should arrange to meet someone involved with the engineering staff for assistance with building operations. Ventilation via breaking out windows is a hazard to persons below.

NOTE: Refer to Chapter 4 for additional information on ventilation, stairs, and elevators.

In early high-rise construction, heating, ventilation and air conditioning (HVAC) systems were not a common utility. Opening windows provided ventilation for daily use and fire fighting operations. In addition, early high-rise buildings used open stairwells and elevator shafts that permitted the vertical travel of smoke and fire. Over time, several disastrous fires demonstrated the need to enclose stairwells and elevators. The first model building codes introduced in the 1920s and 1930s required stairs and elevators to be enclosed. Unfortunately, buildings constructed before those dates were often not required to comply with later standards.

Winecoff Hotel Fire, 1946

The 15-story Winecoff Hotel was built in Atlanta, Georgia in 1913. The hotel was designed in a square shape, with stairs and elevator shafts in the center of the building and hotel rooms around the perimeter. The hotel was advertised as fireproof even though it had no sprinkler system, fire alarms, or fire escapes.

On December 7, 1946, a person sounded an alarm after smelling smoke on the fifth floor of the hotel, not knowing that the second, third, and fourth floors were already engulfed in flames. Another complication: Many doors to the stairwells had been propped open, drawing the fire upward like a chimney. As the stairwells and elevators become impassable, hotel guests had no way to escape. When the fire was finally extinguished, 119 people had died from leaping to their deaths, suffocating, or being overcome by flames. The Winecoff Hotel fire remains the most deadly hotel fire in U.S. history.

Lesson Learned: The public outcry after the disaster led to many changes in fire code enforcement. The findings established that local officials could not be relied upon to make responsible decisions about fire safety, and national safety codes were established and strictly enforced.

High-Rise Construction Type

High-rise buildings use fire-resistive construction. Often a high-rise building will be constructed of a combination of reinforced concrete and a protected steel frame. Tall buildings often have a reinforced concrete core housing the elevator shafts with the remainder of the frame being steel.

The model building code that has been adopted specifies the degree of fire resistance required of structural components. Typically, model building codes require 2- or 3-hour fire resistance for the structural frame of a high-rise building, depending on the number of stories and occupancy, and 2-hour fire resistance for floor construction. In reinforced concrete construction, the floors will be concrete slab. In steel-frame buildings, the floors will be lightweight structural concrete placed over corrugated steel.

Figure 12.6 High rise buildings are intentionally constructed to minimize damage during an incident.

The fire-resistive construction used in high-rise buildings provides a high degree of structural integrity. Serious fires have occurred in high-rise buildings with only minor damage to the structural system **(Figure 12.6)**. Significant structural failure in high-rise buildings is extremely rare.

NOTE: The collapse of the World Trade Center Towers in the attacks of September, 2001 occurred as a result of the structural damage from the aircraft impact and fire fueled by jet fuel.[1]

Figure 12.7 Standpipes provide water access to higher levels of a building.

Fire Protection Systems in High-Rise Buildings

Requirements for new construction, such as automatic sprinkler systems, may not be retroactive; therefore, many older buildings remain without the benefit of modern fire protection features. Automatic sprinklers and communication systems were not commonly provided until the last quarter of the 20th century. In early high-rise buildings, fire protection was usually provided only by standpipe systems. The following sections describe the fire protection features required for modern high-rise buildings.

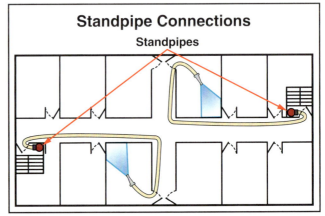

Figure 12.8 Standpipe risers and hose valves are strategically located to reach all parts of the response area when used with the correct length hose.

Standpipes

Standpipes are a crucial aspect of fire protection in high-rise buildings **(Figure 12.7)**. In buildings up to nine or ten stories, it might be possible to advance hoselines manually up stairwells. In taller buildings, however, it is difficult and time-consuming to attempt to advance hoselines in this manner. The taller the building, the more firefighters depend on the availability of standpipes. The standpipe risers and hose valves are located within the stairwells to provide a protected location from which to advance a hoseline **(Figure 12.8)**.

One unavoidable problem with standpipe systems is the variation of pressure in tandem with building height (hydrostatic pressure). Excessive pressure in the lower portion of a standpipe riser can make hoselines difficult or dangerous to handle. NFPA® 14, *Standard for the Installation of Standpipe and Hose Systems*, mandates the use of **pressure-reducing valves** that can be set according to the jurisdiction's needs. Fire inspectors should verify that these devices are properly set at the time of the original installation **(Figure 12.9)**. Periodic tests should be conducted to verify their proper maintenance, as per the manufacturer and AHJ.

Figure 12.9 Detection, suppression, and prevention tools should be installed, maintained, and tested within parameters established by the manufacturer, intended application, and AHJ.

Meridian Plaza Fire, 1991

On February 23, 1991, a fire occurred in the 38-story Meridian Plaza office building in Philadelphia, Pennsylvania, heavily damaging the building and resulting in the deaths of three firefighters. This fire is an example of the deadly consequences of fire protection system inadequacy or failure.

Although the building was initially constructed in 1969 without an automatic sprinkler system, one had been partially installed at the time of the fire. At the time of original construction, the primary fire protection features for the upper portions of the building were a dry standpipe riser with fire department connections (FDCs) and a wet-standpipe system with hose supplied by the domestic water system, intended for occupant use.

During installation of the automatic sprinklers, the dry standpipe had been converted to wet standpipes supplied by two fire pumps. In addition, pressure-reducing valves were installed at the hose outlets of the standpipes.

The fire began on the 22nd floor of the building. Before it was controlled, it spread down to the 21st floor via convenience stairs, and continued up to the 30th floor. Arriving firefighters initially used the building elevators to gain access to the upper floors. Shortly after their arrival, however, a complete electrical failure occurred in the building. This failure prevented firefighters from using the elevators and fire pumps, and also forced them to work in a totally darkened building.

When firefighters reached the fire floor, they connected to the standpipe, but only received poor-quality hose streams of limited reach. The crews were forced to use defensive tactics. The water availability did not improve for four hours, until a sprinkler contractor arrived and adjusted the settings of the pressure-reducing valves on the standpipes. The valves had been improperly adjusted at the time of installation.

Efforts to control the fire became extremely difficult and time-consuming. A 5-inch (125 mm) hoseline was manually advanced up a stairwell in an effort to supply adequate water. The fire's progress through the building was essentially unchecked. Three firefighters became disoriented in the heavy smoke and darkness, and died.

The fire was finally controlled when it reached the 30th floor. A portion of the automatic sprinkler system had been installed, and ten sprinklers operated.

Lesson Learned: Had the pressure-reducing valves on the standpipe system been properly adjusted at the time of installation and the integrity of the building's electrical system been provided, it is likely that the fire could have been controlled through manual fire suppression efforts.

> **Standpipe System** — Wet or dry system of pipes in a large single-story or multistory building, with fire hose outlets installed in different areas or on different levels of a building to be used by firefighters and/or building occupants. This system is used to provide for the quick deployment of hoselines during fire fighting operations.
>
> **Pressure-Reducing Valve** — Valve installed at standpipe connection that is designed to reduce the amount of water pressure at that discharge to a specific pressure, usually 100 psi (700 kPa).

Automatic Sprinklers

Sprinkler and standpipe systems are typically supplied from the same vertical riser **(Figure 12.10, p. 316)**. These systems will be supplied by one or more fire pumps located in the basement of the building. In seismic zones, a secondary on-site water supply is required, usually in the form of a storage tank. Building codes have routinely required that high-rise buildings be equipped with automatic sprinkler systems as well as standpipe systems since the mid-1970s.

NOTE: See the IFSTA **Fire Prevention, Detection, and Suppression Systems** manual for a complete discussion of automatic sprinkler systems.

Figure 12.10 A standpipe riser may include a smaller connecting pipe to supply sprinklers on the same floor.

The sprinkler system in a high-rise building includes individual floor control valves. These valves are important because they permit the rapid shutdown of sprinklers on the floor on which a fire has occurred after the sprinklers have controlled the fire. Rapid shutdown permits the sprinkler system to remain in service on the other floors during overhaul operations and reduces the water damage from a fire. These valves are also useful in reducing water damage resulting from a broken sprinkler.

Fire Alarm Systems

Taller high-rise buildings may have a population of several thousand people: the equivalent of a small town. For this reason, model building and fire codes require fire alarm systems in high-rise buildings. Because of the complex nature of a high-rise, the fire alarm systems are complex and provide more functions than systems used in low-rise buildings. In a high-rise building, a system may include several hundred devices.

NOTE: See the IFSTA **Fire Prevention, Detection, and Suppression Systems** manual for a complete discussion of fire alarm systems.

Many modern high-rise buildings have voice alarm systems that automatically sound an alert tone followed by voice instructions upon actuation of any detector, waterflow device, or manual pull station. These voice evacuation systems are often zoned by floor. Some systems are programmed to evacuate only the floor of origin, the floor above, and the floor below rather than the entire building. These systems will also include voice override capability to broadcast further instructions on a selective or all-call basis.

Detection devices in high-rise buildings, along with waterflow switches, are monitored via the fire alarm system. Smoke detectors in individual residential units are not monitored through the fire alarm system. High-rise buildings typically include:

- Duct detectors arranged to prevent recirculation of smoke to other floors
- Smoke detectors in elevator machine rooms and elevator lobbies to initiate elevator recall
- A circuit breaker linked to heat detection systems to disconnect electrical equipment
- Corridor smoke detectors in residential occupancies

Another unique alarm feature in high-rises is the requirement for a two-way fire department communication system **(Figure 12.11)**. This system operates between locations including:

Figure 12.11 Two way communication systems allow a stranded person to contact someone in another location.

- Fire command center (central control station); spare telephone handsets are often provided in the fire command center
- Landings of enclosed exit stairways
- Areas of refuge
- Elevators and elevator lobbies
- Emergency generator
- Fire pump rooms

Smoke Control Systems

Local or state building codes often require some form of mechanical smoke removal from each floor. For example, some buildings include HVAC systems that have the capability of shutting off airflow to some parts of the building and reversing exhaust to others independently. However, model building codes do not require special mechanical smoke removal provisions from the floor of origin because the requirements for the following systems should be adequate to control smoke movement within a building:

- Shaft construction
- Sealing of floor penetrations
- Automatic sprinklers

All model building codes require smokeproof exit enclosures in all stairs serving floors 75 feet (20 m) or higher. Entrance to these stairways must be made through an open balcony or a pressurized vestibule.

Each fire department should survey all high-rise buildings in their jurisdiction to determine if these buildings have any smoke-control provisions and how they work **(Figure 12.12)**. This information must be incorporated into the preincident plans for each high-rise building.

For example, during the 1970s, model codes typically permitted the use of the building mechanical air handling system to accomplish smoke removal if the building was completely protected by automatic sprinklers. A common approach using the mechanical equipment was called a "pressure sandwich" concept. This approach vented the fire floor and pressurized the floors immediately above and below to contain the smoke.

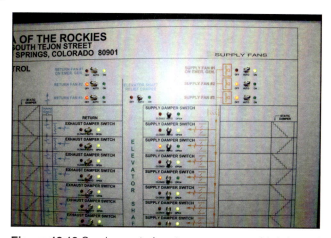

Figure 12.12 Smoke control systems can vary widely based on the complexity of the structure, the features provided by the system, and other factors. *Courtesy of Colorado Springs (CO) Fire Department.*

Fire Command Center/Central Control Station

Model building codes require a room or area in a high-rise building to serve as a fire command center. The fire department must approve the location. Typically, a fire command center is located on the first floor or level of fire department access **(Figure 12.13)**. The room has minimal requirements, often including separation from the rest of the building with 1-hour fire-rating. Many jurisdictions require that the room be accessed directly through an exterior door.

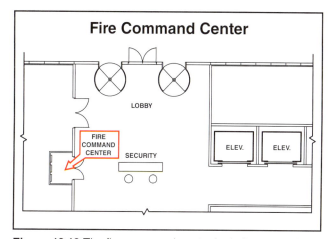

Figure 12.13 The fire command center includes several resources that will aid first responders in determining an appropriate response.

Figure 12.14 Many fire command centers will include similar basic resources.

Typical features of a fire command center include (**Figure 12.14**):

- Emergency voice alarm system control panels
- Fire department two-way telephone system panel
- Fire detection and fire alarm system annunciator panel
- Elevator location and status panel
- Sprinkler valve and waterflow annunciator
- Emergency and standby power status indicators and controls
- Central/status panel for smoke management systems
- Controls for unlocking stairway doors
- Fire pump status indicators
- Telephone for fire department use with access to the public telephone system

One model building code also requires a work table and a set of building plans.

All building components must be maintained to be sure they are in working order during an emergency. Fire personnel complete walk-throughs during preincident planning and inspection visits to verify that maintenance and repair of all fire protection systems are performed regularly. Not all fire command centers look and act alike. Panels and other equipment must be properly labeled to facilitate use.

Fire Extension in High-Rise Buildings

The floor plan of a high-rise building will vary with occupancy and other factors such as site constraints. Many high-rise buildings, especially office buildings and hotels, are designed with a *central core* floor plan. In a central core configuration, building services such as elevators, stairwells, and service shafts are grouped in the center of the floor. This arrangement maximizes the amount of space available for development around the periphery of the building (**Figure 12.15**).

The fire-resistive construction of high-rise buildings provides a certain degree of inherent compartmentalization and barriers to the vertical extension of fire and smoke. Vertical extension of fire and smoke can occur, however, through floor penetrations such as elevator shafts, stairwells, and utility shafts. Consequently, building codes require that vertical shafts be enclosed. Despite the requirement for shaft enclosures, some upward migration of smoke is possible at stairwell doors, utility and elevator shafts, and inadequately protected floor penetrations. For this reason, the HVAC systems in high-rise buildings are designed to manage products of combustion.

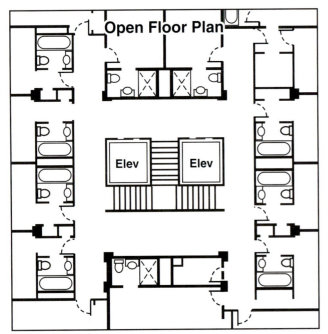

Figure 12.15 An open floor plan arrangement allows more occupancy spaces to have a window.

Exterior fire spread is one means of vertical extension in a high-rise building. Model buildings codes now have strict requirements for sealing voids where floors intersect with curtain walls, because vertical fire spread is particularly likely with uninterrupted floor to ceiling glass curtain walls.

Horizontal fire extension in a high-rise building depends on the partitions that subdivide a floor. The partitions between units and the corridor enclosure will act as barriers to fire spread. Some floor plans, such as those found in hotels and apartment buildings, are inherently subdivided. Other floor plans may be more open. For example, an entire floor may be open with a single office tenant occupying the space.

Disorientation in Open Floor Areas

When a large room is organized with movable partitions, for example cubicles or rack storage, firefighters may have difficulty navigating the area to access the fire. The partitions may increase disorientation in smoke conditions. Preplanning this type of building layout is essential and should happen after the partitions are established because businesses are unlikely to change the layout with much frequency. Firefighters should always enter such areas with either a hoseline or a rope and tagline system to help guide their way back to safety. Air management is complicated in these environments.

Emergency Use of Elevators in High-Rise Buildings

Modern elevators are a critical resource that firefighters use to reach upper floors in high-rise buildings. Dedicated elevators for fire department use in high-rise buildings are now a feature included in modern codes, and many jurisdictions recognize the benefits of elevators for fire service operations. When a structure has more than one dedicated elevator, they may be arranged in banks.

The elevator code requires a **shunt trip** where the elevator hoistway or elevator room is protected by automatic sprinklers. This arrangement will shut down the power to the elevator before a sprinkler discharges water on the elevator equipment. This type of system may stop an elevator between floors, and therefore, some jurisdictions will not allow automatic sprinklers to protect these spaces. Each jurisdiction must establish its own policies and procedures for the use of elevators during fires; firefighters must be familiar with their local requirements. Safe applications of elevators in high-rise construction are explained in the following sections.

Shunt Trip — A circuit breaker used as a safety device in an elevator system. When electrical current surges, the device disconnects the power source.

Safety during Emergency Elevator Use

Elevator use during a fire event is always dangerous. Death and injuries can result from the misuse of elevators during a fire. The decision to use the elevators must be made carefully, and personnel must train on actual local systems to become familiar with the operation of elevators and the relevant emergency procedures.

SOPs/SOGs must be followed for elevator use during an emergency. When using an elevator during an emergency, fire personnel should consider the following:

- Confirm availability of emergency operations.
- Maintain communication (radio or other) at all times.
- Only consider using elevators if the fire is above the 5th floor.
- Stay below the fire floor, according to SOPs.
- Do not use an elevator to travel to the fire floor.
- Never take an elevator below ground level.
- Do not travel above the fire floor in an elevator that serves all floors.
- Do not use elevators for occupant evacuation until the fire is under control.
- Determine the location of the nearest protected stairs in relation to the elevator.
- Account for all elevators to ensure that none are stuck with trapped passengers.
- Never use a fire- or heat-damaged elevator.
- Never use an elevator that has been exposed to water.
- Know the visual signal on the elevator control panel that indicates an impending elevator problem.
- Be aware that, although a minimum of one elevator car may be on emergency power, power may fail at any time during a fire.

Phase I Operation — Emergency operating mode for elevators. Recalls the car to the terminal floor lobby or another floor as specified, and opens the doors.

CAUTION
Electrical power in a building may fail at any time during a fire.

Phase I Elevator Operation

Fire and building officials have long recognized the critical importance of elevators in tall buildings, while noting their susceptibility to interference from factors including:

- Smoke
- Heat
- Flame
- Water

As a result, codes contain mandatory provisions for the recall (Phase I operation) of all passenger elevators with vertical travel greater than 25 feet (7.5 m) in the event of fire. **Phase I operation** can be triggered by the following:

- Activation of automatic smoke detectors
- Activation of automatic sprinkler waterflow alarms
- Activation of manual keyed switch in the terminal floor lobby **(Figure 12.16)**

Figure 12.16 Elevators may be recalled to the lobby via a keyed switch.

Phase I operation is designed to prevent the deaths of civilians who may find themselves in an elevator that is called to the fire floor, as happened in high-rise fires in the 1970s. Phase I operation automatically stops all the cars that serve the fire floor if they are moving away from their terminal floor (the lobby). It also causes the cars to return nonstop to the lobby, or other designated level if the alarm originated from the lobby.

NOTE: The requirement for recall does not apply to freight elevators. Other elevator safety and design features also may not be applicable to freight elevators.

At the lobby, the fire department must account for each car to be certain there are no civilians trapped in a stalled car at or above the fire floor. The elevator control and information panel is usually located adjacent to the elevator bank and can indicate whether anyone may be trapped. Recalling elevators via Phase I operation opens the car doors and keeps them open when the car reaches the recall floor. This visual inspection makes it easy to see which cars are empty and which may be caught on another level **(Figure 12.17)**. During Phase I operation, the elevator car's emergency stop and floor selection buttons are rendered inoperative so that car occupants who may be unaware of the fire or emergency cannot stop the car anywhere but at the terminal floor.

Figure 12.17 Elevator cars that are recalled and open on the terminal floor are ready for firefighter use, and will resist use by passengers.

Phase II Operation — Emergency operating mode for elevators. Allows emergency use of the elevator with certain safeguards and special functions.

Phase II Elevator Operation

Phase II operation is designed to override the recall feature to permit firefighters to use the elevators after they arrive on the scene. Model codes specify that all new elevators must be equipped for Phase II operation. Older elevators may not have any provisions for firefighter service. Individual elevator installations must be evaluated during preincident planning to determine their emergency function capabilities **(Figure 12.18)**.

Typically to activate Phase II operation, a firefighter must insert a key in a three-position switch within a car to place that particular car in "fire service." During this phase, an elevator becomes essentially a manually operated elevator. For example, the floor-select buttons within the car remain operable but the floor-call buttons on the individual floors are inoperable. The elevator doors do not open automatically and the operator must push the "Door Open" button in the car.

The *electric eye safety*, which prevents the doors from closing if there is a person or smoke in the doorway, is disabled during Phase II operations to allow the doors to be closed and the car moved if it inadvertently stops at a smoke-filled floor. The emergency stop button that was inoperable in Phase I should be operable during Phase II. This stop button allows firefighters to stop the

Figure 12.18 Each separate elevator car should be tested separately to ensure proper function.

Figure 12.19 During operations where firefighters will need to use an elevator car, one firefighter must maintain direct access to the controls.

Figure 12.20 When direct access to a building is blocked by any number of obstructions, firefighters may not be able to quickly ventilate the building.

car wherever it is located. Because the car controls are operable only from within a car, it is important that a firefighter remain in the car **(Figure 12.19)**.

Emergency responders should be aware that some local jurisdictions may have specific, unique requirements for certain occupancies such as correctional facilities where the operational features may be different.

NOTE: Additional discussion of special features at correctional facilities is found later in this chapter.

Limited or Controlled Access Buildings

Buildings with limited access must be carefully and routinely pre-planned to maintain the accuracy of the records. Regular inspections of these properties are important to ensure that the emergency access openings are not obstructed on the interior of the building. Building features that limit firefighter access include:

- Solid walls lacking door and window openings
- Obstructions on exterior walls
- Obstructions between the building and the access road
- Features of construction including banked-earth or difficult terrain

Limited access buildings constrict firefighter ability to quickly and efficiently ventilate the building **(Figure 12.20)**. As a result, building codes generally require that these buildings be fully sprinklered.

In addition to sprinklers, limited-access buildings typically must have emergency access openings that meet specific guidelines. For example, upper floors should have emergency access openings on two or more sides in the upper floors. These openings must be readily identifiable and operable from both the exterior and interior, and they must be sized for rescue and ventilation operations. However, there is no consistency in the size requirements; therefore, the local code must be referenced for specific design details.

NOTE: Openings that are operable from the interior and exterior require the use of fire department tools to help maintain building security.

Underground Buildings

Underground buildings may have occupancy areas 30 feet (10 m) or more lower than their primary exit. Underground locations have the advantage of security, relatively constant temperatures, and smaller visual impact. Examples of underground buildings that have existed for many years include:

- Parking facilities
- Subway stations
- Emergency communication/command centers
- Storage facilities

Underground buildings follow the trend toward sustainable (green) building design, and many more underground buildings are being built or planned. These occupancies include:

- Museums
- Libraries
- Academic buildings
- Laboratories
- Industrial facilities
- Offices

Older underground buildings were usually accessed vertically from grade level. However, some modern underground buildings are being built into the side of hills with the primary access being horizontal **(Figure 12.21)**.

Figure 12.21 Horizontal access may be available for some underground buildings.

Examples of Underground Buildings in the US
- Moscone Convention Center, San Francisco, CA
- University of Illinois Library, Urbana, IL
- Underground Art Gallery, Brewster, MA
- New York Transit Museum, Brooklyn, NY
- FedEx, Memphis, TN
- Underman Theater, Dallas, TX
- University of Arizona Integrated Learning Center, Tucson, AZ

Specific types of difficulties for firefighters in underground facilities include:

- Access for fire fighting
- Rescue and evacuation of occupants **(Figure 12.22)**
- Ventilation of heat and smoke
- Water supply and drainage of water from flooding or fire fighting operations

Smoke and Fire Considerations

Probably the greatest single challenge in controlling fires in underground buildings comes from the difficulty in venting heat and smoke. Normal ventilation tactics usually will not work when the roof is entirely below grade.

Figure 12.22 Because rescue activities are more complicated in some structures, special accommodations may be included to aid the process. *Courtesy of Colorado Springs (CO) Fire Department.*

These structures must be thoroughly pre-planned and the plans' information updated as necessary.

Access to an underground structure may take several forms. Large structures may have numerous access points. Underground tunnels such as subways may have stairways, ramps, or even railcar access. Knowing how to gain access and how to remove occupants will be crucial for a coordinated emergency response.

Fire fighting can be extremely difficult when a facility is located below grade, and stairwells or elevators are the only access. Evacuation of occupants from underground locations is more difficult than in high-rise buildings because of the greater physical exertion required for occupants going up stairs and the greater potential for a stairwell being filled with smoke from the fire below. Smokeproof enclosures are now required for buildings with levels more than 30 feet (10 m) below the level of exit discharge.

Underground facilities are not built in the same way as an aboveground building. Underground structures must be excavated. The structural system of an underground facility is massive compared to the framing systems used for aboveground buildings. However, structural damage may still occur in underground structures when a fire has been of long duration. For example, steel support columns may fail in a subway station. The maximum available fire-resistant protection is typically four hours; therefore, fires exceeding four hours are a serious threat.

Special Provisions

The building codes contain special provisions for underground buildings, although they may group underground buildings with windowless buildings. One typical requirement is that the underground portion of the building be of fire-resistive construction. Where buildings have floor levels more than 60 feet (20 m) below the level of exit discharge, separation of each level into two approximately equally sized compartments may be required. Each compartment will be provided with at least one stair and access into the other compartment.

The codes require automatic sprinkler protection for underground buildings, even if a portion of the building extends above the ground and the aboveground portion of the building does not require sprinkler protection.

To address the problem of ventilation of smoke and heat, model codes often require a smoke exhaust system. The depth at which a smoke exhaust system becomes necessary as well as specific requirements for any system will depend on the applicable code.

Below Grade Spaces

Structures may include below grade occupancies such as parking facilities, storage facilities, subway stations, research facilities, and retail stores. These occupancies often include a multitude of hazards, such as:

- Mechanical services powered using natural gas or oil
- High-voltage electrical vaults
- Storage for large quantities of chemical supplies
- Water storage
- Diesel tanks used to power emergency generators

Some structures may have driving surfaces which are located over below grade portions of building. Structures may also be designed with overhangs or areas of low clearance that may impact fire department access. These weight or height limitations may prohibit the use of fire department apparatus due to the collapse potential. Preincident planning of these areas is essential for effective apparatus placement.

Membrane Structures

A membrane structure has an exterior skin of thin, waterproof fabric; often vinyl-coated polyester material. Membrane structures of all types are becoming more common because they are relatively inexpensive and fast to construct. The most significant advantage to membrane structures is the ability to provide a large, unobstructed interior space **(Figure 12.23)**.

Model building codes address a range of membrane structures. In the case of fire exposure, no method of support will prevent the membrane itself from self-venting (melting) under high temperatures. Common structures are described in the following sections.

Figure 12.23 Membrane structures typically use a system of structural supports that leave the interior space unobstructed.

Air-Supported and Air-Inflated Structures

Two types of membrane structures use air pressure to form the shape. The amount of air pressure required to maintain these types of structures is a small fraction above the ambient atmospheric pressure. Fans and air compressors work together to deliver air to the interior of the structure, and accommodate air lost through openings in the membrane **(Figure 12.24)**. Building codes require that the air blowers for pneumatic buildings must be strong, dependable, and redundant to prevent the roof from collapsing on occupants.

Some aspects of life safety addressed in building codes are comparable between these styles of construction and more conventional styles. For example, escape exits and fire suppression resources must be sufficient for the anticipated hazards. In cases where normal access or egress is provided through airlocks or revolving doors, emergency exits may also be required in the building code.

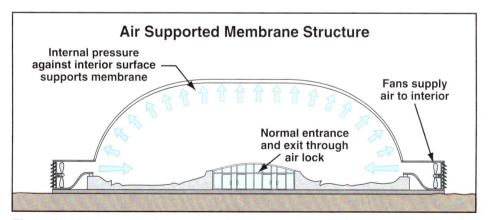

Figure 12.24 Air-supported membrane structures use air control systems to inflate and sustain the shape and size of the occupancy.

> **Air-Inflated Structure** — Membrane structure that uses air pressure to develop its initial shape, but may not use air pressure throughout the entire, high profile, occupancy; enclosed columns or tubes may be inflated to hold the shape of the structure. This type of structure is often intended to be temporary or movable.

> **Air-Supported Structure** — Membrane structure that is fully or partially held up by interior air pressure. This type of occupancy often has a wider footprint than air-inflated structures, and may be secured in place with rigid lower walls and cables. This type of structure may be maintained in place over a long duration.

Air-inflated structures feature a covered space with a fully open floor plan. Air-inflated membrane domes may be used for seasonal "pop-up" shops or as temporary structures used for weather protection while constructing a building inside the membrane structure.

Air-supported structures (domes) are used for occupancies including:

- Sports stadiums
- Tennis courts
- Athletic fields
- Ice skating rinks
- Warehouses
- Casinos
- Churches
- Campus dining facilities

Limitations of Air-Inflated and Supported Structures

Air-inflated or air-supported structures have several limitations including:

- Limited to one story in height.
- Vulnerable to the forces of high winds. Newer structures have computer-controlled fans to automatically adjust to changing atmospheric conditions. For example, when exterior winds increase, the interior pressure is increased.
- The membrane used may be a limited-combustible or noncombustible material. If the material is limited-combustible, it is required to have a low flame spread and low smoke propagation.
- Cannot be used where fire-rated construction is required.

Limitations that ONLY affect air-supported structures include:

- Interior pressure in an air-supported structure can only be slightly greater than the outside pressure to avoid overwhelming occupants.
- Air-supported structures must be secured to some type of foundation to counteract the force of the air-blowing systems. Various anchoring systems have been developed for this purpose.
- Because the interior pressure is greater than the exterior pressure, cables are frequently used to anchor the roof to the ground or substructure.
- Modern air-supported roofs have computer-controlled air-supply systems that adjust for varying external wind loads and internal pressure due to leaks in the membrane. Depending on the manufacturer-specific designs, they may also include cables and low rigid walls.
- Air-supported buildings use a membrane that weighs only a few ounces per square foot for the building skin. Because air-inflated structures do not expose occupants to the supporting pressure, they may use a membrane that is heavier.

Fire Fighting Considerations

Fire fighting in these structures is different from similar activities in different structures for the following reasons:

- Fire suppression systems typically are not installed in air-supported or air-inflated structures due to the flexible nature of the membrane and structural supports.

- Conventional ventilation of an air-inflated or air-supported building is not possible because even a small opening in the roof impairs structural supports.

- Gaining access to the roof is difficult and dangerous: The roof may eventually collapse if the air supply is interrupted or stopped.

Cable- and Frame-Membrane Structures

Cable-membrane structures are supported by external cables fastened to masts (**Figure 12.25**). The structural supports of this type of construction resemble the organization found in a suspension bridge.

Cable-Membrane Structure — Freestanding structure that uses suspension cables for support. *Also known as* Cable Covered Structure.

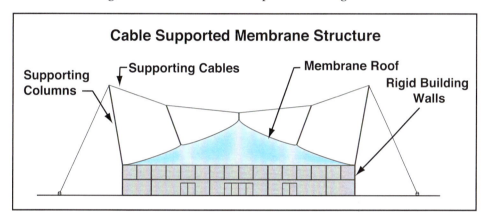

Figure 12.25 Cable membrane structures use a system of uprights and cables to support the membrane from the exterior of the structure.

Frame-Membrane Structure — Structure supported primarily by a frame or skeleton rather than by load-bearing walls. *Also known as* Frame Covered Structure.

Frame-membrane structures feature a rigid frame with a tensioned membrane covering, usually with internal columns (**Figure 12.26**). The structure may include additional internal supports for additional independent compartments. Many states use frame structures to store road salt near highways.

Membrane-covered structures using cable or frame supports are not pressurized, and rely on the configuration of the supports to form the shape of the structure. They are well suited for many uses; however, they cannot be used to provide a large, unobstructed interior space because of the necessary support system. These types of membrane construction are more commonly used than air-inflated or air-supported structures.

As with air-inflated or air-supported membrane structures, membrane-covered cable and frame structures cannot be used where fire-rated construction is required because membranes do not have

Figure 12.26 Frame-membrane structures use a system of internal rigid supports to maintain the shape of the membrane.

a fire-resistance rating. Some membranes are considered noncombustible. The remainder must have a low flame spread, per building codes[2]. This type of construction is also complicated to ventilate, and may collapse quickly.

Covered Mall Buildings

A large covered mall may take the form of a shopping complex with multiple storefront tenants, or a simple covered pedestrian walkway **(Figure 12.27)**. In some large cities, entire original streets may be blocked and developed into multi-block projects **(Figure 12.28)**. The advantage of the covered mall design is that customers may exercise or shop in a comfortable and protected environment.

Figure 12.27 Types of malls include purpose-built structures with a roof.

Figure 12.28 Mall areas may include natural shelter from trees interspersed with the attractions.

Shopping malls are often developed in a suburban community on the edge of a larger city. Sometimes, however, malls are incorporated into redevelopment projects in downtown metropolitan areas as part of mixed-use projects.

As a result of economic changes in neighborhoods, some covered malls that had primarily included retail tenants have been converted to large blocks of offices. Though this is a change in occupancy type, office occupancies tend to have fewer associated hazards than some types of retail, and would therefore still be covered by the mall code provisions.

Hazards and Access

The shopping mall is comparable to the business district of a medium-sized city under one roof, with several commercial blocks roofed over, and the frontage streets turned into pedestrian ways not accessible to emergency vehicles. Any fire department accustomed to working with residential buildings and small- or medium-sized individual stores will have to adjust their operational strategy and tactics to accommodate a shopping mall with multiple occupancy types including:

- Restaurants
- Movie theater complexes
- Professional offices
- Retail stores

Because the smaller stores face into the mall, fire response access to an individual store may be slowed if apparatus cannot directly approach the largest entrance to the store. Some smaller stores may be some distance from a mall entrance, requiring a long hose lay. Codes now require fire department hose outlets in stairs, at major entrances to the mall, and at entrances from the mall to corridors and passageways **(Figure 12.29)**.

Figure 12.29 Covered malls may now be required via code to include fire department connections at strategic places.

Another problem characteristic of covered malls is the periodic change of occupancy in smaller storefronts. This turnover often results in vacant stores and storefronts undergoing renovation. When stores are remodeled, the work is typically done while other stores in the mall are open for business. The stores that are being renovated will have all the hazards associated with construction. In addition, the sprinkler zone protecting that store, and possibly neighboring stores, may be shut off at times during the renovation.

Configuration

Shopping malls are constructed in various sizes and configurations, and typically include one to three levels. When they contain more than one level, covered malls will have multiple openings between the levels. Building codes require that mall walkways be a minimum of 20 feet (6 m) wide. This space permits pedestrian travel and also the use of open storefronts.

Malls are usually designed with one or more large, well-known, perimeter stores that are known as *anchor stores*. The anchor buildings are usually owned and managed as separate entities, and can include nationally known retailers and hotels. The anchor buildings serve to heighten the overall commercial appeal of the mall.

Anchor stores may be separated from the smaller stores by a fire wall; however, codes permit unprotected openings between the anchor stores and the mall. Anchor store buildings function as standalone structures with systems independent from the main mall building, including fire protection systems and utilities.

Construction and Systems

While some shopping malls may be built of fire-resistive construction, many are noncombustible (Type II) or wood (Type V) construction. In recent years, major developers of covered malls have preferred unprotected noncombustible (Type II-b) construction. Current codes do not permit covered malls to be constructed of wood construction.

Figure 12.30 Retail malls may not include fire barriers at every opening.

Sections of covered malls may have been constructed at different times; malls often feature mixed construction. Current codes require malls to be fully sprinklered; however, not all malls maintain full compliance throughout the covered areas. Often the anchor stores have the best compliance and others may have been neglected.

Codes require individual stores within a shopping mall to have 1-hour fire-resistive separations from each other, but they do not require that individual storefronts are separated from the mall itself. Separation between the pedestrian areas and storefronts may have as little separation as a security gate **(Figure 12.30)**. During business hours, the gates or glass doors are open. Products of combustion from a fire occurring within an individual store can readily travel into the mall.

Current codes have eliminated a requirement for smoke control systems in one-story shopping malls; however, a smoke control system may be required in covered mall buildings with three or more stories. Historically, most codes required a smoke control system in all covered mall buildings, regardless of the number of stories.

Detention and Correctional Facilities

Buildings housing detention and correctional facilities differ significantly from most occupancy uses. First of all, the occupants (inmates) are confined, typically in cells. Although they may be physically able to move, they are unable to evacuate in case of a fire until a lock or several locks are opened. In addition, when the occupants are evacuated, they must be relocated to a secure area because they cannot be allowed to escape.

A detention facility is generally a smaller temporary holding facility before release or transfer of inmates to a larger correctional facility. However, some inmates may be kept in a detention facility for several months or longer.

> **Institutional Sprinklers** — Low profile sprinkler system and pendant used with concealed piping in correctional facilities and institutions where tampering of the system must be discouraged or prevented.

For larger correctional facilities located in remote areas, inmates may be evacuated to secure outdoor exercise areas. Some correctional facilities are located in metropolitan areas where large secured outdoor areas are not available. This situation is also the case in many local detention facilities. Where evacuation is a last resort, it is necessary to apply the concept of shelter in place similar to the approach used for hospitals.

Model building code requirements for fire protection and life safety features for detention and correctional facilities vary depending on the level of restraint required at the facility. Types of features may include:

- Remote release of door locks **(Figure 12.31)**
- Smoke compartments
- Areas of refuge on either side of smoke barriers
- Automatic sprinklers
- Smoke control systems
- Manual and automatic fire alarm systems

Newer correctional facilities will likely have a central control center where locking devices are monitored and controlled **(Figure 12.32)**. However, current codes still allow the use of keys under certain conditions. Fire codes have strict flammability requirements for furnishings, including mattresses, to reduce the fire hazard exposure to inmates **(Figure 12.33)**.

Figure 12.31 Correctional facilities may rely on door locking systems that are operated remotely.

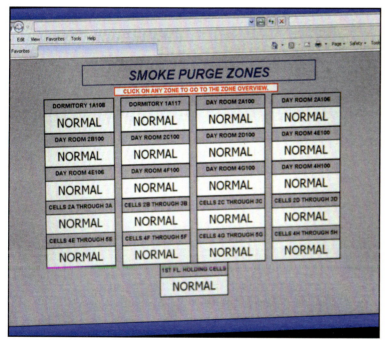

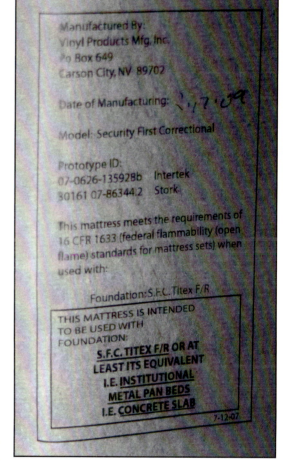

Figure 12.32 (above) Control centers at newer correctional facilities may monitor several systems including smoke control.

Figure 12.33 (right) Flammability requirements for furnishings within some facilities include the use of specially labeled mattresses.

Many newer correctional facilities have automatic sprinklers installed. This fire protection feature specifically addresses the concept of shelter in place. Detention and correctional facilities originally resisted the addition of automatic sprinklers because of the perceived danger of inmates using them incorrectly. This trend changed when the automatic sprinkler industry developed **institutional sprinklers** with a low profile and tamper resistance **(Figure 12.34, p. 332)**.

Figure 12.34 Sprinklers designed for institutional use will break without triggering water flow.

Another key element of the shelter in place concept is creation of one or more compartments on each floor, separated with a fire-rated smoke barrier. This compartmentation allows the inmates to be moved horizontally from the compartment of fire origin to an adjacent compartment on the same floor. Therefore, in most cases, it will not be necessary to use stairs and evacuate inmates.

Older detention and correctional facilities may not have automatic sprinklers installed and may be dependent on keys to open locks. The responding fire department must work closely with the agencies operating these facilities to develop a comprehensive plan of action to guide firefighters during emergency response.

Special Features within Buildings

Some types of building features present unique hazards and challenges for fire fighting operations. The following sections explain unique arrangements that must be preplanned for the best results in an emergency. The special features are largely explained independently from other normal fire scene considerations such as building construction and fire loads, but code-relevant safety features are included.

Atrium — Open area in the center of a building, extending through two or more stories, similar to a courtyard but usually covered by a skylight, to allow natural light and ventilation to interior rooms.

Atriums

Functionally, an **atrium** is a large vertical opening extending through two or more floors of a building that is not used for building services such as enclosed stairs, elevators, or building utilities **(Figure 12.35)**. The code definition of an atrium refers to a covered vertical opening. In an architectural sense, an atrium can have a roof or a ceiling or simply be open to the atmosphere.

Atriums are popular architectural design features used to provide light and ventilate the interior of a building. In contemporary design practice, their appeal lies mainly in the openness they provide within a building. For low-height buildings, an atrium often extends from the first floor up to the roof. In taller buildings, it is common for an atrium to extend only partway up through a building.

From a fire safety standpoint, an atrium poses the same potential as other vertical openings for heat and smoke to travel up through a building **(Figure 12.36)**. There is often a desire to have some floors of a building open to the atrium without any physical separation. In addition, combustible furnishings or other contents are usually found on the floor level of an atrium. Therefore, a fire in floors open to the atrium or on the atrium floor itself has the potential to impact occupants of the other open floors – even upper floors that are otherwise enclosed.

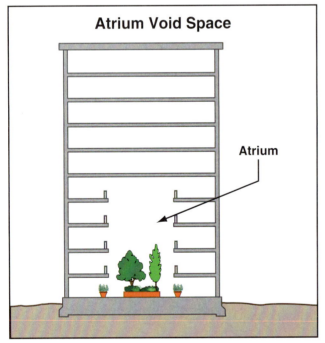

Figure 12.35 Open spaces, such as an atrium, may be used to provide natural light within a structure.

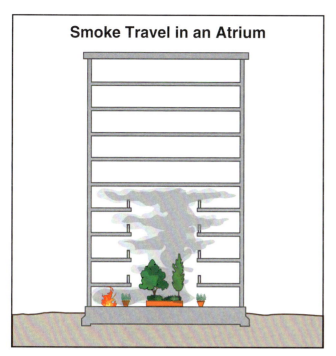

Figure 12.36 Smoke and heat can freely spread in a vertical atrium.

Typical model code requirements for atriums include automatic sprinkler protection **(Figure 12.37)**. Automatic sprinklers may only be required for those floors that the atrium connects. The building codes have a basic requirement that an atrium be enclosed with 1-hour fire-rated construction or a combination of glass and automatic sprinklers. However, codes usually make provision for elimination of the 1-hour enclosure for up to three stories or more when certain conditions are met.

Figure 12.37 Fire safety accommodations in an atrium may include a combination of 1-hour glass enclosures plus closely spaced sprinklers. *Courtesy of Colorado Springs (CO) Fire Department.*

A smoke control system is required to vent the products of combustion to the outside whether floors are enclosed or not. Until recently, requirements for the exhaust capacity reflected the volume of the atrium plus the unenclosed floors connected to the atrium. Current codes calibrate the exhaust capacity to maintain the smoke layer at a specified height above the highest walking level serving the exit system. The required exhaust capacity is based on the magnitude of the expected fire and the height from the floor to the bottom of the lowest-allowable smoke layer. The design of the system, therefore, requires a thorough engineering analysis.

Several different methods of venting atriums can be found, depending on when a particular building was built. For example, some codes now waive the requirements for sprinklers where the ceilings of atriums are more than 55 feet (16.5 m) above the floor.

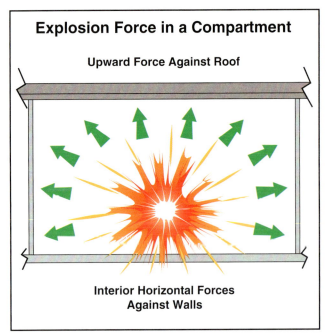

Figure 12.38 The force of an explosion can destroy the structural supports of an enclosed compartment.

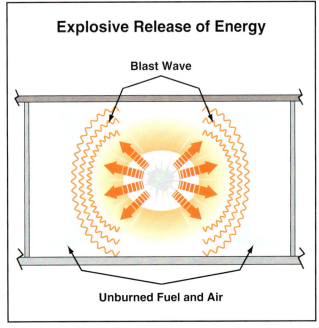

Figure 12.39 During a detonation, blast waves move faster than the speed of sound.

Explosion Venting of Buildings

One type of force that was not discussed in Chapter 3 is the internal force within a building that results from an explosion. An explosion inside a compartment creates an outward pressure on the structural components of the affected space (**Figure 12.38**). In cases of severe explosions, the building can be literally torn apart; exterior structural components such as glass and bricks can be hurled a considerable distance.

For most occupancies, internal explosions are not considered in the design of a building. In specialized industrial occupancies, such as where flammable liquids are processed or where combustible dusts are produced, structural design provisions should be made to reduce the structural damage due to an explosion.

Types of Explosions

An explosion can be defined as an event that produces a rapid release of energy. This sudden release of energy produces outward pressures, often referred to as *blast waves* (**Figure 12.39**). What distinguishes an explosion from other occurrences such as ordinary combustion is the speed with which the process occurs. The damage an explosion may inflict on a structure depends on the maximum pressure developed, the rate of pressure rise, the duration of the peak pressure, and the resistance of the confining structure.

Explosions in buildings occur in a number of ways. Explosions occur because of conditions including:

- A chemical reaction such as the rapid combustion resulting from the ignition of a mixture of air and a flammable vapor (**Figure 12.40**)
- Uncontrolled chemical reactions in processing plants or decomposition of unstable compounds
- Ignition of air and dust from grain or milling/sawing operations
- Boiler explosions in which no chemical reaction occurs

Containment and Venting

Structural damage from an explosion can be mitigated through containment or venting the forces. These two strategies may be used together or separately.

During containment mode, the building enclosure is constructed with adequate reinforcement to contain the pressure resulting from an explosion without failure. Containment is usually expensive because it normally requires reinforcement beyond what is necessary for ordinary structural design purposes. The maximum pressure reached during an explosion may exceed ten times the atmospheric pressure.

Figure 12.40 San Juan, Puerto Rico, 1996. The Humberto Vidal Building was destroyed by a gas mainline explosion. *Courtesy of FEMA/Roman Bas.*

Explosion venting is designed to quickly relieve the pressure before it causes excessive damage **(Figure 12.41)**. Ideally, an explosion vent would be open at all times. However, there are few industrial operations that can be carried out without some kind of an enclosure.

Figure 12.41 The purpose of explosion venting is to provide an escape avenue for pressure.

Some types of explosion vents can be purchased ready to install. Others are custom designed for a specific location. Vent closures must be designed to operate at as low an internal pressure as practical; however, they must still be designed to remain in place when subjected to the forces of external winds.

Because vent panels must operate quickly, they must be relatively light. If the explosion panels are too heavy, their inertia will slow the speed at which they operate resulting in a faster rate of internal pressure rise. Ideally, explosion vent panels should not weigh more than 3 pounds per square foot (16.5 kg/m²). Several different materials, such as lightweight corrugated steel or aluminum sheets, are often used for explosion vents in industrial buildings. Types of explosion vents include:

- Louvered openings
- Hangar-type doors
- Wall panels
- Windows
- Roof vents

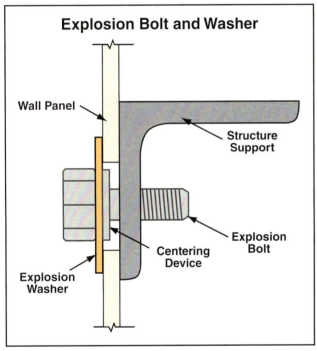

Figure 12.42 Some types of fasteners are designed to release during an explosion.

One method to help ensure rapid operation of vent panels is to attach the panels with explosion vent fasteners, which are designed to release from their attachments under the force of an explosion **(Figure 12.42)**. The panels also may be hinged at one side and fastened at the other so that they swing open in an explosion.

No simple rule exists in regard to the required size of explosion vents. The required explosion vent area varies based on the size and strength of the structure, the expected forces of the potential explosion, and the type of vent. Determination of the actual vent area, therefore, requires an engineering analysis. Generally, a larger vent area results in a lower pressure within the building.

The venting of an explosion is a means of limiting structural damage. Explosion venting is not a substitute for the prevention of explosions and it does not provide for the protection of personnel within a building. The pressure wave developed within the space may be great enough to cause death or injury — even when it is vented — because the pressure wave may come into contact with personnel before the vents open.

When explosion vents are activated, the force of the pressure wave is carried beyond the opening. Therefore, the path of the pressure wave should be identified during preincident planning.

Explosion Control or Deflagration (Fire) Venting

International Fire Code® (IFC®) Section 911 allows the provision of breakaway panels that blow out when the structure is overpressurized to help maintain structural integrity. In the 1970s, the model building codes began requiring breakout panels in exterior walls, but HVAC and sprinkler systems were allowed to be substituted for break-away panels.

Areas of Refuge

An area of refuge for a stairway serving as an accessible means of egress can be located within the stairway on a landing, or near the stairway in an adjacent vestibule. Generally, the area of refuge is designed to accommodate one or two wheelchairs, depending on the occupant load served. The wheelchair space(s) must not obstruct other occupants using the stairway or vestibule for egress. The design of the space must also consider the presence of automatic sprinklers or standpipe risers.

A smoke- and heat-free environment is essential to protect occupants while they are awaiting rescue. Elevator lobbies and enclosed exit stair landings are a logical location for areas of refuge because of the construction features already required in those areas. When a vestibule outside of stairways will be used to provide areas of refuge, the area must be separated from the rest of the floor by a smoke barrier. The typical smoke barrier consists of a minimum 1-hour fire-rated enclosure.

Because of their limited mobility, occupants of an area of refuge could potentially be left unattended or go unnoticed. Therefore, areas of refuge must be provided with some type of two-way communication system connected to a constantly attended location. This system must be designed to accommodate persons with any type of disability. Also, areas of refuge must be well identified from the exterior of the space, and provided on the interior with adequate instructions on the use of the space and the communication system.

Americans with Disabilities Act (ADA) of 1990

As a result of the adoption of the *Americans with Disabilities Act (ADA) of 1990*, significant effort has been dedicated to providing building accessibility and usability for individuals with disabilities. A key element of this effort has been the recognition of the need for special provisions to alert and evacuate people with disabilities if the need arises. For example, if a fire alarm evacuation system is mandated by code in an occupancy or building, the system must provide adequate audible and visual means to alert occupants who are visually or hearing impaired.

Once an alarm is initiated, provisions must include accessible means of egress, especially for occupants who are unable to readily use stairs. Alarm requirements may be reduced or eliminated via code in buildings that are fully protected by automatic sprinklers. When required, accessible means of egress include areas of refuge near stairs or elevators or both. Recent codes require two accessible means of egress from a building, with both routes being continuous to ground level. For buildings with unusual site or configuration restraints, an area of refuge may be needed at the level of stair or elevator discharge.

Rack Storage

Rack storage is a highly efficient use of space. Storage racks are arranged with several horizontal tiers **(Figure 12.43, P. 338)**. While racks may be in single rows, the racks are usually arranged back to back (double-row racks). Warehouses may have multiple rows of racks wider than 12 feet (3.5 m) or with aisles narrower than 3.5 feet (1 m) **(Figure 12.44, P. 338)**.

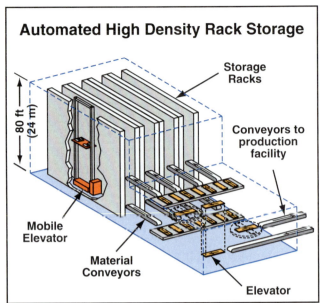

Figure 12.43 (left) Storage rack systems commonly include a series of horizontal shelves that are arranged for the size and shape of the materials they are expected to hold.

Figure 12.44 (above) Rack storage is often configured based on the mechanism used to remove items from shelves, with wider aisles needed for use with forklifts.

The codes regarding the application and design of fire protection features for industrial rack storage include consideration of several variables not limited to:

- Height and style of racks
- Commodity being stored
- Type of containers or palletizing used for the storage
- Public access
- Square footage of the storage area

Rack storage is used in industrial settings for the following reasons:

- The use of multiple-tier racks greatly increases the efficiency of a building's interior volume.
- Rack storage is variable and customizable to the purpose; varying from the simple use of forklifts positioning pallets in the racks to specialized automated warehouses in which unmanned pickers or stackers handle large commodities **(Figure 12.45)**.
- Industrial technology permits precise control of inventory.
- Storage racks can range from a total height of 12 feet (3.5 m) to an excess of 100 feet (30 m).

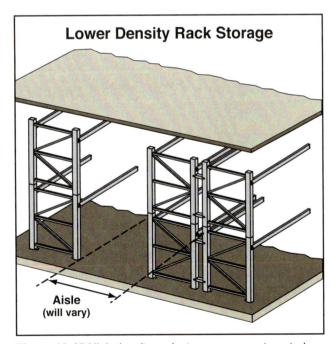

Figure 12.45 High density rack storage uses automated systems that are programmed with the capability to select and deliver specific resources. *Courtesy of Gala and Associates.*

The use of racks for storage has created some unique fire protection problems. First, high density of storage may lead to a high fire load when the stored materials are combustible, such as paper or containers of flammable liquid. This density may obstruct the penetration of water from overhead sprinklers. Second, racks are frequently arranged with narrow aisles. Some fully automated rack storage facilities are not designed to accommodate human access because they are intended to be primarily accessed with robotic picking machinery. Third, some spaces may permit vertical fire travel through the racks.

Sprinklers

Sprinklers are often installed at the ceiling and within high-rack configurations **(Figure 12.46)**. In-rack sprinklers are less effective if the sprinkler discharge is obstructed by the material being stored.

Figure 12.46 Rack storage sprinklers are designed to counter fires within the racks, provided the stored materials are placed appropriately for that use.

Newer ceiling-mounted sprinkler technology includes sprinklers that can operate in control-mode and suppression-mode. These sprinklers are used to control or suppress fires in rack storage, usually without in-rack sprinklers. However, the use of ceiling-mounted sprinklers not only needs to take into account the materials stored and rack arrangement, but also any obstructions from the building elements, such as beams, trusses, ventilation and heating ducts, and slope of the roof.

Structure of Surrounding Building

Normally, storage racks are structurally independent of the building in which they are located, and are often bolted to the floor. In some instances, however, the rack system provides part of the structural support for the building. Because racks consist of unprotected steel members, they may collapse under fire conditions. This situation not only adds to the difficulty of fire suppression, but can also affect the stability of the entire structure when the racks are used as part of the building structural support.

Chapter Summary

While many buildings have similar fire suppression and rescue challenges, others have special characteristics or design features that present unique challenges. This chapter addresses several building types or design features that fall into that category. Many smaller communities may not have any of these special structures within their jurisdiction now; however, they could be constructed at any time. If faced with these buildings or fire-suppression challenges, it is important that firefighters recognize and prepare for the effects they will have on fire suppression efforts. It is highly recommended that preincident plans be prepared for all these locations.

Review Questions

1. List three differences between early and modern high-rise building construction.
2. Name and describe two fire protection systems used in high-rise buildings.
3. What considerations should be made for emergency use of elevators in high-rise buildings?
4. What building features limit firefighters access in limited or controlled access buildings?
5. List types of buildings that have limited or controlled access.
6. What are the basic building codes for construction of atriums?
7. List types of explosion vents.
8. Where are areas of refuge most often required in structures?
9. What hazards can rack storage create?

Chapter Notes

1. For more information on this collapse, the reader is referred to the National Institute of Technology Website at http:/fire.nist.gov/bfrlpubs/.
2. "Special Construction," 2008 New York City Building Code, http://www2.iccsafe.org/states/newyorkcity/Building/PDFs/Chapter%2031_Special%20Construction.pdf.

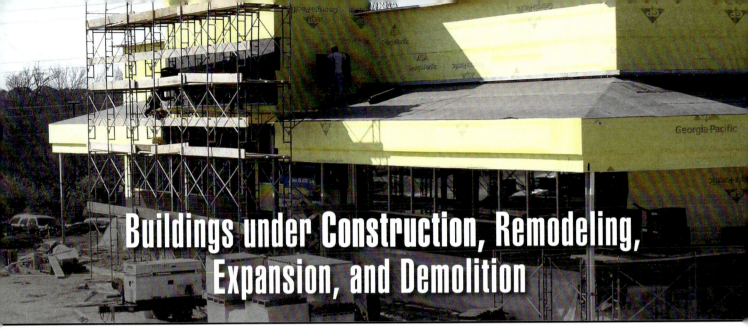

Buildings under Construction, Remodeling, Expansion, and Demolition

Chapter Contents

Case History **345**	Building Expansion 353
Tactical Problems of Construction Sites . 345	Life Safety Features 354
Construction Site Access........................ 346	**Demolition of Buildings** **354**
Fire Hazards at Construction Sites 348	Scavenging Scrap Materials 354
Structural Integrity 350	Unique Hazards of Demolition 355
Fire Protection 351	**Chapter Summary** **355**
Structural Changes and Expansion **352**	**Review Questions** **355**
Building Renovation and Remodeling.... 352	

chapter 13

Key Terms

Fire Department Connection (FDC) 351
Hot Work 350
Liquified Petroleum Gas (LPG) 350
Remodel 352
Renovate 352

FESHE Outcomes Addressed In This Chapter

Fire and Emergency Services Higher Education (FESHE) Outcomes: *Building Construction for Fire Protection*

1. Describe building construction as it relates to firefighter safety, buildings codes, fire prevention, code inspection, firefighting strategy, and tactics.

8. Identify the indicators of potential structural failure as they relate to firefighter safety.

Chapter 13 • Buildings under Construction, Remodeling, Expansion, and Demolition   **343**

Buildings under Construction, Remodeling, Expansion, and Demolition

Learning Objectives

After reading this chapter, students will be able to:

1. Describe conditions at construction sites that impact fire fighting tactics.
2. Identify the methods of providing fire protection at construction sites.
3. Explain how structural changes and expansions may affect fire and life safety.
4. Describe demolition hazards as they relate to fire fighting tactics.

Chapter 13
Buildings under Construction, Remodeling, Expansion, and Demolition

Case History

On March 25, 2014, around 12:30 p.m., a Houston apartment complex caught on fire. The 396-unit apartment complex, which was still under construction, was just three months from completion. The official cause of the fire remains unknown at the time of publishing this manual, but it is suspected that welders on the roof of one of the buildings caused the fire. With sustained winds of 15 to 20 mph (25 to 30 km/h) at the time of the fire, it was considered to be a wind driven fire.

Another significant factor contributing to rapid fire spread was the fact that the building was under construction. With construction still in progress, the structure was essentially a wood frame with some drywall attached. It lacked complete structural integrity, compartmentalization, fire stops (including fire walls and fire doors), and protection systems. The wind drove the fire virtually unabated through the basically open structure.

Nearly 90 companies and 400 firefighters responded to the incident which lasted almost three hours. Approximately 100 construction workers were on site at the time of the fire. Although no major injuries were reported, one dramatic rescue brought this incident to public attention.

The construction process creates special problems for firefighters. Buildings being remodeled, renovated, expanded, or demolished also have unique hazards. This chapter discusses a number of these environments as well as the relevant provisions in building and fire codes. Knowledge of the hazards and code requirements will benefit the firefighter when responding to emergencies at these locations. This chapter includes discussion on the following topics:

- Tactical problems of construction sites
- Structural change and expansion
- Demolition of buildings

Tactical Problems of Construction Sites

Construction sites feature hazards unique to the intended finished project as well as other factors including the unfinished work in progress. A building under construction is particularly vulnerable because fire protection systems and rated barriers may not yet be installed or functional. Emergency responders may be called to construction sites for incidents including:

- Fires, both accidental and intentional
- Non-fire construction accidents
- Debris being blown from upper floors of buildings or around the site
- Structural collapse during construction

In addition, the complexity of a construction project increases with the complexity of the building being constructed. For example, a one-story mercantile building of several thousand square feet may be completed within a few weeks, but a high-rise building can take three years or more to complete. The materials needed during the course of the project may be staged on site starting at the beginning of work, or they may be gathered as needed.

Staging of Raw Materials

NFPA® 241, *Standard for Safeguarding Construction, Alteration, and Demolition Operations*, includes parameters for construction site access and organization, including the storage and staging of combustible materials. The IFC may also include parameters in these environments. The NFPA®, the IFC, and the AHJ may establish rules and protocols to constrain activities and staging at a construction site.

Remodeling work also presents unique challenges. A building's exterior may change in dimension and material as it is remodeled. The interior configuration may be altered through changes in floors, walls, elevator shafts, and stairwells.

Frequent site visits and preincident planning evaluations will help firefighters maintain familiarity with a project, especially when the changing configuration of a large construction project complicates response for reasons including:

- Lack of posted addressing and street signs.
- Road signs may not be current or in place.
- The post office address may not match the lot number assigned via the city, developer, or other AHJ.
- GPS systems and printed maps may not include new-construction roads.

Construction Site Access

First responders commonly have difficulty gaining access to the construction site. Construction sites frequently have fences or barricades surrounding the grounds for security and public safety **(Figure 13.1)**. Gates in fences and barricades may be locked at night and on weekends to prevent unauthorized access, and a watchman may not be available to open the gates. Most construction sites include some type of security measure. Some construction sites may include lock boxes or padlocks to allow emergency access.

Figure 13.1 Barriers around construction sites may indicate hazardous conditions.

Access Roads and Water Supply

Large building projects are typically complex and often built in stages. The fire department should meet with the owner/developer and general contractor before construction starts to coordinate the installation of fire department access and water supply **(Figure 13.2)**.

Reaching the construction site may require long hose lays from existing hydrants located on adjacent streets. Fire codes require that fire hydrants are located near buildings with a water supply capable of meeting the required fire flow for the premises. Codes also allow the fire department to require the installation of necessary mains and hydrants before construction begins.

When permanent roadways and water supply are not available during construction, temporary provisions must be available and sufficient before and during the course of construction. Depending on the condition of the roads and the environment, emergency vehicles may not be able to directly access the building. Restrictions and obstacles associated with access roads include:

- Debris and raw materials
- Vehicles staging on the road as they are loaded/unloaded
- Construction workers' vehicles parked in unauthorized locations
- Damaged roadways from weather and heavy construction equipment
- Construction of the final road may affect temporary access
- Excavations that make access difficult and hazardous **(Figure 13.3)**.

Construction Elevators

Fires frequently occur in the upper floors of high-rise construction, whether or not the work is completed. However, it can be far more difficult and dangerous to access the top of an uncompleted structure. The normal elevators used in a building are usually not in service until shortly before project completion. A construction elevator may be the best available resource to gain access to the upper floors in a high-rise project.

A construction elevator is a temporary elevator usually erected on the outside of a building **(Figure 13.4)**. It is removed when the project is finished. Construction elevators are manually operated. During normal work hours, an operator is stationed in the car and may assist firefighters to gain access to the appropriate level.

Figure 13.2 Water resources should be coordinated early in the process for large construction projects.

Figure 13.3 Excavations in or near access roads may limit access during emergencies.

Figure 13.4 Use of construction elevators during emergency operations may not be possible outside of work hours.

During nonworking hours, an operator is not provided, and the construction site watchman may not be familiar with the operation of the construction elevator. A construction elevator may be disconnected from its power source while not in use. During site visits, firefighters should determine what provision exists for operating the construction elevator during nonworking hours.

Material Hoists

Construction projects may make use of a material hoist as well as a construction elevator. Material hoists are intended only to transport material. They do not have the same safety features as a construction elevator and should never be used to transport personnel. Similarly, the scaffolding systems used during construction are not designed to be used to gain access to upper floors. The maze-like structure of these systems may be extensive enough to present a tactical challenge for firefighters **(Figure 13.5)**.

Figure 13.5 Scaffolding systems are constructed with offset openings for maximum structural stability.

Stairways

Newer building codes require that a minimum of one lighted stairway be provided when building construction reaches a height above four stories or 50 feet (15 m). Temporary stairways or construction ladders can be provided and used when permanent stairways are unavailable.

> **CAUTION**
> The use of temporary stairs and ladders can be difficult and dangerous, especially when a fire occurs several hundred feet up.

Figure 13.6 During low visibility conditions, atypical hazards may not be noticed in time to prevent injury.

A building under construction may have openings in floors for shafts and stairwells. Contemporary safety standards require that these openings, as well as the outside edges of floors, have barricades to help prevent workers from falling. However, firefighters must still maintain situational awareness, particularly under the conditions of limited lighting on a construction site at night. This danger is compounded under fire conditions where smoke may also compromise visibility **(Figure 13.6)**.

Fire Hazards at Construction Sites

Fire hazards at construction sites are often directly related to the unfinished state of the building and its utilities. The following sections describe several common fire hazards at a construction site.

Figure 13.7 Temporary wiring systems may cause a shock hazard.

Figure 13.8 Heating fuels are commonly found on construction sites.

Electrical Wiring

Temporary electrical wiring is often installed on construction projects for lights and power equipment **(Figures 13.7)**. The temporary wiring can become a source of ignition because it is subject to being moved and rearranged in the daily course of the work. Temporary wiring may be damaged via work activities performed in the immediate vicinity.

Uses of Fuels

Flammable and combustible liquids and gases (fuels) are common hazards present on construction sites. Each site may have a unique combination of solids, liquids, and gases, and uses for those materials. Fuels are used for the following applications:

- Heating **(Figure 13.8)**
- Vehicle fuel
- Construction processes

Storage of Fuels

A construction site is a dynamic, changing environment, and the arrangement and storage of fuels will change as the resources are handled and used. Fuels and other materials may be stored in any combination of locations including:

- Inside or outside of the incomplete structure **(Figure 13.9)**
- Above or below grade
- Bulk tanks or in large numbers of smaller cylinders
- Metal shipping containers

NOTE: A full discussion of fuels and other hazardous materials is beyond the scope of this manual. For more information, consult IFSTA's **Hazardous Materials for First Responders** manual.

Figure 13.9 Machinery fuels, such as diesel, may be temporarily stored on construction sites.

Exploding Container Hazard on Construction Sites

Containers holding flammable or non-flammable liquids and gas are found on building construction sites for various processes. The presence of these items can cause an incident or complicate an incident because they may explode if the container is damaged or heated. A typical explosive hazard in this environment comes from liquefied petroleum gas (LPG) tanks.

At a construction site, the risk of hazard from storage containers may be minimized through the following actions:

- Include fuels in preincident surveys
- Watch during any response for fuels in unusual places
- Advise construction personnel to move items as necessary for safety reasons, if authorized to do so.

Liquefied Petroleum Gas (LPG) — Any of several petroleum products, such as propane or butane, stored under pressure as a liquid.

Construction Processes

Construction processes that may increase the fire hazard of a construction site include:

- **Hot work** – Welding, cutting, grinding
- Flammable finishes – Spraying, dipping
- Cleaning – Brushing, spraying
- Testing/commissioning industrial processes – Petrochemical piping, generators

Hot Work — Any operation that requires the use of tools or machines that may produce a source of ignition.

Combustible Debris

A large amount of combustible debris is generated at construction sites **(Figure 13.10)**. At large sites, several truckloads of debris may be removed each day. On a high-rise project, a temporary chute is typically mounted on the building exterior so that debris from the upper floors can be dumped into a container on the ground. A fire in the container can travel up the chute into the building.

Figure 13.10 Combustible debris at construction sites should be maintained as far from an ignition source as possible.

Structural Integrity

Structural fireproofing is often not complete at construction sites **(Figure 13.11)**. Although a building may be designed as fire-resistive construction, it may not have the structural integrity of a fire-resistive building while under construction. For example, in steel-framed buildings, the materials used to provide the fire-resistive insulation must be installed to be effective. In concrete buildings, the ultimate fire resistance of the concrete cannot be ensured until the concrete has cured.

The wooden formwork used in the placing of concrete contributes fuel to a fire. In addition, if the formwork is destroyed, freshly placed concrete will collapse. Firefighters must not be positioned under burning concrete formwork.

Figure 13.11 Because of the nature of construction work, structural fireproofing will not be intact throughout much of the process.

Fire Protection

Like other building systems, such fire protection systems such automatic sprinklers, standpipes, pumps, and hydrants, must be installed before they can provide protection. During construction, firefighters may face an unprotected structure filled with the hazards and combustible materials previously described, but with unfinished fire protection systems. In some cases, the sprinkler system may be one of the last building components to be placed in service.

Temporary Fire Protection Systems

On large, long-duration construction projects, some level of temporary fire protection must be provided. The installation of interim fire protection is essential on high-rise projects, but it is also appropriate for expansive low-rise projects such as regional shopping centers.

The most common temporary fire protection measure is the installation of standpipes with outlets. Systems can also include automatic sprinklers when sufficient progress has been made after the installation of a water supply. Automatic sprinklers sometimes are placed in service to protect completed portions of the building that are used to store construction materials, or to protect the construction offices that may be located within the building.

The most efficient method of providing fire protection on a construction project is to make use of the permanent fire protection systems as they are installed. A separate temporary system can be installed, but this system has the disadvantage of increasing construction costs.

Standpipe risers must be extended up as construction progresses, especially on high-rise buildings, and low-rise buildings more than three stories. Building and fire codes typically require that standpipes be extended before the construction reaches 40 feet (12 m) above the lowest level of fire department access. The top hose outlets should be within one story of the uppermost level that has a secure floor. This coordination requires attention from the contractor installing the system. On some projects, two standpipe risers may be available so one can be maintained in service while the contractor extends the other.

> **Fire Department Connection (FDC)** — Point at which the fire department can connect into a sprinkler or standpipe system to boost the water pressure and flow in the system. This connection consists of a clappered siamese with two or more 2½-inch (65 mm) intakes or one large-diameter (4-inch [100 mm] or larger) intake. *Also known as* Fire Department Sprinkler Connection.

When standpipes are installed in building projects, they cannot be maintained wet (holding water) during freezing weather. Dry standpipes supplied through **fire department connections (FDC)** must then be used **(Figure 13.12)**. Frequent inspections should help ensure that the system will be available when needed. Construction site factors include:

- Workers may try to use standpipes as a source of water for construction purposes.
- Workers may open a hose valve to get water and then leave the valve open when they do not get water.
- A fire department connection charged for a fire will flow water out of any open valve; water flowing out a valve that is not dedicated to fire fighting operations may limit or delay the firefighters' ability to perform fire fighting operations.

Figure 13.12 Standpipes will often be maintained without water during construction work. *Courtesy of McKinney (TX) Fire Department.*

- Obstructions that prevent access to the fire department connection such as construction materials, trucks, or barricades.
- The hose connections can be damaged or even stolen.
- A dry standpipe riser used during cold weather must be drained after use to prevent freezing.

Fire Extinguishers

Fire extinguishers can be useful at construction sites when workers are trained to use them. General ABC extinguishers may address the majority of hazards at a construction site. Specialized extinguishers may be present because of specific fire hazards on the site, such as sensitive electrical equipment or combustible metals. For example, NFPA® 241 requires the presence of a 20 B rated extinguisher during roofing operations as a precaution against the ignition of combustible materials.

When extinguishers are stolen, or likely to be stolen, barrels of water with dedicated buckets can sometimes be substituted, depending on the type of fuel types at the site. Construction workers must be trained to know when water application is an appropriate action.

Structural Changes and Expansion

Over its lifespan, a building may be evaluated for function, style, and new technology. When any aspects are determined to be lacking, the building may be updated. These updates may be limited to changes in the style of wall coverings, or as extensive as changes to structural supports and the external shape of the building **(Figure 13.13)**. The following sections discuss several changes that may be made to a building during renovation, remodeling, and expansion.

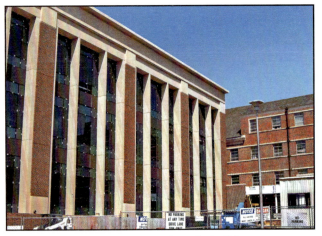

Figure 13.13 Significant expansion of a building may encompass a full city block or more.

Building Renovating and Remodeling

Renovation of a building may be simple or complex, and often addresses modernization or the needs of the occupants. For example, renovation work can consist of replacing bathroom fixtures, or include substantial changes to the color, lighting, and shape of spaces. **Remodel** work may also be simple or complex, ranging from simply removing a nonload-bearing wall to extensive structural and architectural alterations.

Many hazards generated through remodeling and renovating are similar to hazards generated during new construction, including:

- Trash – Combustion and trip hazard
- Temporary wiring – Combustion hazard
- Open flames – Combustion hazard
- Fumes – Inhalation hazard

The primary hazard unique to renovating and remodeling is the disturbance of hazardous substances such as asbestos. Because of the hazardous nature of

Renovate — Restoring or updating a building's features including finishing materials, furnishing, and overall appearance.

Remodel — Restructuring of a building's spaces and occupancy features.

the material, entire areas may be restricted against entrants without specialty clothing and respiratory protection. In addition, removed materials may be stored on site temporarily, with handling requirements per the AHJ.

Because the work often takes place in one portion of a building while the remainder of the building continues to be occupied, remodeling and renovation can introduce unusual hazards.

For example, a hotel may elect to renovate one floor of a building while the other floors are still occupied to minimize the effect on revenue. Renovation or remodeling of an occupied building often includes the erection of construction barricades that can obstruct exits or increase the exit travel distance from the occupied portion of the building. When occupancy continues on other floors, a fire watch is especially important after work stops for the day.

In addition to the other dangers present during remodeling, automatic sprinklers may be disconnected in the area being remodeled. If sprinklers are shut off in the construction area, first aid hose stations and extinguishers must be provided. A renovation project should be planned in such a way that the interruption to sprinkler protection is minimized. In addition, the number of sprinklers shut off should be limited as much as possible.

When a portion of a sprinkler system has been shut off for remodeling, the restoration of the system must be verified when the project is finished. In older construction, sectional control valves may be located in low-traffic corners of old warehouse and factory buildings. In newer buildings with sprinkler systems, building and fire codes require valves controlling the water supply for sprinkler systems with more than twenty sprinklers to be monitored at a constantly attended location.

Building Expansion

Projects that include a significant expansion of a building are typically located in suburban areas, or on a campus-type complex, where adjacent open space is available **(Figure 13.14)**. Expansions of existing buildings often are major construction projects in themselves, and all such projects require building permits. These projects present both the concerns faced in new construction along with some of the concerns of major remodeling projects, including the factors discussed in the section above: Tactical Considerations at Construction Sites. Similar to remodeling work, a common theme in most expansion projects is the need to keep a portion of a building in operation. Therefore, life safety must be maintained for occupants in the existing portion while providing the necessary protection to the construction site.

Some examples of building expansions include:

- Regional shopping centers
- Industrial buildings
- Warehouses

Figure 13.14 Large scale construction projects may affect vehicle and pedestrian traffic.

- Convention centers
- Airports
- Research facilities

The local fire inspector will meet with the owner and contractor to ensure that measures are in place before construction begins. First-due fire companies and other relevant first responders should be made aware of any temporary arrangements and visit the site to become familiar with the project.

Life Safety Features

Construction may affect one or more of the exits for the existing building. Temporary measures must be taken to provide for the continued protection of the occupants in the existing building. These measures may include providing new exits or temporary fire-rated "tunnels" through the new construction zone until occupants can reach a safe location. Arrangements for these provisions need to be developed before the start of construction. The fire inspector assigned to the project must meet with the owner and general contractor to assure that an acceptable approach is in place.

Most expansions involve buildings that already have automatic sprinklers. Buildings with large occupant loads will have a fire alarm evacuation system and possibly a smoke control system installed. The new construction will often affect the existing water supply system on the premises including mains, hydrants, and fire department connections.

As stated earlier in this chapter, temporary provisions may be used to maintain the functionality of fire protection systems. Until the final systems are in place and tested, resources that may be required to maintain the water supply include:

- Temporary mains
- Hydrants
- Fire department connections
- Temporary risers
- Temporary bulk sprinkler piping

Demolition of Buildings

The demolition of a building is even more chaotic than construction. Fires on demolition sites are common, especially in wood-joisted or wood-frame construction. Although the inclination is to not spend money to protect a building in the process of demolition, the neighboring exposures and environmental threat must be considered **(Figure 13.15)**.

Figure 13.15 The hazards common to demolition require careful planning to prevent unanticipated damage to exposures.

Scavenging Scrap Materials

Before demolition activities begin, materials that are salvageable or that have scrap value may be stripped from buildings. These operations may be authorized through the wrecking contractor or unauthorized. Unauthorized removal of materials frequently takes place at night and with few safety precautions. Regardless of authorization, removal of scrap steel often involves cutting with torches, which is a common cause of fires. Items that are frequently removed before demolition include:

- Portions of the fire protection system such as standpipe hose valves and fire department connections.
- Architectural artifacts such as ornate elevator shaft gates, bath tubs, stair railings, and even marble slabs used for stairs.
- Copper elements including wiring and decorative facades and panels.

Unique Hazards of Demolition

Demolition activities systematically undermine and destroy a building's structural integrity. A fire accelerates structural collapse and limits the demolition team's control.

While major fires in buildings being demolished usually involve combustible structures or structures with combustible framing, fire-resistive or noncombustible buildings can contain some unpleasant surprises. Examples include a fuel oil tank with residual oil, or an accumulation of combustible debris at the bottom of an elevator shaft.

Exterior fire fighting tactics from a safe distance are the best course of action. A building being demolished can present a virtual maze consisting of floor openings, an unstable structural system, inoperative fire protection systems, and unknown hazardous materials. Such a structural mess is not worth a firefighter's life. At the same time, situations exist where firefighters must enter buildings being wrecked, including rescues of demolition workers or scavengers who have become trapped or injured.

Chapter Summary

All completed and occupied buildings create a need for the firefighter to know what to expect when arriving at the building during an emergency response. Many target hazards have pre-incident plans and others have been the subject of company inspections. The same respect must be given to buildings that are under construction, being remodeled/renovated or expanded, or are being demolished. These buildings are often full of surprises, and first responders must watch for them.

Review Questions

1. What restrictions or obstacles are associated with access roads?
2. What fire hazards exist at construction sites?
3. What fire protection measures can be taken at a construction site?
4. How do structural changes and expansion affect fire fighting tactics?
5. What unique hazards does a demolition site present to firefighters?

Non-Fire Building Collapse

Chapter Contents

Case History 359	Nature-Related Causes of Building Collapse 365
Human-Related Causes of Building Collapse 360	Earthquakes 365
Inadequate Structural Design 360	Landslides, Subsidence, and Sinkholes 367
Change in Building Use 360	Wind-Related Hazards 369
Poor or Careless Construction Methods 361	Snow and Water Loads 371
Poor or Careless Demolition Methods 362	Floods 372
Explosions 363	**Wide Area Incidents** 373
Other Human-Related Causes 364	**Chapter Summary** 375
	Review Questions 375
	Chapter Notes 375

chapter 14

Key Terms

Aftershock 365	Piecemeal Demolition 363
Controlled Collapse Demolition 363	Voice over Internet Protocol (VoIP) 373
Earthquake 365	
Federal Emergency Management Agency (FEMA) 373	

FESHE Outcomes Addressed In This Chapter

Fire and Emergency Services Higher Education (FESHE) Outcomes: *Building Construction for Fire Protection*

1. Describe building construction as it relates to firefighter safety, buildings codes, fire prevention, code inspection, firefighting strategy, and tactics.

4. Explain the different loads and stresses that are placed on a building and their interrelationships.

8. Identify the indicators of potential structural failure as they relate to firefighter safety.

Non-Fire Building Collapse

Learning Objectives

After reading this chapter, students will be able to:

1. Describe human-related causes of building collapse.
2. Distinguish among nature-related causes of building collapse.
3. Explain the importance of preincident planning for wide area incidents.

Chapter 14
Non-Fire Building Collapse

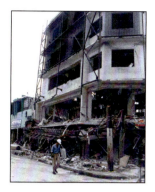

Case History

On May 2, 2009, a non-fire collapse of a structure occurred at an indoor professional football practice facility during a thunderstorm with heavy winds. There were 12 injuries and at least one was serious. The framing of the structure consisted of steel with a gable-roof design and was covered with a fabric under tension. The structure was designed in 2003 and a structural upgrade to selected structural supports was completed in 2008.

The National Institute of Standards and Technology (NIST) cited several factors that contributed to the collapse. The principle findings summarized wind loads used in the original design and the upgraded design differed from wind loads based on the provisions outlined in national standards. The wind speeds at the time of collapse were estimated between 55 to 65 mph (90 to 105 km/h), well below the wind load requirement of 90 mph (145 km/h) as specified in design and capacity standards for that type of framing. In addition, shear forces and bending in the framing was not considered in the original design.

The building was considered fully enclosed instead of partially enclosed. The structure had the vents and openings in the fabric that allowed the pressure in the structure to vary within parameters. Lastly, it was assumed the exterior fabric provided lateral bracing to the outer chords of the framing system.

This collapse highlights how a building and environmental factors are considered during the design phase, and even seemingly structurally sound buildings may collapse under certain conditions. Fire and emergency services personnel must be aware of non-fire factors that can contribute to structural collapse and prepare for such events through preplanning and the knowledge of building construction.

First responders, from recruits to senior officers, must be alert to the potential for building collapse, whether during a fire or due to some other reason. Every response is unique, but three common causes of building collapse can be planned ahead of an incident. The following topics are discussed in this chapter:

- Human-Related Causes of Building Collapse
- Nature-Related Causes of Building Collapse
- Wide Area Incidents

Human-Related Causes of Building Collapse

The causes of building collapse can be put into two broad categories: nature-caused and human-caused. For many of these events, there is no forewarning. For other events, the potential for building collapse can be anticipated, but the specific location will not be known until the event reaches exposed structures.

Whenever possible, specific precautions will be identified for each type of event. When approaching a partially collapsed building, firefighters must assume that the remaining building is seriously weakened. Use caution when performing search and rescue operations when facing this condition.

NOTE: Refer to IFSTA's **Fire Service Technical Search and Rescue** manual for more information on structural collapse.

Inadequate Structural Design

Architects and structural engineers calculate many factors to ensure that a building will have enough structural durability to withstand predictable forces and be constructed in the best possible manner. Although each of the factors are not fully inclusive in themselves, they become rigorous when taken together. Calculations during the design phase include:

- Building code requirements
- Engineering standards and practices
- Local weather, seismic, and flood data
- Redundancies and safeguards as relevant **(Figure 14.1)**

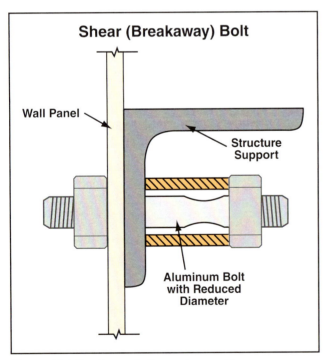

Figure 14.1 Breakaway bolts can be used in some applications as a safety measure to release excess force, such as high wind.

The structural design, including calculations, is typically evaluated during the plan review process before construction begins. The codes also require inspections during construction to ensure that the proper materials and methods of construction are being used. Even with these safeguards, the best practices may be overlooked or disregarded, which may lead to a partial or total collapse.

NOTE: For more information on plans review, consult the IFSTA manual, **Plans Examiner for Fire and Emergency Services**.

Change in Building Use

As discussed in Chapter 3, the structural design of a building includes consideration of the maximum live loads associated with the expected occupancy of the building. If the use changes over the years, it is possible that the new use could result in higher live loads than the original design can accommodate, eventually resulting in structural failure. Although the concern of increased loads may be identified during review of an application for a change in occupancy, all too often these changes occur without the knowledge of the building staff or fire department. For example, upper levels of retail or office buildings may collect storage items, resulting in an increased load over time.

Poor or Careless Construction Methods

Until a building's structural frame is completed, the building will not have the level of structural stability that it will have when the frame is finished. Therefore, there is always a potential for collapse due to poor or hurried construction techniques. Several causes of structural collapse during the course of construction are discussed below.

Temporary Loads

Collapse can result when temporary loads on the structural members exceed final design loads due to careless stockpiling of heavy building materials on upper floors **(Figure 14.2)**. For example, in Los Angeles, California, in December, 1985, a 21-story building under construction collapsed, resulting in the deaths of three workers. Structural steel was stockpiled on one bay on an upper floor. The load of the steel was twice the design load, causing three beams to fail.

Figure 14.2 Staging of large and heavy items must be planned to prevent overloading supports or blocking access.

Sequencing

Another cause of collapse is improper sequencing of the construction process. The order of operations during construction is critical: structural supports must be built before loads can be added.

For example, improper sequencing was a potential contributing factor in Bridgeport, Connecticut, in 1987, when a housing project collapsed during construction, killing 28 workers. At the time of the failure, construction of the shear walls was several floors below the lift-slab erection operation.

Weakness of Building Frame

Failure during construction may result from temporary weakness of the building frame. Poured-in-place concrete structures are especially affected because of the length of time required for concrete to cure and develop its ultimate design strength. If the construction progresses too quickly, the supporting elements may not have sufficient strength to support the new load.

Building Frame Insufficiency
An example of building frame weakness occurred in March, 1973 during the construction of a 26-story condominium building in Bailey's Crossroads, Virginia. The building collapsed, resulting in the death of 14 workers and the injury of 35 others. The collapse was attributed to the removal of shoring before the concrete had cured sufficiently to support the loads above.

Instability of Building Frame

The instability of the building frame during construction may cause failure. Until the final members of the structural frame are in place, the frame is vulnerable to vertical and horizontal loads. The use of temporary bracing is common to all types of building construction **(Figure 14.3)**. The structural engineer or contractor is responsible for identifying and providing temporary bracing.

For example, at the University of Washington, Seattle, Washington in 1987, inadequate temporary bracing affected a grandstand addition to the Husky Stadium. Several of the guy lines being used to provide support during the construction were removed before all structural frame members were in place. Fortunately, there was early warning of the failure and no injuries or deaths occurred.

Figure 14.3 Major structural elements may be temporarily braced during construction while the permanent supports are added. *Courtesy of McKinney (TX) FD.*

Poor or Careless Demolition Methods

The most dangerous time in a building's lifespan is during its demolition. Demolition work is often more haphazard than construction work. Naturally, a building under demolition will gradually lose its stability as its structural supports are systematically removed. When demolition work is conducted with the proper safeguards, exposures are guarded and the targeted materials fall at predictable rates and within established parameters.

Controls on demolition include the tools and strategies used during the work. Both piecemeal demolition and controlled collapse demolition require a well-thought-out plan. **Piecemeal demolition** is performed with hand tools or machines. **Controlled collapse demolition** is performed with larger equipment that may include:

- Crane with a demolition ball
- Hydraulic pusher arms
- Wire rope pulling
- Explosives

Planning during demolition is especially essential when the building being demolished is near other structures. For example, during careless demolition practices, a dry cleaning building in Pennsylvania struck another building and resulted in the death of one person.[1]

Even with the proper safeguards in place, demolition work may undermine the structural stability of nearby structures because of hazards including:

- Shifting soil loads
- Impact against adjacent structures from falling loads
- Impact against the ground from falling loads

When primary structural members are removed during piecemeal demolition, the potential for unexpected collapse increases. Often, this approach will require temporary bracing or props to help ensure that the remaining structure will be able to support the load that may include:

- Workers
- Equipment
- Temporary loads including debris

During piecemeal demolition, an unexpected collapse will likely require rescue response because workers involved in the demolition may be on and in the structure. In contrast, in a controlled collapse demolition, workers should not be near the building as it falls, so rescue should not be required.

Vacant buildings, whether scheduled for demolition or not, are increasingly the site of vandalism and scavenging because of the increased price of salvage materials and architectural artifacts. Amateur scavenging may result in weakening of the structure or an unexpected collapse.

Explosions

Explosions, whether accidental or deliberate, frequently result in building collapse. Except in the rare instance that explosion venting has been provided, explosive forces can cause major structural failure **(Figure 14.4)**. Explosions may or may not include fire, whether before or after the fact.

NOTE: The IFSTA manual **Hazardous Materials for First Responders** includes details on identifying and responding to explosions.

> **Piecemeal Demolition** — Demolition process that uses hand tools and machines to gradually decrease the height of the structure.
>
> **Controlled Collapse Demolition** — Deliberate demolition process that uses large machinery and equipment to reduce an entire structure to ground level.

Figure 14.4 West, Texas, 2013. Many homes near the site of the April 17 fertilizer plant explosion were destroyed. *Courtesy of Norman Lenburg/FEMA.*

Common sources of explosions in buildings include:

- Boiler furnaces
- Flammable gas leaks
- Gasoline vapors
- Finely powdered dust
- Storage of fireworks or blasting agents
- Industrial processes, with or without the proper safeguards in place
- Terrorist or other crime-related activity
- Illicit laboratories
- Oil extraction using flammable liquids and gases

Other Human-Related Causes

Sometimes unexpected events cause a building to collapse. For example, the collision of a motor vehicle with a structure typically results in a partial collapse. Less common, although more significant, is an aircraft crash into a structure. When such a crash occurs, fire almost always follows because of the fuel from the airplane's fuel tanks.

Some older buildings have collapsed due to age and deterioration (**Figure 14.5**). For example, in Philadelphia, Pennsylvania on May 18, 2000, Pier 34 partially collapsed under the nightclub it supported. The collapse resulted in the death of three patrons of the nightclub and injury to 36 patrons and employees. The pier, built in 1909, reportedly failed due to the deterioration of the old piles supporting the deck of the pier. The nightclub had opened the week before this incident, despite earlier indications of structural instability.

Figure 14.5 Ineffective maintenance of an older warehouse resulted in the use of more than 20 tarps for rainwater removal. The dewatering work was conducted in the presence of energized electrical wires. *Courtesy of West Allis (WI) FD.*

Nature-Related Causes of Building Collapse

As indicated in Chapter 3, nature-related forces can exert loads that must be accommodated in building design. Even when a building includes all appropriate measures to prevent damage from expected conditions, extreme incidents can disrupt a building's stability. The following sections describe situations in which a building is unable to withstand the current conditions through no fault of the construction or other human-related factors.

Securing the Ability to Respond

As soon as an event is reported, a general alarm sounds and fire departments secure their ability to respond. Often this action takes the form of staging resources away from the fire station, and surveying the jurisdiction to determine the functionality of the local infrastructure (roads, bridges) and other resources. This action is a best practice, and may be practiced as a training drill.

Earthquakes

Many areas are susceptible to **earthquakes** (**Figure 14.6**). In the United States and Canada, the West Coast, including Alaska and Hawaii, are particularly vulnerable; however, earthquakes occur in other parts of both countries. No proven methods exist for predicting earthquakes.

Earthquake — A sudden release of energy in the Earth's crust that creates seismic forces that shake and sometimes disrupt the ground. Earthquakes are associated with volcanic activity, landslides, and tsunamis.

Figure 14.6 Napa, California, 2014. Even with the addition of retrofitted seismic stabilization systems in 2004-2005, books in the Romanesque Goodman library were scattered during a 6.0 magnitude earthquake. *Courtesy of Christopher Mardorf/FEMA.*

Many earthquakes often include **aftershocks**, some of which may be nearly as strong as the original event. When the events happen close together, buildings damaged during the initial earthquake may not be repaired before the next shock. Severely damaged buildings may further shift during aftershocks, threatening search and rescue operations. Even if a building has not collapsed, a minor aftershock may be strong enough to topple a weakened or damaged cornice or other building element.

Aftershock — A smaller earthquake that occurs in the same area and similar time frame as a larger earthquake.

Model building codes include increasingly stringent requirements for building design that will withstand seismic forces. Because of improvements in the model codes, modern buildings have lower risk of damage from earthquakes than buildings constructed before 1930.

Code requirements account for the expected ground motion in the area where the building is to be located. Maps or tables showing these values are usually included in the applicable code. Seismic design considerations include lateral bracing and other features to provide sufficient resistance to seismic motion in order to minimize damage and avoid collapse **(Figure 14.7)**. Buildings with higher requirements for seismic force resistance include buildings important to public and critical infrastructure.

Figure 14.7 Napa, California, 2014. The 6.0 magnitude earthquake caused minor damage to the structure of the reinforced Goodman library, donated to the city of Napa in 1901. *Courtesy of Christopher Mardorf/FEMA.*

Fire departments in areas subject to earthquakes should have a general plan in place for responding after the event. The fire department should identify in advance buildings that may be more likely to suffer major damage and possible collapse during a major seismic event. One resource that should be consulted is the local (city/province) building department.

Numerous factors contribute to the extent of building damage and potential collapse during earthquakes including:

- Ground motion associated with major earthquakes can cause extensive structural damage to buildings that are near earthquake fault lines, often resulting in partial or total building collapse.
- Unreinforced masonry construction is highly susceptible to seismic events.
- The location of the building relative to the responsible fault and the epicenter of the earthquake.
- The soil conditions beneath the building, especially the potential for liquefaction of loose, sandy soil.

Landslides, Subsidence, and Sinkholes

Unlike most of the other hazards discussed in this manual, there are no specific model building code requirements to address construction in areas prone to landslides, subsidence, and sinkholes. The fire service must develop a close working relationship with public works agencies to ensure notification when problems are noted in the field or where high-risk areas have been identified. Geotechnical investigations must be conducted if a building official requires the work.

The following resources may be consulted for more information while evaluating an area for its likelihood to develop one of these three hazards:

- Recorded history of the area
- Environmental impact reports and zoning regulations
- Soil reports may identify many existing conditions

As a result of the unpredictable nature of many building sites, developers are often required to provide adequate drainage and other measures to ensure ground stability. Firefighters must also be aware of the potential for continued landslide, subsidence, or sinkhole activity after arriving at the scene. The fire service should be aware of the potential hazards of these areas and establish SOPs for responding to incidents of this type. For example, caution must be exercised in parking apparatus to avoid unsafe areas.

Landslides

Landslides are defined as the movement of rock, earth, or debris down a slope **(Figure 14.8)**. Landslides can happen at any time and in many types of places.

Figure 14.8 Lake Delton, Wisconsin, 2008. Flooding caused a dam to break and empty Lake Delton. As the side banks collapsed, the removal of foundational support caused houses to fall. *Courtesy of Robert Kaufmann/FEMA.*

Predictable causes of landslides include:

- Urban expansion that undermines hillsides or uses areas with less stable soil to accommodate building development

- Substantial, sudden weather changes between extremes of wet and dry
- Earthquakes

Indicators of potential landslides may include:

- Damage to underground utilities
- Roadway cracks
- Minor slides in the area
- Wildland fires
- Addition of groundwater through landscape watering or a broken water main

Subsidence

Land subsidence is similar to landslides in that the ground gives way, but usually in the form of gradual sinking. When subsidence occurs under or near buildings, damage or eventual collapse of the building may occur. Cases of subsidence can occur almost anywhere.

The primary cause of subsidence is the removal of large amounts of underground water or oil over many years beneath built-up areas. Subsidence is usually gradual and fairly uniform when the cause is the removal of an underground liquid.

Sinkholes

Sinkholes are considered an extreme form of subsidence, but they usually happen quickly like landslides **(Figure 14.9)**. The primary cause of sinkholes is the collapse of the ground surface into an underground cavity created as ground water dissolves water soluble rock formations. They can also occur over areas that have been subjected to underground mining or more commonly in urban areas as the result of water main breaks.

Figure 14.9 San Diego, California, 1998. El Nino rains collapsed a storm drain pipe into an estimated 850-foot-long hole. *Courtesy of Dave Gatley/FEMA.*

Sinkholes most frequently occur in the U.S. Midwest and Eastern/Southeastern states, especially Florida. They can also occur in all states and throughout most of Canada **(Figure 14.10)**.

Figure 14.10 Red Hook, New York, 2011. Hurricane Irene created conditions that undermined this roadway. *Courtesy of Elissa Jun/FEMA.*

Wind-Related Hazards

Unlike earthquakes and landslides, which usually occur without warning, modern weather forecasting usually enables early warnings about the potential for high winds, tornadoes, and hurricanes. One resource that monitors weather conditions is the National Weather Service (NWS), a component of the National Oceanographic and Atmospheric Administration (NOAA)[2]. Windstorms have been known to occur in most U.S. states and Canadian provinces. However, the paths of these storms are often unpredictable.

Current model building codes include wind loads as part of the structural design requirements. The codes specify minimum design wind speeds to include in the design analysis.

Historically, many buildings were constructed before more stringent requirements appeared in model building codes. Therefore, significant structural damage over a large area can be expected as a result of major windstorms, tornadoes, and hurricanes **(Figure 14.11)**. For example, southern Florida locally adopted more stringent construction requirements after Hurricane Andrew in 1992.

Figure 14.11 Orange Beach, Alabama, 2004. The Windemere Condominiums were severely damaged during the course of Hurricane Ivan's 130 mph winds and 30-foot ocean swells. *Courtesy of Butch Kinerney/FEMA.*

Weather systems that affect large areas may include areas that are more severely affected than neighboring areas. Although some incidents will influence a wide area, each local area will have unique concerns. In some cases, response systems may be unavailable because of inoperable communication systems or the neighboring jurisdictions will have different challenges that they must prioritize. Large, catastrophic events require a highly coordinated multiagency regional plan for response **(Figure 14.12)**.

NOTE: The IFSTA manual **Fire Service Technical Search and Rescue** includes information regarding response to collapsed structures and other related operations.

Figure 14.12 Breezy Point, New York, 2012. The damage caused during Hurricane Sandy was only partially repaired after 10 months. *Courtesy of K.C. Wilsey/FEMA.*

Figure 14.13 Central Oklahoma, 1999. Urban Search and Rescue teams worked to recover missing persons after a widespread system of tornadoes causing significant damage and loss of life. *Courtesy of Andrea Booher/FEMA.*

Tornadoes

Although tornadoes are more likely in the Midwest, South-Central, and Southeastern states and in the prairie/plains areas of Southern Canada, they have been known to occur in most states and provinces. In the case of tornadoes, many structures may be completely destroyed **(Figure 14.13)**. Tornado conditions are largely predictable, but damage may be more extensive than expected.

Hurricanes

In regions that expect wind-borne debris, such as coastal areas subject to hurricanes where the basic wind speed is 110 mph (175 km/h) or greater, window glazing must be impact-resistant. In geographical locations with high probability of hurricanes, structures may include special anchors such as hurricane straps, clips, or brackets to provide additional reinforcement **(Figure 14.14)**.

Hurricanes generally occur only along the Gulf States, Eastern Seaboard, and Hawaii. Hurricanes add the possibility of water surge along immediate adjacent coastal areas, causing additional building damage and destruction **(Figure 14.15)**. The remnants of hurricanes may move into other areas as tropical storms and heavy rainfall.

Figure 14.14 Gulf Breeze, Florida, 2004. Hurricane brackets, also known as wind clips, were used to minimize damage from wind and storm surge associated with Hurricane Ivan. *Courtesy of Mark Wolfe/FEMA.*

Figure 14.15 Rodanthe, North Carolina, 2011. Hurricane Irene caused significant damage from storm surge that included sand and water. *Courtesy of Tim Burkitt/FEMA.*

Snow and Water Loads

Building collapse can occur due to the force associated with accumulated snow, rain water, or a combination of both. This type of collapse is usually associated with major weather events, but may occur after a series of storms **(Figure 14.16)**. These types of collapses often happen without warning and are usually isolated events.

Figure 14.16 Snow and ice load can add enough weight to collapse a large building. *Courtesy of West Allis (WI) FD.*

For example, in Kansas City, Missouri in 1979, the roof of the Kemper Arena collapsed, causing some of the walls to fail. The cause of collapse was a storm with 70 mph (110 km/h) winds and heavy rains, which overwhelmed the roof drainage system. Similarly, the Metrodome in Minnesota collapsed due to the added weight resulting from a heavy snowstorm on December 12, 2010.

Model building codes require that snow and rain loads be addressed as part of the structural design of the building. Roof drains are required to aid the drainage of water from flat roofs. The codes specify the snow loads expected throughout the U.S. and Canada.

NOTE: Chapter 3 includes a discussion of the loads imposed on a structure from weather related forces including snow and water.

Examples of Weather Related Live Loads

Many storms bring combinations of loads that will affect structural integrity. Loads that may occur simultaneously against a structure include:

- Snow
- Rain
- Wind
- Floods
- Waves
- Seismic loads

Floods

Flood loads are another required aspect of structural design considerations for a new building. Floods can be simply described as water flowing where it is not normally expected. This threat exists in all areas and takes on many forms. Examples include overflow of a river bed or body of water resulting from too much rainfall, either over an extended period or from a brief intense downpour **(Figure 14.17)**. Other examples include breaches of dams or levees, earthquake-caused tsunamis, or water surge along coastal areas in conjunction with high winds, especially those associated with hurricanes **(Figure 14.18)**.

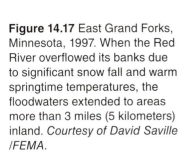

Figure 14.17 East Grand Forks, Minnesota, 1997. When the Red River overflowed its banks due to significant snow fall and warm springtime temperatures, the floodwaters extended to areas more than 3 miles (5 kilometers) inland. *Courtesy of David Saville /FEMA.*

Figure 14.18 New Orleans, 2005. Hurricane Katrina caused significant damage to many buildings. *Courtesy of District Chief Chris E. Mickal, NOFD Photo Unit.*

Damage resulting from floods occurs in several ways. Water can undermine foundations causing partial or total collapse. Or, in the case of storm surges in coastal areas, the house can be swept off its foundation and moved substantial distances from where it originally rested.

U.S. model building codes base requirements for flood loads on **Federal Emergency Management Agency (FEMA)** maps of flood hazard areas. Requirements for construction include more stringent specifications for buildings that are subject to high-velocity wave action that occurs in coastal areas prone to hurricanes. Provisions for buildings in these locations require simultaneous consideration of wind and flood loads on all structural components. Foundations and structures are required to resist flotation, collapse, and lateral movement.

Wide Area Incidents

Natural forces are the primary cause of incidents that affect a wide area. Regardless of the type of incident, these incidents often include wide spread implications for a large geographical region. Service disruptions may persist for days or weeks, and include one or more of the following energy and communication utilities:

- Clean water availability and distribution
- Natural gas distribution
- Electrical energy distribution
- Public communication services including landline, public radio, cellular service
- Emergency services communications
- Voice and data transmission services, including **Voice over Internet Protocol (VoIP)**

Federal Emergency Management Agency (FEMA) — Agency within the U.S. Department of Homeland Security (DHS) that is responsible for emergency preparedness, mitigation, and response activities for events including natural, technological, and attack-related emergencies.

Voice over Internet Protocol (VoIP) — Communication services that utilize an Internet connection to transmit telephone signals.

The fire department must work closely with the appropriate agencies when utilities are lost or damaged for reasons including:

- Damaged electric power systems may ignite combustible materials or energize conductive materials.
- Ruptured natural gas systems may leak into an enclosed area and create an ignition hazard.
- Ruptured water systems may flood low grade spaces and/or deplete water supplies.

Preincident plans for wide-area incidents should include criteria used to determine the proper response when utility, communication, and infrastructure resources are unavailable **(Figure 14.19)**. Fire departments will often receive calls because of the effects of damage to key infrastructure elements including:

Figure 14.19 Oso, Washington, 2014. A landslide killed 43 people, destroyed 49 homes, dammed a nearby river, and blocked State Route 530. *Courtesy of FEMA.*

- Destruction or disruption of multiple buildings and roads
- Multiple, discrete incidents requiring rescue of trapped occupants
- Impairment of building life safety systems
- Fires from accumulation/ignition of vapors from ruptured natural gas delivery systems
- Fires when utilities are restored, especially electrical services
- Arson fires in subsequent days when owners realize that insurance policies may not cover property damage
- Hazardous material or debris removal

Preincident plans can include established actions that will happen after the cause of an incident has ceased. Responses to wide-area incidents must be conducted carefully and with the proper precautions including:

- Carefully determining the placement of apparatus while considering the effects of structural collapse, unstable earth, and potential flooding
- Staging equipment in a safe place depending on the parameters of the incident in order to evaluate the condition and availability of resources
- In-person surveys of infrastructure after an incident to determine the availability of accessibility features including roads and bridges
- Postincident surveys to evaluate accessible amenities or determine the extent of the damage.
- Pre-evacuation of civilians who can be safely moved out of the danger area before the greatest damage is expected

Chapter Summary

There are numerous causes of building collapse other than as a result of fire. Although communities are not likely scenes for some nature-caused emergencies, firefighters and communities need to be prepared for events that may occur. Modern building codes have reduced the vulnerability of buildings to nature-caused collapse, but most jurisdictions have structures that were built before the requirements came about, or before they were strengthened.

Even where modern codes are in effect, mistakes can be made in the design plan review process or on the job site that result in a partial or total collapse. After a partial building collapse, the remaining structure is likely to be weakened. Therefore, the firefighter must exercise extreme care when performing search and rescue operations in these situations.

Review Questions

1. What are some of the human-related causes of building collapse?
2. What poor or careless construction methods may lead to building collapse?
3. What are some of the nature-related causes of building collapse?
4. What design accommodations can be made to prevent building collapse from nature-related causes?
5. What precautions should firefighters take when responding to a wide area incident?

Chapter Notes

1. Dale, Maryclaire, "Contractor charged with murder in Philadelphia building collapse," The Washington Times, November 25, 2013, http://www.washingtontimes.com/news/2013/nov/25/contractor-charged-murder-philadelphia-building-co/.
2. National Oceanic and Atmospheric Administration. http://www.noaa.gov/.

Appendices

Appendix A
Chapter and Page Correlation to FESHE Requirements

FESHE Course Outcomes	Chapter References	Page References
1. Describe building construction as it relates to firefighter safety, buildings codes, fire prevention, code inspection, firefighting strategy, and tactics.	1, 2, 4, 5, 6, 7, 8, 9, 10, 11, 12, 13, 14	9-38, 43-61, 93-132, 137-165, 169-177, 181-212, 217-235, 239-253, 275-290, 295-322, 327-358, 327-337, 341-357
2. Classify major types of building construction in accordance with a local/model building code.	1, 2, 7, 8, 9, 10	9-38, 43-61, 181-212, 217-235, 239-253, 275-290
3. Analyze the hazards and tactical considerations associated with the various types of building construction.	2, 7, 8, 9, 10	43-61, 181-212, 217-235, 239-253, 275-290
4. Explain the different loads and stresses that are placed on a building and their interrelationships.	2, 3, 6, 7, 8, 11, 14	43-61, 65-88, 169-177, 181-212, 217-235, 295-322, 341-357
5. Identify the function of each principle structural component in typical building design.	3, 6, 7, 8, 9, 10, 11, 12	65-88, 169-177, 181-212, 217-235, 239-253, 275-290, 295-322, 327-358
6. Differentiate between fire resistance, flame spread, and describe the testing procedures used to establish ratings for each.	2, 5	43-61, 137-165
7. Classify occupancy designations of the building code.	2, 12	43-61, 327-358
8. Identify the indicators of potential structural failure as they relate to firefighter safety.	1, 6, 7, 8, 9, 10, 11, 12, 13, 14	9-38, 169-177, 181-212, 217-235, 239-253, 275-290, 295-322, 327-358, 327-337, 341-357
9. Identify the role of GIS as it relates to building construction.	1	9-38

Appendix B
Metric Conversions

Metric Conversions

Throughout this manual, U.S. units of measure are converted to metric units for the convenience of our international readers. Be advised that we use the Canadian metric system. It is very similar to the Standard International system, but may have some variation.

We adhere to the following guidelines for metric conversions in this manual:

- Metric conversions are approximated unless the number is used in mathematical equations.
- Centimeters are not used because they are not part of the Canadian metric standard.
- Exact conversions are used when an exact number is necessary such as in construction measurements or hydraulic calculations.
- Set values such as hose diameter, ladder length, and nozzle size use their Canadian counterpart naming conventions and are not mathematically calculated. For example, 1½ inch hose is referred to as 38 mm hose.
- Add metric notes particular to your manual.

The following two tables provide detailed information on IFSTA's conversion conventions. The first table includes examples of our conversion factors for a number of measurements used in the fire service. The second shows examples of exact conversions beside the approximated measurements you will see in this manual.

U.S. to Canadian Measurement Conversion

Measurements	Customary (U.S.)	Metric (Canada)	Conversion Factor
Length/Distance	Inch (in) Foot (ft) [3 or less feet] Foot (ft) [3 or more feet] Mile (mi)	Millimeter (mm) Millimeter (mm) Meter (m) Kilometer (km)	1 in = 25 mm 1 ft = 300 mm 1 ft = 0.3 m 1 mi = 1.6 km
Area	Square Foot (ft^2) Square Mile (mi^2)	Square Meter (m^2) Square Kilometer (km^2)	1 ft^2 = 0.09 m^2 1 mi^2 = 2.6 km^2
Mass/Weight	Dry Ounce (oz) Pound (lb) Ton (T)	gram Kilogram (kg) Ton (T)	1 oz = 28 g 1 lb = 0.5 kg 1 T = 0.9 T
Volume	Cubic Foot (ft^3) Fluid Ounce (fl oz) Quart (qt) Gallon (gal)	Cubic Meter (m^3) Milliliter (mL) Liter (L) Liter (L)	1 ft^3 = 0.03 m^3 1 fl oz = 30 mL 1 qt = 1 L 1 gal = 4 L
Flow	Gallons per Minute (gpm) Cubic Foot per Minute (ft^3/min)	Liters per Minute (L/min) Cubic Meter per Minute (m^3/min)	1 gpm = 4 L/min 1 ft^3/min = 0.03 m^3/min
Flow per Area	Gallons per Minute per Square Foot (gpm/ft^2)	Liters per Square Meters Minute (L/(m^2.min))	1 gpm/ft^2 = 40 L/(m^2.min)
Pressure	Pounds per Square Inch (psi) Pounds per Square Foot (psf) Inches of Mercury (in Hg)	Kilopascal (kPa) Kilopascal (kPa) Kilopascal (kPa)	1 psi = 7 kPa 1 psf = .05 kPa 1 in Hg = 3.4 kPa
Speed/Velocity	Miles per Hour (mph) Feet per Second (ft/sec)	Kilometers per Hour (km/h) Meter per Second (m/s)	1 mph = 1.6 km/h 1 ft/sec = 0.3 m/s
Heat	British Thermal Unit (Btu)	Kilojoule (kJ)	1 Btu = 1 kJ
Heat Flow	British Thermal Unit per Minute (BTU/min)	watt (W)	1 Btu/min = 18 W
Density	Pound per Cubic Foot (lb/ft^3)	Kilogram per Cubic Meter (kg/m^3)	1 lb/ft^3 = 16 kg/m^3
Force	Pound-Force (lbf)	Newton (N)	1 lbf = 0.5 N
Torque	Pound-Force Foot (lbf ft)	Newton Meter (N.m)	1 lbf ft = 1.4 N.m
Dynamic Viscosity	Pound per Foot-Second (lb/ft.s)	Pascal Second (Pa.s)	1 lb/ft.s = 1.5 Pa.s
Surface Tension	Pound per Foot (lb/ft)	Newton per Meter (N/m)	1 lb/ft = 15 N/m

Conversion and Approximation Examples

Measurement	U.S. Unit	Conversion Factor	Exact S.I. Unit	Rounded S.I. Unit
Length/Distance	10 in	1 in = 25 mm	250 mm	250 mm
	25 in	1 in = 25 mm	625 mm	625 mm
	2 ft	1 in = 25 mm	600 mm	600 mm
	17 ft	1 ft = 0.3 m	5.1 m	5 m
	3 mi	1 mi = 1.6 km	4.8 km	5 km
	10 mi	1 mi = 1.6 km	16 km	16 km
Area	36 ft^2	1 ft^2 = 0.09 m^2	3.24 m^2	3 m^2
	300 ft^2	1 ft^2 = 0.09 m^2	27 m^2	30 m^2
	5 mi^2	1 mi^2 = 2.6 km^2	13 km^2	13 km^2
	14 mi^2	1 mi^2 = 2.6 km^2	36.4 km^2	35 km^2
Mass/Weight	16 oz	1 oz = 28 g	448 g	450 g
	20 oz	1 oz = 28 g	560 g	560 g
	3.75 lb	1 lb = 0.5 kg	1.875 kg	2 kg
	2,000 lb	1 lb = 0.5 kg	1 000 kg	1 000 kg
	1 T	1 T = 0.9 T	900 kg	900 kg
	2.5 T	1 T = 0.9 T	2.25 T	2 T
Volume	55 ft^3	1 ft^3 = 0.03 m^3	1.65 m^3	1.5 m^3
	2,000 ft^3	1 ft^3 = 0.03 m^3	60 m^3	60 m^3
	8 fl oz	1 fl oz = 30 mL	240 mL	240 mL
	20 fl oz	1 fl oz = 30 mL	600 mL	600 mL
	10 qt	1 qt = 1 L	10 L	10 L
	22 gal	1 gal = 4 L	88 L	90 L
	500 gal	1 gal = 4 L	2 000 L	2 000 L
Flow	100 gpm	1 gpm = 4 L/min	400 L/min	400 L/min
	500 gpm	1 gpm = 4 L/min	2 000 L/min	2 000 L/min
	16 ft^3/min	1 ft^3/min = 0.03 m^3/min	0.48 m^3/min	0.5 m^3/min
	200 ft^3/min	1 ft^3/min = 0.03 m^3/min	6 m^3/min	6 m^3/min
Flow per Area	50 gpm/ft^2	1 gpm/ft^2 = 40 L/(m^2.min)	2 000 L/(m^2.min)	2 000 L/(m^2.min)
	326 gpm/ft^2	1 gpm/ft^2 = 40 L/(m^2.min)	13 040 L/(m^2.min)	13 000L/(m^2.min)
Pressure	100 psi	1 psi = 7 kPa	700 kPa	700 kPa
	175 psi	1 psi = 7 kPa	1225 kPa	1 200 kPa
	526 psf	1 psf = 0.05 kPa	26.3 kPa	25 kPa
	12,000 psf	1 psf = 0.05 kPa	600 kPa	600 kPa
	5 psi in Hg	1 psi = 3.4 kPa	17 kPa	17 kPa
	20 psi in Hg	1 psi = 3.4 kPa	68 kPa	70 kPa
Speed/Velocity	20 mph	1 mph = 1.6 km/h	32 km/h	30 km/h
	35 mph	1 mph = 1.6 km/h	56 km/h	55 km/h
	10 ft/sec	1 ft/sec = 0.3 m/s	3 m/s	3 m/s
	50 ft/sec	1 ft/sec = 0.3 m/s	15 m/s	15 m/s
Heat	1200 Btu	1 Btu = 1 kJ	1 200 kJ	1 200 kJ
Heat Flow	5 BTU/min	1 Btu/min = 18 W	90 W	90 W
	400 BTU/min	1 Btu/min = 18 W	7 200 W	7 200 W
Density	5 lb/ft^3	1 lb/ft^3 = 16 kg/m^3	80 kg/m^3	80 kg/m^3
	48 lb/ft^3	1 lb/ft^3 = 16 kg/m^3	768 kg/m^3	770 kg/m^3
Force	10 lbf	1 lbf = 0.5 N	5 N	5 N
	1,500 lbf	1 lbf = 0.5 N	750 N	750 N
Torque	100	1 lbf ft = 1.4 N.m	140 N.m	140 N.m
	500	1 lbf ft = 1.4 N.m	700 N.m	700 N.m
Dynamic Viscosity	20 lb/ft.s	1 lb/ft.s = 1.5 Pa.s	30 Pa.s	30 Pa.s
	35 lb/ft.s	1 lb/ft.s = 1.5 Pa.s	52.5 Pa.s	50 Pa.s
Surface Tension	6.5 lb/ft	1 lb/ft = 15 N/m	97.5 N/m	100 N/m
	10 lb/ft	1 lb/ft = 15 N/m	150 N/m	150 N/m

Glossary

Glossary

A

Admixture — Ingredients or chemicals added to concrete mix to produce concrete with specific characteristics.

Aesthetics — Branch of philosophy dealing with the nature of beauty, art, and taste.

Aftershock - A smaller earthquake that occurs in the same area and similar time frame as a larger earthquake.

Aggregate — Particulate material used in construction to provide a stable bedding or reinforce a composition material. Used as an extender in concrete. Can be graded into coarse and fine grain sizes and material types including sand, gravel, stone, etc.

Air-Inflated Structure — Membrane structure that uses air pressure to develop its initial shape, but may not use air pressure throughout the entire, high profile, occupancy: enclosed columns or tubes may be inflated to hold the shape of the structure. This type of structure is often intended to be temporary or movable.

Air-Supported Structure — Membrane structure that is fully or partially held up by interior air pressure. This type of occupancy often has a wider footprint than air-inflated structures, and may be secured in place with rigid lower walls and cables. This type of structure may be maintained in place over a long duration.

Alloy — Substance or mixture composed of two or more metals (or a metal and nonmetallic elements) fused together and dissolved into each other to enhance the properties or usefulness of the base metal.

Alternating Current (AC) Circuit — Electrical circuit in which the current can move through the circuit in both directions and the flow can be constantly reversing.

American Society for Testing and Materials (ASTM) — Voluntary standards-setting organization that sets guidelines on characteristics and performance of materials, products, systems and services; for example, the quality of concrete or the flammability of interior finishes.

Americans with Disabilities Act (ADA) of 1990 - Public Law 101-336 — Federal statute intended to remove barriers, physical and otherwise, that limit access by individuals with disabilities.

Arc — High-temperature luminous electric discharge across a gap or through a medium such as charred insulation.

Arch — Curved structural member in which the interior stresses are primarily compressive. Arches develop inclined reactions at their supports.

Area of Refuge — (1) Space protected from fire in the normal means of egress either by an approved sprinkler system, separation from other spaces within the same building by smokeproof walls, or location in an adjacent building. (2) Area where persons who are unable to use stairs can temporarily wait for instructions or assistance during an emergency building evacuation.

ASTM E-84 — Standard test used to measure the surface burning characteristics of various materials. *Also known as* Steiner Tunnel Test *or* Tunnel Test.

Atrium — (1) Upper chamber of the left or right side of the heart. (2) Open area in the center of a building, extending through two or more stories, similar to a courtyard but usually covered by a skylight, to allow natural light and ventilation to interior rooms.

Authority Having Jurisdiction (AHJ) — An organization, office, or individual responsible for enforcing the requirements of a code or standard, or approving equipment, materials, an installation, or a procedure.

Axial Load — Load applied to the center of the cross-section of a member and perpendicular to that cross-section. It can be either tensile or compressive, and creates uniform stresses across the cross-section of the material.

B

Balloon Frame Construction — Type of structural framing used in some single-story and multistory wood frame buildings; studs are continuous from the foundation to the roof, and there may be no fire stops between the studs.

Bar Joist — Open web truss constructed entirely of steel, with steel bars used as the web members.

Base Isolation — A system of structural elements that create a joint between a building and its base to minimize seismic force effects on the main structure. The type of system may be customized to the type of seismic forces expected in an area.

Beam — Structural component loaded perpendicular to its length. Primarily resists bending stress characterized by compression in the top portion and tension in the bottom portion.

Bearing Wall Structures — Common type of structure that uses the walls of a building to support spanning elements such as beams, trusses, and pre-cast concrete slabs.

Bending Moment — A reaction within a structural component that opposes a vertical load. When the bending moment is exceeded, the component will fail. Bending stress can be calculated from the bending moment.

Bending Stress — Compressive and tensile stresses in a beam. When the stresses are not held in equilibrium, the beam will bend and ultimately fail. Bending stresses are calculated from the Bending Moment.

Blind Hoistway — Used for express elevators that serve only upper floors of tall buildings. There are no entrances to the shaft on floors between the main entrance and the lowest floor served.

Board of Appeals — Group of people, usually five to seven, with experience in fire prevention, building construction, and/or code enforcement, who are legally constituted to arbitrate differences of opinion between fire inspectors and building officials, property owners, occupants or builders.

Bowstring Truss — Lightweight truss design noted by the bow shape, or curve, of the top chord.

British Thermal Unit (Btu) — Amount of heat energy required to raise the temperature of 1lb (0.5 kg) of water 1°F (.55 °C). 1 Btu = 1.055 kilo joules (kJ).

Building Code — A set of rules developed by a standards organization and adopted as law by a governmental body to regulate the minimum requirements for construction, renovation, and maintenance of buildings.

Building Permit — Authorization issued from the appropriate authority having jurisdiction (AHJ) before any new construction, addition, renovation, alteration, or demolition of buildings or structures occurs.

Butt Joint — Connection between two parts made by simply securing ends surfaces together without additional shaping at the ends; a simple but weak joint.

Buttress — Structure projecting from a wall, designed to receive lateral pressure action at a particular point.

C

Cable Membrane Structure — Freestanding structure that uses suspension cables for support. *Also known as* Cable Covered Structure.

Cables — Flexible structural members designed to withstand tension stresses. Commonly used to support roofs, brace tents, and restrain pneumatic structures.

Caisson — Protective sleeve used to keep water out of an excavation for a pier.

Calcination — Process of driving free and chemically bound water out of gypsum; also describes chemical and physical changes to the gypsum component itself.

Calcined — Process that heats a substance to a high temperature but below the melting or fusing point, causing loss of moisture, reduction or oxidation, and decomposition of carbonates and other compounds.

Cantilever — Projecting beam or slab supported at one end.

Capital — Broad top surface of a column or pilaster, designed to spread the load held by a column.

Cast-in-Place Concrete — Common type of concrete construction. Refers to concrete that is poured into forms as a liquid and assumes the shape of the form in the position and location it will be used.

Cement — Any adhesive material or variety of materials which can be made into a paste with adhesive and cohesive properties to bond inert aggregate materials into a solid mass by chemical hardening. For example, portland cement is combined with sand and/or other aggregates and water to produce mortar or concrete.

Chord — Top or bottom longitudinal member of a truss; main members of trusses, as distinguished from diagonals.

Cladding — Exterior finish or skin.

Clean Energy — Energy sources that meet the needs of current consumers without compromising future resources. *Also known as* Sustainable Energy.

Cold Rolled Steel (CRS) — Commercial and drawing steels; shaped after cooling below its recrystallization temperature by being passed through a series of rollers to reduce the thickness incrementally.

Collar Tie — Horizontal roof framing member in the top third of the framing system; braces the roof framing against the uplift of wind.

Column — Vertical member designed to support an axial load and compressive stresses.

Column Footing — Square pad of concrete that supports a column. Footings of decorative columns are often above the bearing surface.

Common Truss — Truss structure with the chords and diagonal members arranged in parallel planes. *Also known as* Monoplane Truss.

Compartment — Any enclosed space without internal fire barriers.

Compartmentation — Series of barriers designed to keep flames, smoke, and heat from spreading between spaces.

Compensated System — Stairwell pressurization system that can modulate the pressure in the stairwell in relation to the interior of the building, or vent excess pressure.

Composite Panels — Produced with parallel external face veneers bonded to a core of reconstituted fibers. *Also known as* Sandwich Panel.

Compression — Vertical and/or horizontal forces that push the mass of a material together; for example, the force exerted on the top chord of a truss.

Concentrated Load — Load that is applied at one point or over a small area.

Concrete — Strong, hard building material produced from a mixture of portland cement and an aggregate filler/binder to which water is added to form a slurry that sets into a rigid building material.

Concrete Block — Large rectangular brick used in construction; the most common type is the hollow concrete block. *Also known as* Concrete Masonry Units (CMU).

Concrete Block Brick Faced (CBBF) — Wall construction system that includes one wythe of concrete blocks with a brick wythe attached to the outside.

Conflagration — Large, uncontrollable fire covering a considerable area and crossing fire barriers such as streets and waterways; usually involves buildings in more than one block and causes a substantial fire loss. Forest fires can also be considered conflagrations.

Controlled Collapse Demolition — Deliberate demolition process that uses large machinery and equipment to reduce an entire structure to ground level.

Convection — Transfer of heat by the movement of heated fluids or gases, usually in an upward direction.

Convenience Stair — Stair that usually connects two floors in a multistory building.

Conventionally Framed Roofs — Roofing system constructed on site; often uses dimensional lumber and nails/screws but can also use preengineered components.

Cooling Tower — Rooftop or independent unit that ejects waste heat into the atmosphere to lower the temperature in a system. Commonly used in HVAC systems.

Corbel — Bracket or ledge made of stone, wood, brick, or other building material projecting from the face of a wall or column used to support a beam, cornice, or arch.

Corbelling — Use of a corbel to provide additional support for an arch.

Cornice — Concealed space near the eave of a building; usually overhanging the area adjacent to exterior walls.

Corrugated — Formed into ridges or grooves; serrated.

Course — Horizontal layer of individual masonry units.

Criterion-Referenced Testing (CRT) — Measurement of one component's tested performance against a set standard or criteria, not against similar components or assemblies. *Similar to* Criterion-Referenced Assessment.

Cross-Section — Theoretical slice of a 3-dimensional structural component to enable area and stress calculations.

Cupola — A type of rooftop projection historically used for ventilation and lighting, and modernly added for aesthetics.

Curtain Wall — Nonload-bearing exterior wall attached to the outside of a building with a rigid steel frame. Usually the front exterior wall of a building intended to provide a certain appearance.

D

Damping Mechanism — Structural element designed to control vibration from resonance.

Dead Load — Weight of the structure, structural members, building components, and any other features permanently attached to the building that are constant and immobile.

Design Principles — Guidelines applied to basic units of a project that cause the items to work together as a unified, completely finished item that serves a purpose within established parameters. Units can include the materials, concepts, and setting.

Design-Build — The use of a single organization to both design and build a facility to minimize risks for the project owner. May also refer to a firm specializing in design-build.

Dewatering — Process of removing water from a vessel or building.

Dielectric — Material that is a poor conductor of electricity, usually applied to tools that are used to handle energized electrical wires or equipment.

Dimensional Lumber — Lumber with standard, nominal measurements for use in building construction. Dimensional lumber is also available in rough, green components with actual dimensions that match the nominal dimensions.

Direct Current (DC) Circuit — Electrical circuit in which the current moves through the circuit in only one direction.

Door Closer — Mechanical device that closes a door. *Also known as* Self-Closing Door.

Door Hold-Open Device — Mechanical device that holds a door open and releases it upon a signal. Mechanism may be a fusible link that releases under fire conditions, or an electromagnet connected to a smoke detector. *Also known as* Door Holder.

Draft Curtains — Noncombustible barriers or dividers hung from the ceiling in large open areas that are designed to minimize the mushrooming effect of heat and smoke and impede the flow of heat. *Also known as* Curtain Boards *and* Draft Stops.

Drop Panel — Type of concrete floor construction in which the portion of the floor above each column is dropped below the bottom level of the rest of the slab, increasing the floor thickness at the column.

Ductility — A measure of a metal's ability to be drawn, hammered thin, or rolled into shapes without breaking. The high ductility of steel makes it very versatile for use in constructing buildings.

Dumbwaiter — Small freight elevators that carry items, not people, and generally have a small weight and size capacity.

Dynamic Load — Loads that involve motion, including impact from wind, falling objects, and vibration. *Also known as* Shock Loading.

E

Earthquake — A sudden release of energy in the Earth's crust that creates seismic forces that shake and sometimes disrupt the ground. Earthquakes are associated with volcanic activity, landslides, and tsunamis.

Eccentric Load — Load perpendicular to the cross-section of the structural member, but which does not pass through the center of the cross-section. An eccentric load creates stresses that vary across the cross-section and may be both tensile and compressive.

Elastomer — Generic term for rubber-like materials including natural rubber, butyl rubber, neoprene, and silicone rubber used in facepiece seals, low-pressure hoses, and similar SCBA components.

Elevator — Mechanical system that travels vertically and is used to transport people and items in a multistory building.

Elevator Pit — Depression at the base of an elevator hoistway that contains equipment and maintenance access.

Engineered Wood — A material manufactured by bonding pieces of wood with glue or resin to form finished shapes.

Equilibrium — Condition of balance that exists when a structural system is capable of supporting the applied load.

Escalator — Belt-driven moving stairs that move in one direction at a fixed rate of speed.

Exhaust System — Ventilation system designed to remove stale air, smoke, vapors, or other airborne contaminants from an area.

Expanded Polystyrene (EPS) — Closed-cell foam used for a growing number of purposes including building insulation. Properties include rigidity, low weight, and formability.

Expansion Joint — Flexible joint in concrete used to prevent cracking or breaking because of expansion and contraction due to temperature changes.

Exposure — Structure surfaces or separate parts of the fireground to which a fire or products of combustion could spread.

Exterior Insulation and Finish Systems (EIFS) — Exterior cladding or covering systems composed of an adhesively or mechanically fastened foam insulation board, reinforcing mesh, a base coat, and an outer finish coat. *Also known as* Synthetic Stucco.

Exterior Stairs — Stairs separated from the interior of a building by walls.

F

Facade — Fascia added to some buildings with flat roofs to create the appearance of a mansard roof. *Also known as* False Roof *or* Fascia.

Factor of Safety — Ratio of the failure point of a material to the maximum design stress; indicates the strength of a structure beyond the expected or actual loads.

Failure Point — Point at which material ceases to perform satisfactorily; depending on the application, this can involve breaking, permanent deformation, excessive deflection, or vibration.

Fascia — (1) Flat horizontal or vertical board located at the outer face of a cornice. (2) Broad flat surface over a storefront or below a cornice.

Fast-Track Construction — Strategy to reduce the overall time for completion of a project by merging the design and construction phases. Often used in conjunction with design-build.

Fault — Area of discontinuity in the Earth's crust associated with movement by tectonic plates.

Federal Emergency Management Agency (FEMA) — Agency within the U.S. Department of Homeland Security (DHS) that is responsible for emergency preparedness, mitigation, and response activities for events including natural, technological, and attack-related emergencies.

Finger Joint — Connection between two parts made by cutting complementary mating parts, and then securing the joint with glue.

Fire Area — One of a set of sections in a building separated from each other by fire-resistant partitions.

Fire Cut — Angled cut made at the end of a wood joist or wood beam that rests in a masonry wall to allow the beam to fall away freely from the wall in case of failure of the beam. This helps prevent the beam from acting as a lever to push against the masonry.

Fire Damper — Device that automatically restricts the flow of air through all or part of an air-handling system; usually activated by the building's fire alarm signaling system.

Fire Department Connection (FDC) — Point at which the fire department can connect into a sprinkler or standpipe system to boost the water pressure and flow in the system. This connection consists of a clappered siamese with two or more 2½-inch (65 mm) intakes or one large-diameter (4-inch [100 mm] or larger) intake. *Also known as* Fire Department Sprinkler Connection.

Fire Door — Specially constructed, tested, and approved fire-rated assembly designed and installed to prevent fire spread by automatically sealing an opening in a fire wall to block the spread of fire.

Fire Escape — Means of escaping from a building in case of fire; usually an interior or exterior stairway or slide, independently supported and made of fire-resistive material.

Fire Flow — The amount of water required to extinguish a fire in a timely manner.

Fire Load — Maximum amount of heat that can be released if all fuel in a given area is consumed; expressed in pounds per square foot and obtained by dividing the amount of fuel present by the floor area. Used as a measure of the potential heat release of a fire within a compartment. *Similar to* Fuel Load *and* Heat of Combustion.

Fire Partition — Fire barrier that extends from one floor to the bottom of the floor above or to the underside of a fire-rated ceiling assembly; provides a lower level of protection than a fire wall. An example is a one-hour rated corridor wall.

Fire Resistance — The ability of a structural assembly or material to maintain its load-bearing ability under fire conditions.

Fire Resistance Rating — Rating assigned to a material or assembly after standardized testing by an independent testing organization; identifies the amount of time a material or assembly will resist a typical fire, as measured on a standard time-temperature curve.

Fire Retardant — Any substance, except plain water, that when applied to another material or substance will reduce the flammability of fuels or slow their rate of combustion by chemical or physical action.

Fire Spread — The movement of fire from one material (source) to another (exposure). May occur within a compartment or across a break.

Fire Stop — Solid materials, such as wood blocks, used to prevent or limit the vertical and horizontal spread of fire and the products of combustion; installed in hollow walls or floors, above false ceilings, in penetrations for plumbing or electrical installations, in penetrations of a fire-rated assembly, or in cocklofts and crawl spaces.

Fire Wall — Fire rated wall with a specified degree of fire resistance, built of fire-resistive materials and usually extending from the foundation up to and through the roof of a building that is designed to limit the spread of a fire within a structure or between adjacent structures.

Firefighter's Smoke Control Station (FSCS) — Interface between the smoke management system and the fire response forces.

Flame Spread — Movement of a flame away from the ignition source.

Flame Spread Rating — (1) Numerical rating assigned to a material based on the speed and extent to which flame travels over its surface. (2) Measurement of the propagation of flame on the surface of materials or their assemblies as determined by recognized standard tests.

Flange — Single or paired external ridges or rims on a beam that do most of the work of supporting a load.

Flat Plate — Plain floor slab about 8 inches (200 mm) thick that rests on columns spaced up to 22 feet (6.5 m) apart and depends on diagonal and orthogonal patterns of reinforcing bars for structural support because the slab lacks beams; simplest and most economical floor system.

Flat-Slab Concrete Frame — Construction technique using concrete slabs supported by concrete columns.

Floating Foundation — Foundation for which the volume of earth excavated will approximately equal the weight of the building supported. Thus, the total weight supported by the soil beneath the foundation remains about the same, and settlement is minimized because of the weight of the building.

Footing — Part of the building in contact with the bearing soil. Footings are thicker (deeper) than the column or foundation wall and are often embedded below the surface of the soil to rest on bedrock.

Force — 1) Simple measure of weight, usually expressed in pounds (kilograms). 2) In physics: Any interaction that may change the motion of an object.

Forced–Air System — A building heating and cooling system that uses air as the heat transfer medium.

Foundation Wall — Vertical element of a foundation; rests on the foundation footers. May be full-story height as in a basement, or partial height. Materials often include poured concrete, or mortar elements such as block, brick, or stone.

Frame — Internal system of structural supports within a building.

Frame Membrane Structure — Structure supported primarily by a frame or skeleton rather than by load-bearing walls. *Also known as* Frame Covered Structure.

Freestanding Walls — Self-supporting fire walls independent of the structure's frame. Must resist a lateral load of 5 pounds per square foot (.25 kPa per square meter).

Frost Line — Common depth at which ground water in soil will freeze. Influential variables include climate, soil properties, and nearby heat sources.

Fuel Load — Total quantity of fuel (combustible material) in a compartment; can include structural elements, interior finish, and trim. Expressed in heat units of the equivalent weight in wood. *Also known as* Fuel Loading.

Fusible Link — Connecting link device that fuses or melts when exposed to fire temperatures; used to activate individual elements in active and passive fire suppression systems. Benefits include: inexpensive, rugged, easy to maintain. Disadvantages include: slower to activate than automated systems.

G

Generator — Portable device for generating auxiliary electrical power; generators are powered by gasoline or diesel engines and typically have 110- and/or 220-volt capacity outlets.

Gentrification — Process of restoring rundown or deteriorated properties by more affluent people, often displacing poorer residents.

Geographic Information Systems (GIS) — Computer software application that relates physical features on the earth to a database to be used for mapping and analysis. The system captures, stores, analyzes, manages, and presents data that refers to or is linked to a location.

Glazing — Glass or thermoplastic panel in a wall or other barrier that allows light to pass through.

Glue-Laminated Beam — (1) Wooden structural member composed of many relatively short pieces of lumber glued and laminated together under pressure to form a long, extremely strong beam. (2) Term used to describe wood members produced by joining small, flat strips of wood together with glue. *Also known as* Glued-Laminated Beam *or* Glulam Beam.

Grain — Direction of growth of a tree. Loads aligned perpendicular to the grain are more sturdily supported; lumber will split more easily when cut parallel to the grain.

Gravity (G) — Force acting to draw an object toward the earth's center; force is equal to the object's weight.

Green Design — Incorporation of environmental principles including energy efficiency and environmentally friendly building materials into design and construction.

Green Roof — Roof of a building that is partially or completely covered with vegetation and a growing medium, planted over waterproof roofing elements. Term can also indicate the presence of green design technology including photovoltaic systems and reflective surfaces.

Grillage Footing — Footing consisting of layers of beams placed at right angles to each other and usually encased in concrete.

Grout — A mixture of cement, aggregate, and water that hardens over time; used to embed reinforcement materials in masonry walls. Similar to mortar.

Gusset Plates — Metal or wooden plates used to connect and strengthen the joints of two or more separate components (such as metal or wooden truss components or roof or floor components) into a load-bearing unit.

H

Hardware — General term for small pieces of equipment made of metal, including ancillary equipment affixed to another medium to aid the use of the primary tool. Fire door hardware includes: door knobs, hinges, and door closure devices.

Heat of Combustion — Total amount of thermal energy (heat) that could be generated by the combustion (oxidation) reaction if a fuel were completely burned. The heat of combustion is measured in British Thermal Units (Btu) per pound, kilojoules per gram, or Megajoules per kilogram.

Heat of Hydration — During the hardening of concrete, heat is given off by the chemical process.

Heat Release Rate (HRR) — Total amount of heat released per unit time. The heat release rate is typically measured in kilowatts (kW) or Megawatts(MW) of output.

Heat Transfer — Flow of heat from a hot substance to a cold substance; may be accomplished by convection, conduction, or radiation.

Heating, Ventilating, and Air Conditioning (HVAC) System — Mechanical system used to provide environmental control within a structure, and the equipment necessary to make it function; usually a single, integrated unit with a complex system of ducts throughout the building. *Also known as* Air-Handling System.

Heaving — Upward deformation of a building's structural elements

High-Rise Building — Building that requires fire fighting on levels above the reach of the department's equipment. *Also known as* High-Rise.

Hoistway — The vertical shaft in which the elevator car travels; includes the elevator pit.

Horizontal Motion — Side-to-side, swaying motion.

Hot Work — Any operation that requires the use of tools or machines that may produce a source of ignition.

Hurricane Glazing — Protective treatment for exterior windows designed to withstand hurricane conditions including high wind and impact.

Hydronic System — A building heating and cooling system that uses water as the heat-transfer medium.

Hygroscopic — Ability of a substance to absorb moisture from the air.

I

Ignition Source — Mechanism or initial energy source employed to initiate combustion, such as a spark that provides a means for the initiation of self-sustained combustion.

I-Joist — Engineered wood joists with an "I" shaped cross section. Commonly used in modern roof and floor construction.

Institutional Sprinklers — Low profile sprinkler system and pendant used with concealed piping in correctional facilities and institutions where tampering of the system must be discouraged or prevented.

Insulated Concrete Form (ICF) Construction — Construction technique that uses hollow foam blocks with predetermined sizes and shapes. The blocks lock together and are filled with concrete to form structural supports.

International Building Code® (IBC®) — Code that is dedicated to providing safety regulations for life safety, structural, and fire protection issues that occur throughout the life of a building.

International Code Council (ICC) — Organization that develops the *International Building Code® (IBC®)* and the *International Fire Code® (IFC®)*, for city and state adoption. Was formed by the merger of the Building Officials and Code Administrators (BOCA) International, Inc., the International Conference of Building Officials (ICBO), and the Southern Building Code Congress International (SBCCI). See Building Officials and Code Administrators (BOCA), *International Building Code®(IBC®)*, International Conference of Building Officials (ICBO), *International Fire Code® (IFC®)*, and Southern Building Code Congress International (SBCCI).

Intumescent Coating — Coating or paintlike product that expands when exposed to the heat of a fire; creates an insulating barrier that protects the material underneath.

Inverted Truss — Truss support system that is constructed with a deep triangular portion projecting down instead of up, and the portions of a standard truss are under compression instead of tension.

J

Joists — Horizontal structural members used to support a ceiling or floor. Drywall materials are nailed or screwed to the ceiling joists, and the subfloor is nailed or screwed to the floor joists.

K

Kinetic Energy — Energy possessed by a moving object because of its motion.

L

Lamella Arch — Special type of arch constructed of short pieces of wood called lamellas.

Laminated Wood — Material made of wood strips and resin, shaped, and bonded with heat and/or pressure.

Landing — Horizontal platform where a flight of stairs begins or ends.

Lateral Displacement — Sideways deformation of a building's structural elements.

Lateral Load — Load that exerts a horizontal force against a structure. Calculated as a live load; includes seismic activity and soil pressure against vertical restraints such as retaining walls and foundations.

Ledger Board — Horizontal framework member, especially one attached to a beam side that supports the joists. *Also known as* Ribbon Board.

Lintel — Support for masonry over an opening; usually made of steel angles or other rolled shapes, singularly or in combination.

Liquified Petroleum Gas (LPG) — Any of several petroleum products, such as propane or butane, stored under pressure as a liquid.

Listed — Refers to a device or material that has been tested by any of several testing laboratories (including the Underwriters' Laboratories Factory Mutual System) and certified as having met minimum criteria.

Live Load — (1) Items within a building that are movable but are not included as a permanent part of the structure. (2) Force placed upon a structure by the addition of people, objects, or weather.

Load — Any effect that a structure must be designed to resist, including the forces of gravity, wind, earthquakes, or soil pressure.

Load-Bearing Wall — Wall that supports itself, the weight of the roof, and/or other internal structural framing components, such as the floor beams and trusses above it; used for structural support. *Also known as* Bearing Wall.

Louvers — A series of horizontal slats that are angled to permit easy ventilation in one direction of flow and restricted ventilation in the opposite direction. Louvers are commonly used in applications where the restrictive side blocks sunshine, rain, or products of combustion.

Lumber — Lengths of wood prepared for use in construction; items are graded for strength and appearance.

M

Machine Room-Less (MRL) — Elevator hoistway that includes all components, including motors, mounted within the hoistway itself to eliminate the need for a machine room at the top of the hoistway. The elevator controls may be located remotely from the elevator system.

Manufactured Components — Structural elements constructed in a factory and shipped to the construction site.

Masonry — Bricks, blocks, stones, and unreinforced and reinforced concrete products.

Mastics — Heat resistant construction adhesive that bonds with most materials; can be used as a fire retardant coating.

Mat Slab Foundation — Thick slab beneath the entire area of a building; thicker and more reinforced than a simple slab-on-grade foundation.

Means of Egress — Continuous and unobstructed path of exit travel from any point in a building or structure to a public way; consists of three separate and distinct parts: exit access, exit, and exit discharge. (Source: NFPA 101, *Life Safety Code®*).

Membrane Ceiling — Usually refers to a suspended, insulating ceiling tile system.

Membrane Structure — (1) Structure with an enclosing surface of a thin stretched flexible material. (2) Weather-resistant, flexible or semiflexible covering consisting of layers of materials over a supporting framework.

Metal-Clad Door — Wood core door protected with galvanized sheet metal steel or other heavy metal exterior. *Also known as* Kalamein Door.

Mortar — Cement-like material that hardens over time. Used to bond individual masonry units together into a solid mass and transmit compressive forces between masonry units.

Multiple-Injection System — Stairwell pressurization system that uses an air supply shaft that discharges supply air at a uniform rate along several points within the stairwell.

Mushrooming — Tendency of heat, smoke, and other products of combustion to rise until they encounter a horizontal obstruction; at this point they will spread laterally until they encounter vertical obstructions and begin to bank downward.

N

Nailability — Property of a material that allows it to accept a fastener, such as a nail. Nailable materials include wood, gypsum, and some thin metals.

Negative Pressure — Air pressure less than that of the surrounding atmosphere; a partial vacuum.

NFPA 265 — Large scale test used to evaluate the performance of textile wall coverings under fire conditions. Older test, succeeded by NFPA 286. *Similar to* ASTM E-84.

NFPA 286 — Large scale test used to evaluate the performance of textile wall coverings under fire conditions. Designed to accommodate materials that may not remain in place during ASTM E-84 testing. Also includes the capacity of attaching materials to the ceiling. Newer test, preceded by NFPA 265. *Similar to* ASTM E-84.

Nominal Dimension of Lumber — Actual dimensions of processed lumber do not match the nominal dimensions, within defined parameters. Historically, the two sets of dimensions were identical.

Noncombustible — Incapable of supporting combustion under normal circumstances.

Nonload-Bearing Wall — Wall, usually interior, that supports only its own weight. These walls can be breached or removed without compromising the structural integrity of the building. *Also known as* Nonbearing Wall.

Nonveneered Panel — Lightweight wood construction panel manufactured from wood chips, strands, wafers, or sawdust and a bonding agent such as glue or resin. Used as sheathing, reinforcement of structural elements, and sub-flooring. Includes OSB, particleboard, waferboard.

O

Occupancy — Building code classification based on the use to which owners or tenants put buildings or portions of buildings. Regulated by the various building and fire codes. *Also known as* Occupancy Classification.

Oriented Strand Board (OSB) — Wooden structural panel formed by gluing and compressing wood strands together under pressure. This material has largely replaced plywood and planking in applications including roof decks, walls, and subfloors.

Overhead Door — Door that opens and closes above a large opening, such as in a warehouse or garage, and is usually of the rolling, hinged-panel, or slab type. *Also known as* Rolling (Overhead) Door.

Overpressure — Air pressure above normal or atmospheric pressure.

P

Parapet Wall — Portion of the exterior walls of a building that extends above the roof. A low wall at the edge of a roof.

Particleboard — Wooden structural panel formed from wood particles and synthetic resins. *Also known as* Flakeboard, Chipboard, *or* Shavings board.

Passive Smoke Control — Smoke control strategies that incorporate fixed components that provide protection against the spread of smoke and fire. Passive smoke control components include fire doors, fire walls, fire stopping of barrier penetrations, and stair and elevator vestibules.

Phase I Operation — Emergency operating mode for elevators. Recalls the car to the terminal floor lobby or another floor as specified, and opens the doors.

Phase II Operation — Emergency operating mode for elevators. Allows emergency use of the elevator with certain safeguards and special functions.

Photovoltaic (PV) System — An arrangement of components that convey electrical power to an energy system by converting solar energy into direct current (DC) electricity.

Piecemeal Demolition — Demolition process that uses hand tools and machines to gradually decrease the height of the structure.

Pier — Deep foundation type that uses beams mounted on concrete wedges/blocks to support loads. *Similar to* Caissons *and* Belled Piers.

Pilaster — Rectangular masonry pillar that extends from the face of a wall to provide additional support for the wall. Decorative pilasters may not provide any support.

Piles — Deep foundation type that uses beams used to support loads. Develop load-carrying ability either through friction with the surrounding soil or by being driven into contact with rock or a load-bearing soil layer.

Pipe Chase — Concealed vertical channel in which pipes and other utility conduits are housed. Pipe chases that are not properly protected can be major contributors to the vertical spread of smoke and fire in a building. *Also known as* Chase.

Platform Frame Construction — (1) Type of framing in which each floor is built as a separate platform, and the studs are not continuous beyond each floor. *Also known as* Western Frame Construction. (2) A construction method in which a floor assembly creates an individual platform that rest on the foundation. Wall assemblies the height of one story are placed on this platform and a second platform rests on top of the wall unit. Each platform creates fire stops at each floor level restricting the spread of fire within the wall cavity.

Plywood — Wood sheet product made from several thin veneer layers that are sliced from logs and glued together.

Polychlorinated Biphenyl (PCB) — Toxic compound found in some older oil-filled electric transformers.

Polyurethane — A polymer formed by reacting an isocyanate with a polyol; used in many applications including floating insulating foams and floating ropes.

Polyvinyl Chloride (PVC) — Synthetic chemical used in the manufacture of plastics and single-ply membrane roofs.

Portland Cement — Most commonly used cement, consisting chiefly of calcium and aluminum silicate. It is mixed with water to form mortar, a paste that hardens, and is therefore known as a hydraulic cement.

Post and Beam Construction — Construction style using vertical elements to support horizontal elements. Associated with heavy beams and columns; historically constructed of wood.

Posttensioned Reinforcement (Concrete) — Concrete reinforcement method. Reinforcing steel strands placed in protective sleeves in the concrete are tensioned after the concrete has hardened.

Precast Concrete — Method of building construction where the concrete building member is poured and set according to specification in a controlled environment and is then shipped to the construction site for use.

Preincident Planning — Act of preparing to manage an incident at a particular location or a particular type of incident before an incident occurs. *Also known as* Prefire Inspection, Prefire Planning, Preincident Inspection, Preincident Survey, *or* Preplanning.

Preincident Survey — Assessment of a facility or location made before an emergency occurs, in order to prepare for an appropriate emergency response. *Also known as* Preplan.

Pressure-Reducing Valve — Valve installed at standpipe connection that is designed to reduce the amount of water pressure at that discharge to a specific pressure, usually 100 psi (700 kPa).

Prestressing — Stress introduced to the concrete before the load is applied; accomplished by applying tension to reinforcing bars before the concrete is poured.

Pretensioned Reinforcement (Concrete) — Concrete reinforcement method. Steel strands are stretched, producing a tensile force in the steel. Concrete is then placed around the steel strands and allowed to harden.

Products of Combustion — Materials produced and released during burning.

Purlin — Horizontal member between trusses that support the roof.

Pyrolysis — The chemical decomposition of a solid material by heating. Pyrolysis precedes combustion of a solid fuel.

R

Rafter — Inclined beam that supports a roof, runs parallel to the slope of the roof, and to which the roof decking is attached.

Rafter Tie — Horizontal roof framing member at the bottom of the roof framing system; helps keep walls from spreading due to the weight of the roof.

Rated Assembly — Assemblies of building components such as doors, walls, roofs, and other structural features that may be, because of the occupancy, required by code to have a minimum fire-resistance rating from an independent testing agency. *Also known as* Labeled Assembly *and* Fire-Rated.

Rated Fire Door Assembly — Door, frame, and hardware assembly that has a fire-resistive rating from an independent testing agency.

Recirculation — Movement of air back into a ventilation system after being ejected.

Refuse Chute — Vertical shaft with a self-closing access door on every floor; usually extending from the basement or ground floor to the top floor of multistory buildings.

Reinforced Concrete — Concrete that is internally fortified with steel reinforcement bars or mesh placed within the concrete before it hardens. Reinforcement allows the concrete to resist tensile forces.

Reinforcing Bars (Rebar) — Steel bars placed in concrete forms before the cement is poured. When the concrete sets (hardens), the rebar within it adds considerable strength and reinforcement.

Remodel — Restructuring of a building's spaces and occupancy features.

Renovate — Restoring or updating a building's features including finishing materials, furnishing, and overall appearance.

Resonance – Movements of relatively large amplitude resulting from a small force applied at the natural frequency of a structure.

Return-Air Plenum — Unoccupied space within a building through which air flows back to the heating, ventilating, and air-conditioning (HVAC) system; normally immediately above a ceiling and below an insulated roof or the floor above.

Ridge Beam — Highest horizontal member in a pitched roof to which the upper ends of the rafters attach. *Also known as* Ridge Board *or* Ridgepole.

Rigid Frame — Load bearing system constructed with a skeletal frame and reinforcement between a column and beam.

Rise — Vertical distance between the treads of a stairway, or the height of the entire stairway.

Riser — Vertical part of a stair step.

Roll Roofing — Roof covering made of flexible material that may be applied to the roof deck as a continuous sheet. Commonly used on shallow pitch roofs.

Rolling — Process of forming metal stock into shapes including sheets by passing thick bars of metal through a pair of rollers. Cold rolling occurs at temperatures above recrystallization temperature.

Run —The horizontal measurement of a stair tread or the distance of the entire stair length.

R-Value — A measure of the ability of a material to insulate. Used in structural engineering and construction. Insulators with higher R-values are more effective.

S

Scarf Joint — Connection between two parts made by the cutting of overlapping mating parts and securing them by glue or fasteners so that the joint is not enlarged and the patterns are complementary.

Seismic Effect — Movement of a shock wave through the ground or structure after a large detonation; may cause additional damage to surrounding structures.

Seismic Forces — Forces produced by earthquakes travel in waves. These are the most complex forces that can be exerted on a building.

Seismic Load — Application of forces caused by earthquakes.

Self-Closing Door — Door equipped with a door closer.

Setback — Distance from the street line to the front of a building.

Settlement — Downward deformation of a building's structural elements. *Also known as* Settling.

Shear Stress — Stress resulting when two forces act on a body in opposite directions in parallel adjacent planes.

Shear Wall — Wall panels that are braced against lateral loads. May be load-bearing or nonload-bearing.

Shell Structure — Rigid, three-dimensional structure with an outer "skin" thickness that is small compared to other dimensions.

Shelter in Place — Having occupants remain in a structure or vehicle in order to provide protection from a rapidly approaching hazard, such as a fire or hazardous gas cloud. *Opposite of* Evacuation. *Also known as* Protection-in-Place, Defending-in-Place, Sheltering, *and* Taking Refuge.

Shoring — General term used for lengths of timber, screw jacks, hydraulic and pneumatic jacks, and other devices that can be used as temporary support for formwork or structural components or used to hold sheeting against trench walls. Individual supports are called shores, cross braces, and struts. Commonly used in conjunction with cribbing.

Shunt Trip — A circuit breaker used as a safety device in an elevator system. When electrical current surges, the device disconnects the power source.

Single-Injection System – Stairwell pressurization system that uses one point of supply air; pressurization can be lost if the system becomes unsealed through the use of doors.

Slab and Beam Frame — Construction technique using concrete slabs supported by concrete beams.

Slenderness Ratio — Comparison of the height or length of a structural component and the width/thickness of the component. Used to determine the load that can be supported by the component; lower ratios indicate components are more stable.

Sliding Door — Door that opens and closes by sliding across its opening, usually on rollers.

Slump Test — Method of evaluating the moisture content of wet concrete by measuring the amount that a small, cone-shaped sample of the concrete slumps after it is removed from a standard-sized test mold.

Smoke Control — Strategic use of passive and active devices and systems to direct or stop the movement of smoke and other products of combustion.

Smoke Control Mode — Setting on an HVAC system or Fire Alarm Control Unit system that can be activated automatically or manually to initiate a programmed smoke control procedure.

Smoke Damper — Device that automatically restricts the flow of smoke through all or part of an air-handling system; usually activated by the building's fire alarm signaling system.

Smoke Developed Rating — The measure of the relative visual obscurity created during the testing process by a known material.

Smoke Tower — Fully enclosed escape stairway that exits directly onto a public way; these enclosures are either mechanically pressurized or they require the user to exit the building onto an outside balcony before entering the stairway. *Also known as* Smokeproof Enclosure *or* Smokeproof Stairway.

Smokeproof Stair Enclosures — Stairways that are designed to limit the penetration of products of combustion into a stairway enclosure that serves as part of a means of egress.

Soil Property — Physical qualities of the materials at the surface of the earth. Affects a building's foundation and size. Influential variables include texture, structure, density, porosity, and consistency.

Space Frame — Aluminum skeleton upon which an aluminum, plastic, or composite skin is attached. The internal structure provides structural support, while the skin provides styling and protection from the elements.

Spalling — Expansion of excess moisture within masonry materials due to exposure to the heat of a fire, resulting in tensile forces within the material, and causing it to break apart. The expansion causes sections of the material's surface to violently disintegrate, resulting in explosive pitting or chipping of the material's surface.

Spec Building — Building built before securing a tenant or occupant. *Spec* is short for *speculation*.

Specific Gravity — Mass (weight) of a substance compared to the weight of an equal volume of water at a given temperature. A specific gravity less than 1 indicates a substance lighter than water; a specific gravity greater than 1 indicates a substance heavier than water.

Spray-Applied Fire Resistive Material (SRFM) — Coating used to increase the fire resistance rating of structural components. Materials commonly include mineral fiber or aggregates such as vermiculite and perlite.

Standpipe System — Wet or dry system of pipes in a large single-story or multistory building, with fire hose outlets installed in different areas or on different levels of a building to be used by firefighters and/or building occupants. This system is used to provide for the quick deployment of hoselines during fire fighting operations.

Static Load — Load that is steady, motionless, constant, or applied gradually.

Stationary Storage Battery System — A system including a battery, a charger, and electrical equipment for a particular application. This type of system can include a lead-acid battery or a safer type of battery.

Steel — An alloy of iron and carbon; proportions and additional elements affect the characteristics of the finished material. Used widely in the construction of buildings and other infrastructure.

Steiner Tunnel — Test apparatus used in the determination of flame spread ratings; consists of a horizontal test furnace 25 feet (7.5 m) long, 17½ inches (440 mm) wide, and 12 inches (300 mm) high that is used to observe flame travel. A 5,000 Btu (5 000 kJ) flame is produced in the tunnel, and the extent of flame travel across the surface of the test material is observed through ports in the side of the furnace. Used with ASTM E-84, also known as the "Tunnel Test."

Stratum — Sheet-like layer of rock or earth; numerous other layers, each with different characteristics, are typically found above and below. *Plural:* Strata.

Stress — Factors that work against the strength of any piece of apparatus, equipment, or structural support. Measurement of intensity is calculated as force divided by area.

Structural Insulated Panel (SIP) — A composite panel used in structural applications; made of plastic foam between two outer wood panels, often oriented strand board (OSB).

Structural Stiffness — The use or addition of structural supports to improve the ability of a structure to withstand forces imposed by loads. Often indicates supplemental reinforcement to accommodate specific types of loads, such as earthquake forces. *Also known as* Stiffening.

Stud — Vertical structural member within a wall in frame buildings; most are made of wood, but some are made of light-gauge metal.

Superplasticizer — Admixture used with concrete or mortar mix to make it workable, pliable, and soft while using relatively little water.

Surface Systems — System of construction in which the building consists primarily of an enclosing surface, and in which the stresses resulting from the applied loads occur within the bearing wall structures.

Surface-Burning Characteristic — Speed at which flame will spread over the surface of a material.

Surface-To-Mass Ratio — Relationship between the available surface area of the fuel and the mass of the fuel; used to predict the rate of fire consumption of combustible material.

Swinging Door — Door that opens and closes by swinging from one side of its opening, usually on hinges. *Also known as* Hinged Door.

T

Tensile Stress — Stress in a structural member that tends to stretch the member or pull it apart; often used to denote the greatest amount of force a component can withstand without failure.

Tension — Vertical or horizontal force that pulls material apart; for example, the force exerted on the bottom chord of a truss.

Thermal Radiation — Transmission or transfer of heat energy, from one body to another body at a lower temperature, through intervening space by electromagnetic waves similar to radio waves or X-rays.

Thermoplastic — Plastic that softens with an increase of temperature and hardens with a decrease of temperature but does not undergo any chemical change. Synthetic material made from the polymerization of organic compounds that become soft when heated and hard when cooled.

Tied Walls — Fire walls connected to a line of columns or steel structural supports with the same degree of fire resistance. Must resist lateral collapse on either side of the structure.

Tilt-Up Construction — Type of construction in which concrete wall sections (slabs) are cast on the concrete floor of the building, then tilted up into the vertical position. *Also known as* Tilt-Slab Construction.

Tin-Clad Door — Similar to a metal-clad door, except covered with a lighter-gauge metal, often an alloy of tin and lead.

Torsional Load — Load aligned off-center from the cross-section of the structural component and at an angle to or in the same plane as the cross-section; produces a twisting effect that creates shear stresses in a material.

Transformer — Device that uses coils and magnetic fields to increase (step-up) or decrease (step-down) incoming voltages.

Transverse Load — Structural load that exerts a force perpendicular to structural members.

Tread — Horizontal face of a step.

Truss — Structural member used to support a roof or floor with triangles or combinations of triangles to provide maximum load-bearing capacity with a minimum amount of material. Connections are likely to fail in intense heat.

Two-Way Slab Construction — Concrete construction framework type that uses reinforcing steel placed on the bottom of the framework that provides reinforcement in two directions. *Also known as* Waffle Construction.

U

Underpinning — The use of permanent supports to strengthening an existing foundation.

Unprotected Steel — Steel structural members that are not protected against exposure to heat.

Utility Chase — Vertical pathway (shaft) in a building that contains utility services such as laundry or refuse chutes, and grease ducts.

V

Veneered Walls — Walls with a surface layer of attractive material laid over a base of a common material.

Voice over Internet Protocol (VoIP) — Communication services that utilize an Internet connection to transmit telephone signals.

W

Wall Footing — Type of shallow foundation that includes a wide, thick area to distribute the weight of a wall on the bearing soil. *Also known as* Strip Footing.

Water Table — The highest level of ground water saturation of subsurface materials. Influential variables include the season, soil properties, and topography.

Web — (1) Wide vertical part of a beam between thick horizontal flanges at the top and bottom of the beam. (2) Secondary member of a truss contained between the chords. *Also known as* Diagonals.

Wildland/Urban Interface — Line, area, or zone where an undeveloped wildland area meets a human development area. *Also known as* Urban/Wildland Interface.

Wind — Horizontal movement of air relative to the surface of the earth.

Wired Glass — Flat sheet of glass or fire glazing containing an embedded wire mesh that increases its resistance to breakage and penetration; installed to increase interior illumination without compromising fire resistance and security. May be transparent or translucent.

Wythe — Single vertical row of a series of rows of masonry units in a wall; usually brick or concrete block.

Index

Index

A

AC (alternating current) circuit, 106
Access to construction sites, 347–348
Acoustic board, 194
Acoustic tile in dropped ceilings, 245
Active barriers, 33
Active fire protection, 99
Active smokeproof enclosures, 100
Active soil pressure, 78
ADA. *See* Americans with Disabilities Act (ADA) of 1990
Admixture, 258
Aesthetics, 29–30
Aftershocks, 365
Age of construction
    advantages of older construction, 25
    building condition and, 25
    gentrification, 26
    maintenance and upgrading of buildings, 25
    World War II influences on codes and styles, 25
Aggregate, defined, 257, 258
AHJ. *See* Authority Having Jurisdiction (AHJ)
Air ducts, 119
Air filtration systems, 118
Air handling systems, 116–128
    cupola, 117
    exhaust systems, 120
    forced-air system, 120–121
    HVAC. *See* Heating, Ventilating, and Air Conditioning (HVAC) system
    pressurized stairwells, 126–128
    smoke and heat vents, 124–125
    smoke control systems, 121–124
    smoke towers, 125–126
    ventilation systems, 120
Air intakes, 118
Air-cooled chiller, 118, 119
Air-cooled transformers, 129
Air-supported and air-inflated structures, 325–327
Alarm systems in high-rise buildings, 316–317
Alloy, 240
Alternating current (AC) circuit, 106
American Society of Civil Engineers (ASCE), 60
American Society of Mechanical Engineers (ASME), 103
Americans with Disabilities Act (ADA) of 1990
    accessibility requirements, 21–22, 337
    area of refuge, 21
    defined, 20
    elevators in multistory buildings, 103
Anchor stores, 329–330
Apartment complex fire, Houston, TX (2014), 345
Arc, defined, 129
Arch
    defined, 81
    hinges, 81
    lamella arch, 282
    roof architecture, 280
    steel, 249–250
    structural design, 80–81
    support systems, 289
    trussed, 250

Architect
    aesthetics and design, 30
    owner's needs and desires, 28
    Sullivan, Louis A., 13
    Wright, Frank Lloyd, 13
Area of refuge
    accessibility requirements, 21–22, 337
    defined, 20
    locations for, 337
    smoke barriers, 337
    in a stairway, 337
    two-way communication system, 337
Asbestos, 192–193, 352–353
ASCE (American Society of Civil Engineers), 60
ASCE/SFPE 29, *Standard Calculation Methods for Structural Fire Protection*, 60
ASME (American Society of Mechanical Engineers), 103
ASME Standard A17.4, *Guide for Emergency Personnel*, 112
ASME/ANSI A17.1, *Safety Code for Elevators*, 103
Asphalt shingles and tiles, 294–295
ASTM A36, structural steel, 241
ASTM D-2859, Reference Radiant Panel Test, 143
ASTM E 136, *Standard Test Method for Behavior of Materials in a Vertical Tube Furnace at 750°C*, 54
ASTM E-84 UL 723, *Test for Surface Burning Characteristics of Building Materials*, 141–143
ASTM E-108, roof covering evaluation, 298–299
ASTM E-119 test, 55, 58–59, 201
ASTM E-152 test, 162–163
ASTM Standard 1529, Standard Test Methods for Determining Effects of Large Hydrocarbon Pool Fires on Structural Members and Assemblies, 58
Atriums
    automatic sprinklers, 333
    building codes, 333
    defined, 332
    Hyatt Regency Hotel, 33
    impact on fire and smoke, 23
    purpose of, 332
    smoke travel, 332, 333
Authority Having Jurisdiction (AHJ)
    asbestos remediation, 193
    building permits, 15
    defined, 12
    elevator keys, 114
    raw materials staging, 346
    responsibilities, 12
    standpipes, 314
    void spaces in roof construction, 287
Auto body shop fire (2013), 239
Automatic fire suppression systems construction design, 23
Automatic smoke control, 123
Automatic sprinkler systems. *See also* Sprinklers
    atriums, 333
    high-rise buildings, 315–316
    institutional sprinklers, 330, 331–332
    limited access building requirements, 322, 324
    rack storage, 339
Axial load, 69

B

Balloon-frame construction, 203, 204
Bar joist, 83, 249
Barriers, passive and active, 32–33
Base isolation, 77
Basement fires (1961, 2006), 9–10, 210
Batteries, 131
Beam
    beam and girder frames, 247–248
        rigid frame, 247
        semi-rigid frame, 247–248
        simple frame, 247
    beam pocket, 227, 228
    box beams, 208, 284–285
    cantilever, 78, 79
    continuous, 79
    defined, 78, 79
    glulam, 184, 185
    I-beams, 80, 208, 284–285
    overhanging, 79
    post and beam framing, 86, 208
    restrained, 79
    simply supported, 79
    slab and beam frame, 87, 268
    steel, 242
    stresses, 80
    T-shaped concrete, 260
Bearing plates, 232–233
Bearing wall, 85
Belled piers, 173
Below grade spaces, 324–325
Bending moment, 67, 79
Bending stress, 67, 79
Beverly Hills Supper Club fire, Southgate, KY (1977), 138
Bids, 15
Blast waves, 334
Blind hoistways, 111, 112
Board of Appeals, 15
Boate Kiss nightclub fire, Santa Maria, Brazil (2013), 93
BOCA. *See* Building Officials and Code Administrators (BOCA) International, Inc.
Bowstring truss
    collapse, 9
    defined, 83
    pre-engineered roof framing, 288
Box beams, 208, 284–285
Breakaway bolt, 360
Breakout panels for explosion control, 336
Breezy Point, NY, hurricane damage (2012), 370
Bricks
    manufacturing methods, 219
    material properties, 219
    veneer, 193
British Thermal Unit (Btu), 197
Brown roofs, 300
Buffers on elevators, 108
Building classifications, 43–51
    basis of, 44
    mixed construction, 51
    NFPA® 220 classification requirements, 44–45
    purpose of, 44
    Type I – Fire Resistive, 20, 45, 46–47
    Type II – Protected Noncombustible or Noncombustible construction, 20, 45, 47–48
    Type III – Exterior Protected (Masonry or Ordinary) construction, 20, 45, 48–49
    Type IV – Heavy Timber construction, 20, 45, 49–50, 205–206, 207
    Type V – Wood Frame construction, 20, 45, 50–51
Building code
    building classification numerical designations, 44
    common sense requirements, 19
    construction type, 20
    defined, 13, 18
    exemptions, 17
    fire safety provisions, 19
    International Building Code. *See International Building Code® (IBC®)*
    International Existing Building Code, 17
    life safety codes, 19–20
    National Building Code of Canada, 18
    National Fire Protection Association®, 18. *See also* National Fire Protection Association® (NFPA®)
    occupancy and use, 21
    World War II influences, 25
Building collapse. *See* Collapse of buildings
Building Construction and Safety Code. *See* NFPA® 5000, *Building Construction and Safety Code*
Building frame
    instability, 362
    insufficiency, 362
    weakness, 361–362
Building materials. *See also* Concrete; Masonry; Steel; Wood
    design elements, 13
    hoists, 348
    scavenging scrap, 354–355
Building Officials and Code Administrators (BOCA) International, Inc.
    BOCA Basic Building Code, 25
    International Code Council and, 18
Building permit
    appeals, 15
    building plan review before construction begins, 15
    defined, 15
    for large projects, 15
    obtaining of, 15
    renovation and remodeling, 17
Building settlement, 175–176
Building systems, 93–132
    air handling systems, 116–128
        HVAC, 116–124
        pressurized stairwells, 126–128
        smoke and heat vents, 124–125
        smoke towers, 125–126
    electrical equipment, 128–131
        emergency and standby power supplies, 130–131
        transformers, 128–130
    electrical systems, 35
    elevators, 102–114
        access panels, 112
        defined, 103
        doors, 111–112, 113
        emergency use of, 103
        hoistways, 109–111
        safety features, 108–109
        shafts, 114, 150
        types, 104–108

failure, 34–35
mechanical conveyor systems, 101–102
to prevent combustion, 35
stairs, 94–101
    circular, 95, 96
    components, 94
    folding, 95, 97
    landings, 95
    as means of egress, 98–99
    open stairs, 101
    prefabricated, 95
    return, 95
    scissor, 95, 96
    smokeproof enclosures, 99–100
    spiral, 95, 97
    straight run, 95
vertical shafts and utility chases, 114–116
Building wrap, 190–191
Built-up membrane, 292
Butt joint, 184, 185
Butterfly roof, 280, 281
Buttress, 226, 227

C

Cable covered structure, 327–328
Cable membrane structure, 327–328
Cables, 82, 83
CAD (Computer Aided Dispatch), 36
Caissons, 173, 174
Calcination, 244
Calcined gypsum, 244
Calculating structural endurance under fire conditions, 201–202
Canada
    National Building Code of Canada, 18
    National Research Council of Canada, 18
    voltage supply to buildings, 128
Cantilever beam, 78, 79
Capital, 87
Car safeties on elevators, 109
Carbon in steel, 240
Cast iron, 240
Cast-in-place concrete, 263
Cavity wall, 226
CBBF (concrete block brick faced), 226, 227
Ceilings
    acoustic tile, 245
    concealed spaces, 145
    dropped ceiling hazards, 49
    fire resistance rating, 54
    functions, 145
    membrane, 245–246
    restrained assemblies, 56
Cement. *See also* Concrete
    defined, 257, 258
    tile roofs, 296–297
Cementitious, 244
Central control station in high-rise buildings, 317–318
Central core floor plan, 318
Chase, 116
Chimney fire and ceiling collapse, 65
Chipboard, 188
Chlorinated polyethylene (CPE), 293
Chord, 82, 83

Circular stairs, 95, 96
Civil engineering, 13
Cladding, 192
Class A fire doors, 153
Class B fire doors, 153
Class C fire doors, 153
Class D fire doors, 153
Class E fire doors, 153
Classes of buildings. *See* Building classifications
Clay tile blocks, 220
Clay tile roofs, 296–297
Clean energy, 301
CMU (concrete masonry unit), 85
Cold rolled steel (CRS), 241
Collapse of buildings, 359–375
    bowstring truss collapse, 9
    chimney fire and ceiling collapse, 65
    collapse control zones, 230, 231
    condominium, Bailey's Crossroads, VA (1973), 362
    design-caused structural failure, 33–36
    Firefighter Nation research, 196
    football practice facility (2009), 359
    high-rise, Shanghai, China (2009), 169
    housing project, Bridgeport, CT (1987), 361
    human-related causes, 360–364
        building frame weakness, 361–362
        change in building use, 360
        construction methods, 361–362
        demolition methods, 362–363
        explosions, 363–364
        other causes, 364
        poor maintenance, 364
        sequencing, 361
        structural design inadequacy, 360
        temporary loads, 361
    Hyatt Regency collapse (1981), 33–34
    Kemper Arena, Kansas City, MO (1979), 371
    masonry construction, 230–231
    Metrodome collapse, MN (2010), 371
    nature-related causes, 365–373
        earthquakes, 365–366
        floods, 372–373
        hurricanes, 370–371
        landslides, 367–368
        sinkholes, 367, 368–369
        snow and water loads, 371–372
        subsidence, 367, 368
        tornadoes, 370
        wind, 369–371
    NFPA® statistics, 196
    Pier 34, Philadelphia, PA (2000), 364
    prestressed concrete, 263
    steel structures, 252
    structural collapse, 10
    Tropicana Casino parking garage, Atlantic City, NJ (2003), 217
    wide area incidents, 373–375
    wood construction, 210–211
    World Trade Center Towers (2001), 313
Collar tie, 285
Column
    connections, 251
    defined, 80, 81
    footing, 171

materials used in, 80
slab and column frames, 87
slenderness ratio, 250
steel, 250–251
vertical reinforcing bars, 260, 261
Combustion
combustible debris at construction sites, 350
combustible materials, 47
defined, 35
heat of combustion, 54, 197
International Building Code® criteria, 54
testing for combustibility, 54
wood materials, 196–200
fire-retardant treatment of wood, 198–200
heat of combustion, 197
ignition temperature, 196–197
life safety and fire fighting tactics, 196
surface area and mass, 198
void spaces, 200
Common truss, 287
Community fire defense, 30–33
conflagration, 30
exposures and fire spread factors, 31–33
fire spread, 30
heat transfer, 30–31
Compartment
compartmentation, 145–146
defined, 139
full height partition walls, 309
surface burning characteristics, 139
Compensated system, 128
Composite panels, 189
Compression, 68
Compression testing of concrete, 265
Computer Aided Dispatch (CAD), 36
Concealed spaces
in ceilings, 145
dropped ceilings, 49
in Type III construction, 49
void spaces. *See* Void spaces
Concentrated load, 72
Concrete, 257–272. *See also* Masonry; Mortar
applications, 263–264
blocks. *See* Concrete blocks
cement, 257, 258, 296–297
composition, 257–258
defined, 257, 258
fire resistance, 266–267
foundation walls, 174
framing systems, 267–272
concrete plus structural steel, 268
flat-slab concrete frame, 267
precast concrete, 268–272
slab and beam frame, 268
waffle construction, 268
heat sink effect, 267
joist construction, 268
material properties, 257–267
as noncombustible building material, 46–47
quality control, 264–265
compression testing, 265
hydration, 264, 265
slump test, 265

temperature, 264–265
water-to-cement ratio, 264
reinforced, 259–263
defined, 259
ordinary reinforcing, 259–261
posttensioning, 262–263
prestressing, 261–263
pretensioning, 262
rebar, 259, 260
spalling, 267
types, 258
Concrete blocks
for bearing walls, 84
concrete block brick faced (CBBF), 226, 227
defined, 85
material properties, 220
Concrete masonry unit (CMU), 85
Condominium collapse, Bailey's Crossroads, VA (1973), 362
Configuration of internal spaces, 23
Conflagration, 30
Construction process
coordination and scheduling, 15–16
fast-track construction, 16
Construction sites, 345–352
access, 346–348
access roads, 347
construction elevators, 347–348
difficulties, 346
material hoists, 348
stairways, 348
water supply, 347
apartment complex fire, Houston, TX (2014), 345
fire hazards, 348–350
combustible debris, 350
construction processes, 350
electrical wiring, 349
fuel usage, 349
storage of fuels, 349–350
fire protection, 351–352
fire extinguishers, 352
temporary systems, 351–352
incidents requiring emergency response, 345–346
life safety features, 354
raw materials staging, 346
remodeling, 346
structural integrity, 350
water supply concerns, 347
Construction types, 20
Construction variables
aesthetics and culture, 29–30
economics-based, 27–28
building use, 27
existing infrastructure, 27
fire loss management, 28
engineering-based, 22–26
age of construction, 25–26
automatic fire suppression systems, 23
building site properties, 22–23
climate, 22
gentrification, 26, 27
green design, 26, 27
internal space configuration, 23, 24
investment of wealth, 28–29

law-based, 18–22
    accessibility requirements, 21–22
    building code requirements, 18–21
    construction type, 20
    life safety codes, 19–20
    occupancy and use, 21
  owner's needs and desires, 28
Containment of explosions, 334–336
Continuous beams, 79
Controlled access buildings. *See* Limited or controlled access buildings
Controlled collapse demolition, 363
Convection, 30, 31
Convenience stair, 94
Conventional framed roofs, 285–287
Cook County Administration Building fire, Chicago, IL (2003), 309
Cool roofs, 300
Cooling tower, 120, 121
Corbel, 228
Corbelling, 228
Corner tests, 144
Cornice, 230
Correctional facilities, 330–332
Corrugated steel, 251
Course of masonry units, 225
Covered mall buildings, 328–330
  anchor stores, 329–330
  change in occupancy, 329
  configurations, 329–330
  construction and systems, 330
  forms of, 328
  hazards and access, 329
CPE (chlorinated polyethylene), 293
Criterion-referenced assessment, 141
Criterion-referenced testing (CRT), 141, 163–164
Cross bracing, 85, 176
Cross-bracing reinforcements, 77
Cross-section, 68
CRS (cold rolled steel), 241
CRT (criterion-referenced testing), 141, 163–164
Cultural characteristics of buildings, 29
Cupola, 117
Curtain boards, 124, 125
Curtain wall
  defined, 150
  functions, 150
  materials and combinations, 150–151
  nonfire-resistive, 151
  nonload-bearing, 151
Curved roof, 281–282

D

Damping mechanisms, 76, 77
DC (direct current) circuit, 106
Dead load, 70
Debris at construction sites, 350
Deck roof, 280–281
Deep foundations, 172–174
Defending-in-place, 146
Defensive fire fighting strategy, 37
Delta truss, 248
Demolition of buildings, 354–355, 362–363

Department of Homeland Security (DHS), 373
Design and construction process, 12–17
  bids, 15
  building permits, 15
  concept, 12–14
  construction process, 15–16
  design principles, 13
  documentation, 14–15
  engineering specialties, 13–14
  financing, 14
  inspection and testing, 16–17
  materials, 13
  professional design, 13
  renovation and remodeling, 17
  resources, 12
Design principles, 13
Design-build, 12
Design-build firm, 12
Design-caused structural failure, 33–36
  building system failure, 34–35
  causes of, 33
  combustion and, 35
  design deficiencies, 35–36
  Hyatt Regency collapse, 33–34
  loss of structural integrity, 34
  meaning of, 33–34
Detection devices in high-rise buildings, 316–317
Detention facilities, 330–332
Dewatering, 73
DHS (U.S. Department of Homeland Security), 373
Diagonals, 81, 82, 85
Dielectric properties, 129
Dimensional lumber, 182
Direct current (DC) circuit, 106
Distributed load, 72
Documentation, engineering design, 14–15
Dome roof, 281, 282
Doors
  clutch for elevator doors, 113
  door closer, 160
  door holder, 159
  elevator, 111–112, 113
  fire doors, 152–165
    classifications, 152–157
    hardware and features, 158–162
    maintenance, 162
    tactical uses of, 152
    testing, 162–165
Dormers, 283
Draft curtains, 124, 125
Draft stops, 124
Drainage layer of roof coverings, 294
Drop panel, 87
Dropped ceilings, 49
Drum elevators, 105–106
Dry transformers, 129
Ductility of steel, 241
Ductwork, 119
Dumbwaiter, 108
Dupont Plaza hotel fire, Puerto Rico, (1986), 24
Dynamic load, 71–72

E

E2 nightclub disaster, 53
E-119 test, 55, 58–59, 201
Earthquakes
    aftershocks, 365
    building code requirements, 366
    cause of, 74
    as cause of building collapse, 365–366
    defined, 365
    factors contributing to building damage, 366
    high risk locations, 74–75
    Napa, CA (2014), 365, 366
    seismic stabilization systems, 365
East Grand Forks, MN, flood (1997), 372
Eccentric load, 69
Economics-based construction variables, 27–28
    building use, 27
    existing infrastructure, 27
    fire loss management, 28
Egress, means of, 94, 98
EIFS (exterior insulation and finishing system), 191, 229
Elastomer, 77
Electric
    elevators, 104–108
    emergency power, 35
    emergency power batteries, 131
    fire stops in openings, 35
    generators, 130–131
    lock-out/tag-out, 106
    wiring hazards at construction sites, 349
Electrical engineering, 14
Electrical equipment, 128–131
    air-cooled transformers, 129
    emergency power batteries, 131
    generators, 130–131
    oil-cooled transformers, 129–130
    stationary storage battery system, 131
    transformers, 128–130
    voltage supply to buildings, 128
Elevator, 102–114
    access panels, 112, 113
    blind hoistway, 112
    construction site, 347–348
    defined, 103
    doors, 111–112, 113
    dumbwaiter, 108
    electric, 104–108
    elevator hoistway, 109–111
    elevator pit, 109
    emergency exits, 112
    emergency use for fire operations, 103
    emergency use in high-rise buildings, 319–322
        electric eye safety, 321
        keyed switch, 320–321
        Phase I operation, 320–321
        Phase II operation, 321–322
        safety, 319–320
        shunt trip, 319
    features, 102
    freight, 104
    hoistways, 109–111
    hydraulic, 104
    keys, 114
    passenger, 104
    regulations, 103
    safety features, 108–109
    service elevators, 104
    shafts, 114, 150
    traction, 105, 106–107
Enclosure walls, 149–150
Energy conservation, 26. *See also* Green design
Engineered wood, 183–187
    defined, 183
    glue-laminated beams, 184
    glulam beams, 184, 185
    laminated wood, 184–185
    structural composite lumber, 186
    thermoplastic composite lumber, 187
Engineering specialties
    civil engineering, 13
    electrical engineering, 14
    fire protection engineering, 14
    mechanical engineering, 14
    structural engineering, 14
Engineering-based construction variables, 22–26
    age of construction, 25–26
    automatic fire suppression systems, 23
    building site properties, 22–23
    climate, 22
    gentrification, 26, 27
    green design, 26, 27
    internal space configuration, 23, 24
EPDM (ethylene propylene diene monomer), 293
EPS (expanded polystyrene) foundation walls, 174–175
Equilibrium, defined, 66
Escalator, 101–102
Ethylene propylene diene monomer (EPDM), 293
Everyone Goes Home® program, 19
Exhaust system, 120
Existing/non-conforming structure, 17
Exits
    E2 nightclub disaster, 53
    elevator, 112
    means of egress, 94, 98
Expanded polystyrene (EPS) foundation walls, 174–175
Expansion joints, 76, 77
Expansion of buildings, 353–354
Explosions
    blast waves, 334
    as cause of building collapse, 363–364
    containment, 334–336
    explosion vent fasteners, 336
    fuel container hazards on construction sites, 350
    Humberto Vidal Building, Puerto Rico (1996), 266, 335
    sources, 364
    types, 334
    venting of buildings, 334–336
Exposure, 31–33
    defined, 31
    fire spread factors, 31–33
Exterior insulation and finishing system (EIFS), 191, 229
Exterior stairs, 98, 99
Exterior wall materials, 190–193
    building wrap, 190–191
    foam insulation, 191–192
    sheathing, 190
    siding, 192–193

F

Facade, 230
Factor of safety, 69
Factory Mutual System, listed coatings, 140
Failure point, 69
False fronts, 230
False roof, 230
Fans for HVAC systems, 118
Fascia, 230
Fast-track construction, 16
Fault, 74
FDC (fire department connection), 351
Federal Emergency Management Agency (FEMA), 373
FEMA (Federal Emergency Management Agency), 373
Financing for construction, 14
Finger joint, 184, 185
Fink truss, 289
Fire alarm pull stations, 21
Fire alarm systems in high-rise buildings, 316–317
Fire areas, 146
Fire command center in high-rise buildings, 317–318
Fire cut, 228
Fire damper, 119
Fire department connection (FDC), 351
Fire department sprinkler connection, 351
Fire detection and suppression systems, minimum requirements, 32
Fire doors, 152–165
    classifications, 152–157
        fire door requirements, 153
        horizontal sliding fire doors, 155, 157
        rolling (overhead) doors, 154–155
        special-purpose fire doors, 157
        swinging fire doors, 156, 158
    hardware and features, 158–162
        closing devices, 159–160
        defined, 158
        door hold-open device, 159
        glazing, 161–162
        louvers, 162
    maintenance, 162
    tactical uses of, 152
    testing, 162–165
        ASTM E-152, 162–163
        criterion referenced testing, 163–164
        marking rated fire doors, 164–165
Fire escapes, 98–99
Fire extension in high-rise buildings, 318–319
Fire extinguishers at construction sites, 352
Fire fighting
    high-rise buildings, 310
    membrane structures, 327
    roofs and, 278
    strategy for, 37
    tactic research, 196
Fire flow, 146
Fire hazards at construction sites, 348–350
    combustible debris, 350
    construction processes, 350
    electrical wiring, 349
    fuel usage, 349
    storage of fuels, 349–350
Fire load
    defined, 54
    structural load vs., 54
Fire loss management, 28
Fire partition, 149. *See also* Walls
Fire protection
    active barriers, 33
    at construction sites, 351–352
        fire extinguishers, 352
        temporary systems, 351–352
    engineering, 14
    fire detection and suppression systems, 32
    high-rise buildings, 314–318
        automatic sprinklers, 315–316
        fire alarm systems, 316–317
        fire command center, 317–318
        Meridian Plaza fire, Philadelphia, PA (1991), 315
        smoke control systems, 317
        standpipes, 314
    passive barriers, 32–33
    rack storage, 339
    steel, 243–246
        cementitious, 244
        gypsum, 244–245
        intumescent materials, 245
        mastic coatings, 245
        membrane ceilings, 245–246
        spray-applied fire resistive material, 243–244
Fire resistance, 55–61
    apartment complex, Houston, TX (2014), 345
    ASTM-E 119 test, 55, 58–59
    concrete construction, 266–267
    defined, 55
    failure criteria, 57
    fire resistance rating, 55
    fire tests, history of, 55
    floor and ceiling assemblies, 54
    high-rise buildings, 313
    laboratory-tested data, 56–59
    masonry walls, 221
    material properties, 55
    mathematical models, 60, 61
    publishing fire test results, 59
    test finding limitations, 58
    testing laboratories, 59
    underground building materials, 324
Fire Resistance Design Manual, 145
Fire Resistance Directory
    annual listing of assemblies, 59
    fire wall fire resistance ratings, 145
    floor and ceiling assembly, 54
    gypsum board, 194
Fire retardant, 47
Fire spread, 30
Fire stop, 49
Fire wall, 146–149
    defined, 146
    fire areas, 146
    fire resistance ratings, 147–148
    freestanding walls, 146–147
    negative perception of fire walls, 148–149
    parapet walls, 147, 148
    tied walls, 147, 148
    uses of, 149
Fired clay tile, 220
Firefighter Nation, 196

Firefighter's smoke control station (FSCS), 123–124
Fire-rated assembly, 146
Fire-retardant
   coatings, 140–141
   wood treatment, 198–200
Fires
   apartment complex, Houston, TX (2014), 345
   auto body shop (2013), 239
   basement fire (1991), 9–10
   basement fire (2006), 210
   Beverly Hills Supper Club, Southgate, KY (1977), 138
   Boate Kiss nightclub, Santa Maria, Brazil (2013), 93
   chimney fire and ceiling collapse, 65
   Cook County Administration Building, Chicago, IL (2003), 309
   Dupont Plaza hotel, Puerto Rico (1986), 24
   failure of unprotected engineered trusses, 210
   Great Chicago Fire (1871), 30
   Hayman Fire, Colorado Springs, Co (2002), 277
   K-Mart fire, removal of fire doors, 149
   Lame Horse nightclub, Perm, Russia (2009), 137
   LaSalle Hotel, Chicago, IL (1946), 138
   Meridian Plaza, Philadelphia, PA (1991), 35, 315
   MGM Grand, Las Vegas, NV (1980), 77
   pyrotechnics, 137
   Station Night Club, West Warwick, RI (2003), 138
   Windsor Tower, Madrid, Spain (2005), 43
   Winecoff Hotel, Atlanta, GA (1913), 313
Firestopping wood materials, 189–190
Flakeboard, 188
Flame spread, 139
Flame spread rating, 142–143
Flange, 80, 81
Flat plate, 266, 267
Flat roofs
   architecture, 279, 280
   built-up tar-and-gravel roof, 292, 294
   coverings, 292–294
      drainage layer, 294
      membrane, 292–294
      thermal insulation, 292, 293
      vapor barrier, 292
      wear course, 294
   support systems, 283–285
      box beams and I-beams, 284–285
      joists, 283–284
Flat-slab concrete frame, 266, 267
Floating foundation, 172
Floods, 372–373
Floors
   fire resistance rating, 54
   flame spread ratings, 143
   floor plans
      central core, 318
      open floor plans in high-rise buildings, 318–319
   restrained assemblies, 56
   surface burning characteristics, 140
Fluid-applied membrane, 293
Foam insulation, 191–192
Folding stairs, 95, 97
Football practice facility collapse (2009), 359
Footings, 171–172
Force
   defined, 66

   gravity, 67
   shrinkage, 67
   temperature, 67
   vibration, 67
Forced-air system, 120–121
Forest fires, 30
"Form follows function," 13
Formulas
   kinetic energy of a falling object, 71
   soil pressure, 79
Foundations, 169–177
   building settlement, 175–176
   deep foundations, 172–174
   factors influencing the type and depth of, 170
   shallow foundations, 171–172
   shoring, 176–177
   soil properties and, 169–170
   underpinning, 176–177
   walls, 174–175
Frame
   building, 361–362
   construction, 85
   covered structure, 327–328
   defined, 85
   frame structural systems, 85–87
      post and beam construction, 86
      rigid frame, 86
      slab and beam frame, 87
      slab and column frames, 87
      steel stud walls, 85
   membrane structure, 327–328
Freestanding wall, 146–147, 148
Freight elevators, 104
Frost line, 170
FSCS (firefighter's smoke control station), 123–124
Fuel load
   defined, 20, 54
   occupancy and use, 21
Fuels at construction sites, 349–350
Fusible link, 154

G

Gable roofs, 280, 285, 286
Gabled rigid frames, 249
Gambrel roofs, 280, 286
Garage exposures, 32
Gas springs on folding stairs, 97
Generators, 130–131
Gentrification, 26, 27
Geodesic domes, 282
Geographic information system (GIS), 36–37
Girders
   beam and girder frames, 247–248
   joint girder, 248
GIS (geographic information system), 36–37
Glass block, 220
Glazing, 161–162
Global positioning system (GPS), 36
Glued-laminated beam, 184
Glue-laminated beam, 184
Glulam beam, 184, 185
Golden Gate Bridge, special emergency resources needed for, 22
Goodman library, earthquake damage, 365, 366
GPS (global positioning system), 36

Grain of wood, 183
Gravity, 67
Grease ducts, 115-116
Great Chicago Fire (1871), 30
Green design
    defined, 27
    hazards of, 26
    purpose of, 26
    roofs, 300-302
        defined, 300, 302
        photovoltaic roofs, 301-302
        solar cells, 301
        vegetative roof systems, 302
    underground buildings, 323
Grillage footing, 171, 172
Grout, 226, 227
Guide for Emergency Personnel (ASME Standard A17.4), 112
Guide for Fire and Explosion Investigations (NFPA® 921-2011), 35
Gusset plates, 83, 209, 252
Gypsum
    calcination, 244
    calcined, 244
    fire walls, 145
    for firestopping, 190, 194
    as interior covering, 48
    nailable, for roof decks, 290
    regular, 244
    steel fire protection, 244-245
    type X, 244
Gypsum Association, 145
Gypsum blocks, 220

H
Hardware for fire doors
    closing devices, 159-160
    defined, 158
    door closers, 160
    door hold-open device, 159
    metal- and tin-clad doors, 158-159
    self-closing door, 160
    for wood swinging fire doors, 158
Hayman Fire, Colorado Springs, Co (2002), 277
Header course, 225
Heat of combustion, 54, 197
Heat of hydration, 264
Heat release rate (HRR)
    defined, 20
    fire load and, 54
    occupancy and use, 21
Heat sink effect, 267
Heat transfer, 30-31
Heating, Ventilating, and Air Conditioning (HVAC) system. *See also* Air handling systems
    components, 118-119
        air ducts, 119
        air filtration, 118
        air heating and cooling equipment, 119
        fans, 118
        outside air intakes, 118
        return-air plenum, 119
        smoke and fire dampers, 119
    defined, 116
    forced-air system, 120-121
    functions, 116-117
    as life-support system, 117
    purpose of, 116
    smoke and heat vents, 124-125
    smoke control systems, 121-124, 317
    ventilation and exhaust systems, 120
Heaving, 175
Heavy timber construction. *See* Type IV - Heavy Timber construction
Heavy timber framing, 205-207, 209
High-rise buildings, 310-322
    collapse in Shanghai, China (2009), 169
    defined, 310
    early vs. modern buildings, 311-313
        height of construction, 311
        occupancy and use, 311, 312
        ventilation and vertical enclosures, 311-312
        Winecoff Hotel fire, Atlanta, GA (1913), 313
    elevators, emergency use of, 319-322
        electric eye safety, 321
        keyed switch, 320-321
        Phase I operation, 320-321
        Phase II operation, 321-322
        safety during use, 319-320
        shunt trip, 319
    fire extension, 318-319
    fire fighting challenges, 310
    fire protection systems, 314-318
        automatic sprinklers, 315-316
        fire alarm systems, 316-317
        fire command center, 317-318
        Meridian Plaza fire, Philadelphia, PA (1991), 315
        smoke control systems, 317
        standpipes, 314, 315
        two-way communication system, 316
    fire-resistive construction, 313
    open floor plan, 318-319
Hinged door, 156
Hinges on arches, 81
Hip roof, 280, 285, 286
History of building construction, 11-12
Hoist, material, 348
Hoistway
    blind, 111, 112
    defined, 105
    elevator, 109-111
    fire spread in, 110
    innovations, 111
    purpose of, 105
Horizontal motion, 76, 77
Horizontal sliding fire doors, 155, 157
Hot work, 350
Housing project collapse, Bridgeport, CT (1987), 361
HRR. *See* Heat release rate (HRR)
Human-related causes of building collapse, 360-364
    building frame weakness, 361-362
    change in building use, 360
    construction methods, 361-362
    demolition methods, 362-363
    explosions, 363-364
    other causes, 364
    poor maintenance, 364

sequencing, 361
structural design inadequacy, 360
temporary loads, 361
Humberto Vidal Building explosion, Puerto Rico (1996), 266, 335
Hurricanes
Breezy Point, NY damage (2012), 370
Hurricane Andrew, 369
hurricane brackets, 370, 371
hurricane glazing, 121
Hurricane Irene, 371
Hurricane Ivan, 369, 371
Hurricane Katrina, 373
Hurricane Sandy, 370
New Orleans, LA, damage (2005), 373
Windemere Condominiums, Orange Beach, AL, damage (2004), 369
HVAC. *See* Heating, Ventilating, and Air Conditioning (HVAC) system
Hyatt Regency collapse (1981), 33–34
Hydration of concrete, 264, 265
Hydraulic cement, 220
Hydraulic elevators, 104
Hydronic system, 120, 121
Hygroscopic fire-retardant treatment, 200

I

IBC®. *See International Building Code® (IBC®)*
I-beams, 80, 208, 284–285
ICBO (International Conference of Building Officials), 18
ICC. *See* International Code Council® (ICC)
ICF (insulated concrete form) construction, 174, 175
IEBC (International Existing Building Code), 17
IFC®. See International Fire Code® (IFC®)
Ignition source, 197
Ignition temperature, 196–197
Ignition-resistant construction, 200–201
I-joists, 208
Inclined forces, 80–81
Infrastructure as construction variable, 27
Inspection and testing
entities performing inspections, 16
preincident planning, 16–17
preincident survey, 16
testing of building features, 16
Institutional sprinklers, 330, 331–332
Insulation
exterior finish, 271
exterior insulation and finishing system, 191, 229
fiberglass, 191
foam, 191–192
insulated concrete form construction, 174, 175
loose-fill, 191
noncombustible, 191
R-value, 189
sandwich panels with foam core, 269
solid-fill foam, 192
structural insulated panel, 189
thermal insulation of flat roof coverings, 292, 293
Interior finishes, 137–165
ceilings, 145
common finishes and trim, 138
defined, 138
fire doors, 152–165

classifications, 152–157
hardware and features, 158–162
maintenance, 162
testing, 162–165
fire-retardant coatings, 140–141
surface burning characteristics, 139–140
testing, 141–145
ASTM E-84, 141–143
criterion-referenced testing, 141
flame spread ratings, 142–143
limitations of findings, 144–145
NFPA® tests, 143–144
smoke developed ratings, 142, 143
walls and partitions, 145–151
assembly parameters, 145
compartmentation, 145–146, 147
curtain walls, 150–151
enclosure and shaft walls, 149–150
fire partitions, 149
fire walls, 146–149
wood materials, 194
Interior framing, 227–228
Interior lining, 138
Internal space configurations, 23
International Association of Fire Chiefs, annual safety stand-down, 19
International Building Code® (IBC®)
construction types, 20
defined, 18
fire wall fire resistance ratings, 147–148
fire-resistance rating requirements, 45
fire-retardant treatment of wood, 198
interior finish material tests, 144
live loads, 71
noncombustible material, defined, 54
occupancy classifications, 51–52
Type IV fire resistance requirements, 207
International Code Council® (ICC)
fire wall fire resistance ratings, 147
IBC. *See International Building Code® (IBC®)*
International Wildland-Urban Interface Code, 201
International Conference of Building Officials (ICBO), 18
International Existing Building Code (IEBC), 17
International Fire Code® (IFC®)
explosion control, 336
purpose of, 18
raw materials staging, 346
vent requirements, 124
International Residential Code (IRC), 52
International Style aesthetic, 29
International Wildland-Urban Interface Code, 201
Intumescent coatings, 140, 245
Inverted truss, 285
Investment of wealth, 28–29
IRC (International Residential Code), 52
Iron, 240. *See also* Steel

J

John Hancock Center zone occupancy, 111
Joint girder, 248
Joists
bar joist, 83, 249
beams, 79

concrete joist construction, 268
defined, 78, 283
flat roof support, 283–284
I-joists, 208
one-way reinforced slab, 268
open-web, 248–249, 251, 283
steel beams and light-gauge steel, 251
truss joists, 83

K

Kemper Arena collapse, Kansas City, MO (1979), 371
Kilojoules (kJ/g), 197
Kinetic energy, 71, 73
K-Mart fire, removal of fire doors, 149
Knee joint, 252–253

L

Labeled assembly, 146
Laboratories, testing, 59
Laboratory fire-resistance tests, 56–59
Lake Delton, Wisconsin, landslide (2008), 367
Lame Horse nightclub fire, Perm, Russia, (2009), 137
Lamella arch, 282
Lamella washer, 282
Lamellas, 282
Laminated strand lumber (LSL), 186
Laminated veneer lumber (LVL), 186
Laminated wood, 184
Landing, 95
Landslides, 367–368, 374
LaSalle Hotel fire, Chicago, IL (1946), 138
Lateral displacement, 175
Lateral loads, 76, 77
Laundry chute, 114–115
Law-based construction variables, 18–22
  accessibility requirements, 21–22
  building code requirements, 18–21
  construction type, 20
  life safety codes, 19–20
  occupancy and use, 21
Ledger board, 203
Life safety and fire fighting tactic research, 196
Life Safety Code. *See* NFPA® 101, *Life Safety Code®*
Life safety codes
  development of, 19
  fire responder safety, 19–20
  occupant safety, 19
Life safety during renovation and remodeling, 354
Light wood framing, 203–205
Lightweight construction, 184
Limited or controlled access buildings, 322–332
  building code requirements, 322
  features limiting firefighter access, 322
  membrane structures, 325–327
    air-supported and air-inflated structures, 325–326
    cable membrane structures, 327–328
    characteristics, 325
    covered mall buildings, 328–330
    detention and correctional facilities, 330–332
    fire fighting considerations, 327
    frame membrane structures, 327–328
  underground buildings, 322–325
    automatic sprinklers, 324

    below grade spaces, 324–325
    difficulties for firefighters, 323
    examples, 322–323
    fire-resistive construction, 324
    green design, 323
    horizontal access, 323
    smoke and fire considerations, 323–324
    smoke exhaust system, 324
Line of Duty Death (LODD), 196
Linear coefficient of thermal expansion of steel, 242
Lintel, 228, 229
Liquefied petroleum gas (LPG), 350
Listed coatings, 140
Live load, 70, 71, 372
Load
  axial, 69
  concentrated, 72
  dead, 70
  defined, 66
  distributed, 72
  dynamic, 71–72
  eccentric, 69
  fire load, 54
  fuel load, 20, 21, 54
  lateral, 76, 77
  live loads, 70, 71, 372
  rain, 72
  seismic, 74–78
  snow, 72, 371–372
  soil pressure, 78–79
  static, 70–71
  structural, 54
  structural accommodations, 79–84
    arches, 80–81
    beams, 79–80
    cables, 82
    columns, 80
    space frames, 84
    trusses, 82–84
  temporary, 361
  torsional, 69
  transverse, 86
  water, 73
  wind, 73–74
Load-bearing structures, 56
Load-bearing walls
  defined, 85
  masonry, 223–225
  purpose of, 84
LODD (Line of Duty Death), 196
Louvers, 162
LPG (liquefied petroleum gas), 350
LSL (laminated strand lumber), 186
Lumber. *See also* Wood
  defined, 195
  grading stamps, 195
  quality control, 195
LVL (laminated veneer lumber), 186

M

Machine Room-Less (MRL) elevators, 108
"Machines for living," 13
Maintenance
  age of construction and, 25

fire doors, 162
poor maintenance and collapse of buildings, 364
Malls. *See* Covered mall buildings
Mansard roof, 280–281, 286
Manual smoke control, 123–124
Manufactured components, 194–195
Map of fire fatalities, 19
Masonry
    code classifications, 222
    false fronts and voids, 230
    foundation walls, 174
    interior framing, 227–228
    material properties, 217–221
        bricks, 219
        clay tile blocks, 220
        compressive strengths, 218
        concrete blocks, 220
        density, 218
        drawbacks of use, 218
        fire resistance, 221
        fired clay tile, 220
        glass block, 220
        gypsum blocks, 220
        mortar, 218, 221
        stone, 219
        structural glazed tile, 220
    parapets, 229–230
    spalling, 220
    structural failure, 230–235
        collapse, 230–231
        indicators of, 235
        nonfire-related deterioration, 233–235
        tie rods and bearing plates, 232–233
        wall breaching, 232
    wall construction, 223–226
        load-bearing, 223–225
        nonload-bearing, 223
        nonreinforced, 224
        reinforced, 226, 231
    wall openings, 228–229
Mastics, 140, 245
Mat slab foundation, 172
Materials. *See* Building materials
Mathematical models based on collected data, 60, 61
Means of egress
    defined, 94
    stairs as, 94, 98
Mechanical conveyor systems, 101–102
Mechanical engineering, 14
Member, defined, 44
Membrane structure
    air-supported and air-inflated structures
        building codes, 325
        defined, 326
        fire fighting considerations, 327
        limitations, 326
    ceilings, 245–246
    characteristics, 325
    defined, 87
    frames, 87–88
    roofing, 292–293
    shell structure, 88
Meridian Plaza fire, Philadelphia, PA (1991), 35, 315

Metal roof coverings, 297–298
Metal-clad door, 155, 156, 158–159
Metrodome collapse, MN (2010), 371
MGM Grand fire, Las Vegas, NV (1980), 77
Mill construction, 49, 206, 207. *See also* Type IV – Heavy Timber construction
Mixed occupancies, 52–53
Modern mansard roof, 280–281
Monadnock building, Chicago, IL, 224
Monitor roof, 280, 281
Monoplane truss, 287
Mortar
    decay rate, 218
    defined, 174
    foundation walls, 174
    functions, 221
    portland cement, 220, 221
Mortise and tenon joint, 209
Moving stairs, 101–102
Moving walkways, 102
MRL (Machine Room-Less) elevators, 108
Multiple-injection system, 126, 127
Mushrooming, 110

N

Nailable gypsum, 290
Napa, CA, earthquake (2014), 365, 366
National Building Code, 18
National Building Code of Canada, 18
National Fallen Firefighters Foundation, Everyone Goes Home® program, 19
National Fire Protection Association® (NFPA®). *See also specific NFPA® standard*
    building codes, 18
    Fire Analysis and Research Department, 196
    life safety and fire fighting tactic research, 196
    life safety codes, 19
    occupancy classifications, 52
National Geographic, 74
National Institute for Occupational Safety and Health (NIOSH), 196
National Institute of Standards and Technology (NIST)
    building collapse factors, 359
    life safety and fire fighting tactic research, 196
National Oceanographic and Atmospheric Administration (NOAA), 369
National Research Council of Canada, 18
National Weather Service (NWS), 369
Nature-related causes of building collapse, 365–373
    earthquakes, 365–366
    floods, 372–373
    hurricanes, 370–371
    landslides, 367–368
    sinkholes, 367, 368–369
    snow and water loads, 371–372
    subsidence, 367, 368
    tornadoes, 370
    wind, 369–371
Near Miss reports, 196
Negative pressure, 73
Neutral axis, 80
New Orleans, LA, hurricane damage (2005), 373
NFPA®. *See* National Fire Protection Association® (NFPA®)
NFPA® 1, *Uniform Fire Code*, 18, 153

NFPA® 14, *Standard for the Installation of Standpipe and Hose Systems*, 314
NFPA® 80, *Standard for Fire Doors and Other Opening Protectives*, 153, 161
NFPA® 80A, *Recommended Practice for Protection from Exterior Fire Exposure*, 32
NFPA® 90A, *Standard for the Installation of Air-Conditioning and Ventilating Systems*, 120
NFPA® 92A, *Standard for Smoke-Control Systems Utilizing Barriers and Pressure Differences*, 126
NFPA® 101, *Life Safety Code®*
    fire door requirements, 153
    means of egress, 94
    occupancy classifications, 52
    provisions, 18
NFPA® 204, *Standard for Smoke and Heat Venting*, 124
NFPA® 220, *Standard on Types of Building Construction*, 44–45
NFPA® 241, *Standard for Safeguarding Construction, Alteration, and Demolition Operations*, 346, 352
NFPA® 251, *Standard Method of Tests of Fire Endurance of Building Construction and Materials*, 55, 60
NFPA® 252, *Standard Methods of Fire Tests of Door Assemblies*, 162
NFPA® 253, wall and ceiling covering tests, 143
NFPA® 256, *Standard Methods of Fire Tests of Roof Coverings*, 298–299
NFPA® 265, *Standard Methods of Fire Tests for Evaluating Contribution of Wall and Ceiling Interior Finish to Room Fire Growth*, 143, 144
NFPA® 286, interior finish materials tests, 143, 144
NFPA® 921, fire spread, 30
NFPA® 921-2011, *Guide for Fire and Explosion Investigations*, 35
NFPA® 1851, *Standard of Selection, Care, and Maintenance of Protective Ensembles, Structural Fire Fighting and Proximity Fire Fighting*, 193
NFPA® 5000, *Building Construction and Safety Code*
    fire door requirements, 153
    jurisdictions, adoption of codes, 18
    occupancy classifications, 52
NIOSH (National Institute for Occupational Safety and Health), 196
NIST. *See* National Institute of Standards and Technology (NIST)
NOAA (National Oceanographic and Atmospheric Administration), 369
Nominal dimension of lumber, 182
Nonbearing wall, 151
Noncombustible construction
    construction types, 20
    defined, 20
    materials, 46–47, 54
    protected steel frame or reinforced concrete construction, 46–47
    Type II construction, 47–48
Non-conforming structure, 17
Nonload-bearing structure, 56
Nonload-bearing wall, 151, 223
Nonreinforced bearing wall, 224
Nonveneered panels, 188
NWS (National Weather Service), 369

O

Occupancy and use of buildings
    change of occupancy and compromised safety, 53
    change of occupancy as cause of building collapse, 360
    classifications, 51–53
    covered mall buildings, 329
    economics-based construction variables, 27
    fuel load and, 21
    heat release rate, 21
    high-rise buildings, 311, 312
    International Building Code® classifications, 51–52
    mixed occupancies, 52–53
    model codes, 21
    NFPA® classifications, 52
    occupancy, defined, 51
Occupational Safety and Health Administration (OSHA), 19
Offensive fire fighting strategy, 37
Oil-cooled transformers, 129–130
One-way reinforced slab, 268
Open floor plans in high-rise buildings, 318
Open stairs, 101
Open-web joists, 248–249, 251, 283
Ordinary construction. *See* Type III – Exterior Protected (Masonry or Ordinary) construction
Ordinary reinforcing, 259–261
Oriented strand board (OSB), 188
OSB (oriented strand board), 188
OSHA (Occupational Safety and Health Administration), 19
Oso, WA, landslide (2014), 374
Outside air intakes, 118
Overhanging beams, 79
Overhead (rolling) doors, 154–155
Overpressure in pressurized stairwells, 128
Overspeed switch on elevators, 108
Owner's needs and desires for building design, 28

P

Panels, wood, 187–189
    composite panels, 189
    nonveneered panels, 188
    oriented strand board, 188
    particleboard, 188
    plywood, 187
    waferboard, 188, 189
Parallel strand lumber (PSL), 186
Parapet wall, 147, 148, 229–230
Parking garages, 52, 271
Particleboard, 188
Partitions, 149. *See also* Walls
Passenger elevators, 104
Passive barriers, 32–33
Passive fire protection, 99
Passive smoke control, 99
Passive smokeproof enclosures, 100
Passive soil pressure, 78
PCB (polychlorinated biphenyl), 129
Penthouses, 303
Permits, 15, 17
Phase I elevator operation, 320–321
Phase II elevator operation, 321–322
Photovoltaic (PV) system, 301–302
Piecemeal demolition, 363
Pier 34 building collapse, Philadelphia, PA (2000), 364
Piers in foundations, 172–173
Pilaster, 226, 227
Piles in foundations, 172–173

Pipe chase, 116
Pitched roofs
    architecture, 279–281
    coverings, 294–298
        asphalt shingles and tiles, 294–295
        cement tiles, 296–297
        clay tiles, 296–297
        metal, 297–298
        slate tiles, 296–297
        wood shingles and shakes, 295–296
    reinforcements, 286
    rise and run, 279–280
Platform frame construction, 204–205
Plywood, 187
Polychlorinated Biphenyl (PCB), 129
Polyurethane, 189
Polyvinyl chloride (PVC), 187, 293
Ponding of water, 72
Portland cement, 220, 221
Post and beam construction, 86, 208
Posttensioned reinforcement (concrete), 262–263
Pratt truss, 289
Precast concrete
    advantages of use, 269
    connections, 270, 272
    defined, 263
    disadvantages of use, 269
    identification of, 271
    parking garages, 271
    production of, 263, 268
    sandwich panels with foam core, 269
    standard shapes, 270
    tilt-up construction, 270, 271
Pre-engineered roof framing, 287–289
Prefabricated stairs, 95
Prefire inspection, 16
Prefire planning, 16
Preincident inspection, 16
Preincident planning
    in building construction, 36–37
    defined, 16
    fire fighting strategy, 37
    geographic information systems, 36–37
Preincident survey, 16
Preplan, 16
Preplanning, 16
Pressure impregnation of wood, 199
Pressure-reducing valve, 314, 315
Pressurized stairwells, 126–128
    calibration, 126, 128
    compensated system, 128
    multiple-injection system, 126, 127
    overpressure, 128
    parameters for, 126
    single-injection system, 126, 127
Prestressing
    defined, 261
    ordinary vs. prestressed reinforcement, 261
    posttensioning, 262–263
    pretensioning, 262
    process, 262
    reinforcing steel cutting dangers, 261
Pretensioned reinforcement (concrete), 262

Products of combustion, 98
Protected stairs, 98
Protection-in-place, 146
PSL (parallel strand lumber), 186
Public Law 101-336, 20
Purlin, 289
PV (photovoltaic) system, 301–302
PVC (polyvinyl chloride), 187, 293
Pyrolysis, 197
Pyrolysis process, 197
Pyrotechnics, 137

R

Rack storage, 337–339
    building code requirements, 338
    configurations, 337, 338
    fire protection problems, 339
    sprinklers, 339
    structure of surrounding building, 339
Rafter, 285
Rafter tie, 285
Rain loads, 72
Rain roofs, 299–300
Rated assemblies, 146
Rated fire door assembly, 153
Reactions R, 66
Rebar (reinforcing bars), 259, 260
Recirculation of air, 120, 121
Recommended Practice for Protection from Exterior Fire Exposure (NFPA® 80A), 32
Red Hook, NY, sinkhole (2011), 369
Redundant structural supports, 78
Reference Radiant Panel Test (ASTM D-2859), 143
Refuse chute, 114–115
Regular gypsum, 244
Reinforced concrete
    defined, 259
    ordinary reinforcing, 259–261
    posttensioned reinforcement, 262–263
    prestressing reinforcing, 261–262
    pretensioned reinforcement, 262
    rebar, 259, 260
Reinforcing bars (rebar), 259, 260
Remodeling. *See* Renovation and remodeling
Renovation and remodeling. *See also* Construction sites
    asbestos hazards, 192–193, 352–353
    building expansion, 353–354
    changing occupancy type, 21
    construction sites, 346
    dangerous changes, 17
    defined, 352
    demolition of buildings, 354–355, 362–363
    E2 nightclub disaster, exit violations, 53
    exemptions from codes, 17
    existing/non-conforming structure, 17
    gentrification, 26, 27
    hazards at construction sites, 352–353
    life safety features, 354
    misleading exteriors, 26
    permits, 17
    Windsor Tower fire (2005), 43
Residence
    apartment complex fire, Houston, TX (2014), 345

basement fires, 210
housing project collapse, Bridgeport, CT (1987), 361
International Residential Code, 52
Resonance, 76, 77
Restrained beams, 79
Restrained floor and ceiling assemblies, 56
Return stairs, 95
Return-air plenum, 119
Ribbon board, 203
Ridge board, 285
Ridgepole, 285
Rigid frame, 86, 247, 260
Rise of stairs, 94
Riser of stairs, 94
Roll roofing, 289
Rolling (overhead) doors, 154–155
Rolling of metal, 241
Roofs, 277–304
    arches, 289
    architectural styles, 279–283
        curved roofs, 281–282
        dormers, 283
        flat roofs, 279
        pitched roofs, 279–281
    coverings, 291–300
        factors in choice of, 291
        fire ratings, 298–299
        flat roofs, 292–294
        layers, 291
        pitched roofs, 294–298
        rain roofs, 299–300
        weather conditions to resist, 291
    curved roofs
        architecture, 281–282
        geodesic domes, 282
        lamella arch, 282
    dormers, 283
    false roof, 230
    fire fighting and, 278
    flat roofs
        architecture, 279
        coverings, 292–294
    functions, 278
    green design, 300–302
    penthouses, 303
    pitched roofs
        architecture, 279–281
        coverings, 294–298
        types, 280–281
    rain roofs, 299–300
    rise and run, 279–280
    roll roofing, 289
    roof decks, 289–291
    skylights, 303–304
    support systems, 283–289
        arches, 289
        conventional roof framing, 285–287
        flat roof support, 283–285
        pre-engineered, 287–289
Rooftop garden, 302
Run of stairs, 94
R-value, 189

S

Safety Code for Elevators (ASME/ANSI A17.1), 103
St. Louis Gateway Arch, special emergency resources needed for, 22
San Diego, CA sinkhole (1998), 368
Sandwich panel, 189
Sawtooth roof, 280, 281
SBCCI (Southern Building Code Congress International), 18
Scaffolding, 348
Scarf joint, 184, 185
Scissor stairs, 95, 96
SCL (structural composite lumber), 186
Sears Tower, special emergency resources needed for, 22
Seismic effect, 74
Seismic forces, 74
Seismic loads, 74–78
    defined, 76
    earthquakes, 74, 75
    horizontal motion, 76
    lateral loads, 76
    location of seismic activity, 74–75
    resonance, 76
    structural accommodations, 76–77
    structural stiffening accommodations, 77–78
Seismic maps, 74
Self-closing door, 160
Semi-rigid frame, 247–248
Sequencing, 361
Service elevators, 104
Setback, 23
Settlement, 175–176
Settling, 175–176
SFPE (Society of Fire Protection Engineers), 60
SFRM (spray-applied fire-resistive material), 243–244
Shaft walls, 149–150
Shallow foundations, 171–172
Shavings board, 188
Shear stress, 68, 69
Shear systems, 77
Shear wall, 110
Sheathing, 190
Shed roof, 280, 286
Shell structure, 88
Sheltering in place, 146, 147
Shingles
    asphalt, 294–295
    wood, 295–296
Shock loading, 71
Shopping mall. *See* Covered mall buildings
Shoring, 176–177
Shrinkage forces, 67
Shunt trip in elevators, 319
Siding materials, 192–193
Simple frame, 247
Simply supported beams, 79
Single-injection system, 126, 127
Single-ply membrane, 292–293
Sinkholes, 367, 368–369
SIP (structural insulated panel), 189
Site properties variables, 22–23
Skylights, 303–304
Slab and beam frame, 87, 268
Slab and column frame, 87

Slate tile roofs, 296-297
Slenderness ratio, 250
Sliding fire door, 155
Sliding systems, 77
Slump test of concrete, 265
Smoke barriers in areas of refuge, 337
Smoke control
    defined, 121
    mode, 121
    systems, 121-124
        atriums, 333
        automatic smoke control, 123
        fire-mode operation of HVAC system, 122
        high-rise buildings, 317
        manual smoke control, 123-124
        smoke control mode, 121
        underground buildings, 323-324
Smoke damper, 119
Smoke developed rating, 142, 143
Smoke exhaust systems in limited access buildings, 324
Smoke tower, 125-126
Smokeproof enclosure, 125
Smokeproof stair enclosure, 99-100
Smokeproof stairway, 125
Snow loads, 72, 371-372
Society of Fire Protection Engineers (SFPE), 60
Soil liquefaction, 78
Soil pressure load, 78-79
Soil properties
    defined, 170
    engineering-based construction variables, 22
    as foundation and building factor, 169
    frost line, 170
    stratum, 170
    water table, 170
Solar cells, 301
Solar panels, 301-302
Soldier course, 225
Solid lumber, 182-183
SOPs/SOGs, elevator use in emergencies, 320
Southern Building Code Congress International (SBCCI), 18
Space frames, 84
Spalling, 220, 221, 267
Spec building, 28
Special-purpose fire doors, 157
Specific gravity, 183
Speed governor on elevators, 108
Speed-reducing switch on elevators, 108
Spiral stairs, 95, 97
Split-ring connector, 209, 210
Spray-applied fire resistive material (SFRM), 243-244
Sprinklers. *See also* Automatic sprinkler systems
    in escalator protection systems, 102
    high-rise buildings, 315-316
Stairs, 94-101
    circular, 95, 96
    components, 94
    construction site, 348
    convenience stairs, 94
    exterior, 98, 99
    fire escapes, 98-99
    folding, 95, 97
    landing, 95
    as means of egress, 94, 98
    moving stairs (escalators), 101-102
    open stairs, 101
    prefabricated, 95
    pressurized stairwells, 126-128
    protected stairs, 98
    purpose of, 94
    return, 95
    scissor, 95, 96
    smokeproof enclosures, 99-100
    smokeproof stairway, 125
    spiral, 95, 97
    straight run, 95
Standard Building Code, 18
Standard Calculation Methods for Structural Fire Protection (ASCE/SFPE 29), 60
Standard for Fire Doors and Other Opening Protectives (NFPA® 80), 153, 161
Standard for Fire Tests of Joint Systems (UL Standard 2079), 58
Standard for Safeguarding Construction, Alteration, and Demolition Operations (NFPA® 241), 346, 352
Standard for Smoke and Heat Venting (NFPA® 204), 124
Standard for Smoke-Control Systems Utilizing Barriers and Pressure Differences (NFPA® 92A), 126
Standard for the Installation of Air-Conditioning and Ventilating Systems (NFPA® 90A), 120
Standard for the Installation of Standpipe and Hose Systems (NFPA® 14), 314
Standard Method of Tests of Fire Endurance of Building Construction and Materials (NFPA® 251), 55, 60
Standard Methods of Fire Tests for Evaluating Contribution of Wall and Ceiling Interior Finish to Room Fire Growth (NFPA® 265), 143, 144
Standard Methods of Fire Tests of Door Assemblies (NFPA® 252), 162
Standard Methods of Fire Tests of Roof Coverings (NFPA® 256), 298-299
Standard of Selection, Care, and Maintenance of Protective Ensembles, Structural Fire Fighting and Proximity Fire Fighting (NFPA® 1851), 193
Standard on Types of Building Construction (NFPA® 220), 44-45
Standard operating procedures/standard operating guidelines (SOPs/SOGs), elevator use in emergencies, 320
Standard Test Method for Behavior of Materials in a Vertical Tube Furnace at 750°C (ASTM E 136), 54
Standard Test Methods for Determining Effects of Large Hydrocarbon Pool Fires on Structural Members and Assemblies (ASTM Standard 1529), 58
Standpipe system
    at construction sites, 351
    defined, 314, 315
    in high-rise buildings, 314
    Meridian Plaza fire, Philadelphia, PA (1991), 315
Static load, 70-71
Station Night Club fire, West Warwick, RI (2003), 138
Stationary storage battery system, 131
Steel, 239-253
    acoustic board, 194
    alloy, 240
    arches, 249-250
    beam and girder frames, 247-248
    code modifications, 251-252
    cold rolled steel, 241

    collapse, 252
    columns, 250–251
    concrete plus structural steel, 268
    corrugated, 251
    defined, 240
    failure point temperature, 57
    fire protection, 243–246
        cementitious, 244
        gypsum, 244–245
        intumescent materials, 245
        mastic coatings, 245
        membrane ceilings, 245–246
        spray-applied fire resistive material, 243–244
    floor systems in steel-framed buildings, 251
    gabled rigid frames, 249
    gusset plates, 252
    heat conduction of, 242
    knee joint, 252–253
    material properties, 240–246
        ductility, 241
        expansion and deterioration, 242–243
        fire protection, 243–246
    protected steel frames, 46
    rigid frame, 247, 260
    roof deck materials, 290
    semi-rigid frame, 247–248
    simple frame, 247
    stud walls, 85
    suspension systems, 250
    trusses
        for roofs, 246, 289
        uses for, 248–249, 266
    unprotected, 46, 242, 243
Stefan-Boltzmann law, 31
Steiner tunnel test, 141
Step chain on moving stairs, 101
Stiffening, 77
Stirrups, 260
Stone
    foundation walls, 174
    material properties, 219
    veneer, 193, 234
Storage. *See* Rack storage
Straight-run stairs, 95
Strain of steel, 241
Stratum, 170
Stress
    axial load, 69
    bending stress, 67, 79
    compression, 68
    cross-section, 68
    defined, 66
    eccentric load, 69
    factor of safety, 69
    failure point, 69
    shear stress, 68, 69
    steel, 241
    tensile stress, 68
    tension, 68
    torsional load, 69
Stretcher course, 225
Strip footing, 171
Structural bearing walls, 84–85

Structural changes and expansion, 352–354
Structural collapse. *See* Collapse of buildings
Structural components, 44
Structural composite lumber (SCL), 186
Structural design, 65–88
    arches, 80–81
    beams, 79–80
    bending moment, 67, 79
    cables, 82
    as cause of building collapse, 360
    columns, 80
    concentrated loads, 72
    dead loads, 70
    distributed loads, 72
    dynamic loads, 71–72
    equilibrium, 66
    forces, 66, 67
    live loads, 70, 71
    loads, defined, 66
    rain and snow loads, 72
    seismic loads, 74–78
    soil pressure loads, 78–79
    space frames, 84
    static loads, 70–71
    stresses, 66, 68–69
    structural bearing walls, 84–88
    trusses, 82–84
    water loads, 73
    wind loads, 73–74
Structural endurance, calculating under fire conditions, 201–202
Structural engineering, 14
Structural failure, design-caused, 33–36
    building system failure, 34–35
    causes of, 33
    combustion and, 35
    design deficiencies, 35–36
    Hyatt Regency collapse, 33–34
    loss of structural integrity, 34
    meaning of, 33–34
Structural glazed tile, 220
Structural insulated panel (SIP), 189
Structural integrity
    at construction sites, 350
    loss of, 34
Structural load vs. fire load, 54
Structural stiffness, 77–78
Structural systems, wood, 202–210
    box beams and I-beams, 208
    heavy timber framing, 205–207
    light wood framing, 203–205
    post and beam framing, 208
    trusses, 209–210
Structural terra cotta, 220
Struts
    on folding stairs, 97
    foundation shoring, 176
Stud, 85
Sublimation, 197
Subsidence, 367, 368
Sullivan, Louis A., 13
Superplasticizer, 258
Surface burning characteristics of interior finishes, 139–140
    defined, 139

factors, 139–140
    floor coverings, 140
        thin surface treatments, 140
Surface system, 87
Surface-to-mass ratio, 198
Suspension systems, steel, 250
Sustainable energy, 301
Swinging fire door, 156, 158
Synthetic stucco, 191
Systems for buildings. *See* Building systems

T

Taking refuge, 146
Tar and gravel roof, 292, 294
Technology of building construction, 11
Temperature forces, 67
Temporary loads on structures during construction, 361
Tensile stress, 68
Tension, 68
Terminal device on elevators, 108
Test borings, 170
Test for Surface Burning Characteristics of Building Materials
  (ASTM E-84 UL 723), 141
Tests
    ASTM E-84, 141–143
        flame spread ratings, 142–143
        smoke developed ratings, 142, 143
    ASTM E-119, 55, 58–59, 201
    building features, 16
    combustibility, 54
    compression testing of concrete, 265
    corner tests, 144
    criterion-referenced testing, 141, 163–164
    fire doors, 162–165
        ASTM E-152, 162–163
        criterion referenced testing, 163–164
        marking rated fire doors, 164–165
    fire resistance, 55–59
    floor coverings, 143
    interior finishes, 141–145
        ASTM E-84, 141–143
        limitations of findings, 144–145
        NFPA® tests, 143–144
    laboratories, 56–59
    NFPA® interior finish tests, 143–144
    Reference Radiant Panel Test (ASTM D-2859), 143
    roof coverings, 298–299
    slump test, 265
    Steiner tunnel, 141
    test fire enclosure, 144
    test pits, 170
Theater smoke vents, 124
Thermal insulation of flat roof coverings, 292, 293
Thermal radiation, 30, 31
Thermoplastic composite lumber, 187
Thin surface treatments, 140
Tie rods, 232–233
Tied wall, 147, 148
Tiles, roof
    asphalt, 294–295
    cement, 296–297
    clay, 296–297
    slate, 296–297
    wood, 295–296

Tilt-slab construction, 271
Tilt-up construction, 270, 271
Tin-clad door, 155
Tornadoes, 370
Torsional load, 69
Traction elevators, 105, 106–107
Transfer switch, 131
Transformers
    air-cooled, 129
    defined, 128
    oil-cooled, 129–130
    purpose of, 129
Transitional fire fighting strategy, 37
Transverse load, 86
Tread of stairs, 94
Tropicana Casino parking garage collapse, Atlantic City, NJ
  (2003), 217
Trusses
    bowstring, 9, 83, 288
    common, 287
    configurations, 82
    defined, 82, 83
    delta, 248
    Fink truss, 289
    gusset plates, 209
    heavy timber, 209
    inverted, 285
    light wood frame, 209–210
    loads and failure, 84
    monoplane, 287
    mortise and tenon joint, 209
    Pratt truss, 289
    roof trusses, 287–289
    split-ring connector, 209, 210
    steel
        for roofs, 246, 289
        uses for, 248–249, 266
    structural configurations, 85
    unprotected engineered trusses, failure of, 210
    wood, 222, 289
Tunnel test, 141
Two-way communication system, 316, 337
Two-way slab construction, 268
Type I – Fire Resistive construction
    characteristics, 46
    combustible materials, 47
    fire retardant materials, 47
    IBC® fire-resistance rating requirements, 45
    IBC® numerical designations, 20
    noncombustible materials, 46–47
    uses for, 46
Type II – Protected Noncombustible or Noncombustible
  construction
    characteristics, 47
    IBC® fire-resistance rating requirements, 45
    IBC® numerical designations, 20
    Type II-A (protected), 47
    Type II-B (unprotected), 48
Type III – Exterior Protected (Masonry or Ordinary)
  construction
    characteristics, 48
    concealed space fire concerns, 49
    IBC® fire-resistance rating requirements, 45

IBC® numerical designations, 20
Type III 2-1-1 construction, 48
Type III A construction, 48
uses for, 48
Type IV – Heavy Timber construction
   characteristics, 49, 205, 207
   features, 49–50, 205–206
   fire hazards, 50
   fire-resistance requirements, 207
   IBC® fire-resistance rating requirements, 45
   IBC® numerical designations, 20
   mill construction and, 206
   uses for, 50
Type V – Wood Frame construction
   characteristics, 50
   construction methods, 51
   IBC® fire-resistance rating requirements, 45
   IBC® numerical designations, 20
   limitations of use, 50–51
Type X gypsum, 244

U
UBC (Uniform Building Code), 18
UL. *See* Underwriters Laboratories, Inc. (UL)
Ultimate stress of steel, 241
Underground buildings, 322–325
   automatic sprinklers, 324
   below grade spaces, 324–325
   difficulties for firefighters, 323
   examples, 322–323
   fire-resistive construction, 324
   green design, 323
   horizontal access, 323
   smoke and fire considerations, 323–324
   smoke exhaust system, 324
Underlayment, 294
Underpinning, 176–177
Underwriters Laboratories, Inc. (UL)
   Fire Resistance Directory
      annual listing of assemblies, 59
      fire wall fire resistance ratings, 145
      floor and ceiling assembly, 54
      gypsum board, 194
   fire resistance rating, 54
   fire walls, 145
   life safety and fire fighting tactic research, 196
   listed coatings, 140
   roof covering tests, 299
   test furnace, 58
   testing materials, 55
   UL Standard 2079, *Standard for Fire Tests of Joint Systems*, 58
Uniform Building Code (UBC), 18
Uniform Fire Code (NFPA® 1), 18, 153
United States Department of Homeland Security (DHS), 373
United States Fire Administration (USFA), 19
United States Geological Survey (USGS), 74
United States Occupational Safety and Health Administration (OSHA), 19
Unprotected steel, 46, 242, 243
Unrestrained floor and ceiling assemblies, 56
Use of buildings. *See* Occupancy and use of buildings
USFA (United States Fire Administration), 19
USGS (United States Geological Survey), 74

Utilities
   economics-based construction variables, 27
   electrical lock-out/tag-out, 106
   utility chases, 114–116

V
Vacant buildings, vandalism and scavenging of, 363
Valves, pressure-reducing, 314, 315
van der Rohe, Mies, 29
Vapor barrier of flat roof coverings, 292
Variables. *See* Construction variables
Vegetative roof systems, 302
Veneer, 193
Veneered walls, 193
Ventilation
   atriums, 333
   draft curtains, 124, 125
   explosion vents, 334–336
   external vents, 118
   high-rise buildings, 311–312
   smoke and heat vents, 124–125
   underground buildings, 323–324
   vent hazards, 125
   vent limitations, 125
   ventilation and exhaust systems, 120
Vertical shaft enclosures
   atriums, 332. *See also* Atriums
   grease ducts, 115–116
   high-rise buildings, 311–312
   rated smoke enclosures, 150
   refuse and laundry chutes, 114–115
Vibration forces, 67
Vinyl siding, 192
Voice over Internet Protocol (VoIP), 373
Void spaces
   atriums, 332. *See also* Atriums
   ceilings, 49, 145
   combustion in, 200. *See also* Concealed spaces
   masonry building, 230
   truss roof construction, 287
VoIP (Voice over Internet Protocol), 373
Voltage supply to buildings, 128

W
Waferboard, 188, 189
Waffle construction, 268
Walls
   assembly parameters, 145
   bearing wall structures, 85
   compartmentation, 145–146, 147
   curtain walls
      defined, 150
      functions, 150
      materials and combinations, 150–151
      nonfire-resistive, 151
      nonload-bearing, 151
   enclosure and shaft walls, 149–150
   exterior wall materials, 190–193
      building wrap, 190–191
      foam insulation, 191–192
      sheathing, 190
      siding, 192–193
   fire partitions, 149

fire walls, 146–149
    defined, 146
    fire areas, 146
    fire resistance ratings, 147–148
    freestanding walls, 146–147, 148
    negative perception of fire walls, 148–149
    parapet walls, 147, 148
    tied walls, 147, 148
    uses of, 149
foundation walls, 174–175
full height partition walls, 309
load-bearing, 84, 85
masonry
    bearing walls, 220
    breaching, 232
    building classifications, 222
    cavity wall, 226
    fire resistance, 221
    as floor and roof support, 222
    load-bearing, 223–225
    nonfire-related deterioration, 233–235
    nonload-bearing, 223
    nonreinforced, 224
    openings, 228–229
    parapet, 229–230
    reinforced, 226, 231
rated assemblies, 146
shear wall, 110
steel stud walls, 85
textile covering tests, 144
veneered, 193
wall footing, 171
Water
    as cause of building collapse, 371–372
    dewatering, 73
    floods as cause of building collapse, 372–373
    loads, 73
    ponding, 72
    rain and snow loads, 72
    supplies at construction sites, 347
    utilities, economics-based construction variables, 27
    water table, 170
Wear course or roof coverings, 294
Web, 80, 81, 82
Western frame construction, 204
Wide are incidents, 373–375
Wildland/urban interface
    defined, 33
    exposures, 33
    forest fires, 30
    International Wildland-Urban Interface Code, 201
Willis Tower, special emergency resources needed for, 22
Wind
    as cause of building collapse, 369–371
    defined, 67
    hurricanes
        Breezy Point, NY damage (2012), 370
        Hurricane Andrew, 369
        hurricane brackets, 370, 371
        hurricane glazing, 121
        Hurricane Irene, 371
        Hurricane Ivan, 369, 371
        Hurricane Katrina, 373
        Hurricane Sandy, 370
        New Orleans, LA, damage (2005), 373
        Windemere Condominiums, Orange Beach, AL, damage (2004), 369
    kinetic energy of, 73
    loads, 73–74
    negative pressure, 73
    tornadoes, 370
Windemere Condominiums, Orange Beach, AL, hurricane damage (2004), 369
Windows, hurricane glazing, 121
Windsor Tower fire, Madrid, Spain (2005), 43
Winecoff Hotel fire, Atlanta, GA (1913), 313
Wired glass, 161
Wood, 181–211
    combustion properties, 196–200
        fire-retardant treatment of wood, 198–200
        heat of combustion, 197
        ignition temperature, 196–197
        life safety and fire fighting tactics, 196
        surface area and mass, 198
        void spaces, 200
    foundation walls, 174
    grain, 183
    joints, 184–185
    lumber
        defined, 195
        grading stamps, 195
        quality control, 195
    material properties, 181–202
        brick or stone veneer, 193
        combustion properties of wood, 196–200
        engineered wood, 183–187
        exterior walls, 190–193
        firestopping, 189–190
        ignition-resistant construction, 200–201
        interior finish materials, 194
        manufactured components, 194–195
        panels, 187–189
        quality control of lumber, 195
        solid lumber, 182–183
        structural endurance under fire conditions, 201–202
    methods for connecting, 202
    pressure impregnation, 199
    shingles and shakes, 295–296
    siding, 192
    specific gravity, 183
    structural collapse, 210–211
    structural systems, 202–210
        box beams and I-beams, 208
        heavy timber framing, 205–207
        light wood framing, 203–205
        post and beam framing, 208
        trusses, 209–210
    trusses, 289
World Trade Center Towers collapse (2001), 313
World War II influences on codes and styles, 25
Wright, Frank Lloyd, 13
Wythe, 223–224, 225

Y

Yield point stress of steel, 241

Z

Zones
    collapse control, 230, 231
    John Hancock Center zone occupancy, 111

Indexed by Nancy Kopper

Notes